Perspectives on
Caribbean Law

Perspectives on
Caribbean Law

A Compendium of Legal Essays

Edited by
**Shazeeda Ali and
Stephen Vasciannie**

The University of the West Indies Press
Mona • St Augustine • Cave Hill • Global • Five Islands

First published in Jamaica, 2024 by
The University of the West indies Press
7A Gibraltar Hall Road,
The UWI, Mona Campus,
Kingston 7, Jamaica
www.uwipress.com

© 2024
ISBN: 978-976-640-963-0 (paperback)
        978-976-640-964-7 (Epub)

A catalogue record of this book is available from
the National Library of Jamaica.

Cover and Book Design by Christina Moore Fuller
Printed and Bound in the United States of America

Contents

Foreword

Derrick McKoy

Except for two short excursions away from the University of the West Indies, first to act as Contractor-General and then as Attorney General, I have served most of my life in the Faculty of Law at the UWI. I entered as a student, became a lecturer, and left as dean at the Mona campus. It is, therefore, with considerable pleasure that I write the foreword to this compendium of essays collected by Professors Shazeeda Ali and Stephen Vasciannie in celebration of the fiftieth anniversary of UWI's Faculty of Law. This work is especially meaningful to me, as I have interacted with every contributor to this volume – as a former student, a fellow lecturer or a colleague administrator.

Long before Dorcas White joined the faculty as a lecturer, then a senior tutor at the Norman Manley Law School, we were students together at Cave Hill. Over the years, with her sterling contribution to legal education, Dorcas has demonstrated that she is, indeed, the doyenne of law teaching in the region. There is no better authority on Commonwealth Caribbean legal education and nothing more beneficial than Dorcas' reflections on fifty years of teaching law.

Professor Shazeeda Ali – former student, fellow lecturer and successor as dean – introduces us to that most elusive personality, the eudaimonic attorney. This pursuit of the highest ideals must be the object of our educational system. While Dr Jason Haynes puts the focus on an intersectional approach to fairness in sport, Dr Celia Blake's chapter introduces her unique speciality, the role of language in law and justice.

Suzanne Ffolkes-Goldson brings us back to the confines of good corporate governance, focusing on the evolving laws in this field. In his chapter on the juridification of good governance in CARICOM law, Dr Neto Waite demonstrates that governance in the region has moved beyond the concerns of national laws.

André Sheckleford continues the discussion by reminding us of the limitations of the emerging regional legal regime and the exceptions of the CARICOM treaty. At the same time, Professor Stephen Vasciannie offers a variation on the theme and discusses the transnational law enforcement arrangements of the region with a reconsideration of the Shiprider agreements.

The law of torts occupies a lot of our attention. Professor Gilbert Kodilinye discusses aspects of tort in the hospitality sector. Rose Cameron's chapter is on consent to medical treatment for children. Coleen Lewis' contribution is the lessons for Jamaica from recent developments in defamation laws in Australia as well as England and Wales, while Gabrielle Elliot-Williams ties in defamation law with the enforcement of morals.

The compendium contains the contribution of the Honourable Mr Justice Andrew Burgess of the Caribbean Court of Justice. Lecturer, lawyer, former law professor, former Dean of the Faculty of Law and constant friend, Justice Burgess is the best representation of legal education in the region. Therefore, it is appropriate that the collection includes a discussion by him of the pinnacle of our justice system, the appellate advocate and the appellate function in our court system.

Fifty years is a significant period in the life of any institution and it is appropriate that our legal scholars seek to mark that accomplishment. More importantly, the editors have brought together a body of work that will endure for many more years. This book will become a necessary feature of all libraries interested in Commonwealth Caribbean law and legal education.

I am grateful to Professors Ali and Vasciannie for the opportunity to partake in this celebration. It is reassuring that not only have they achieved the heights of their profession, but they have put together this compendium that continues to shape the development of legal scholarship in the region. Furthermore, I am deeply honoured that they allowed me to be associated with it.

Introduction: Panoramic Perspectives on Caribbean Law

Shazeeda Ali and Stephen Vasciannie

In September 1970, the University of the West Indies welcomed its first cohort of students into the newly established Faculty of Law. Although the faculty was based at the Cave Hill campus in Barbados, Jamaican students were permitted to do year one of the Bachelor of Laws programme at home on the Mona campus. Today, three law faculties exist at the UWI – in 2012, one was established at the St Augustine campus in Trinidad and another at the Jamaican campus, the latter affectionately called "MonaLaw". In celebration of the faculty's fiftieth anniversary, academic staff connected with MonaLaw at various stages of its evolution have united to produce a peer-reviewed collection of essays on a range of diverse legal topics. The essays, written by emerging and established academics, seek to expose the reader to a panoramic landscape of legal scholarship concerning national, regional and international issues.

Perspectives on Caribbean Law comprises twelve chapters and is designed to reflect the level and range of scholarship associated with some colleagues who have contributed over the years to the mission of MonaLaw. The book features, inter alia, articles on corporate law, tort law, international law, family law and ethics. Of significance, the chapters include discourse on matters that are unique to the region. For instance, the chapters by André Sheckleford and Neto Waite focus on issues that have emerged from the Caribbean regional integration movement (CARICOM), while Celia Brown-Blake examines socio-legal questions associated with the use of the Creole language in the Caribbean justice system. Issues concerning legal liability in the Caribbean tourism sector are explored by Gilbert Kodilinye, while Jason Haynes focuses on fairness in sports, again with emphasis on the Caribbean. Suzanne Ffolkes-Goldson writes on matters of corporate governance, particularly as it relates to directors' duties. Two chapters deal with defamation – one by Coleen Lewis, the other by Gabrielle Elliott-Williams. Child law is explored by Rose Cameron, who looks at consent to medical treatment for children. Judge Andrew Burgess of the Caribbean Court of Justice, writing extra-judicially, analyses the region's appellate court system, while Stephen Vasciannie provides insights into jurisdictional issues for Jamaica, with special reference to the United Nations Law of the Sea Convention. At the same time, Dorcas White reflects authoritatively on teaching law at Mona, and Shazeeda Ali investigates critically the responsibilities of attorneys to the greater good.

As MonaLaw strives to contribute to the development of legal scholarship in the Caribbean, the editors wish to thank all the authors for their valuable essays in this publication – without them, the book would not have come into port. We would also like to express our gratitude to the MonaLaw research assistants, Dr Rohan Clarke and Dr Yentyl Williams, who assisted the editors in the compilation of this volume at different stages of its production.

Shazeeda Ali and Stephen Vasciannie
MonaLaw
May 2023

Reflections on Fifty Years of Teaching Law
Dorcas White

The UWI Faculty of Law started out as one. Out of that one (Cave Hill) has come three faculties – Cave Hill, St Augustine and Mona. The mother faculty was four years old when I was recruited to join the teaching staff in July 1974. Incidentally, I was co-editor of a publication to mark its tenth anniversary. Now I have the divinely approved privilege of taking part in a publication to celebrate fifty years of teaching law in the region. The Cave Hill faculty today may not be identical in every way to the institution that was established in 1970. It was then the UWI law faculty, with headquarters at the Cave Hill campus. Neither the Mona nor the St Augustine incarnation was in existence at the inception of the programme of law teaching in the Caribbean.

However, there were satellite programmes on these campuses, which in time had the capacity to become full-fledged faculties and have become such.

It is not an alternative fact to say that the Faculty of Law Cave Hill, as it stands today, was not in existence fifty years ago. Whatever the decision-making strategy to accomplish this feat – one faculty becoming three – this does not negate the fact that we are therefore celebrating *fifty years* of law teaching by the UWI on its three campuses and institutional modalities cannot deny but rather affirm this.

Congratulations to the UWI on its triversity structure. Congratulations to Dr Shazeeda Ali, Dean of MonaLaw, and her team for organizing and coordinating the rich celebratory agenda and for doing so in a time of great difficulty. Congratulations to all staff members of the three faculties.

I do thank God, in the Lord Jesus Christ, that by His grace and mercy I am still teaching law, albeit at the Norman Manley Law

School, at this stage of the life of the law faculty and this juncture in my life.

Cave Hill, the mother of law teaching in the region, was the mecca to which all disciples in the region flowed. They flowed from the islands. They flowed in groups from the first-year satellite programmes at the Mona and St Augustine campuses. After three years they flowed out from Cave Hill to either Hugh Wooding in Trinidad or Norman Manley in Jamaica for final preparation, before returning home to serve. These were homegrown professionals who had been fed on a diet of English law. They read and memorized English judicial decisions and English texts. They were familiar with the *dicta* and ways of English judges and the commentaries of English authors.

For the most part, the students did not know the law of their own territories or the names of the judges of their courts and there were no textbooks by Commonwealth Caribbean authors, save an unpublished monograph on Caribbean legal systems by Edward Laing, a Belizean, and articles in English journals by the late A.R. Carnegie.

The faculty members came from English universities. The first dean – an Englishman, K.W. Patchett – was from Sheffield University; the deputy dean, A.R. Carnegie, an eminent law teacher, later the second dean, was a Jamaican and a graduate of Oxford. There were also faculty members from French, American, Nigerian, Australian and New Zealand universities. At Cave Hill, it was a rich melting pot and there was much energy as all grappled with the Herculean task of nursing a newborn regional institution to enable it to carry out the mandate given by the founding fathers.

For the most part, teaching the law of a number of island states of varying degrees of constitutional development was not an easy task. Not only that, but the reception clauses were not uniform in relation to time and date and the particular body of English law that had been received. The next best thing was to bend to the strong wind of the cumulative disorganization manifested by the several receptions of law provisions, which provided for the reception of English law in the Anglophone Caribbean territories. These provisions were satisfied in a simplistic way of general application without seeking meticulously to ascertain what body of English common law was received and the dates of reception closure for each territory. It was easy to take a generalized approach. After all, the English-trained barristers, the solicitors and the judges were taking the same approach. Further, the English approach to the interpretation of statutes was fully embraced and passed on.

The law library at Cave Hill was the premier law library in the region, although the bulk of the materials stocked was of English or Commonwealth origin, with a few volumes of the *West Indian Law Reports*. Was all this institutional wrongdoing? Hardly. Our history reveals that our region was forged out of conflict between nations and law was the fingerprint of each antagonist. The region saw the imposition from the two great families of law —common and civil. The English common law prevailed over Spanish law in Trinidad.[1] English law prevailed almost totally over Roman Dutch law in Guyana.[2] English law prevailed almost entirely over French civil law in St Lucia.[3]

Examination of the global legal landscape should reveal that legal systems belong to one or the other of these two great families of law, either wholly or in combination, as well as in combination with indigenous rules where these existed.

In addition, examination of judicial decisions reveals a conformity to one or the other legal family. Also, the writings of legal scholars, the arguments of counsel at the bar show clearly to which of the legal families they belong. The common lawyer is governed by the common law thought-ways and techniques of argument that originated in England. We, the products of the UWI law faculty, are common lawyers belonging to one of the great legal traditions. We should not be ashamed or discouraged, but make the best of the import in this age of globalization when courts are not ashamed of reason borrowing to meet the justice of situations confronting them.

---

1.   Carl Campbell, "The Transition from Spanish Law to English Law in Trinidad Before and After Emancipation," in *Some Papers on Social, Political and Economic Adjustments to the Ending of Slavery in the Caribbean* (1975), 25–32, 132–38, presented at the Seventh Annual Conference of Caribbean Historians.

2.   See Mohamed Shahabuddeen, The Legal System of Guyana (Georgetown, 1973).

3.   See Dorcas White, "Some Problems of a Hybrid Legal System: A Case Study of St Lucia," International and Comparative Law Quarterly 30: 862; see generally, Sir Dennis Byron, Coming of Age in the Caribbean, a Norman Manley Lecture, West Indian Law Journal [special commemorative issue] (August 2012): 55.

Social institutions and interactions reveal very little if any conceptual differences between the legal families. People from all nations and races enter into contracts; they commit crimes; they cause harm one to another; they borrow money; they charge real property; they devise property to their loved ones; people wrangle over succession; they marry, and so on.

Every legal family has rules designed to solve these problems. Since there are at least two sides to every problem, there must be a loser. That loser in a legal battle may desire to have the law changed so that they could be winners. But what about the party who had conducted their business according to the existing law? For the loser the argument is that the applicable law is not relevant and should be changed. But who should be the instrument of change? Should law teachers be the ones to seed the change? Bearing in mind that they are usually far removed from reality and are usually wrapped up in fanciful ideas, the failure of which is not costly to them or to any third party. Should the judges make the change? In such a case the one who relied on the existing law is put in the wrong and has to pay costs. The issue of the fairness or otherwise of judicial lawmaking so as to make law relevant comes into question.

Judicial Changes in Law

At this time, this should be left to the legislature, who has the constitutional obligation to make laws for the peace, order and good governance of the state. Law reform committees and the parliamentary drafting office should be so resourced that appropriate consideration should be given to any need for change, the change that should be made and how. The issue of relevance will be addressed in the context of all relevant circumstances.

Publications – Books, Journals and Law Reports

Naturally, there are more of these than when law teaching began. *The West Indian Reports, Jamaica Law Reports, Barbados Law Reports* and *The Law Reports of British Guiana* were in existence before law teaching at tertiary level began. *The West Indian Reports* have continued with strength and vitality. *Belize Law Reports* and *Cayman Islands Law Reports* came into being over the last fifty years. *Jamaica Law Journal* has been absorbed by *West Indian Law*

Journal, the premier law journal in the region, published by the Norman Manley Law School. Each of the three faculties has its own publications.

Bar associations in the region have taken seriously their role of participating in the development of the law by maintaining publications and undertaking public interest litigation. See, for example, *Bar Association of Belize v AG of Belize* [2017] CCJ 4 (AJ); *Jamaica Bar Association v AG of Jamaica and the General Legal Council* [2017] J.M.F.C. 02.

Fifty years of law teaching has produced a large number of law teachers, practitioners on the bench, at the bar, in government and the media. However, the writings are replicative of the content and thought-ways of inherited law. This is not a criticism; it is a statement of fact. It is a fact of life that one cannot go too far from family resemblances and traits.

Newest World Court

The Caribbean Court of Justice, the newest world court, was established in 2001.[4] As an appellate court, it is a common law court of co-ordinate jurisdiction with the Privy Council (UKPC), the Supreme Court of the United Kingdom (UKSC), USSC and other world appellate courts. In its original jurisdiction, it is coordinate with other world courts adjudicating on matters of international law. The UWI Faculty of Law played a role in sensitizing law students to the need for the replacement of the Judicial Committee of the Privy Council. Further, there are graduates of the faculty on the bench of the CCJ. The current president is a graduate.

Scholarly criticism tends to be subtle to the point of non-existence. It is usually perceived that because the legal systems are so small that scholarly criticism of judicial decisions could have effects other than what was intended. This is one reason why many prefer the ultimate appellate court to be in a far place where judge, litigant, lawyer or scholar would be just a name on paper and the opportunity to bruise egg-shell egos would be diminished to vanishing point.

---

4.   Byron, Norman Manley Lecture 2012, 55–58; Andrew Maharaj, *Cornell International Law Journal* 235 (2015): 47.

The change to online delivery of education should not have caught the UWI off-guard. This institution had been in the vanguard of development of online capability since the 1970s. I remember delivering a lecture to students simultaneously at Mona, Cave Hill and St Augustine campuses on the "Law of Public Mischief" via UWIDITE. It was a great experiment.

It is my firm belief that institutions exist for the glory of Jesus Christ, and should function accordingly. Happy fiftieth anniversary to a great law faculty.

Cases

Aaron v Baptiste DM 2014 HC 13 (Carilaw, Eastern Caribbean Supreme Court).

Aberdeen v Blaikie (1854) 1 Macq 461 HL Sc.

Aberdeen v Blaikie Bros. [1843-60] All ER Rep. 249, 2 Eq. Rep. 1281 (HL).

Abramson v Ritz-Carlton Hotel Co. D.C. Civil No. 09-cv-03264 (2012).

Albright v Morton on 321 F Supp 2d 130, 136 (D Mass 2004).

Ali Samatar and Others v France (Judgment), App. No. 17110/10 and 17301/10, Eru 2014, Eur. Ct. H.R.

Barrow v Bolt [2014] VSC 599.

BCE Inc. v 1976 Debentureholders [2008] 3 S.C.R. 560, 2008 SCC 69.

Bell v Lever Bros. [1932] AC 161 Eng HL.

Benkley Northover v Eric Northover and Rohan Northover and Godfrey Dixon and Winston G. Berkoff v Burchill [1996] 4 All ER 1008.

Bhullar v Bhullar, Re Bhullar Bros. Ltd. [2003] 2 BCLC 241 Eng CA.

Bowen v Independent Publishing Co. 96 SE2d 564, 230 SC 509 (1957) 513.

BTI 2014 LLC *(Appellant) v Sequana SA and others* (Respondents) [2022] UKSC 25.

Byrne v Dean [1937] KB 818.

Cabral Douglas v Commonwealth of Dominica [2017] CCJ 1 (OJ).

Canadian Aero Services Ltd. v O'Malley [1974] S.C.R. 592, 40 D.L.R. (3d) 371.

Carnival Cruise Lines, Inc. v Shute 499 US 585, 111 S. Ct. 1522, 113 L. Ed. 2d 622 (1991).

Percival v Wright [1902] 2 Ch. 421 Eng Ch D.

Phillips v The Commonwealth [1964] 110 CLR 347 (HCA).

Philip Morris Brands Sàrl, Philip Morris Products S.A. and Abal Hermanos S.A. v Oriental Republic of Uruguay, ICSID Case No. ARB/10/7, Award, 8 July 2016.

Pianka and Hylton v R [1977] 15 J.L.R. 175.

Pinder v Moscetti, 666 F. Supp. 2d 1313, 1318 (S.D. Fla.2008).

Piper Aircraft Co. v Reyno 454 US 235.

Polygram Records, Inc. v Superior Court 170 Cal. App. 3d 543 (1985).

Powell v Streatham Manor Nursing Home [1935] AC 243.

Punt v Symons [1903] 2 Ch. 506 Eng Ch D.

R. v Central Criminal Court ex parte Francis & Francis (A Firm) [1989] A.C. 346

R v Cox and Railton [1884] 14 QBD 153.

R v Thomas Dakin [1978] 15 J.L.R. 302.

Rajkumar v Ali and T&T News Centre Ltd. TT [2010] HC 146 (Carilaw TT HC).

Rea v Wildeboer [2015] ONCA 373.

Re City Equitable Fire Insurance Co. [1925] 1 Ch 407 (CA) 428.

Re Hydrodam (Corby) Ltd. [1994] 2 BCLC 180, 183 Eng.Ch D.

Re MDA Investment Management Ltd. [2005] BCC 783 [70].

Regal (Hastings) Ltd. v Gulliver [1967] 2 AC 134n, Eng HL.

Revenue and Customs Commissioners v Holland [2010] UKSC 51.

Reynolds v Times Newspapers Ltd. and others [1998] 3 WLR 862.

Rock Hard Cement Ltd. v Barbados and Caribbean Community Judgment [2020] CCJ 2 (OJ).

Rudisa Beverages & Juices NV and Caribbean International Distributors Ltd. v Republic of Guyana [2014] CCJ 1 (OJ).

Sally Ann Fulton v Chas E Ramson Ltd. [2016] JMSC Comm. 14.

Sanfarraro v Bay Roc Ltd. [2011] Supreme Court, Jamaica, No. 220 of 2004.

Secretary of State for Trade and Industry v Deverell [2000] 2 BCLC 133, 146 Eng. CA.

Semenya v Switzerland (App. no. 10934/21).

Sempra Energy International v Argentine Republic, ICSID Case No. ARB/02/16, Award, 28 September 2007.

Sim v Stretch [1936] 2 All ER 1237.

Sequana S.A. v BAR Industries Plc and Others [2019] EWCA Civ. 112.

Shanique Myrie v Barbados, Judgment [2013] CCJ 3 (OJ).

SM Jaleel & Co. Ltd. and Guyana Beverages Inc. v Guyana Son v Kerzner International Resorts Inc. [2008] US Dist. Lexis 67482 [2017] CCJ 2(OJ).

Smithton v Naggar [2013] EWHC 1961 (Ch.).

Smith v Leech Brain &Co. Ltd. [1962] 2 QB 405.

Sullivan v Jack Tar Village Management Co. [2002] High Court, St Kitts/Nevis, No. 203 of 1995.

Sun Trust Bank v Sun International Hotels Ltd. 184 F. Supp. 2d 1246 S.D. Fla. 2001.

Tamika Gilbert, Lynnel Gilbert, Royston Gilbert and Glennor Gilbert v Barbados [2019] CCJ 2 (OJ).

TCL v CARICOM (merits) [2009] CCJ 4 (OJ).

Teck Corp. v Millar 33 DLR (3d) 288 (B.C.S.C.).

Tele2 Sverige AB v Post-och telestyrelsen and Others [2016] ECR I-970.

Attorney General and General Legal Council v Jamaican Bar Association [2023] UKPC 6.

Liquidator of Wendy Fair (Heritage) Ltd. v Hobday [2006] EWHC 5803.

Thomason v Times-Journal 190 Ga. App. 601, 603 (1989).

Thompson v Renmote Mews Ltd. [2006] Supreme Court, Jamaica, No. CLT-138 of 2001.

Thornton v Shoe Lane Parking Ltd. [1971] 1 All ER 686.

Thornton v Telegraph Media Group Ltd. [2010] EWHC 1414 (QB), [2011] 1 WLR 1985.

Tolofson v Jensen [1995] 120 DLR (4th).

Tomlinson v Belize and Trinidad & Tobago, Judgment [2016] CCJ 1 (OJ).

Transvaal Lands Co. v New Belgium (Transvaal) Land and Development Co. [1914] 2 Ch. 488, 84 L.J. Ch. 94 (CA).

Trinidad Cement Ltd. v Caribbean Community, Judgment [2009] CCJ 2 (OJ).

Trinidad Cement Ltd. v CARICOM [2009] CCJ 4 (OJ).

Trinidad Cement Ltd. v Competition Commission, Judgment [2012] CCJ 4 (OJ).

Trinidad Cement Ltd. v Trinidad & Tobago; Trinidad Cement Ltd. & Arawak Cement Ltd. v Barbados [2019] CCJ 1 (OJ).

Trinidad Cement Ltd. v Caribbean Community, Judgment [2009] CCJ 2 (OJ), 5 February 2009.

Legislation

Antigua and Barbuda Companies Act, 1995

Australia Companies Act, 1961

Australian Uniformed Defamation Laws, 2005

Barbados Companies Act, 1985

Canada Business Corporations Act, 1985

Canada Immigration Act, 1952

Company Directors Disqualification Act, 1986

Corporations Act, 2001 (Commonwealth)

Defamation Act of New South Wales, 1974 (repealed)

Dominica Companies Act, 1994

German Stock Corporation Act (Aktiengesetz), 1965

German's Liability Companies Act (GmbHG), 2008

Guyana Criminal Law (Procedure) Act, 1998

Hotelkeeper's Liability Act, 1950

Jamaica Companies Act, 2005

Jamaica Defamation Act, 2013

Jamaican Exclusive Economic Act, 1991

Jamaica's Extradition Act, 2006

Jamaica Jury Act, 2016

Limitation Act, 1969

Maritime Areas Act, 1998

Maritime Drug Trafficking (Suppression) Act, 2016

Treaties

List of Abbreviations

AML/CFT	Anti-Money Laundering and Counter Financing of Terrorism
BCA	Barbados Companies Act
CARICOM	Caribbean Community
CAS	Court of Arbitration for Sport
CBCA	Canada Business Corporation Act
CDDA	Company Directors Disqualification Act
COTED	Council for Trade and Economic Development
CSME	Caribbean Single Market and Economy
DSD	Differences of Sex Development
EC	European Community
ECHR	European Convention on Human Rights
ECtHR	European Court of Human Rights
ESG	Environmental, Social, and Governance
GATS	General Agreement on Trade in Services
GATT	General Agreement on Tariffs and Trade
IAAF	International Amateur Athletic Federation (now World Athletics)
ICSID	International Centre for Settlement of Investment Disputes
ISDS	Investor-State Dispute Settlement
JBA	Jamaica Bar Association
JCA	Jamaica Companies Act

JEITT	Judicial Education Institute of Trinidad and Tobago
NAAATT	National Association of Athletics Administration of Trinidad and Tobago
NCAA	National Collegiate Athletics Association
NZCA	New Zealand Companies Act
OCA	Office of the Children's Advocate
OSAC	Overseas Security Advisory Council
POCA	Proceeds of Crime Act
RTC	Revised Treaty of Chaguaramas
TTCA	Trinidad and Tobago Companies Act
UKCA	United Kingdom Companies Act
UNCRC	United Nations Convention of the Rights of the Child
USADA	United States Anti-Doping Agency
WADA	World Anti-Doping Agency
WTO	World Trade Organization

CHAPTER 1

The Eudaimonic Attorney –
The Virtuous Pursuit of the Greater Good

Shazeeda Ali

The duties of lawyers to their clients and the court are well documented in legislation, case law and the various codes or Canons of legal professional ethics. In the same vein, the obligations of attorneys to the legal profession and the administration of justice are appropriately articulated. Perhaps, what is less acknowledged are the roles and responsibilities of lawyers in society and, indeed, their contribution to the greater good. In light of this omission, the objective of this chapter is to explore the role of the legal profession in enhancing the well-being of society.

Since so many lawyers occupy positions of significance and tremendous influence, it is important for members of the legal profession to "cultivate the good that each…can bring to our legal system, society and humanity".[1] By so doing, each member can help the profession to "steer into law's eudaimonic turn".[2]

This is no trifling feat and, in order to appreciate the implications of this trajectory, one must first examine the notion of eudaimonia.

The concept of eudaimonia is derived from Aristotle's *Nicomachean Ethics*, his seminal philosophical work on the 'science of happiness'.[3] Eudaimonia may be translated literally from ancient Greek, as good demons, "a vivid imagistic expression of what happiness is: life governed by an infestation of good spirits."[4] In its simplest form, it is often taken to mean welfare,

---

1. H. Brown, "The Eudaimonic Turn: How We Can Help Lawyers Flourish," *ABA Journal* (7 September 2021).
2. Ibid.
3. Catherine Moore, "What is Eudaimonia? Aristotle and Eudaimonic Wellbeing," *Positive Psychology* (8 April 2019). https://positivepsychology.com/.
4. Daniel Bowling, "Lawyers and Their Elusive Pursuit of Happiness: Does It Matter?" *Duke Forum for Law & Social Change* 7 (2015): 37–52.

happiness, flourishing or well-being.[5] Indeed, the etymology helps to provide more context as the prefix "eu" means "good" or "well" and "daimon" means "self" or "spirit".[6]

Aristotle used the term as a broad concept to describe the highest good humans could strive toward – or a life 'well lived' – and his conception of eudaimonia reflects the idea of the "pursuit of virtue, excellence, and the best within us", all of which foster human flourishing.[7]

For Aristotle, this meant practising virtues like courage, wisdom, good humour, moderation and kindness.[8] Virtue ethics was advanced by Aristotle but initially asserted by Socrates and Plato who, respectively, advocated the pursuit of the "ultimate good" and "the highest and ultimate aim of both moral thought and behaviour".[9]

In the context of the legal profession, one might ask whether the practice of law is compatible with eudaimonia. The answer should be in the affirmative if "the predominant purpose of one assuming a career in law is to further the aims of justice, and to vigorously promote public order and the common good".[10] In this regard, a eudaimonic approach would hold that true well-being arises from the pursuit of virtue, or *arête*, in one's legal career.[11]

This quest would entail the use of one's legal skills to the best of one's ability; that is, the seeking of excellence. This means that any matter that a lawyer assumes should reflect her belief that the excellence of her actions can help advance the cause of her client and promote the administration of justice.[12]

Further, this approach would involve the pursuit of a goal that has an intrinsically moral value, purpose or cause.[13] For many lawyers, seeking moral virtue in one's career is consistent with

---

5.   Moore, "Eudaimonia".
6.   Ibid.
7.   Ibid.
8.   The Ethics Centre, Ethics Explainer: Eudaimonia (4 August 2016). https://ethics.org.
       au/ethics-explainer-eudaimonia/.
9.   Moore, "Eudaimonia".
10.   Angelo Nicolaides and Stella Vettori, "The Duty of Lawyers: Virtue Ethics and Pursuing
       a Hopeless Legal Case," *Athens Journal of Law* 5, no. 2 (April 2019): 149.
11.   Bowling, "Lawyers".
12.   Ibid.
13.   Ibid.

the idea that law is a public calling.[14] However, throughout their professional career, some lawyers simply pursue extrinsic goals, such as financial success.[15]

Perhaps the apotheosis of eudaimonia may be found within the sphere of professional responsibility. Here, it "can best be understood as relating to character strengths and virtues and their employment in the civic good."[16] Indeed, the virtuous efforts of lawyers to promote the public good can occur in a variety of circumstances connected to professional social responsibility, including engaging in *pro bono* legal work and furthering other public interest objectives.

If, in essence, "the eudaimon life is one dedicated to developing the excellences of being human",[17] then, within this framework, the eudaimonic attorney-at-law may be described as one who possesses and practices the virtues of the legal profession. With this in mind, the focus of this chapter is on the pursuit of eudaimonia by lawyers practising the virtue of professional social responsibility.

If one were to unpack the idea of the social responsibility of lawyers, it could be understood as strategies that combine business, human and social elements, where the more outward-looking aspects involve the responsibilities of lawyers to the community at large.[18]

To appreciate this point of view, one might ask, "what are a lawyer's obligations to the society she lives in while she goes about trying to ply her trade and make a living?"[19] In response, there is a very strong argument to the effect that "the key way in which lawyers serve society – their key social responsibility – is by serving their clients well."[20] Here, one might also consider the limited obligations of lawyers to the public good as those contained in their duties to the court and justice system.[21] Thus, historically, it has

---

14. Ibid.
15. Ibid.
16. Ibid.
17. Ethics Centre, Ethics Explainer.
18. Varsha Aithala and Siddharth Peter de Souza, "Lending a Hand," *India Business Law Journal* (15 October 2018).
19. C. MacDonald, "The Social Responsibilities of Lawyers," *Canadian Business* (17 November 2011).
20. Ibid.
21. Jonathan Herring, *Legal Ethics*, 2nd ed (Oxford: Oxford University Press, 2017).

been believed that the "primary social responsibility of all lawyers is to provide guidance to their clients to enable them to comply with the law or achieve their desired goals in a lawful manner."[22]

However, lawyers "play too important a role in modern society for them to think of themselves as solely beholden to their clients."[23] Moreover, these limited formulations do not embrace the imperative of lawyers giving back to the society a portion of the benefit they receive from it. Indeed, there are increasing expectations on the functions of lawyers in relation to society at large, to identify and define the role they play in the delivery of legal services, promoting access to justice and building a culture of social responsibility.[24]

To put in perspective the role of the lawyer in society, one should not think strictly in terms of "the human micro-implications of a particular situation" but should also look carefully at "the roles individuals play in important social structures, and the roles those structures play in society as a whole."[25] Lawyers are officers of the court and viewed as zealous advocates for their clients, but they are also perceived as "trustees for the public good".[26] Nonetheless, our legal culture appears to have "mostly fallen out of the habit of thinking about its public obligations".[27]

Thus, it is important to steer the legal profession into the eudaimonic turn.[28] By so doing, eudaimonic attorneys can demonstrate social responsibility and act for the good of society by, *inter alia,* engaging in pro bono activities, implementing effective corporate governance and sustainability initiatives in their law practice, whilst advancing public interest strategies.

Professional Responsibility as a Social Contract

There is a school of thought that there exists an implied social contract between legal professionals and the rest of society.[29]

22. R. Garrett, "The Social Responsibility of Lawyers in Their Professional Capacity," *University of Miami Law Review* 30 (1975–1976): 879.
23. MacDonald, "Social Responsibilities".
24. Aithala and Siddharth, "Lending a Hand".
25. MacDonald, "Social Responsibilities".
26. Robert Gordon, "Why Lawyers Can't Just be Hired Guns," in *Ethics in Practice: Lawyers' Roles, Responsibilities, and Regulation,* ed. Deborah Rhode (Oxford: Oxford University Press, 2000).
27. Ibid.
28. Brown, "Eudaimonic Turn".
29. Heineman, Ben, William Lee, and David Wilkins, Lawyers as Professionals and as

Accordingly, it has been suggested that a more appropriate way to view legal education, and the nature of the law itself, is as a social contract between legal educators, lawyers and society.[30]

In *Du Contrat Social*, Jean-Jacques Rousseau proposed that all participants in a society must surrender an equal amount of rights and impose the same degree of duties in return for the privileges and benefits of freedom and a free society.[31] Rousseau, *philosophe*, believed in the possibility of a genuine social contract – one in which, in exchange for their independence, people would receive a greater freedom; that is, "true political, or republican, liberty."[32] According to Rousseau, such liberty is to be found in obedience to what he described as the *volonté générale*, in which this "general will" is "a collectively held will that aims at the common good or the common interest".[33]

Therefore, given the critical role it performs in the governance of a society, the legal profession can be said to have assumed a form of social contract. Undoubtedly, lawyers have contributed to state formation and continue to play an important part in enhancing the governability of society.[34] Certainly, as part of civil society, lawyers constitute a professional body that is "interposed between the powerless individual and the state itself or a variety of powerful private organisations."[35] Generally, it can be said that lawyers help to "maintain and refresh the public sphere, the infrastructure of law and cultural convention that constitutes the cement of society."[36]

In fact, most lawyers are privileged to earn an income that allows them to enjoy a relatively good standard of living. Further, while the profession operates largely in the private sector, it also

---

Citizens: Key Roles and Responsibilities in the 21st Century (Harvard Law School Center on the Legal Profession, 2014), https://clp.law.harvard.edu/wp-content/uploads/2022/10/Professionalism-Project-Essay_11.20.14.pdf.

30. Robert Adler, "Renewing the 'Social Contract' Between Law Schools, Lawyers, and Society," Utah OnLaw: *Utah Law Review Online Supplement* 1 (2014).

31. Ibid.

32. The Social Contract in Rousseau, https://www.britannica.com/topic/social-contract/The-social-contract-in-Rousseau.

33. Ibid.

34. C. Arup, "The Social Responsibilities of Lawyers: The Future of Regulation," Sino-Australian Seminar Lawyers Practice and Ethics, Ministry of Justice, People's Republic of China (27–28 September 2004).

35. Ibid.

36. Gordon, "Hired Guns".

receives protection and status from the state.[37] This relationship reinforces the idea of a social contract in which, in addition to the more tangible professional benefits, attorneys embrace the intrinsic rewards inherent in providing service to others.[38]

Consequently, in return for the substantial privileges that attorneys enjoy, it follows that they should assume a proportionate degree of duties to society.[39] When one considers the social contract between businesses and society today, it is typically found that society expects commercial entities to be good corporate citizens.[40] Likewise, from a eudaimonic perspective, the social contract involving the legal profession and society would dictate that lawyers ought to be socially responsible professionals who contribute to the greater good.

Traditionally, the most common form of law practice has been the sole practitioner or a small partnership. The development of large law firms, while still nominally a partnership, has enabled lawyers to organize on a much more functional basis.[41] Since these firms are usually operated along corporate lines, it is suggested that the concept of corporate social responsibility (CSR) may be adapted to meet the social responsibility of lawyers, in accordance with the essential role that lawyers play in society.

CSR is a form of self-regulation that reflects a company's commitment to contributing to the well-being of society through various environmental and social measures.[42] CSR defines the business model and degree of responsibility that companies should maintain in order to have a positive impact on the world.[43] The CSR model outlines how a company can be accountable to its staff, clients, the public, as well as local and global environments.[44] Overall, to be a good corporate citizen, the expectation is that a company

37.   Arup, "Social Responsibilities".
38.   Ibid.
39.   Adler, "Social Contract".
40.   Archie Carroll, "Carroll's Pyramid of CSR: Taking Another Look," *International Journal of Corporate Social Responsibility* 1, no. 3 (2016).
41.   Arup, "Social Responsibilities".
42.   Nadia Reckmann, "What Is Corporate Social Responsibility?" Business News Daily (29 June 2022), https://www.businessnewsdaily.com/4679-corporate-social-responsibility.html.
43.   Victoria University, "Corporate Social Responsibility in Action: The Good and the Bad," 4 February 2020, https://online.vu.edu.au/blog/what-is-corporate-social-responsibility.
44.   Ibid.

should take part in initiatives that will contribute to an improved society and quality of life. One might add that this emphasis on the well-being of society is consistent with a eudaimonic approach.

In 1962, noted economist Milton Friedman argued that social issues are not the concern of businesspeople and that these problems should be resolved by the unfettered workings of the free market system.[45] For instance, Friedman contended that if the corporate executives make expenditures on reducing pollution "beyond the amount that is in the best interests of the corporation or that is required by law in order to contribute to the social objective of improving the environment", they would be spending someone else's money, that is, the shareholders' money.[46] This would undermine their primary responsibility to conduct business in a manner that would "make as much money as possible while conforming to the basic rules of the society".[47] Today, however, businesses are increasingly expected to be accountable for how their practices impact society and the environment. For instance, in 2022, increased pressure was exerted on bauxite company, Windalco, after effluent from its plant polluted the Rio Cobre in St Catherine, Jamaica and caused a fish kill. Environmental groups demanded all of Windalco's environmental permits suspended until it implemented corrective measures to prevent further pollution of the river.[48]

This type of action makes it clear that CSR is no longer just a respected business practice but a consumer-driven demand by society. Therefore, as more socially conscious people choose businesses that are focused on social responsibility, implementing a CSR model is essential for the maintenance and growth of a law firm's reputation and clientele.

Pyramid of Corporate Social Responsibility

An important construct of CSR is Carroll's *Pyramid of Corporate*

---

45.   Archie Carroll, Jill Brown, and Ann Buchholtz, *Business & Society: Ethics, Sustainability & Stakeholder Management*, 11th ed. (Boston: Cengage, 2022).

46.   M. Friedman, "The Social Responsibility of Business Is to Increase Its Profits," in *Corporate Ethics and Corporate Governance*, eds. W.C. Zimmerli, M. Holzinger, and K. Richter (Berlin: Springer, 2007).

47.   Ibid.

48.   Radio Jamaica News, "Environment lobbyist wants Windalco's environmental permit suspended" (2 August 2022).

Social Responsibility.[49] This theory holds that firms should engage in decisions, actions, policies and practices that simultaneously fulfil the four component parts of the CSR pyramid. Essentially, these four modules form a conceptual framework that comprises the economic, legal, ethical and philanthropic or discretionary responsibilities that society places on businesses at a given point in time.[50]

In terms of understanding each type of responsibility, Carroll notes that the economic responsibility is "required" of business by society. As CSR is built upon the premise of an economically sound and sustainable business, it is a foundational requirement that the base of the pyramid is economic responsibility.[51] According to Carroll, just as the footings of a building must be strong to support the entire edifice, sustained profitability must be strong to support society's other expectations of enterprises.[52] For Carroll, the legal responsibility is also "required" by society; the ethical responsibility is "expected" by society; and the philanthropic responsibility is "expected/desired" by society.[53]

However, it is submitted that for lawyers, as officers of the court, it should not simply be an expectation but it should be a requirement that they would operate in both a lawful and ethical fashion. Thus, for the legal profession, it is suggested that the legal and ethical responsibilities should co-exist at the base, alongside economic responsibility.

Philanthropy is at the apex of Carroll's pyramid since, although not a responsibility in a literal sense, it has become a part of the everyday expectations of a business by the public.[54] In principle, corporate philanthropy embraces a company's voluntary or discretionary activities that are guided by its desire to participate in social activities that are not mandated by law or ethics.[55] To fulfil its philanthropic objectives, businesses engage in a variety of activities, including monetary gifts, product and service donations, volunteerism by staff, community development and other

49.   Carroll, "Pyramid".
50.   Ibid.
51.   Ibid.
52.   Ibid.
53.   Ibid.
54.   Ibid.
55.   Ibid.

discretionary contribution to the community.[56] Hence, this category is often thought of as good "corporate citizenship" as these actions would touch the lives of other citizens in many ways.[57]

A recent example is Wata, the Wisynco water brand, which is celebrating Jamaica's sixtieth independence anniversary by giving back through the Wata Jamaica 60th Education Initiative. The Wata bottles are wrapped in a bright yellow label which boasts the official "Jamaica 60" logo and displays a pledge to contribute JM$1 from the sale of each bottle, up to JM$12 million, to an education initiative that will benefit students and teachers.[58]

Some cynics assert that businesses pursue strategic philanthropic activities as a utilitarian decision and not necessarily for noble or self-sacrificing reasons.[59] They claim that this is done to be seen as a good corporate citizen, simply to enhance the company's reputation. Nonetheless, many companies do pursue philanthropy for altruistic reasons, which they consider to be the virtuous thing to do.[60]

Regardless of the motive, it remains one of the most important elements of CSR because the public wants and expects businesses to engage in discretionary philanthropic acts. Furthermore, for the eudaimonic law firm acting consistently with the CSR model, this would mean that it has the expectation, and even responsibility, to do "what is right, just, and fair and to avoid or minimize harm to all the stakeholders with whom it interacts".[61]

Indicators of CSR would involve an evaluation of institutional aspects of a firm, including sustainability of operations, inclusivity of the working environment, quality of work life, as well as community engagement efforts.

A law firm can implement several types of CSR initiatives; the most common activities relate to environmental efforts, charity work, ethical labour practices and volunteer projects.[62] These measures help to promote a eudaimonic culture that recognizes

56.   Ibid.
57.   Ibid.
58.   *Jamaica Observer*, "WATA marks Jamaica 60th with $12m in education grants," 30 August 2022.
59.   Carroll, "Pyramid".
60.   Ibid.
61.   Ibid.
62.   Reckmann, "Corporate Social Responsibility".

and rewards excellent professional conduct, which should foster honesty, integrity and fairness. The following section involves a review of some of the key components of CSR that may indicate whether a law firm is a good corporate citizen.

Diversity and Inclusion

Diversity is achieved through programmes and policies that encourage increased representation of varied races, cultural backgrounds, religions, genders, sexual orientation, ages, abilities and disabilities. Essentially, diversity refers to the wide variation in personal, physical and social characteristics that exist, "while inclusion refers to the procedures organizations implement to integrate everyone in the workplace".[63]

These policies should safeguard staff from being discriminated against in terms of recruitment and career progression, including appointment, compensation, promotion and professional development. To this end, some law firms have drawn up specific policies covering anti-discrimination, prevention of sexual harassment and promotion of diversity to ensure that staff receive equality in treatment.

In order to ensure their broad application, such policies should also extend to the clients and service providers with whom the firm does business. Lawyers have a responsibility to the society to include everyone, regardless of race, culture, religion or societal class; and, as such, a law firm should not victimize a client or third-party contractor based on any prejudice.

In essence, law firms should place a strong emphasis on ensuring a diverse and inclusive work environment that prevents any form of discrimination in their practice, and issues of diversity, equality and social justice should be incorporated into the firm's business strategies.

Environmental Impact

This criterion refers to a firm's attempts to reduce its ecological footprint and not cause harm to the environment. Concerns about climate change should be addressed by a firm's environmental

---

63.   https://resources.workable.com/hr-terms/diversity-vs-inclusion.

initiatives and such sustainability policies should be systematically ingrained at all levels, including at the supply chain end.[64] This means that firms need to be responsible and choose business relationships in a discerning manner. Indeed, it is important for firms to consistently evaluate their energy-consumption and waste-generation habits and use suppliers with an established record of compliance with responsible standards.

In any office environment, opportunities to become greener include adopting renewable energy sources, reducing reliance on paper products, and using more energy-efficient equipment, appliances and light fixtures.[65] The increased usage of technology in the legal industry, and the facilitation of e-filing and e-service in some jurisdictions, has also made it possible for law firms to become more sustainable with resources.[66]

Overall, economic and ecological sustainability practices may be assessed through energy conservation, waste reduction and recycling efforts, as well as ethical supply-chain management.

Pro Bono Service

In some jurisdictions, driven in part by cuts to legal aid and public sector services, many law firms are engaged in activities that support access to justice for the homeless and other socially disadvantaged groups.[67] One could contend that many lawyers recognize an obligation to the greater good by means of their pro bono work. However, such retainers are not undertaken by every lawyer and, for a number of law firms, pro bono legal aid matters are handled on an *ad hoc* basis with minimal systemic or institutional support.

Nonetheless, attempts are being made in some jurisdictions to embed the importance of pro bono work. This is reflected in the American Bar Association's rules which state that "every lawyer,

---

64. E.K. Tekin, A. Ertürk, and H. Tozan, "Corporate Social Responsibility in Supply Chains," in *Applications of Contemporary Management Approaches in Supply Chains*, eds. H. Tozan and A. Erturk (London: IntechOpen, 2015), DOI: 10.5772/59582.

65. L. Dean, "Corporate social responsibility in the legal industry: Trends and opportunities," 24 August 2017, https://www.onelegal.com/blog/corporate-social-responsibility-in-the-legal-industry-trends-and-opportunities/.

66. Ibid.

67. J. Goodman, "Corporate social responsibility – community spirit", 24 October 2016, https://www.lawgazette.co.uk/features/corporate-social-responsibility-community-spirit/5058438.article.

regardless of professional prominence or professional workload, has a responsibility to provide legal services to those unable to pay, and personal involvement in the problems of the disadvantaged can be one of the most rewarding experiences in the life of a lawyer".[68] To this end, the ABA urges all lawyers to provide a minimum of fifty hours of pro bono services annually.[69]

Since the early 2000s, the Bar Human Rights Committee of England and Wales has facilitated barrister volunteers going to Jamaica to support local lawyers undertaking death row cases.[70] Their involvement has been made possible through funding from various chambers in the UK.[71] There are other positive signs in Jamaica where, for example, following the signing of a memorandum of understanding between the Jamaican Bar Association and Woman Incorporated, women who are victims of domestic violence will be able to receive free legal services.[72] The assistance will be in the nature of representation in the civil courts for protection orders, custody, maintenance and financial provision applications. Also, the human rights group, Jamaicans for Justice (JFJ) provides direct legal support in human rights matters, including pro bono legal advice to low-income and marginalized persons.

Volunteerism

An important aspect of CSR relates to volunteerism, which includes activities such as volunteering one's time in the community or participating in fundraising activities. However, it has been contended that some firms penalize lawyers for clocking up insufficient billable hours in circumstances where they have been volunteering for charity work.[73]

Volunteer service in the community could involve cleaning up a beach, sorting donations at a food or clothes charity, or painting crosswalks. All of these efforts would make a positive impact on the people in the surrounding neighbourhoods, while helping to

---

68.   ABA Model Rule 6.1.
69.   https://www.americanbar.org/groups/probono_public_service/policy/aba_model_
      rule_6_1/.
70.   https://barhumanrights.org.uk/project/jamaican-death-row-pro-bono/.
71.   Ibid.
72.   J. Murphy, "Bar Assn to offer free legal services to domestic violence victims," Gleaner,
      13 November 2021).
73.   Goodman, "Community Spirit".

build camaraderie in the law firm. One Jamaican law firm's website showcases its "responsibility as a good corporate citizen" to the community, where it frequently lends support to meaningful projects and activities that focus on improving the lives of the youth.[74] This includes the firm's provision, for many years, of material support for a day-care centre serving the downtown community, as well as an outreach programme to help meet the pressing educational and recreational needs of the children living in the immediate environs of their Kingston office.[75]

Another dimension of the giving back component of volunteerism could involve attorneys setting up funds for scholarships, prizes or other grants for law students. For instance, some firms have actively supported legal education in the region by being a contributor to the UWI Endowment Fund. Others have promoted academic excellence by awarding scholarships, bursaries, prizes and internships to students pursuing the LLB degree at the UWI or the Legal Education Certificate at the regional law schools.

Apart from these activities, professional associations of lawyers should endorse programmes to inform the public about their rights and duties under the law and the important role of lawyers in protecting their fundamental freedoms.[76] Special attention should be given to assisting the poor and other disadvantaged persons to enable them to assert their rights and, where necessary, call upon the assistance of lawyers.[77]

Benefits of Social Responsibility

CSR is a complex concept that permeates every stage of the life cycle of a legal practice. Although many of the measures appear expensive and burdensome, they would yield several long-term benefits to legal practices and their clients. This is because CSR plays a crucial role in a firm's brand perception, attractiveness to clients, employees, talent retention and overall success.[78] Some of

---

74.   https://dunncox.com/why-dunncox/.
75.   Ibid.
76.   United Nations. Basic Principles on the Role of Lawyers, adopted by the Eighth UN Congress on the Prevention of Crime and the Treatment of Offenders, Havana, Cuba, 27 August to 7 September, 1990.
77.   Ibid.
78.   Reckmann, "Corporate Social Responsibility".

these benefits include[79]:

    i. Brand recognition: engaging in CSR has a great impact on a client's public image as clients often feel more emotionally connected and loyal to a brand that aligns with their values.

    ii. Increased profits: many firms with a well-thought-out CSR strategy experience higher profit margins. As people become more aware of local, national and international issues, a firm's CSR policies can have a huge impact on their potential clients as, by proving they can be socially responsible, the firm would motivate clients to do business with them.

    iii. Increased employee retention and recruitment: CSR practices also help to boost employee morale as employees and employers gain a greater sense of purpose and connection to their work. Indeed, knowing their actions will help the world in a positive way would motivate employees and provide an incentive to continue working with the firm.[80]

Apart from these benefits, the emergence of the ESG (environmental, social, and governance) movement in the late 2010s has brought focus on the sustainability of a firm with regard to these pillars.[81] The ESG metrics embody the CSR principles and may be used by stakeholders to evaluate a firm's environmental and social impact. It may also be invoked to assess key elements about a firm's governance structure to determine if it is formulated to promote transparency, accountability and greater professional social responsibility.

Consequently, by adopting a CSR approach, a firm can establish a comprehensive framework that maximizes the well-being of its stakeholders, including its clients, employees and suppliers. Significantly, the focus on well-being would direct the law firm towards a eudaimonic path.

---

79. Jason Fernando, "What is CSR? Corporate Social Responsibility Explained," https://www.investopedia.com/terms/c/corp-social-responsibility.asp.
80. Victoria University, "Corporate Social Responsibility".
81. Kyle Peterdy, "ESG (Environmental, Social and Governance): A framework for understanding and measuring how sustainably an organization is operating," 26 October 2022, https://corporatefinanceinstitute.com/resources/esg/esg-environmental-social-governance/.

Lawyers as Gatekeepers

Up to this point, the discussion has focused on the conventional attributes of lawyers as professionally responsible citizens within the ambit of the CSR model. The next part of the chapter will direct the spotlight on that aspect of professional responsibility that relates to the role of the lawyer as a gatekeeper in the international financial system.

Gatekeepers are an essential component of any effective corporate governance regime. Since corporate and commercial lawyers are involved in "overseeing the ultimate passage of their clients' transactions from planning to fruition", this gives them access to information that would allow them to detect and disrupt wrongful conduct, thereby qualifying them as effective gatekeepers.[82]

As an attorney's role has always included a substantial gatekeeper facet, it follows that they can play a significant part in preventing client misconduct. Consequently, to require lawyers to respond to client misconduct is not automatically equivalent to enlisting them as secret police, "cops on the beat" or whistleblowers for the government.[83]

Undoubtedly, based on their function, lawyers represent major sources of information for persons investigating serious financial crime, as they are often the medium through which miscreant clients, including corrupt politicians, terrorists and other criminals, seek to gain access to various corporate and commercial services. As such, given the responsibility of lawyers as gatekeepers, "it is important to avoid the misconception that lawyers should have no role to play in preventing client misconduct."[84]

In this regard, virtue ethics dictate that, as professionals, lawyers "should consider their options carefully before embarking on a legal venture with a client".[85] In this process, lawyers should be guided by a moral compass which should put virtue ahead of the

---

82. Stephane Rousseau, Julie Biron, and Ejan Mackaay, "Lawyers as Gatekeepers," in *Company Lawyers Independent by Design: An ECLA White Paper*, eds. P. Coen and C. Roquilly (Paris: Lexis Nexis, 2014).
83. Fred C. Zacharias, "Lawyers as Gatekeepers," *University of San Diego Public Law and Legal Theory Research Paper Series* 20 (2004), https://digital.sandiego.edu/lwps_public/art20.
84. Zacharias, "Gatekeepers".
85. Nicolaides, "Duty of Lawyers".

demands of their profession.[86]

Therefore, although lawyers should not be discriminatory in their decision to accept a retainer, law firms must be increasingly mindful of the clients they take on and ensure that they are not "furthering corruption, propping up authoritarian regimes or inadvertently assisting with money laundering".[87]

In fact, the actions of members of the profession to decline to act for certain persons can send a strong message. For instance, the recent "flight of top-tier legal capacity" from Russia, following Putin's invasion of Ukraine, mirrored the larger movement of Western companies out of the country.[88] The legal withdrawal from Russia marks a major shift as it demonstrates that law firms are re-examining their clients' ethical standards and their moral standing.[89] This reaction is consistent with changing public sentiment, as many clients are becoming increasingly outraged at the unscrupulous enablers of global corruption.[90] In response, more law firms are resisting representing the world's kleptocrats.[91]

Lawyers often face criticism where they hide behind and, sometimes, abuse key principles of the profession, notably the protection afforded by client confidentiality and legal professional privilege (LPP), in order to shield the ethically questionable (and at times criminal) behaviour of their clients.[92] However, LPP is not absolute as it is subject to an illicit purpose exception where the client is seeking to use the attorney to further an unlawful purpose, such as money laundering.[93] This exception to LPP demonstrates that attorneys are precluded from protecting the confidence of clients who seek to invoke their services to engage in criminality.[94] The exception is necessary to "preserve interests that society has

---

86.   Ibid.
87.   Alexandra Wrage, "Mind your client: law firms must choose to be responsible gatekeepers, International Bar Association, 25 April 2022, https://www.ibanet.org/mind-your-client-law-firms-must-choose-responsible-gatekeepers.
88.   Ibid.
89.   Ibid.
90.   Ibid.
91.   Ibid.
92.   International Bar Association, "IBA launches new project examining the role of lawyers as ethical gatekeepers," 2 June 2022, https://www.ibanet.org/IBA-launches-new-project-examining-the-role-of-lawyers-as-ethical-gatekeepers.
93.   *R. v Central Criminal Court ex parte Francis & Francis (A Firm)* [1989] A.C. 346.
94.   For example, *R. v Cox and Railton* (1884) 14 QBD 153.

deemed more important than the client's".[95]

In the sphere of the criminal law, it is obvious that lawyers should not engage directly in criminal activity nor participate in crimes, including conspiring with clients or aiding or abetting illegal conduct. Otherwise, they will be held culpable under the criminal law. In addition, under the relevant codes or canons of legal professional ethics, an attorney has a duty to "not act contrary to the laws of the land, or aid, counsel or assist any man to break those laws".[96] Such a violation of the criminal law could lead to disciplinary action for professional misconduct. One might consider these duties of lawyers to refrain from participation in the illicit activity of their clients as being consistent with their social responsibilities and obligations to the public good.

Apart from exercising such restraint, positive duties to detect and deter criminal conduct have been imposed on lawyers within the ambit of the anti-money laundering and counter financing of terrorism (AML/CFT) regime. This is because it has long been recognized that, given their role and function in the financial system, lawyers are vulnerable to becoming embroiled in a money laundering or terrorist financing scheme. In reality, as gatekeepers to the financial system, they are well poised to assist in the prevention and detection of these unlawful activities.

Consequently, in many jurisdictions, attorneys are required to implement programmes, policies and procedures, such as client due diligence and risk-profiling measures, record-keeping and reporting obligations. These requirements are not intended to transform lawyers into police officers or financial investigators, nor are they meant to place them in harm's way.[97] The idea is that, given their status in the financial system, lawyers should have a responsibility to exercise vigilance in ensuring that transactions in which they are involved do not further or facilitate serious financial crimes.[98]

However, not all lawyers are content with these responsibilities

---

95.   Zacharias, "Gatekeepers".
96.   For example, Canon III(f) Legal Profession (Canons of Professional Ethics) Rules, Jamaica
97.   General Legal Council of Jamaica, *Anti-Money* Laundering Guidance for the Legal Profession (May 2014).
98.   Ibid.

that they believe have been foisted upon the profession. In 2013, in Jamaica, the Proceeds of Crime (Designation of Non-Financial Institution) (Attorneys-at-Law) Order designated attorneys-at-law, engaged in certain specified activities, to be a part of the regulated sector for the purpose of the Proceeds of Crime Act (POCA). Shortly after the designation, the Jamaican Bar Association sought and obtained an injunction to suspend the operation of this order.[99] The thrust of their claim was that the order was "unconstitutional, overboard, unenforceable or otherwise vague and unlawful".[100]

The JBA contended, inter alia, that the regime conflicted with the integral and essential role played by attorneys-at-law in the proper administration of justice and maintenance of the rule of law. On appeal, they further challenged whether the disclosure, identification, verification and record-keeping requirements of the regime are within proper limits, and contended that they breach the constitutional rights of regulated attorneys-at-law and their duty of commitment to their client's cause.[101]

Much of the case involved issues surrounding the impact of the POCA provisions on the attorney-client relationship, particularly as relates to confidentiality and legal professional privilege, as well as the constitutionality of such provisions. It is beyond the scope of this chapter to evaluate the merits of the arguments proffered or the decisions of the courts. However, the case raises a broader concern as relates to the role of lawyers, as gatekeepers, in the prevention and detection of serious crime and the apparent reluctance of the profession to assume such responsibility.

The JBA case must be viewed within the context of Jamaica, which has one of the highest crime rates in the world.[102] Much of the crime and violence are associated with organized criminal activity, which generates several million dollars annually. These illicit proceeds are often laundered in Jamaica, using various financial vehicles, including the purchase of real estate, as well as investment in other high-value assets. It is evident that many of these money-

---

99. *Jamaican Bar Association v Attorney General and General Legal Council* [2014] JMSC Civ. 179; [2017] JMFC Full 02.
100. Ibid.
101. [2020] JMCA Civ 37.
102. Overseas Security Advisory Council, Jamaica 2020 Crime & Safety Report, US Department of State, https://www.osac.gov/Country/Jamaica/Content/Detail/Report/d4b8403a-3feb-427b-bd36-18f1af0b746a.

laundering devices would involve the services of attorneys.

While the financial sector has long been placed on the AML/ CFT frontline, and other non-financial professionals, such as accountants, real estate brokers and gaming operators, have accepted their role as gatekeepers within the regulated sector, the legal profession has fought tooth and nail to avoid several of the obligations under POCA.

In the course of the litigation, the Court of Appeal declared a number of provisions null and void for infringement of certain fundamental rights, but accepted that the identification, verification and record-keeping requirements, although intrusive on the client's privacy rights, served a public purpose and would be useful to prevent regulated attorneys from being used as pawns in money-laundering schemes.[103]

The appellate court also agreed that the state's decision to extend the AML/CFT measures to regulated attorneys had a legitimate aim and was not irrational in light of global concerns surrounding money laundering and terrorist financing, particularly because there was ample evidence to show the importance of their role in the international fight against organized crime.[104]

On appeal to the Judicial Committee of the Privy Council, it was held that in terms of combatting criminality, as well as Jamaica's economic prosperity and international standing, the objectives of the AML regime and its application to attorneys are of first importance.[105] Where disciplinary regulation is insufficient in addressing the facilitation of money laundering by lawyers, in the interest of effective detection, prevention and enforcement, making the regime part of the criminal law is within the legislature's margin of appreciation and the range of reasonable options open to it – a course of action taken in many countries.[106] Overall, the AML regime was not considered to be arbitrary and legal professional privilege was deemed sufficiently protected by a number of safeguards built into the regime.[107] Having regard to the importance of the

103. [2020] JMCA Civ 37.
104. Ibid.
105. *Attorney General and General Legal Council v Jamaican Bar Association* [2023] UKPC 6.
106. Ibid.
107. Ibid.

objectives of the AML regime, for Jamaican society and economy, the board held that a fair balance has been struck; the regime is a proportionate measure that does not breach the constitutional rights of attorneys or their clients; and, moreover, any infringement of rights of privacy has been demonstrably justified.[108]

As such, one might ponder why the legal profession in Jamaica would have been so averse, or even antagonistic, to assuming its role in the fight against serious crime in the country. Some lawyers have pointed to a fear of retaliation from their clients. Nonetheless, one may cynically suggest that the general reluctance of the profession to accept their role in the AML/CFT regime highlights a deficiency in the culture of social responsibility within the profession. Perhaps, if virtue ethics were more fully ingrained in the profession, attorneys would better value the contribution that they can make to the public good by playing their part in the detection and prevention of financial crime.

Globally, given the potential magnitude of the function of lawyers as gatekeepers, the International Bar Association (IBA) announced in 2022 that it had embarked on a project to examine the role of lawyers as professional and ethical gatekeepers within wider society, to help clarify their ethical responsibilities when providing services.[109]

The IBA's action is in response to criticisms of the profession in relation to perceived facilitation of illicit financial activity; enabling climate change; frustrating the achievement of the United Nation's Sustainable Development Goals (SDGs); and, the most recent reproach, legal services provided to individuals and entities associated with Russia's invasion of Ukraine.[110]

Indeed, irrespective of a positive legal obligation to do so, as responsible professionals, attorneys should conduct due diligence on all clients and the source of their funds, verify ultimate beneficial ownership and double-check account holders. Generally, it is critical for lawyers to "establish robust money laundering controls, develop internal ethical guidelines about the types of work the firm will and will not take on, and routinely review clients and matters

---

108. Ibid.
109. International Bar Association, "Ethical gatekeepers".
110. Ibid.

to confirm that they are not inadvertently furthering illegal or, even, anti-democratic conduct".[111]

At root, it is a good thing for lawyers to screen client misconduct as it keeps them honest, serves societal interests in preventing harm and enhances judicial administration.[112] By making lawyers think about the morality and legality of clients' conduct, as well as their own, it encourages them to help clients recognize and pursue appropriate behaviour.[113] All of these are valid functions for lawyers and have always been understood to play a part in their everyday dealings with clients.[114]

Ultimately, "[I]t is time for ethical and competent lawyers to prevail in a spirit in which they become co-creators of a virtuous society."[115] A virtuous lawyer "adheres to ingrained and objective moral norms or character traits which impact and direct his or her capacity to judge between what action is right or wrong and to then act accordingly".[116] In so doing, they will "take on the mantle of responsible gatekeeper"[117] and fulfil their role in promoting justice.

Eudaimonia and Legal Professional Ethics

In return for their rights of practice, there are standards of professional conduct by which the legal practitioner assumes duties to their clients, the court, the legal profession and the community.[118] These principles encompass honesty, candour, confidentiality, diligence, courtesy and fairness.[119] However, some commentators bemoan the disappearance of the "lawyer statesman",[120] an earlier ideal whose "traits of openness, learning, and prudence caused the citizenry" to look to him for guidance in a challenging matter.[121]

In most jurisdictions, admission to the Bar requires character and fitness evaluations of potential attorneys. Nevertheless, these

---

111. Wrage, "Mind your client".
112. Zacharias, "Gatekeepers".
113. Ibid.
114. Ibid.
115. Nicolaides, "Duty of Lawyers".
116. Ibid.
117. Wrage, "Mind your client".
118. Arup, "Social Responsibilities".
119. Ibid.
120. Anthony Kronman, former Dean of Yale Law School, quoted in Bowling, "Lawyers".
121. Bowling, "Lawyers".

assessments are often viewed as assets a person either has or does not have, rather than virtues one can cultivate.[122] It has been suggested that what is required is a deeper consideration of what it means to have and cultivate character and "a more holistic definition of fitness to practice law".[123]

In this regard, from an ethical standpoint, lawyers should learn how "to step into the eustress zone and take a proactive, eudaimonic approach toward multidimensional fitness to practice law".[124] In considering the consequences of an action, lawyers should take into account their impact on the flourishing of others and should do their best "to eliminate as many barriers to flourishing" as possible.[125]

This goal comports with the overarching objective of legal professional ethics, which purports that an attorney shall "at all times maintain the honour and dignity of the profession and shall abstain from behaviour which may tend to discredit the profession of which he is a member".[126] In fact, it has become somewhat of a truism that it is "required of lawyers practising in this country that they should discharge their professional duties with integrity, probity and complete trustworthiness".[127]

Therefore, an ethical legal practice should not be considered an option, but rather, it should form "an indispensable and integral part of the justice system".[128] Against this background, virtue ethics would help lawyers facing moral dilemmas to decide between what is right and wrong. In summary, the ethical lawyer is "a person who possesses the traits of character that together comprise the moral quality commonly associated with the most morally praiseworthy among us: the quality of integrity".[129]

For many, it is believed that law is no longer a calling and is "just a job with ridiculous hours, stress and unpaid law school debt".[130]

---

122. Brown, "Eudaimonic Turn".
123. Ibid.
124. Ibid.
125. Ethics Centre, Ethics Explainer.
126. For example, Canon 1(b) Legal Profession (Canons of Professional Ethics) Rules, Jamaica.
127. Per Sir Thomas Bingham, MR in *Bolton v Law Society* [1994] 2 All ER 486.
128. Nicolaides, "Duty of Lawyers".
129. Dolovich, S., "Ethical Lawyering and the Possibility of Integrity" (2002) 70(5) *Fordham Law Review* 1629.
130. Bowling, "Lawyers".

As a whole, lawyers suffer from higher rates of depression than other professions, along with accompanying social maladies, such as substance abuse and suicide.[131]

The result is that legal professionalism is said to be in decline, along with the well-being of lawyers.[132] However, "if more lawyers re-discover why they became lawyers in the first place and rededicate themselves to those intrinsic goals", then it would be possible to have "a happier, healthier, and more ethical profession".[133]

Although the legal profession "wrestles with myriad problems and challenges, instead of solely ruminating about brokenness, harm and damage", lawyers "can become healthier practitioners, individually and collectively" by adopting a eudaimonic approach to the practice of law.[134] Hence, it has been suggested that encouraging and promoting well-being beyond merely the treatment of illness will help to increase professional competence, professionalism and work satisfaction.[135] To this end, there seems to be a slow, eudaimonic turn in the profession as an increasing number of scholars and groups are focused on lawyer well-being.[136]

This is a pivotal development as well-being forms an important component of legal professionalism. Thus, it is in the interests of enhancing the profession and its role in society that its leaders should institute measures to better understand and promote well-being.[137] Overall, one might say that a happier lawyer is a better lawyer.

As Aristotle purported, well-being is the end to which all actions aim and well-being resides in fulfilling our own proper function. Therefore, some scholars believe that well-being and professionalism are inextricably bound.[138] Indeed, it has been argued that "the values that promote professionalism - integrity, collegiality, honesty, decency – are the same that promote well-

---

131.   Ibid.
132.   Ibid.
133.   Ibid.
134.   Brown, "Eudaimonic Turn".
135.   Bowling, "Lawyers".
136.   Ibid.
137.   Ibid.
138.   Ibid.

being, and their absence is shown to correlate with distress."[139]

According to Aristotle, he is happy who lives in accordance with complete virtue.[140] Regrettably, the pursuit of happiness has proved futile for many members of the legal profession. However, if character and virtue are the drivers of happiness, one can choose happiness by seeking to cultivate one's character through ethical behaviour.[141]

At the end of the day, a happy lawyer will be a more ethical and effective advocate for her clients.

Towards a Eudaimonic Profession

It is said that attorneys-at-law should have the characteristics of a technical expert, wise counsellor and effective leader.[142] These qualities are essential because an attorney has a responsibility to act in a manner that contributes to the administration of justice, promotes the protection of rights and preserves the rule of law.

At the same time, "lawyers need to be courageous enough" to integrate their professional endeavours into a good or well-lived life, while maintaining a "continuity" and "interdependence between the virtues required for good lawyering" and those necessary for "a good human life".[143]

The starting point in the responsibility to cultivate a happy eudaimonic lawyer should reside in the faculty of law, in which future attorneys commence their legal education, and this journey should continue at the professional law school. In these settings, as one commentator opined, law students should be deemed to be the clients of their lecturers.[144]

At an early stage, students should be immersed into an understanding of the demands and responsibilities of the legal profession. It should be the duty of legal educators to determine and impart the skills and content that will allow students to identify and correct injustice.[145] In this context, students should be

---

139. Ibid.
140. Moore, "Eudaimonia".
141. Bowling, "Lawyers".
142. Heineman, Lee, and Wilkins, Lawyers as Professionals.
143. Nicolaides, "Duty of Lawyers".
144. Karen Tokarz, "Access to Justice: The Social Responsibility of Lawyers," *Washington University Journal of Law & Policy* 16, no. 1 (2004): 1.
145. Ibid.

provided with the opportunity to engage in social justice work.[146] This methodology would help to generate more socially conscious lawyers, through educational opportunities that are tailored to the pursuit of justice.[147] It would also be consistent with the vision of legal education as an integral component of the social contract between law schools, lawyers and society.

In the Caribbean, the curricula of the faculties of law of the University of the West Indies, as well as the Council of Legal Education law schools, have sought to incorporate these core principles. However, more emphasis would need to be placed on attaining the broader objective of shaping the eudaimonic attorney.

Significantly, a key tenet of eudaimonia is that of intrinsic motivation, that is, "wanting to do something because you want it for itself, not what it represents".[148] In other words, self-actualization and living virtuously need to be their own reward. One may contend that these virtues cannot be instilled solely by the delivery of the law programmes, but must be bolstered by the exemplar of a socially conscious legal profession.

However, for far too long, the legal profession has been criticized for the selfish pursuit, by some of its members, of personal financial gain at all cost. Unfortunately, the unethical behaviour of a few lawyers has caused irreparable damage to the entire profession's reputation and consequential loss of respect. Perhaps, if more practising lawyers act with "complete trustworthiness", adopt the guiding principles of CSR and embrace their role as gatekeepers within the international financial system, the legal profession would, once more, be considered noble. This paradigm shift would inspire the next generation of lawyers and the moulding of the socially responsible attorney would be more than just an aspirational goal.

Inspired by the overarching idea to cultivate the eudaimonic attorney, the legal profession must consistently embrace the elements of virtue ethics, and recognize the higher role it has to play in advancing society and contributing to the greater good. Overall, in seeking to build a culture of social responsibility motivated by the pursuits of excellence and integrity, the legal profession would not only flourish but would, ultimately, safeguard the well-being of society.

---

146. Ibid.
147. Ibid.
148. Bowling, "Lawyers".

CHAPTER 2

Caribbean Republicanism: Values and Vernaculars

Celia Brown-Blake

The milestone that this volume commemorates coincides generally with the revival of the movement towards republicanism in the independent states of the Commonwealth Caribbean. While Guyana and Trinidad and Tobago long consummated their political independence with the adoption of new constitutional arrangements for a republican form of government in 1970 and 1976 respectively, and Dominica achieved independence and republic status simultaneously in 1978, the move to a republican parliamentary democracy has just been undertaken by Barbados, symbolically on this country's fifty-fifth independence anniversary. The finalization of this process has re-opened debates in the public arena in Jamaica and the wider Caribbean about the meaning of republicanism and the emblems appropriate for marking it.[1] It is proposed, in this chapter, to situate the language question in the Commonwealth Caribbean, particularly within the domain of law and justice, against the backdrop of these debates. The focus on this domain is apt because the status of being a republic rests entirely on a legal act rooted in the very *grundnorm* of the legal system, the various constitutional instruments, so critical in the birth of our independent nations. Thus, constitutions, in particular, and the law more generally, are fundamental not only as the route via which independent, and ultimately republican status are achieved, but also because these instruments, as embodiments of that status,

---

1. See, for example, Phillip Paulwell, 'Jamaican republicanism – more than empty symbolism' *The Sunday Gleaner* (9 January 2022) H4; 'In full support: Panellists examine move to a republic' The Barbados Advocate (17 August 2021) <www. barbadosadvocate.com/news/full-support-0 > accessed 17 July 2022; 'Discussion on republic move should be taken to the people: Lecturer' *The Barbados Advocate* (9 August 2021) <www.barbadosadvocate.com/news/discussion-republic-move-should-be-taken-people-lecturer >accessed 17 July 2022

tend to enshrine the symbols of that status and to signal the broad philosophical underpinnings and direction of the emergent independent-republican state.

The sub-discipline of sociolinguistics, the study of language in its social context, theorizes that social phenomena are reflected in the linguistic order. There is thus a connection between language and society in the sense that correlates may be identified between features of the language situation of a speech community and the nature of that community's social construct. Social meaning is thus carried in the language landscape. In this article, the social phenomenon under examination is the republican movement situated within the wider ambit of the thrust for independence in the Commonwealth Caribbean. The article considers the main principles and values promoted by this movement and analyses the extent to which those values are, or may be mirrored in the nature of the language policy in the law and justice domain.

The Meaning of Caribbean Republicanism

Popular Meaning

Across the independent Commonwealth Caribbean, republicanism is popularly conceived as acquiring the political status of a republic by jettisoning the British monarch as the head of state coupled with instituting, in her stead, "our own man at the top."[2] This perception is consistent with the way in which the question of republicanism has been brought to the people in public outreach events hosted by various review commissions set up to consider constitutional reform in these Caribbean territories. The discussion in Chapter 7 of the Final Report of the Political Reform Commission 2000, for Belize, under the sub-heading "British Monarch or Belizean Head of State", typifies the focal point in public consultations on the question of republicanism:

> Representations made on the issue of the Governor-General focused largely on whether or not Belize should replace the British monarch with a citizen of Belize while at the same time keeping the existing functions of the present Head of State. Such a change would effectively mean that Belize

---

2.   (Barbados) *Report of the Commission Appointed to Review the Constitution* (1979) (hereafter, the Cox Commission Report) para 40.

would cut its ties to the British monarchy and become a parliamentary *republic* with its own Head of State. The term «republic» in this case would refer simply to the fact that the Head of State is no longer a monarch but selected by Belize.[3]

Several reports emanating from these commissions contain segments which capture the popular views for and against the removal of the British monarch as head of state and the adoption of a republican form of government in this sense.[4] Views coalesce around some common themes. The position in favour of becoming a republic has been informed particularly by issues of national identity, consciousness and pride as well as advancing the decolonization process. The Wooding Report of Trinidad and Tobago, in documenting the strong societal support for converting to a republic, states that:

> It is no more than an expression of the fact that independence must involve the creation of indigenous symbols of nationhood…The thrust since Independence has been towards the discovery of a new identity which involves leaving behind the colonial heritage of subjection, imitation and external dependence.[5]

This sentiment is echoed in other commission reports such as the Belize Commission Report, which states that a "Belizean Head of State should increase people's sense of ownership and identification with the Belizean nation."[6] Similarly, the Forde Commission Report for Barbados records the argument that "the Head of State should be the focal point of national unity and patriotism" and that this "is more likely to be achieved if the Head of State is a citizen of the country… resides in the country and is familiar with its history, customs, traditions and culture".[7] It is indeed difficult to reconcile values associated with patriotism and national pride with the fact that a country's pre-eminent figure, from the point of view

---

3.   (Belize) *Final Report of the Political Reform Commission* (2000) (hereafter, the Belize Commission Report) para 7.2.
4.   Ibid paras 7.4-7.5; The Cox Commission Report (n 1) paras 25-43; (Barbados) *Report of the Constitution Review Committee* (1998) (hereafter, the Forde Commission Report) paras 8.3-8.8; (Trinidad and Tobago) *Report of the Constitution Commission* (1974) (hereafter, the Wooding Report) paras 138–40.
5.   Wooding Report (n 4) para 138.
6.   Belize Commission Report (n 3) para 7.5
7.   Forde Commission Report (n 4) para 8.8.4.

of constitutional state organization, is not a citizen of the state. If a constitution not merely regulates the state but, at its most fundamental, articulates who a people are and what they aspire to be as a community,[8] then holding out successive monarchs who are British as a symbol of that identity and aspiration is problematic.

Linked to the question of the assumption of a discrete identity is the notion of continuing the process of delinking from the colonial past – another principled basis put forward for transitioning to a republic. Most Caribbean independence constitutions contemplated only partial severing with forms and institutions of the colonial government. Not only is there "the shadow of the UK Constitution,"[9] lurking behind the constitutions of the independent territories of the Commonwealth Caribbean, there has been, too, the explicit retention of colonial institutions in the form of Her or His Majesty as the holder of executive authority, and of Her or His Majesty in Council, i.e., the Judicial Committee of the Privy Council as the highest appellate court. Acquiring republican status then represents another step in the decolonization process.[10]

Another rationale advanced by the publics of the independent states of the Commonwealth Caribbean for the move towards republicanism is that it augments the democratic character of the political life of those countries.[11] As revealed in various commission reports,[12] this democratic character would be reflected both in a negative and a positive way. The former way manifests in the rejection of a constitutional arrangement via which hereditary rights determine the head of state to which office, therefore, no native can

---

8. Simeon C R McIntosh, *Caribbean Constitutional Reform: Rethinking the West Indian Polity* (Caribbean Law Publishing Company 2002) 37–41.

9. Tracy Robinson, Arif Bulkan and Adrian Saunders, *Fundamentals of Caribbean Constitutional Law* (1st edn, Sweet & Maxwell 2015) 66. This refers to the fact that independence constitutions in the Commonwealth Caribbean essentially mimicked the British structure of government.

10. A former Prime Minister of Jamaica, Portia Simpson-Miller, in her inaugural address in 2012, spoke of "complet[ing] the circle of independence" in her government's resolve (or promise) to "initiate the process of our detachment from the monarchy to become a republic".<www.youtube.com/watch?v=Nx9D_t33_CY > accessed 17 July 2022.

11. Democratic, certainly in the sense of the right of a people to elect the representatives who will carry out the functions of the state, but also extending to the ability a people to contest what government does. See, Philip Pettit, *Republicanism: A Theory of Freedom and Government* (Clarendon Press 1997).

12. For example, the Forde Commission Report (n4) para 8.8.1 and the Belize Commission Report (n 3) para 7.5(2) and (4).

aspire; and the latter way gains expression through the adoption of a system in which the populace has a role in determining the office holder.

Theoretical Interpretation

In the Caribbean then, the popular perspective of republicanism is underpinned, not necessarily exhaustively, by notions of identity, decolonization and democratic practices. This latter element, in particular, dovetails into perhaps a more esoteric concept of republicanism. Simeon McIntosh, a Caribbean constitutional theorist, states that the republican archetype must be taken to mean a representative, democratic state limited by constitutional tenets.[13] Drawing on the work of Philip Pettit who grounds republicanism in the principle of freedom as non-domination (rather than mere non-interference), McIntosh writes that republicanism rests on certain values, including citizenship as opposed to *subjecthood*, in which concept inheres the notion of subordination.[14] The value of citizenship then recognizes parity in the moral importance and standing of each person in the polity. This ties in with the values of equality and justice, on which, as McIntosh explains, republicanism is also grounded. These values are complex in nature and he does not elaborate on the meanings of these values in his description of republicanism. The work of other scholars, though, have elucidated these values.

Equality is a concept embedded expressly or implicitly in the constitutions of the territories of the Commonwealth Caribbean.[15] These constitutions have largely given expression to equality as non-discrimination on specified grounds whereby differential treatment wholly or mainly attributable to any of those grounds is proscribed.[16] This is a contracted interpretation, contemplating only direct discrimination or formal (in)equality. Scholars of Commonwealth Caribbean constitutional law[17] who have explored

---

13.   Simeon C R McIntosh (n 8) 123–27.
14.   Ibid., 123.
15.   For a discussion of the ways in which the equality principle is given expression in these constitutions, see Arif Bulkan, 'The Poverty of Equality Jurisprudence in the Commonwealth Caribbean' (2013) 10 *The Equal Rights Review* 11–32.
16.   Margaret DeMerieux, *Fundamental Rights in Commonwealth Caribbean Constitutions* (Faculty of Law Library, The UWI 1992) 413–52.
17.   For example, Arif Bulkan and Tracy Robinson, 'Equality and Social Inclusion' in

the concept have alluded to the various meanings of equality and have favoured wider and more expansive interpretations which foster substantive, not just formal equality, as well as social inclusion. Egalitarian principles are intrinsic to theories of the republican ideal and indeed to democracy. These theories, however, do not necessarily subscribe to the broader notions associated with substantive equality.[18] Pettit, for example, in his exposition on republican democracy,[19] explicates a modest version of equality in support of (social) justice as a requisite component of a republican model. It contemplates only the equal status of free (undominated) citizens to which the state must have regard, but he writes, "it is not driven by a concern with furthering substantive equality."[20] Robert Post agrees that democracy, *per se*, compels only this limited concept of equality.[21] He argues, though, that while robust egalitarian principles are not a core value of democracy, there is nonetheless "an intimate relationship" between the two because "[a]s these principles become politically salient, as they make inequities oppressive, as they prompt citizens to experience these inequities as alienating, they prepare the way for the eventual emergence of democracy-based arguments for the amelioration of these inequities".[22] Supporting this, is the view, articulated by Donnelly, that strong egalitarian principles, as reflected in international human rights norms, and democracy are "mutually reinforcing" in the context of a *liberal* democratic framework.[23] Liberal democracies, he says, tend to give preference to human rights in resolving tensions between such rights and democratic ideals. Commonwealth Caribbean independent territories, which

---

Janeille Zorina Matthews and Jewel Amoah (eds), *Securing Equality for All in the Administration of Justice* (Faculty of Law, The UWI 2019).

18. While there may be varying meanings of the term, substantive equality, this article adopts the substantive equality framework as advanced by Sandra Fredman in 'Substantive Equality Revisited' (2016) 14 *International Journal of Constitutional Law* 3, 712–38. The framework contemplates four dimensions along the following objectives: redress disadvantage; redress stigma and prejudice; enhance voice and participation; and accommodate difference and realize structural change.

19. Philip Pettit, *On the People's Terms* (CUP 2012).

20. Ibid., 89.

21. Robert Post, 'Democracy and Equality' (2006) 603 *The Annals of the American Academy of Political and Social Science* 1, 24–36, esp 28–31.

22. Ibid., 34.

23. Jack Donnelly, 'Human Rights, Democracy and Development' (1999) 21 *Human Rights Quarterly* 3, 608–32, 621.

may be regarded as espousing liberal democratic traditions,[24] may thus be taken as subscribing to robust egalitarianism or substantive equality.[25]

Equality principles are also inherent in the value of justice, another pillar of republicanism. Pettit characterizes this pillar as *social* justice which he confines to what needs to be achieved if citizens are to experience freedom equally. While concepts of justice may be grounded in equality, they typically permit certain inequalities if fairness is to be achieved. Rawls, for example, in his exposition of justice as fairness,[26] accounts for this in his second principle, the so-called difference principle, which states that inequalities are allowable (and therefore not arbitrary) if they work to everyone's benefit. Similarly, sociologist, Wendell Bell, recognizes that social justice cannot be defined on the basis of equality alone.[27] He construes social justice as equity which, he argues, calls for evaluations as to "whether or not a given equality or amount of inequality is fair or just."[28] Bell, whose early research spanned questions of sovereignty and nationalism in the Caribbean, has argued that social justice was critical to the Commonwealth Caribbean's movement for political independence which was the vehicle via which inequalities spawned by colonialism were to be redressed.[29] This is arguably reflected in the lyrical plaint of the late Jamaican reggae artiste, Peter Tosh, "*I need equal rights and justice*," which may be said to have been the popular anthem of the Jamaican people in the early post-independence period in which Tosh's music rose to prominence. It is submitted then, that values of equality and justice, foundational to the republican ideal, are embedded in the psyche of the nations of the Commonwealth Caribbean.

---

24.   Jorge Domínguez, 'The Caribbean Question: Why Has Liberal Democracy (Surprisingly) Flourished?' In Jorge Domínguez, Robert Pastor and Delisle Worrell (eds), *Democracy in the Caribbean* (Johns Hopkins University Press 1993) 1–28.

25.   The Caribbean Court of Justice has assertively stated that in order to "safeguard equality rights, courts must adopt a substantive approach". See, *McEwan v AG* [2018] CCJ 30 (AJ) para 66 per Saunders, P.

26.   John Rawls, 'Justice as Fairness' (1958) reprinted in Robert Goodin and Philip Pettit (ed), *Contemporary Political Philosophy* (Blackwell 1997) 187–202.

27.   Bell writes that "there are unfair equalities and unfair inequalities and there are fair equalities *and* fair inequalities". 'Equity and Social Justice: Foundations of Nationalism in the Caribbean' (1980) 20 *Caribbean Studies* 2, 5–36, 23.

28.   Ibid., 20.

29.   Ibid., 27.

A Caribbean Precept of Republicanism

The foregoing discussion suggests that a model of Caribbean republicanism may be analyzed at two levels. Firstly, there is a popular sense which, at its simplest, means an alteration of a constitutional arrangement having the effect of removing the British sovereign as head of state which office would then be held by a citizen of the relevant Caribbean state. It has been shown, though, that such a constitutional act must be seen as being imbued with notions of identity, decolonization and democracy. Secondly, there is the theoretical sense which indicates that the concept is intricately linked to values of freedom (non-domination), and hence citizenship, within the political construct of a (liberal) democracy in which equality and justice are constitutive elements. There is, however, in actuality, a fusion of these two senses in the national consciousness of the peoples of the independent countries of the Commonwealth Caribbean. Arguably, too, there is a strong conceptual relationship between the notions associated with the popular perception of republicanism on the one hand, and the values of republicanism advanced in the academic literature, on the other hand. For the independent nation-states of the Commonwealth Caribbean, republicanism may be viewed as a political construct in which nationalism - the mission for a distinct collective identity, the collective sentiment among a citizenry of a strong affinity with, and loyalty to one's country - is articulated. Given the historical colonial realities of the independent countries of the Commonwealth Caribbean, values of democracy, citizenship, equality and justice are conjoined with the nationalist vision in a rejection of the colonial order and its vestiges.[30] This, it is submitted, is the essence of the meaning of a Caribbean republicanism.

Sociolinguistics and the Law

Linguistics, the study of language, intersects society. At this confluence, called sociolinguistics, language is not just a means of labelling or analyzing social phenomena, it is a reflection of how society is ordered and is a factor that itself contributes to the

---

30.   It is noted that these values are largely reflected in the Charter of Barbados, 2021, a document setting out a vision of Barbadian citizenship under a republican state. The Charter, while approved by Parliament, is not legally binding.

way in which society is ordered. This is what Dell Hymes, who was instrumental in laying some of the groundwork of the sub-discipline, refers to as "socially constituted linguistics" – the notion that "social function gives form to the ways in which linguistic features are encountered in actual life".[31] Language is thus a mirror of social phenomena, and at the same time, it helps to construct the social order. Sociolinguistics is thus concerned with the relationship between the structure of language use and the social condition. For instance, a people's beliefs about themselves, their identity, is expressed at the level of language which may signal social cohesion or social exclusion, depending on the nature of the language practices within a speech community. At the same time, language practices may help shape or consolidate a people's sense of identity or signal cultural disaffection. A contemporary example of the nature of the relationship between language and society seems to be baldly unfolding in Ukraine since the start of the invasion by the Russian Federation towards the end of February 2022. Under the by-line David Stern, Robert Klemko and Robyn Dixon, *The Washington Post* electronically reported on April 12, 2022 that many Ukrainians, who are linguistically proficient in the Ukrainian as well as the Russian language, were refusing to speak Russian in the wake of the Russian Federation's hostilities against Ukraine.[32] In this context, refusal by Ukrainians to speak Russian signifies a determined dissociation with, and contempt for the Russian Federation in response to the invasion. At the same time, their refusal to speak Russian also helps to intensify 'de-Russification' in Ukraine,[33] in the bid to assert a discrete Ukrainian identity and citizenship[34] in the post-Soviet era.

The carving out of a distinct national identity in decolonization processes has also been articulated on the level of language. A very

---

31.   Dell Hymes, *Foundations in Sociolinguistics* (University of Pennsylvania Press 1974) 196.
32.   See, 'War Impels Many in Ukraine to Abandon Russian Language and Culture' *The Washington Post*, 22 April 2022 <www.washingtonpost.com/world/2022/04/12/ ukrainians-abandon-russian-language/ > accessed 16 June 2022.
33.   See, Volodymyr Kulyk, 'Shedding Russianness, Recasting Ukrainness: The post-Euromaidan Dynamics of Ethnonational Identifications in Ukraine' (2018) 34 *Post-Soviet Affairs* 2–3, 119–38.
34.   In *Law and Language: Effective Symbols of Community* (CUP 2013) 44, Harold Berman states that "[b]y speaking, we affirm our membership in the various communities... which have given us our language". Conversely, we disaffirm our membership in a community by refusing to speak languages associated with that community.

useful example of this particular relationship is seen in the role of Kiswahili, an East African language, in the independence movement in Tanzania as a symbol of national unity, of disengagement with the colonial order, and in consolidating the national culture.[35] The desire to have a language that was representative of a synthesis of Indian culture was also a feature of the independence-republican movement in India.[36]

Language is also a marker of privilege and social inequalities. Additionally, language practices may perpetuate social inequalities and relationships of power and control. Given this, the linguistic order may become a battle ground for social justice, on which racial, ethnic, class or other tensions are actuated and exhibited. This role of language is readily exemplified in apartheid and post-apartheid South Africa. During the apartheid era, language policies, backed legislatively by the Bantu Education Act, 1953, were deployed to support the maintenance of the apartheid regime, key aims of which were white hegemony, racial segregation cum Black oppression.[37] In the aftermath of the termination of the apartheid regime, official language policy changed to promote multilingualism, including, significantly, the indigenous African languages which were given official recognition, on par with English and Afrikaans, via South Africa's Constitution. This was designed to reflect, and indeed help instrumentalize the sociopolitical change towards racial equality and political democratization.[38] This example from South Africa takes us neatly into a discussion of how sociolinguistics may interact with the law.

Law, as a body of rules with its unique method, may be regarded as an internally autonomous discipline. But like language, law is intimately connected with society.[39] The law does not only regulate the behaviour of persons within the society, but it is also supportive

---

35.   See, Wilfred Whiteley, *Swahili: The Rise of a National Language* (Methuen, 1969.)

36.   See, J R Siwach, 'Nehru and the Language Problem' (1987) 48 *The Indian Journal of Political Science* 2, 251–65.

37.   See, Timothy Reagan, 'The Politics of Linguistic Apartheid: Language Policies in Black Education in South Africa' (1987) 56 *Journal of Negro Education* 3, 299–312; Nkonko Kamwangamalu, 'Social Change and Language Shift: South Africa' (2003) 23 *Annual Review of Applied Linguistics* 225–42.

38.   Nkonko Kamwangamalu (n 37).

39.   There is a long tradition of scholarship on the sociology of law both by legal intellectuals (Eugene Ehlrich and Roscoe Pound are notable ones) as well as sociologists (such as Philip Selznick and Donald Black).

of the sociopolitical organization, typically protecting the interests of the controllers of the state and the dominant social groups.[40] Law, therefore, is itself a social institution, a part of the apparatus of systems and conventions ordering, if not controlling, the society in the interests of the dominant social classes. There are debates regarding whether the law is merely supportive and therefore only reflective of the extant sociopolitical order, or whether it is also an instrument of social engineering via which fundamental social adjustment and re-ordering may be triggered and achieved. It is submitted that the function of law put forward by both sides of the debate is evidenced in actuality in Caribbean contexts and beyond. The law is thus both a reflective and agentive social institution, and is germane to sociolinguistic analysis.

The aim in this chapter is to examine language in the domain of the law and the justice system with a view to evaluating, whether, and to what extent the popular and theoretical values of Caribbean republicanism are transmitted and constructed at the level of language. What can a sociolinguistic analysis of law and the justice system tell us about the enhancement of republican values in the independent states of the Commonwealth Caribbean? This question is addressed in the next section.

Republican Values and Language
Outline of the Language Situation

A brief overview of the language situation in the independent territories of the Commonwealth Caribbean is necessary to contextualize the analysis of the relationship between language and Caribbean republican values in the context of the law and the justice system. English, a colonial linguistic legacy, is the acceptable language variety in public formal domains and, as a matter of practice, is the language generally used, if not prescribed for use in

---

40.   Independent Commonwealth Caribbean territories share a common history in which the laws and the legal system were designed to sustain the socioeconomic system of the slave plantation. See, for example, the work of historian, Elsa Goveia, 'The West Indian Slave Laws of the Eighteenth Century' (1960) 4 *Revista de Ciencias Sociales* 75–105. With particular reference to Guyana, see, too, David J Dodd 'The Role of Law in Plantation Society: Reflections on the Development of a Caribbean Legal System' (1979) 7 *International Journal of the Sociology of Law* 275–96.

state institutions and agencies.[41] By virtue of such practices, it is the de facto official language of the various independent states of the Commonwealth Caribbean. English, however, is not the only language spoken in these territories. Vernacular languages also exist, and are the languages of wider communication in the sense that the majority of people in the respective territories speak a vernacular language in ordinary speech. Many of these vernaculars are creole language varieties. They emerged out of the historical language contact situation between European settlers and African slaves in the plantation societies of the Caribbean. A significant portion of the vocabulary of the creole varieties which emerged derives from the languages of the colonizing Europeans, English for the most part, but also French,[42] and Dutch.[43] However, these creoles, at the deeper levels of language analysis such as syntax and morphology, are structurally discrete from their respective European superstrates and are regarded as separate languages by several scholars of Caribbean linguistics.[44]

Questions of languagehood, though, are essentially socially, rather than empirically, determined, based on a society's ideology about the relevant linguistic varieties. The contention by such scholars that these Caribbean creoles are languages is itself, therefore, reflective of a particular ideology they share in respect of these creole languages. Arguably, their ideology is embedded in some of the republican values under discussion. Advocating the languagehood of Caribbean creole varieties may be taken as

---

41. See, for example, Jamaica House of Representatives, Standing Orders, standing order 6, which provides that proceedings and debates of the House and petitions shall be in English. This standing order is replicated, *mutatis mutandis*, in the Standing Orders of the Senate of Jamaica.

42. Examples of Commonwealth Caribbean countries where French-based creoles are spoken are St Lucia and Dominica. French-based creoles are also spoken in the wider Caribbean such as in Haiti and in the territories of France in the Eastern Caribbean.

43. See, for example, Ian Robertston, 'Guyana's Dutch-lexicon creoles: The Demerara (dis) connection' (2009) 5 *Arts Journal: Critical Perspectives on Contemporary Literature, Art and Culture of Guyana and the Caribbean* 1&2, 81–91.

44. Such linguists include Mervyn Alleyne, *Comparative Afro-American* (Karoma 1980); David Lawton, 'The Implications of Tone for Jamaican Creole' (1968) 10 *Anthropological Linguistics* 6, 22–26; Douglas Taylor, 'The Origins of West Indian Creole Languages: Evidence from Grammatical Categories' (1963) 65 *American Anthropologist* 4, 800– 14; Hubert Devonish, On the Existence of Autonomous Varieties in "Creole Continuum Situations" in Pauline Christie, Barbara Lalla, Velma Pollard and Lawrence Carrington (eds) *Studies in Caribbean Language II* (Society for Caribbean Linguistics 1998).

signifying that these creoles are *equal* with languages – that they are worthy constituents of the set of systems of human communication regarded as 'languages' including, of course, English. In addition, maintaining that Caribbean creoles are languages separate from their European superstrates may also be seen as related to the republican values of identity differentiation and delinking from the colonial order.

The orthodox use of vernacular languages in the independent countries of the Commonwealth Caribbean has been in private informal domains, and the orthodox overt ideology is, generally, a negative societal evaluation of these languages vis-à-vis their European superstrates. There has, though, over the years, been a significant expansion in the use of these languages which have, to some degree, invaded public domains.[45] Besides, the public/private dichotomy of domains is becoming blurred with the explosion of social media where there is abundant use of Caribbean vernacular languages.[46] Additionally, attitudes towards the vernacular languages have shifted considerably, with increasingly more favourable overt attitudes towards the vernacular languages.[47] English, though, retains a margin of functional near-exclusivity in the most formal public domains.

In addition to English and the creole vernaculars, there are, in some territories, indigenous languages. While much of the indigenous populations of the Caribbean were obliterated with European conquest and settlement, there remain areas in which indigenous languages are spoken. Salient examples of these are the Amerindian communities of Guyana and the Mayan and Garifuna communities of Belize.

---

45. See, Lawrence Carrington, 'The Status of Creole in the Caribbean' (1999) 45 *Caribbean Quarterly* 2/3, 41–51; for a discussion of the status shift in relation to St Lucia specifically, see Aonghas St Hilaire, *Kwéyòl in Postcolonial St Lucia* (John Benjamins 2011) 193–210.

46. Regarding the use of the Jamaican vernacular in cyberspace, see, for example, Andrea Moll, *Jamaican Creole Goes Web* (John Benjamins 2015) and Joseph Farquharson, 'The Black man's burden: Language and Political Economy in a Diglossic State and Beyond' (2015) 63 *Zeitschrift für Anglistik und Amerikanistik: Leipzig* 2, 157–77 esp 172–73.

47. See, for example, Jamaican Language Unit, Department of Language, Linguistics & Philosopy, The Language Attitude Survey of Jamaica (2005). <https://kitlv-docs.library.leiden.edu/open/333434234.pdf>

Vernaculars as Value Conveyors
Identity, Citizenship and Decolonisation

For the purpose of this discussion, identity refers to *national identity*, which, as a concept, may have varied interpretations in the scholarly literature. I draw on the work of Wodak et al.,[48] and consider it to be a form of social representation at the level of the collective of the nation, primarily in its political sense but extending as well to the cultural nation. National identity incorporates the notions of sameness as well as of difference.[49] It rises above the divergences of individual and group identities and locates unifying characteristics which are melded into a common national spirit. This collective notion of sameness, however, also serves as a point of difference, of national uniqueness which distinguishes and excludes others external to the particular nation ('othering'). Thus, intra-nation consistency combines with inter-nation distinctiveness in the concept of a national identity.

Language is one factor that may be indicative or symbolic of national identity;[50] in many instances, it can signal whether a speaker belongs or does not belong to a polity.[51] Given the centrality of language to culture, language is a means by which cultural identity is represented and constructed. Where cultural identity overlaps with a certain political nation state or states, then language provides an indication of national identity. It is notable that in several countries, proficiency in a culturally symbolic language is a requirement for citizenship.[52] This idea of citizenship betokens a cultural affinity

---

48. Ruth Wodak, Rudolf De Cillia, Martin Reisigl and Karin Liebhart, *The Discursive Construction of National Identity* (Edinburgh University Press 2009).
49. Stuart Hall, a sociologist who has grappled with the nature of Caribbean cultural identity, also conceives of identity as a relationship between similarity and difference. See, Stuart Hall, Cultural Identity and Diaspora in Jonathan Rutherford (ed) *Identity: Community, Culture, Difference* (Lawrence & Wishart 1990) 222–37.
50. The relationship between speech/language and place of origin/nationality is the premise of the deployment of LADO – linguistic analysis for the determination of origin – by immigration authorities across Europe.
51. Even where persons of different nationalities speak a common language, linguistic features, e.g., accent, peculiar to the varieties spoken by persons of these different nationalities become markers of belonging or othering.
52. The UK, for example, has, since 2013, introduced English language requirements for immigrants as part of a civic integration test. See, Anne-Marie Fortier, 'On (Not) Speaking English: Colonial Legacies in Language Requirements for British Citizenship' (2018) 52 *Sociology* 6, 1254–69. For the position in Europe, see, *Report on the 2018 Council of Europe and ALTE Survey on Language and Knowledge of Society Policy for*

with a wider national community and, in this sense, the concept overlaps with the notion of national identity.

Citizenship, however, is a highly contested concept and admits of different strands of meaning.[53] The notion of citizenship adopted for the purposes of this chapter departs from the inegalitarianism inherent in Caribbean colonial societies which were predicated on the superior status of whites versus the inferior status of non-whites. In this chapter, citizenship involves a particular legal relationship between a state and an individual in which such an individual is held to be equal to all others in the polity and possesses, on par with all such persons, all the rights and responsibilities arising from the status of being a citizen of that state. As intimated in the previous discussion on the theoretical approach of Caribbean Republicanism, citizenship must be seen in contrast to subjecthood. Indeed, slave revolts may be regarded as demands for recognition as citizens – for freedom as non-domination and for equal treatment which were impossible to achieve within the framework of colonial societies. This therefore ties in with the notion of decolonization – detachment and disengagement from the colonial order which goes beyond a mere transference of power, and extends to a dismantling of colonial institutions and ideas. The movements to republicanism may be seen as part and parcel of this process of dismantling. Arguably, both decolonization and citizenship may be seen as continuing processes. The appeal on the part of peoples in the independent territories of the Commonwealth Caribbean to be recognized as citizens persists even in the post-independence period as calls for social inclusion within the body politic.

The question of emblems to give expression to nationalistic sentiments typically accompanies movements towards independence and republicanism. Guyana, led by the then prime minister, Forbes Burnham, transitioned to republicanism within four years of gaining independence. His PNC[54] party conceived a novel species of republic, the Co-operative Republic, which, as he stated, was "the means of making the small man a real man and changing, in a revolutionary fashion, the social and economic relationships

---

Migrants. <www.coe.int/en/web/lang-migrants/surveys> accessed 22 June 2022.

53.   See, John Clarke, Kathleen Coll, Evelina Dagnino and Catherine Neveu, *Disputing Citizenship* (Bristol University Press 2014).

54.   People's National Congress.

to which we have been heir as part of our monarchical legacy."[55] This vision was accompanied by announcements to bring into effect certain changes symbolic of decolonisation – disbanding the legacy of English honours and titles, removal from public spaces of statues and other likenesses of notable Europeans, and making Cuffy, an historical figure regarded as being relevant to Guyana's independence movement, a national hero. The date on which the country became a republic, February 23, 1970, was deliberately made to coincide with the anniversary of the Berbice slave revolt of 1763 which Cuffy, a house slave, had led. Mr Burnham, in an address to the country's National Assembly on the republic motion, stated that this would symbolize the need to give "substance and content to the concept of independence and mature nationhood."[56] Barbados, in similar trajectory, declared a daughter of its soil, Rihanna, internationally renowned singer and entrepreneur, a national hero on the day it became a republic in November 2021. Rihanna retains an unmistakable Bajan accent – a fact highlighted in the remarks which introduced her at Barbados' National Independence Honours Ceremony in 2021. Rihanna's short speech,[57] her first as national hero in which she herself makes reference to the distinctiveness of the Bajan accent, reveals linguistic features characteristic of the Barbadian vernacular.

It is noteworthy, though, that in the quest for distinctive emblems of nationhood in the independence and republican movements in Commonwealth Caribbean territories, language does not appear to have featured in a formal or official way. There is a glaring absence of constitutional as well as statutory provisions[58] or policy documents which officially recognize a language as a symbol of national cohesion. Given the relationship between language and national identity, Caribbean vernaculars are arguably good candidates for symbolizing the identity of the various Caribbean territories. Unlike English, and indeed indigenous languages

---

55.   Forbes Burnham, 'The Small Man A Real Man' Speech by the Prime Minister in moving the motion in the National Assembly to declare Guyana a republic, 28 August 1969.

56.   Ibid.

57.   (Barbados)   The   National   Honours   Ceremony   <www.youtube.com/watch?v=EGqpgv53nUY> accessed 17 July 2022.

58.   It is worth noting that constitutional recognition of languages as official in franco- and creolophone Haiti came only in 1987 (see, art. 5 of Haiti's Constitution), more than 180 years after the country proclaimed its independence.

where they still exist, the respective vernaculars are spoken and understood by most, if not all citizens residing in the relevant state. In addition, and again unlike English, and notwithstanding the traditional negative overt attitudes on the part of creole speakers toward their languages, there has been, customarily, covert positive attitudes to these languages which speakers have considered to be the language of "solidarity or friendship."[59] This then, is the common thread, the emblematic community of a people,[60] which fulfils one requirement for a national identity. The other is the fact that the vernacular of each territory acts as a unique differentiator – both in respect of another Caribbean territory as well as polities external to the independent Commonwealth Caribbean. So that Creolese of Guyana, Bajan of Barbados, Patois of Jamaica, by way of examples, seem capable of essentializing the concept of national identity. The origin of these vernaculars, languages arising from the clash of African and European cultures on plantation societies, lies deep within the Caribbean historical experience. This produced, according to Stuart Hall,[61] "specific roots of identity", part of the "cultural resources" from which a Caribbean identity may be constructed. Arguably, Creolese of Guyana, provides not just a diachronic marker, as does Cuffy, for national identity, but is also capable of constituting a synchronic and continuing symbol via which that identity may be articulated, even reconstructed.

This argument raises the question of how the omission or failure to deploy Caribbean vernacular languages as formal national symbols in the independence-republican movement

---

59.   John Rickford, 'Standard and Non-standard Language Attitudes in a Creole Continuum' in N Wolfson and J Manes (eds) (Walter de Gruyter 1985) 145–62; see, too, Alicia Beckford Wassink, 'Historic Low Prestige and Seeds of Change Towards Jamaican Creole' (1999) 28 *Language in Society* 57–92.

60.   It is worth pointing out that this is in contrast to several other British colonies in their transition to independence which faced the problem of identifying a common language that could serve as a symbol of a composite national identity. Some countries in Africa, such as Kenya and Uganda, opted for English as a unifying language in the face of tribal allegiances exhibited at the level of language (see, Wilfred Whiteley (n 35) 97–98). The problem also arose in India, where the choice of Hindi as the constitutionally designated official language engendered considerable controversy in view of the fact that there is a large non-Hindi speaking population in the south of the country (see, J R Siwach (n 36) 259-263. The equivocal nature of the language-related provisions in India's Constitution (art. 343-347) attests to the dilemma and the compromise arrived at on the official language question.

61.   Stuart Hall, 'Negotiating Caribbean Identities' (1995) 209 *New Left Review* 3–14.

may be explained. It is suggested that sociolinguistic analysis can contribute to an understanding of this failure or omission. The wave of the independence movement in the Commonwealth Caribbean coincided with a period during which the predominant language ideology was that the vernaculars were not genuine languages; at best, they were merely distorted forms of their European superstrates, and were negatively evaluated. This is part of the plantation society hangover – the inferiority, barbarity and non-human-ness with which slaves were regarded were projected onto their speech. The result of such a projection is that the speech of slaves has been historically described as deficient, a linguistic corruption, without grammatical consistency.[62] This psychology has been imprinted upon the Afro-Caribbean, and the culture of self-denigration, powerfully conveyed by Frantz Fanon in *Black Skin, White Masks*, survived the colonial era.[63] In this context, 'broken English,'[64] as the English-lexicon vernaculars have been called, burdened with sentiments of humiliation and subordination, spurned because they were not even 'languages', could not be conceived as being worthy of symbolizing the nascent national identity. It is suggested that this ideology is likely to have plagued Guyanese leadership in the transition to republicanism, notwithstanding the displays of ardent nationalism on the part of the leadership during that period. Forbes Burnham's "goal to make the small man a real man", symbolized by venerating Cuffy, a bane of the Dutch colonizers, as a hero, could have no linguistic analog. Historiographical accounts have been recasting the images of slave leaders like Cuffy, from violent slave

---

62.   See, Mervyn Alleyne (n 44) 2–3.
63.   Rex Nettleford refers to this psychology when he wrote about "the noxious notion that all things drawn from the experience of Europe, the land of the masters, are good and all or most things drawn from elsewhere (and particularly from the experience of people of African ancestry or from Africa itself) are less than good". *Caribbean Cultural Identity: The Case of Jamaica* (Institute of Jamaica 1978) 13.
64.   Edward Long, author of an historical treatise on Jamaica published in 1774, in recommending that a school be established in a particular part of the island, suggested that a certain number of white servants be kept on the compound so that boarders "might not, by a too early familiarity and intercourse with Negroes, adopt their vices and broken English". *The History of Jamaica Vol II* (Lowndes 1774).

insurgents[65] into statesmen,[66] with whom the "small man" could positively identify. However, nationalist leaders did not dare revere the creole languages that these slave leaders must have spoken,[67] even though the legal recognition of these language varieties would have been powerfully emblematic of a rejection of the colonial order, of an assertion of citizenship in the respective new nations, and of an intent to re-value and de-stigmatize things Caribbean.

In the case of Guyana, the indigenous Amerindian languages would also not have presented an option as a national symbol at the time the country became a republic. While their languagehood would not have been in doubt, the social tensions between their speakers and much of the rest of the population would have precluded these Amerindian languages from acting as appropriate symbols of national identity. These tensions were rooted historically in Amerindian alignment with European colonizers in suppressing slave rebellions. Additionally, given the very low regard in which Amerindians were held by the two main ethnic groups in Guyana,[68] Amerindian languages would not have inspired national pride at the time of Guyana's transition to a republic.

Brown-Blake[69] reports that while the issue of language was

---

65.   See, for example, discussion on Dutch newspaper reports on the 1763 revolt in Esther Baakman, "'Their power has been broken, the danger has passed' Dutch newspaper coverage of the Berbice slave revolt, 1763" (2018) 2 *Early Modern Low Countries* 1, 45–67. And see, more generally, Hilary Beckles, 'Caribbean Anti-slavery: The Self-liberation Ethos of Enslaved Blacks' (1988) 22 *Journal of Caribbean History* 1–2, 1–19.

66.   In his speech on 28 August 1969 in which the motion in the National Assembly to declare Guyana a republic is moved, Forbes Burnham (n 55) speaks of respecting the "statesmanship and insight" which Cuffy showed during his leadership of the 1763 revolution.

67.   It is reasonable to conclude, based on Mervyn Alleyne's theory (n 44, 184) that occupational stratification on slave plantations affected the linguistic acculturation of slaves, that Cuffy, for example, was a speaker of Creole Dutch. This can be deduced from the fact that he was a house slave and described as a "highly creolized, and assimilated, African" in Marjoleine Kars, 'Dodging Rebellion: Politics and Gender in the Berbice Slave Uprising of 1763' (2016) 121 *American Historical Review* 1, 39–69, 48. In addition, commentary by Ursy Lichtveld and Jan Voorhoeve on some of the letters Cuffy is reported to have written to the Dutch authorities suggests that he spoke Creole Dutch. See, *Suriname: Spiegel der Vaderlandse Kooplieden* (1980) 72–88. <www.dbnl.org/tekst/voor007suri01_01/> accessed 17 July 2022

68.   Andrew Sanders, 'Amerindians in Guyana: A Minority Group in a Multi-ethnic Society' (1972) 12 *Caribbean Studies* 2, 31–51.

69.   Celia Brown-Blake, 'The Right to Linguistic Non-discrimination and Creole Language Situations: The Case of Jamaica' (2008) 23 *Journal of Pidgin and Creole Studies* 1, 32–74.

broached in parliamentary debates in 1962 on what was to become Jamaica's Constitution, there was no suggestion that Jamaican (Patois) should be constitutionally recognized. Instead, it was suggested that "some thought should be given to the language of some of the African countries from which the majority of us came."[70] This strengthens the claim that Jamaican, like Creolese in Guyana, was not considered fit for purpose – it was not perceived as a language, was something that brought shame, and thus incongruous with the ethos of national pride which was being cultivated in the fledgling nation. The vernacular languages, understandably during the early independence movement, could not have presented useful symbols of nationhood. It is submitted that even if the idea had been conceived by leaders of the nationalistic movements across the Commonwealth Caribbean, it would, in all likelihood, have been stillborn, even sparked public outrage, given the prevailing language ideology during the currency of the independence movement.

Transitions to independence in the Commonwealth Caribbean have been criticized as not ushering in any fundamental structural change. Independence constitutions of the Commonwealth Caribbean, birthed in the UK at Westminster, were not designed to be transformative but preservative,[71] merely to transfer command of the state apparatus to the local elite, the middle class, "within the sphere of British dominance."[72] Political scientist, Louis Lindsay, stated that "perhaps because of formal constitutional changes, the content and spirit of Jamaican politics continue to reflect the major assumptions, values and practices which typified...colonial rule."[73] Paralleling this substantive retention of the colonial order, but with local middle class leadership, was the maintenance of the linguistic state of affairs. The state apparatus continued to function entirely in English. Local leadership, though, by virtue of their competence

70.   Jamaica Hansard cited in Celia Brown-Blake, ibid., 38.
71.   The inclusion of the notorious saving law clauses in the constitutions of Commonwealth Caribbean independent states is both a symbol, and an agent of the retention of the colonial status quo.
72.   Richard Drayton, 'Whose Constitution? Law, Justice and History in the Caribbean' JEITT Sixth Distinguished Jurist Lecture 2016. <https://www.ttlawcourts.org/jeibooks/books/djl2016_final.pdf> accessed 17 July 2022.
73.   Louis Lindsay, 'The Myth of Independence: Middle Class Politics and Non-mobilization in Jamaica' (SALISES 1975) Working Paper No. 6 <https://papers.ssrn.com/sol3/papers.cfm?abstract_id=1822826> accessed 17 July 2022.

in, and diglossic use of both English and the respective vernaculars, was able to consolidate their leadership position by acting as communication brokers between the local, largely vernacular-monolingual masses and the English-speaking colonial authorities. The linguistic abilities of the local middle class supported their emergent dominance of politics, the state bureaucracy and the professional class. Trevor Munroe, in his treatise, *The Politics of Constitutional Decolonisation*, references Norman Manley, barrister and a leader in Jamaica's independence movement, as having cited the difficulty that "ordinary" Jamaicans experienced in understanding the constitutional change to independence.[74] And Alleyne, in an early post-independence examination of the use of language in the domain of politics, explains that campaigning politicians in Jamaica in 1962 advanced the importance of their ability to "go abroad and talk on equal level with equal ability with leaders of other independent nations".[75] The middle class thus possessed a social advantage very much tied into language.

The absence of meaningful social and, significantly, constitutional change was reflected in the neglect on the part of national leaders of the role that the respective vernaculars could play in forging distinct national identities and establishing the new citizenship. The independence constitutions were essentially superficial acts of decolonization which were designed to retain the status quo, as intimated in the Belize Commission Report, 2000 which alludes to a mere swapping of the British monarch for a local citizen while "keeping the existing functions of the present Head of State."[76] The failure to adopt, particularly via constitutional instruments, a non-colonial language as a national language that would signal a break with the colonial order was consistent with the intention on the part of Caribbean independence leaders to continue to govern in the same vein as had the British. This is in contrast to India, for example, whose independence-republican constitution which took effect in 1950, designated a local language, Hindi, as the official language of the Union. This constitutional designation of Hindi arguably reflects an ideological shift away from the colonial

---

74.   Trevor Munroe, *The Politics of Constitutional Decolonisation* (ISER 1972) 71.
75.   Mervyn Alleyne, 'Communications and Politics in Jamaica' (1963) 3 *Caribbean Studies* 2, 22–61, 29.
76.   See text accompanying n 3.

order among the leaders of India's independence movement – a shift captured in the words of Jawaharlal Nehru, a leader of the movement, and the country's first prime minister. Conceding that English was "a great language", he nonetheless is reported to have stated:

> ...no nation can become great on the basis of a foreign language. Why? Because a foreign language can never be the language of the people, for you will have two strata or more – Those who live in thought and action of a foreign language and those who live in another world. So we must do our work more and more in our language.[77]

In India though, colonialism was engrafted on the existing indigenous culture which survived the colonial period. In the Caribbean, on the other hand, indigenous cultures, for the most part, were annihilated. This, according to Stuart Hall, created a crisis of identity because, if "the search for identity always involves the search for origins, it is impossible to locate in the Caribbean an origin for its peoples."[78] Colonialism in the Caribbean entailed a clash of foreign cultures from which Caribbean societies are now constructing their identities. The (perceived) absence of a clear, firm linguistic grounding which could emblematically support nationhood mirrors the fact that Caribbean nations, at the point of gaining independence, were merely in the beginning stages of defining their identities. Arguably, this stands in contrast to what obtained in other colonized territories such as India where indigenous languages pre-dated the onset of, and survived the colonial experience.

The sociolinguistic analysis that has been offered in this paper thus far explains the omission during the intensity of the independence movement to harness the unique character of the vernacular languages. That analysis is less convincing in relation to the recent renewed thrusts to complete the "circle of independence"[79] by becoming parliamentary republics. This is because, as discussed in the outline of the language situation, independent Commonwealth Caribbean nations have become more secure in the languagehood

---

77.   Jawarharlal Nehru, cited in J R Siwach (n 36) 256.
78.   Hall (n 61) 5.
79.   See, n 10.

of the respective vernacular languages,[80] and overt attitudes to these languages are shifting positively.[81] This shift in language ideology accords with the fact both Rihanna and the person who introduced her at the Barbados National Independence Honours Ceremony in 2021 proudly highlighted Bajan as nationally distinctive. This has not been transmitted into a definitive formal or official policy or law, nor is there any clear indication that there will be such a policy. The Charter of Barbados, 2021, a parliamentary-approved but legally non-binding document which envisions the nature of "active citizenship" under a republican system of government, does reveal references to language in a generic way,[82] without express mention of the Barbadian vernacular. As the country undertakes the task of re-crafting its constitution in the wake of its new republican status, it remains to be seen whether these references will be honed into specific legal provisions to facilitate official recognition of Bajan as emblematic of national identity and citizenship within a republican state.

Jamaica has, in its sixtieth year of independence and on the heels of Barbados' transition to a republican government, again expressed its commitment to become a parliamentary republic. There has yet been no official proposal to formulate an explicit policy or law regarding the use of Jamaican as emblematic of national identity, or to address substantive and systemic problems of access to justice. In fact, Jamaica's Prime Minister, in his most recent public pronouncements on the language question, is reported to have said:

> Take away all the cultural issues about language being a

---

80. The Language Attitude Survey of Jamaica (n 47) carried out in 2005 by the Jamaican Language Unit at The University of the West Indies, Mona, shows that nearly 80% of respondents believe that Jamaican (Patois) is a language. <https://kitlv-docs.library.leiden.edu/open/333434234.pdf> at 35.
81. The Language Attitude Survey of Jamaica (ibid) shows that while negative stereotypical attitudes persist (for example, a significant majority felt that a speaker of English would be more intelligent), the break-out analysis indicates that younger (50 years and under) people tend to have healthier attitudes to Jamaican than do older people. One daily newspaper in Jamaica, *The Gleaner*, has been consistently of the view that Jamaican should be respected by the government and given legal recognition. See, for example, the recent editorial, 'English of course, but...' *The Gleaner* (30 May 2022).
82. See, Charter of Barbados, 2021, Article I which acknowledges the divisive way in which languages were used historically, the connection between language and certain values, and pledges to embrace "the many languages represented". <https://www.barbadosparliament.com/bills/details/596 > accessed 17 July 2022.

barrier to access... We need to get over that and ensure that we protect the English language in our country as discrete from our Jamaican language... But get over this nonsense that one is going to block you from access in the society.[83]

The newspaper article also reports that the Prime Minister intends to explore the possibility of Jamaica adopting Spanish as a second language.[84] While there seems to be acceptance on his part that Jamaican is a language, he does not appear to favour its status promotion, and seems to be of the view that the current linguistic order does not contribute to social exclusion. In addition, Jamaica's Prime Minister seems inclined toward a policy of embracing another colonial language without official recognition of the first language of the vast majority of Jamaicans. This unwillingness to legally recognize Jamaican not only goes against the grain of current popular attitudes,[85] but ignores the role that the Jamaican language has played, and continues to play in constructing and fortifying national identity,[86] and contributing to one's sense of citizenship. I contend that the adoption of Spanish as a second language, without official recognition of the native language of Jamaicans, would be to repeat the error of our independence leaders of overlooking the centrality of language to nationhood and to citizenship in the cultural sense. It is submitted that it would be a missed opportunity, a display, this time around, of wilful ignorance, and dissonant with republican values should independent countries of the Commonwealth Caribbean, in executing the constitutional act of de-linking from the British Crown, decline to grant official,

---

83. 'Protect English as language of labour forces, says PM' *The Gleaner* (26 May 2022) <https://jamaica-gleaner.com/article/news/20220526/protect-english-language-labour-force-says-pm> accessed 17 July 2022

84. There is precedent in the independent Commonwealth Caribbean for such an initiative. In 2005, Trinidad and Tobago implemented, via its Ministry of Education, a government directive to establish Spanish as a first foreign language of that country. <www.moe.gov.tt/spanish-implementation-secretariat-sis%EF%BF%BC/> accessed 17 July 2022.

85. The Language Attitude Survey of Jamaica, 2005 (n 47), indicates that nearly 69% of survey respondents said that Parliament should make Patois an official language.

86. Hubert Devonish and Byron Jones, in an illuminating discussion on the use and significance of language in Jamaican music, sound a warning about the need for the Jamaican state to be a "truer manifestation" of the Jamaican nation which could be facilitated by formal recognition of Jamaican as an official language. 'Jamaica: A State of Language, Music and Crisis of Nation' (2017) 13 *Volume!* 2 https://journals.openedition.org/volume/5321 accessed 11 May 2022.

indeed constitutional recognition to the languages via which Caribbean peoples have largely negotiated their identities, to borrow phraseology from Stuart Hall.

The question remains as to a plausible explanation for the reluctance on the part of Caribbean governments in the contemporary republican movement to squarely confront the language question. As already discussed, language did not only reflect class differentiations in the immediate post-colonial period, but was also a factor in the social ascendancy of the middle class. It is submitted that language continues to be an index of class, and is a platform on which class interests are articulated. Race and economic standing have traditionally been determinative of social class in Jamaica and indeed across the independent Commonwealth Caribbean, with language being generally correlative of class. Arguably, though, economic status while still important, has become a less decisive marker of the conventional middle class. This, perhaps shrinking but vocal segment of the society, is defined by certain values and conduct. Linguistic behaviour, involving the ability to use English where 'required' according the social rules embedded in the orthodox language ideology, is a key value of this class.[87] They generally are in control of the state which steadfastly holds to the English official language policy. Elevation of the Jamaican language then, beyond the limits imposed by this class of its cultural charm could, according to Devonish and Carpenter, "threaten the very survival of the state."[88] This class therefore has a vested interest in the retention of the linguistic status quo. Constitutional recognition of Caribbean vernaculars in the independent countries of the Commonwealth Caribbean, even as only emblematic of national identity, would tend to unsettle this status quo and a crucial social foundation of this class. Reluctance or refusal to take the step toward this recognition must be situated in this sociolinguistic context. It may be that we should not see failure to give our vernaculars constitutional recognition as a resistance to decolonization, but rather as a preservation of local vested interests. Indeed, linguists have identified a standard variety

---

87. Hubert Devonish and Karen Carpenter refer to this segment of the society as the "chateratti". *Language, Race and the Global Jamaican* (Palgrave Macmillan 2020) 55.
88. Ibid., 12.

of English used in Jamaica, Standard Jamaican English (SJE), which possesses features distinct from the British standard. This may be regarded as being reflective of a fissure between colonial values and post-independence values. The linguistic differentiation though between SJE and vernacular varieties is now perhaps more symptomatic of a colonial-inspired neo-elitism in which "a good command of the English language" is privileged and forms the basis of exclusionary policies governing certain work positions.[89]

Democracy, Equality and Justice

The discussion so far has focussed on the use of the law to carry out a symbolic function – official endorsement, via constitutional instruments, of the respective vernaculars as symbols of the republican values of national identity, citizenship and decolonization. This section considers the republican values of democracy, equality and justice and goes beyond symbolism. Through the lens of language, it will examine the citizen's ability to effectively participate in the law and justice domain, whether disadvantages and thus inequalities accrue on account of how justice is administered, and how these impact notions of fairness.

As is the case for the rest of the state machinery, English is the official language of the justice system. This is a de facto status determined by practice,[90] and supported by certain laws.[91] There is no formal policy on the use of the vernaculars in the administration of justice. Of course, users of the justice system who are vernacular-dominant speak their vernacular languages as they navigate the system. However, no professional interpreters are provided for these vernacular speakers, unlike other speakers of languages other than English. This may be attributed to the traditional language ideology that the Caribbean vernaculars are not real languages themselves but are merely dialects of their respective superstrates. In practice, navigation of the justice system by these vernacular speakers is aided by bilingual, diglossic professionals who perform the role

---

89.   See, Alison Irvine, 'A Good Command of the English language: Phonological Variation in the Jamaican Acrolect' (2004) 19 *Journal of Pidgin and Creole Languages* 1, 41–76.
90.   Statutes are published, and judgments written routinely in English.
91.   For example, laws governing eligibility for jury service typically require that a person speak, read and write English. See, (Guyana) Criminal Law (Procedure) Act, Cap 10:01, s 20; (Jamaica) Jury Act, s 2(2); (Trinidad) Jury Act, Cap 6:53, s 4.

of language and communication brokers on an ad hoc basis. In this way, the justice system proceeds, but arguably unsatisfactorily when viewed against the backdrop of core legal principles.

All law and legal proceedings are language-sensitive events. Where, in particular, accused persons are not proficient in the language in which the proceedings are carried out, the law requires interpretation services for such an accused. This is reflected in the constitutions of the independent countries of the Commonwealth Caribbean which enshrine the due process right of an accused to have the assistance of an interpreter free of cost if he cannot understand or speak the language used in court.[92] Justice systems place a premium on an accused person being able to understand the charge and the case against him or her especially because this has an impact on other rights within the bundle of due process rights in criminal proceedings, such as the right to examine the witnesses against him or her and the right to be cognitively present at one's trial. These are rights that ultimately affect the values of participation, inclusion and overall fairness.

The Chief Justice of Jamaica is reported as having acknowledged that the *majority* of litigants in the parish courts are Patois speakers.[93] An issue that confronts the justice system in Jamaica and across the independent Commonwealth Caribbean is whether these systems are adequately honouring the constitutionally enshrined due process rights in respect of vernacular-dominant speakers, comprising the mass of users of the lower courts. It is notable that a survey carried out in Trinidad and Tobago in the mid 20-teens indicates lack of understanding of court proceedings on the part of certain users of the justice system. The study reports one user as having said, "…[Y]ou don't understand what's going on. You just hearing certain terminologies being used. You don't understand what it means."[94] There is, too, research which demonstrates likely misunderstandings on the part of users of the court system who

---

92. See, for example, (Jamaica) Constitution, s 16(6); (Guyana) Constitution, art 144(2); (Barbados) Constitution, s 18(2).

93. Editorial, 'Justice Sykes rules for Patois', *Gleaner* (9 March 2020).

94. Dylan Kerrigan, Peter Jamadar, Elron Elahie and Tori Sinanan, 'Securing Equality for All: The Evidence and Recommendations. In Janeille Zorina Matthews and Jewel Amoah (eds), *Security Equality for All in the Administration of Justice* (Faculty of Law, The UWI 2019) 61–98, 88.

are vernacular-dominant speakers[95] who are likely to feel insecure and trapped in a linguistic bubble. It should not be assumed that it is only these speakers who are prone to have language-related misunderstandings and communication difficulties in court proceedings. The variation in the continuum of vernacular varieties existing in Jamaica and Guyana, for example, and the fact that speakers' competence may span only a range of varieties on this continuum open the door for misunderstandings to occur where the variety spoken by one person does not overlap with the varieties understood or spoken by the interlocutor(s). Despite the role that bilingual, diglossic professionals may play in the justice system of mediating language-based communication problems, they are themselves also liable to misunderstandings because of the nature of the language situation. This situation is exacerbated where a vernacular-dominant national of one jurisdiction in the Commonwealth Caribbean is obliged to appear in the courts of another jurisdiction within the region. Eastern Caribbean judicial officers, in personal communication with the author, have pointed to the need to have competent Jamaican Patois interpreters in their courts where the need arises.

The communication problem is also not confined to court proceedings but may arise at other points in the administration of justice. The everyday event in police operations of administering the caution to suspects may also present comprehension difficulties. This in turn may affect the legal protection that the caution is designed to offer. Sandra Evans has demonstrated, in the context of St Lucia, how Kwéyòl-dominant speakers are at a disadvantage because the police caution is, in several instances, incompetently interpreted to them by untrained police officers.[96] Denial of the protection intended by the caution is compounded by a failure to accord the Kwéyòl language, and by extension its speakers, the same treatment that the justice system would accord speakers of 'real' languages, i.e. the provision of competent, professional interpretation. This treatment of Kwéyòl and its speakers in St Lucia

---

95. See, for example, Celia Brown-Blake, 'Supporting Justice Reform in Jamaica through Language Policy Change' (2017) 45 *Caribbean Studies* 1–2, 183–215, 198.
96. R Sandra Evans, '"Ou ni right-la pou remain silans": The Case for a Standard Kwéyòl Translation of the Pre-trial Right to Silence' (2021) 36 *Journal of Pidgin and Creole Languages* 1, 175–200.

brings into stark focus the relegation of creole vernaculars in the linguistic landscape of the independent Commonwealth Caribbean. This is because the dissimilarity of French-lexicalized Kwéyòl from English, the official language of the country, while patently differentiating these languages, does not make Kwéyòl 'real'. Like its English-lexicalized counterparts in the Commonwealth Caribbean which traditionally have been disguised as mere dialects or forms of the official language, Kwéyòl is excluded from official recognition in St Lucia. This converts into unfair and substantively unequal treatment of its speakers in the law and justice domain.

Justice systems of independent countries in the Commonwealth Caribbean have, for a long time, concealed the vernacular languages under a cloak of invisibility; the languages, necessarily, appear, but like an unrobed attorney, cannot be seen and may not be acknowledged by courts. The difficulty with this concealment is its potential to compromise the rights and notions of fairness that are at the heart of our justice system; the very rights counsel are expected to enforce and judges have sworn to uphold. This policy of concealment has perpetuated an inequality of treatment as between court users competent in English versus those who are vernacular-dominant speakers. Subscribing to a policy which recognizes English only while tacitly relegating vernacular languages has the effect of benefitting one linguistic group while presenting a handicap to another. This is substantive inequality which weakens the principles foundational to our justice systems and is inimical to the republican values of democracy, equality and justice. Aligned with this suggestion is the empirically established perception on the part of the public in Trinidad and Tobago that someone who speaks 'proper English' is more likely to receive favourable treatment in the justice system than someone who speaks 'heavy dialect'. The survey showed that nearly 67% of members of the public participating in the survey agreed with this viewpoint. It is also notable that some 60% of attorneys surveyed were also in agreement with the statement.[97] The real prospect of unequal treatment, unfairness and exclusion is thus matched by perceptions of language-based discrimination and marginalisation.

---

97.   Dylan Kerrigan, Peter Jamadar, Elron Elahie and Tori Sinanan (n 94) 95.

Acknowledgements by Jamaica's Chief Justice about the reality of the language situation in courts must be seen as a positive first step against the traditional culture of vernacular concealment and linguistic discrimination. It is submitted, however, that if effect is to be given to the republican values of equality, justice and democracy, steps must be taken to translate the Chief Justice's acknowledgements into legislative action and a formal language policy for the justice system. Guyana appears to be the only country in the independent Commonwealth Caribbean which, since 2003, has included language as a basis on which discrimination is constitutionally prohibited.[98] The provision states that "no person shall be treated in a discriminatory manner" by any person performing public functions. The meaning ascribed to "discriminatory" in art. 149(2) of the Constitution,[99] which includes language as a prohibited factor, among others, appears to proscribe direct discrimination only. The question thus arises as to whether the provision may be of value in situations involving a formally neutral policy which has a disparate impact because of the different conditions in which this policy may apply. As has been discussed, having English as the language of the court, without adequate recognition of Caribbean vernaculars and appropriate facilitation of their speakers, amounts to indirect discrimination and has an exclusionary effect. Republican constitutions which intend to be more than tokens of dismantling the colonial order must redress the disadvantage to which vernacular-dominant speakers are exposed, and institutionalize the values of equality, justice and democracy in the context of the language situation in which the majority of court users, certainly in the lower courts, are vernacular-dominant speakers. In the emerging republican dispensations of the modern era, courts as well as citizens should be assured that vernacular-

---

98.   (Guyana) Constitution, s 149. Jamaica, in 2011 when it undertook a major revision of the fundamental rights in its constitution, declined to include language as a prohibited ground in the anti-discrimination provision in the new Charter of Fundamental Rights and Freedoms.

99.   This provision of the Constitution of Guyana states, "'Discriminatory' means affording different treatment to different persons attributable wholly or mainly to their or their parents' or their guardians' respective description by...language...whereby persons with one such description are subjected to disabilities or restrictions to which other persons of the same or another such description are not made subject or are accorded privileges or advantages which are not afforded to other persons of the same or another such description."

dominant speakers are not at legal risk and are not disadvantaged by virtue of the continued concealment of their languages in the administration of justice.

Notably, the Constitution of Guyana provides indigenous peoples with "the right to the protection, preservation and promulgation of their languages, cultural heritage and way of life".[100] The scheme of the Constitution suggests that the term 'indigenous peoples' means the Amerindians so that the provision contemplates only the Amerindian languages. Although it appears that Creolese continues to be overlooked in Guyana's 2003 amended Constitution, the provision of legal rights in respect of Amerindian languages marks an important step in Guyana's republicanism.[101] In explicitly acknowledging the pre-colonial, it signals a de-focusing on the colonial, and a re-orienting towards Caribbean origins which are critical in the search for, and construction of identity. The grant of rights connected with traditionally marginalized languages is also perhaps indicative of a move towards achieving a measure of linguistic justice given (a) the endangerment of Amerindian languages associated with the diminution in the Amerindian populations in the wake of colonial intervention, and (b) the general alienation of Amerindians and their culture in the post-independence era.[102]

Conclusion

It has been argued that language should be seen as a key factor in the new thrust towards republicanism in the independent countries of the Commonwealth Caribbean. Because this thrust is typically operationalized via constitutional acts, these legal instruments become important in signalling and agentivising the new direction involved in assuming the status of being a republic. This involves

---

100. (Guyana) Constitution, s.149G.
101. In support of the constitutional provisions regarding protection of indigenous languages is Guyana's Amerindian Act 2006, s. 41(f) which stipulates that one function of the National Toshaos Council (a statutory organization comprising Amerindian village leaders) is to "promote the recognition and use of the Amerindian languages'.
102. See, Janette Bulkan, "'Original Lords of the Soil"? The Erosion of Amerindian Territorial Rights in Guyana' (2016) 22 *Environment & History* 3, 351–91 and 'The Struggle for Recognition of the Indigenous Voice: Amerindians in Guyanese Politics' (2013) 102 *The Roundtable* 4, 367–80.

an effective alignment with the republican values contemplated by Caribbean republicanism. It has been demonstrated that language is important both at the symbolic and the substantive level of these values. Constitutional recognition of these languages, like the re-making of slave rebels into national heroes, would be a symbolic response to the contempt with which these languages, their speakers and culture were regarded by colonizers. In addition, because of the nexus between language and national identity, legal recognition of the vernaculars would be an expression of the 'smaddification'[103] of traditionally dominated, depersonalized Caribbean natives, both at the individual and the collective level. It would be emblematic not only of discarding the colonial values and structures which have contributed, among other things, to linguistic self-degradation, but also of becoming 'somebody' distinct from a mere embodiment of colonial values. It would not only be symbolic of casting off disaffirming colonial values, but it would symbolize and play a role in re-defining and re-shaping Caribbean identity and aspirations. Certainly in the case of Jamaican, Caribbean vernaculars are gaining in linguistic capital and global recognition and imitation.[104] This is a departure from the traditional notion that it was a sign of poverty and a mere parochial idiosyncrasy. The developing economic value is likely to accelerate and strengthen the evolving positive overt ideology toward Jamaican. This, in turn, is likely to have an impact on self-image and the desire to associate with the language variety. Constitutions, as the instruments which usher in republicanism, should not repeat the half-hearted attempts at decolonization which the independence constitutions symbolize and actively support; they should deploy language as a means of giving effect to the new citizens of the Caribbean and of bearing witness to the identities which are being re-constructed.

---

103. Rex Nettleford has been credited with coining this term, rooted in the Jamaican language word, smadi (English: somebody). The term is taken to mean the "affirmation of personhood". See, Norman Girvan, 'Caribbean Integration: Can Cultural Production Succeed Where Politics and Economics Have Failed?' Keynote address delivered at the St Martin Book Fair (31 May 2012). <https://sta.uwi.edu/iir/normangirvanlibrary/sites/default/files/normangirvanlibrary/images/Caribbean%20integration%20can%20cultural%20production%20succeed%20where%20politics%20and%20economics%20have%20failed.pdf> accessed 17 July 2022. Charles Mills is known for using the term "smadditizin" which has a comparable meaning. See, Charles Mills, 'Smadditizin' (1997) 43 Caribbean Quarterly 2, 54–68.

104. Joseph Farquharson (n 46).

The functionality of our justice system, particularly in the context of republicanism, also demands effective participation, fairness and substantive equality for users of the system. The discussion has raised the question of whether the justice systems, in their current *modus operandi*, are honouring certain fundamental rights of many of their users who are vernacular-dominant speakers. There is a patent risk of sacrificing fairness in the trial process on the altar of a linguistic ideology that elects to camouflage vernaculars with English. It is an ideology that also supports linguistic discrimination against, and domination of vernacular-dominant speakers. Language-based unfairness and discrimination which are repugnant to republican values should be upended in Caribbean republican constitutions with bold provisions galvanized by purposive judicial interpretation. The sociolinguistic analysis has suggested that framers of the independence constitutions and leaders of the early republican movement may be excused for omitting to tackle the language question. It is submitted that in the context of the sociolinguistic evolution that has occurred in the Commonwealth Caribbean post-independence, leaders of the renewed republican movement have a duty to redress the disadvantage and unfairness to which vernacular-dominant speakers have been exposed, and to make them substantive citizens. The architects of the modern republican constitutions would do a great injustice if they proceeded with eyes wide shut to the language issue.

CHAPTER 3

The Appellate Advocate and the Appellate Function in our Court System

Andrew Burgess

Why does our system provide for one group of judicial actors, appellate judges, to review the work of another group of judicial actors, trial judges?[1] Or phrased another way: What is the rationale behind creating courts with appellate jurisdiction? And as a corollary to that question, what is the role of the appellate attorney in the appellate process, other than seeking to win the case being appealed for his client?

These questions are rarely ever given even the briefest thought by most lawyers, including appellate advocates. Legal scholars, teaching and researching judgments of appellate courts, never find any reason to contemplate those questions. The appellate function, including the role of the appellate lawyer, is taken as a given. It is not surprising then, that even though our region has produced, and continues to produce, world-class judges, lawyers and academics, apart from a lecture by president of the Caribbean Court of Justice, Justice Adrian Saunders, entitled "The Role of the Court of Appeal in Developing and Preserving an Independent and Just Society,"[2] this subject has not engaged the attention of any of these luminaries.

The loud echo of the regional silence on this subject makes it necessary to turn to the impressive body of high-level scholarship on this subject to be found in law review articles, books, case law dicta and even on the internet, especially from the United States, Canada, Australia and the United Kingdom. This learning is of vital importance in better understanding the role of a judge of appeal and the role of the advocates who appear before them.

---

1. This chapter is based on a presentation to the Barbados Bar Association on 26 August 2022.
2. Distinguished Jurist Lecture Series (2012) of the Judicial Education Institute of Trinidad and Tobago.

Research firmly suggests that to really understand the appellate system, including the crucial role of the appellate lawyer, it must be seen in institutional terms – as a social agency with a specific function. This function is what may be called the appellate function.

This study is divided into two parts: the first seeks to explore and explain the appellate function, while the second proposes some practical ways in which the appellate advocate can best contribute to the challenging demands of the appellate function in our country.

Before going any further, it must be stressed that this paper is not intended to be a manual for appellate advocates on how to best persuade an appellate court to decide a case in their favour. It is not about the art and techniques of efficacious appellate advocacy.[3] Its sole aim is to present observations on how the appellate attorney in Barbados can best assist our Court of Appeal and the CCJ in their discharge of the appellate function.

Part 1: Hierarchical Appellate Court Structure

It may be advantageous to begin with some basics on the appellate court structure in Barbados.

As Goodridge, JA pointed out in the Court of Appeal decision in *Oscar Maloney v Commissioner of Police,* Magisterial Application No. 6 of 2014 (Unreported), our law, grounded as it is in the English common law system, does not recognize any general or inherent right to appeal. Under our law, a right to appeal can only be asserted in so far as it is granted by the constitution, statute or with statutory authority.

The constitution establishes two appellate courts in Barbados. These are the Court of Appeal and the CCJ. Appellate jurisdiction and powers are conferred on these two courts by the constitution and by other laws.

The appellate jurisdiction of the Court of Appeal is amplified in section 52 of the Supreme Court of Judicature Act, Cap 117A, in other statutes and in the Supreme Court (Civil Procedure) Rules, 2008 (CPR). Section 52 of Cap 117A confers on the Court of Appeal

---

3.   Two books which are widely regarded as classics on the art and techniques of appellate advocacy are Frederick Weiner's book, *Effective Appellate Advocacy* (New York: American Bar Association, 1955), and Ruggero J. Aldisert's *Winning on Appeal: Better Briefs and Oral Arguments* (New York: Clark Boardman Callaghan, 1992).

general jurisdiction to hear appeals from any judgment or order of the High Court or any judge thereof. The Court of Appeal also has jurisdiction vested in it by the Magistrate Court Jurisdiction and Procedure Act, Cap 116 to hear appeals from the magistrate courts; and jurisdiction to hear appeals from decisions of certain tribunals under the particular Acts establishing such tribunals.

The appellate jurisdiction of the CCJ is laid out in the constitution, the agreement establishing the CCJ. signed in Bridgetown on 14 February 2001, the Caribbean Court of Justice Act, Cap 117 and in the Caribbean Court of Justice Appellate Jurisdiction Rules 2017. Pursuant to section 79 D. (1) (c) of the constitution, sections 6, 7 and 8 of the CCJ Act and Part III of the agreement, the CCJ is invested with jurisdiction to hear appeals from decisions of the Court of Appeal. In sum, our court system consists of a hierarchical structure with the trial courts at the bottom, the Court of Appeal above the trial courts and the CCJ at the apex.

So, what is the purpose of our appellate system? Most appellate judges acknowledge that the purpose or rationale of an appellate function in relation to a decision of a trial court is twofold. The first is the private purpose, which is to correct any error made by the trial court in a particular case. This is what may be called the error-correcting purpose. The second is the public purpose, which is to delineate, clarify and develop the law to ensure the law's universal application by courts within the court hierarchy. This may be called the universal application of law purpose or law-making rationale.

It should be noticed here that the universal application of law purpose takes precedence over the error-correcting purpose. The extent to which this is so in the apex appellate court is evident in the House of Lords' decision in *Scandinavian Trading Tanker Co. AB v Flota Petrolera* [1983] 2 AC 694. This was an application for leave to appeal to the House of Lords in a case concerning relief from forfeiture in the context of a charter party. The House of Lords granted leave to appeal, not because there was any need to give fuller consideration of the decision of the Court of Appeal, but "in order that a matter of such practical importance to the shipping world should, by a decision of the highest appellate court, be put beyond reach of further challenge".[4]

---

4.   *Scandinavian Trading Tanker Co. AB v Flota Petrolera* [1983] 2 AC 694 at 700.

Our Court of Appeal decision in *Financial Service Commission and BIPA Inc v British American Insurance Co. (Barbados) Ltd.* (Claim No. 4 of 2012) illustrates the same principle in an intermediate appellate court. That case concerned an application by BIPA Inc. seeking leave to appeal to the Court of Appeal the decision of Beckles, J (acting) denying an application by BIPA that BIPA be joined as a party in the judicial management proceedings initiated by the Financial Services Commission against British American. The Court of Appeal held that BIPA had not established that Beckles, J had incorrectly applied the law and that consequently there was no realistic prospect of success of the intended appeal before the Court of Appeal. In other words, there was no error by Beckles, J for the Court of Appeal to correct. This notwithstanding, the court granted leave to appeal because: "[T]he case undeniably raises for the first time the narrow but important question of who, other than the Supervisor of Insurance and the company in question, may be parties in judicial management proceedings after the appointment of a judicial manager. The intended appeal affords an opportunity for the Court of Appeal to clarify the law on this matter."[5]

Before exploring the error-correcting and law-making rationales, however, it should be mentioned that some commentators suggest other purposes for the appellate function. Two of these, most often asserted, deserve a quick comment. The first is that the function is necessary to ensure justice. Justice Cordozo's admonition in *The Nature of the Judicial Process* is a caution against too readily embracing the ensuring justice rationale. He wrote in rather flowery language:

> The judge, even when he is free, is still not wholly free. He is not to innovate at pleasure. He is not a knight-errant, roaming at will in pursuit of his own ideal of beauty or of goodness. He is to draw his inspiration from consecrated principles. He is not to yield to spasmodic sentiment, to vague and unregulated benevolence. He is to exercise a discretion informed by tradition, methodized by analogy, disciplined by system, and subordinated to 'the primordial necessity of order in the social life'.[6]

5.   *Financial Service Commission and BIPA Inc. v British American Insurance Co. (Barbados) Ltd.* (Claim No. 4 of 2012).
6.   Benjamin Cardozo, *The Nature of the Judicial Process* (New Haven, CT: Yale University Press, 1921), 141.

Unless, then, justice is understood as meaning the even-handed justice explicated by John Rawls in *A Theory of Justice*, the appellate function risks yielding "to spasmodic sentiment, to vague and unregulated benevolence", as warned by Cardozo.[7] Rawlsian justice avoids this risk because justice is achieved by deciding like cases alike in accordance with the applicable law. Stated another way, Rawlsian justice inheres in the consistent application of the law which, as we will see presently, coincides with "the universal application of law purpose". In other words, justice properly understood is already ensured by "the universal application of law purpose".

The second rationale for the appellate function is to enhance judicial accountability. In this regard, a senior judge in the region has propounded: "Exposing decisions made by first instance judges to the scrutiny of a panel of more experienced judges is one aspect of judicial accountability. An appeal affords the opportunity to test first instance decisions."[8]

The logical extension of this argument is that the accountability of the Court of Appeal is ensured by appeal to the apex court, the CCJ. The major problem with this view is that it does not require any accountability from the apex appellate court.

In the end, it is suggested that the "error correcting rationale" and the "the universal application of law rationale" best answer the question why there exists an appellate system. These two rationales

The Error-Correcting Rationale

It is universally accepted that the primary purpose of the appellate process is the correcting of any error made by a lower court or other lower adjudicative body. Indeed, the express statutory language establishing both the CCJ, and the Court of Appeal appear to embrace error correction as the sole appellate function.

The error-correcting function of appeals was accepted and advanced by the distinguished American legal scholar Roscoe Pound, who wrote in 1941 that: "Appeals are needful because they

---

7.   John Rawls, *A Theory of Justice* (Cambridge, MA: Harvard University Press, 1971).
8.   This chapter is based on a presentation to the Barbados Bar Association, 26 August 2022.

correct the unfairness or unskillfulness of those who adjudicate."[9] Pound's explication of the need for error correction as resulting from "the unskillfulness of those who adjudicate" is now largely discredited.

The more modern explanation for the error-correcting appellate function is the fallibility of judges as mere humans. Put differently, error from time to time is an intrinsic aspect of the human condition and this truth is equally evident in the adjudication of disputes by judges, no matter how experienced and supremely qualified. Accordingly, the modern explanation of the need for an appellate process to correct errors by lower adjudicative bodies is not due to the "unskilfulness" of the trial judge; rather it is their inherent fallibility.

Iacobucci and Major, in the oft-cited Supreme Court of Canada decision in *Housen v Nikolaisen*,[10] have added reinforcement to the modern view. They insist that appellate error correcting is not in any way predicated on any notion that appellate judges, as judges, are somehow superior to or "smarter" than trial judges. They point out that a bedrock assumption of our hierarchical system of judicial decision-making is that trial courts "can decide in a fair manner matters of fact, including witness choices and inferences, and can fairly balance competing factors when the law so requires".[11] Indeed, the qualification and experience required of a trial judge[12] make it abundantly clear that the objective of our adjudicative system is the expectation that a just result will be achieved at the trial stage. The sole justification for the error correcting jurisdiction vested in the Court of Appeal and the CCJ is therefore the inevitability of human error by judges.

The types of errors made by a trial court fall into three broad categories: errors on questions of law, questions of fact, and questions of mixed law and fact. The first are questions about what the correct legal rule is; questions of fact relate to what actually

---

9.   Roscoe Pound, *Appellate Procedure in Civil Cases* (Boston: Little, Brown, 1941), reprinted in Robert Martineau et al., *Cases and Materials on Appellate Practice and Procedure* (St Paul, MN: West Publishing, 1987).
10.   *Housen v Nikolaisen* (2002) SCR 235 CSC 33.
11.   See Roger Kerrans and Kim Willey, *Standards of Review Employed by Appellate Courts* (Edmonton: Juriliber, 2006), 14.
12.   Compare Section 7 of the Supreme Court of Judicature Act, Cap 117A and Art IV Paragraph 10 of the Agreement Establishing the Caribbean Court of Justice.

took place between the parties; and questions of mixed law and fact refer to the application of the legal rule to the facts.

On an appeal on an error of law, an appellate court is free to review a trial judge's findings and to replace the opinion of the trial judge with its own. On such an appeal, the appellate court is exercising its primary function, which is to correct errors of law.

Where the appeal is that the trial judge's error is one of fact, the settled law in our jurisdiction is that a distinction is to be drawn between primary facts and inferences from primary facts. The process of finding primary facts involves the trial judge assessing the credibility of witnesses. Inferences are concerned with the judge's evaluation of the primary facts.

An appellate court will only interfere with the trial judge's finding of primary facts where there was no evidence at all or only a scintilla of evidence to support the finding. In respect of the trial judge's inferences from the primary facts, an appellate court will generally regard itself as being in as good a position to draw inferences from or to evaluate facts as the trial judge.

Where an appeal is that the error of the trial judge involves a question of mixed law and fact, the settled law is that an appellate court in our jurisdiction is free to draw legal or factual inferences and to interfere with the findings of the trial judge.

It will be seen later why these basic principles are of crucial importance to the appellate advocate in the drafting of the notice of appeal. Meanwhile, the second rationale for the appellate function, the universal application of law rationale, must now be considered.

Though it is not expressly provided for by statute, the appellate process also exists for the purpose of ensuring the universal acceptance and application of the law. This objective is achieved through the functioning of the doctrine of *stare decisis,* whereby the view of the law propounded by the appellate court prevails, whatever the view of the lower court.

This point is very well captured in a statement in the 1966 Practice Statement of the House of Lords: "Their Lordships regard the use of precedent as an indispensable foundation upon which to decide what is the law and its application to individual cases. It provides at least some degree of certainty upon which individuals can rely in the conduct of their affairs, as well as a basis for orderly development of legal rules."[13]

The importance of the universal acceptance and application of the law was also underlined by the Supreme Court of Canada in the case of *Woods Manufacturing Co. Ltd. v The King*:

> It is fundamental to the due administration of justice that the authority of decisions be scrupulously respected by all courts upon which they are binding. Without this uniform and consistent adherence, the administration of justice becomes disordered, the law becomes uncertain, and the confidence of the public in it undermined. Nothing is more important than that the law as pronounced...should be accepted and applied as our tradition requires; and even at the risk of that fallibility to which all judges are liable, we must maintain the complete integrity of that relationship between the courts.[14]

The value of universal acceptance and application of the law identified in *Woods Manufacturing Co. Ltd. v The King* and the Practice Statement is demonstrably a crucial aspect of the appellate function. An equally important aspect of the universal acceptance and application of the law function is the law-making role of the appellate function, which is acknowledged in the 1996 Practice Statement. That statement declares that in a small but still significant number of cases where the rules or principles arguably applicable are unclear or out of touch with the needs of contemporary society or have not been applied to similar facts, the courts must "make" law. This acknowledgement calls into serious question the once fashionable oracular or declaratory theory of judging, where the court simply "finds" the relevant rule and mechanically applies it to the factual situation. This theory of judging, championed by Coke, Hale, Blackstone and other legal luminaries, was castigated by Lord Reid as a fairy tale.

So that it is now widely accepted that judicial law-making is a critical part of the appellate function. The sentencing guidelines laid down by Sir David Simmons in the Court of Appeal in the *Pierre Lord* case are without doubt an example of judicial law-making. Similarly, the reformulation of the American Cyanimid principle

---

13.   House of Lords, Practice Statement, 3 All ER 77, [1966] 1 WLR 1234.
14.   *Woods Manufacturing Co. Ltd. v The King* [1951] SCR 504 at 515.

in the Court of Appeal decision of *Toojays Ltd. v Westhaven Ltd.* may also be viewed as another example of judicial law-making by our Court of Appeal.[15]

These examples raise a very interesting question: should law-making be a part of the appellate function of our Court of Appeal, which, after all, is merely an intermediate appellate court? An influential school of thought championed by Justice James D. Hopkins in "The Rule of an Intermediate Appellate Court" argues that the only function of an intermediate court of appeal, such as our Court of Appeal, is to correct departures from the existing rules by trial judges – and not to make or remake the rules themselves.[16] According to this school, judicial law-making in our system should be the preserve of the CCJ, the apex court.

The Hopkins school of thought is not entirely persuasive. Needless to say, our Court of Appeal, as an intermediate court, cannot make law as freely as the CCJ, which is the ultimate court of appeal in our system. However, this does not mean that the Court of Appeal should not have a law-making function less than that of the CCJ. This is so because only a very small percentage of the cases decided in Barbados are appealed to the CCJ, as compared to those appealed to the Court of Appeal from trial courts. This means that in many cases where the law is unclear, it is preferable that the Court of Appeal seeks to clarify the law than that the law remain unclear in the hope that a case reaches the CCJ sometime in the future! This is especially so since the operation of the doctrine of precedent makes the Court of Appeal's decision subject to review by the CCJ. Another reason why the Court of Appeal should have a law-making function is because it is arguably better able to take judicial notice of some local or specialized matters which affect the articulation of what the law should be. In any event, it appears that the Court of Appeal has, for better or for worse, always considered itself as having a law-making function subject only to review by the CCJ.

This raises an interesting question concerning the law-making appellate function of the CCJ in our courts. Where the law made

---

15.   [2012] 2 LRC 65.
16.   James D. Hopkins, "The Rule of an Intermediate Appellate Court," *Brooklyn Law Review* 41, no. 3 (1975): 459–60.

by the CCJ is in an appeal from Barbados, there can be no doubt that that law binds our courts. The situation is slightly more complicated where the law is made in an appeal from Guyana or Belize or Dominica. Does a statement of law by the CCJ in such an appeal, which conflicts with say, settled Barbados Court of Appeal precedent, overrule that precedent by implication?

That question is not easily answered. However, the issue raised by the question cautions that where the CCJ is exercising its law-making function, the CCJ must have regard to relevant precedent from all the territories adhering to its appellate jurisdiction.

The Exercise of the Appellate Function

As has been seen, the primary role of trial courts is to resolve individual disputes based on the application of settled law to the facts before them. On the other hand, the role of appellate courts is not only to correct errors of the trial court, but also to delineate and refine legal rules and ensure their universal application. Given this description of the role of the appellate court, a question of some moment for the appellate advocate is this: How does the appellate court approach the decision appealed to it from the lower court? Put more directly, does the appellate function involve a rehearing or a review of the decision of the lower court?

Cap 117A confers appellate jurisdiction on the Court of Appeal. However, that Act is silent as to whether that jurisdiction is exercised by way of a review or a rehearing. By contrast, CPR 62.5 (1) provides that: "An appeal to the court shall be way of rehearing". Given the silence of the Act and the declaration of the rules, the question as to what the appellate process in appeals from a trial court is has obvious implications for the appellate advocate and so merits deeper examination.

In the decision of *Fair Trading Commission v Barbados National Oil Co. Ltd.*,[17] the Court of Appeal addressed the issue of the nature of its appellate function. There, the court noted that, broadly speaking, appeals are generally accepted as falling into two categories. These are *de novo* appeals and appeals on the record.

In a *de novo* appeal, the appellate court re-hears the case. The particular procedure by which the case is re-heard may vary.

---

17.   *Fair Trading Commission v Barbados National Oil Co. Ltd.* Civil Appeal No. 20 of 2009.

However, what defines a re-hearing is that there may be a retrial, for instance, either on the evidence in the trial record or on new evidence adduced before the appeal court. A *de novo* appeal is therefore an appeal by way of a re-hearing in the sense of a retrial by the appellate court.

The notion of an appeal by way of a re-hearing in the common law system is explained best within the historical origins of appeals. Historically, the notion of an appeal arose out of the development of an appeal in Chancery. Such an appeal was a re-hearing of a dispute delegated by the Lord Chancellor to the lower judges. In *Re Chennell*,[18] an appeal was described as a re-hearing in the sense of a "trial over again on the evidence used in the Court below; but there [was] special power to receive further evidence".[19]

In appeals on the record, the decision of the trial court is challenged by arguing that, for instance, the trial judge misapplied the law; came to an incorrect factual finding; considered evidence which they should not have considered; or failed to consider evidence that should have been considered. The Court of Appeal then examines the trial record to determine whether to uphold the challenge. The Court of Appeal can only consider evidence other than that adduced before the trial judge in very narrowly circumscribed circumstances. An appeal on the record is therefore in the nature of a review.

The appeal by way of review is of more recent vintage than appeals by way of re-hearing. Indeed, an appeal by way of review is the more modern acceptance of the meaning of what is an appeal. It is not surprising, therefore, that in the Australian High Court case of *Builders Licensing Board v Sperway Construction (Syd) Property Ltd.*, Mason, J referred to an appeal by way of review as "an appeal *stricto sensu*".[20] He emphasized that "upon an appeal *stricto sensu*, the question is whether the order or decision appealed from was correct on the material which the lower court had before it".[21]

In the interest of completeness, it is important to point out

---

18.   *Re Chennell, Jones v Chennell* (1878) 8 Ch D 492 at 505.
19.   Ibid.
20.   *Builders Licensing Board v Sperway Construction (Syd) Property Ltd.* (1976) 135 CLR 616 at 620.
21.   *Ponnamma v Arumogam* [1905] AC 383 at 388.

that in reviewing the decision of the trial judge, the appellate judge observes the principle of appellate deference. The principle of appellate deference holds that an appeal court will pay due deference to the decision of the trial judge and will interfere only where there is clear error.

This principle is usefully captured by May, LJ in the English Court of Appeal decision of *Dupont de Nemours v Dupont*.[22] In describing what is involved in an appeal by way of a review, May, LJ said:

> The review will engage the merits of the appeal. It will accord appropriate respect to the decision of the lower court. Appropriate respect will be tempered by the nature of the lower court and its decision-making process. There will also be a spectrum of appropriate respect depending on the nature of the decision of the lower court which is challenged.[23]

When regard is had to the powers of the Court of Appeal expressly stated in Cap 117A, and in particular the power in section 62 to order new trials, the appeal contemplated by Cap 117A is more consistent with an appeal by way of review than by way of re-hearing. This appears to be the way in which it has been understood the Court of Appeal. The provision in CPR 62.5 (1) that an appeal shall be by way of a re-hearing has been disregarded by the Court of Appeal as the CPR does not contain any procedures for a re-hearing. Instead, notwithstanding CPR 62.5 (1), all the rules in CPR seem to assume that an appeal is to be by way of review.

The jurisprudential basis for viewing an appeal under Cap 117A as being by way of review may be found in the judgment of Iacobucci and Major JJ in the Supreme Court of Canada decision in *Housen v Nikolaisen*.[24] They stated:

> The role of the appellate court was aptly defined in Underwood v Ocean City Realty Ltd. (1987), 12 B.C.L.R. (2d) 199 (C.A.), at p. 204, where it was stated: The appellate court must not retry a case and must not substitute its views for the views of the trial judge according to what the appellate court thinks the evidence establishes on its view of the balance of probabilities.

---

22.   *Dupont de Nemours v Dupont* [2006] 1 WLR 2793 at 94.
23.   Ibid., 2799.
24.   *Housen v Nikolaisen* (2002) SCR 235 CSC 33.

...The foundation of the principle is as sound today as one hundred years ago. It is premised on the notion that finality is an important aim of litigation. There is no suggestion that appellate court judges are somehow smarter and thus capable of reaching a better result. Their role is not to write better judgments but to review the reasons in light of the arguments of the parties and the relevant evidence, and then to uphold the decision unless a palpable error leading to a wrong result has been made by the trial judge.[25]

In light of the foregoing, it seems that the correct view of the law is that appeals in Barbados pursuant to Cap 117A is by way of review and not by way of re-hearing.

Statutory Provision for Appeal by Re-hearing

Notwithstanding the nature of an appeal under Cap 117A, appellate counsel must always remember that an appeal is not a common law proceeding. It is a remedy given by statute. So that a particular statute, in conferring a right of appeal, may therefore provide that such an appeal be by way of a re-hearing.

In approaching a statutory provision for an appeal by way of a re-hearing, appellate counsel would do well to remember the observation by Viscount Sankey LC in *Powell v Streatham Manor Nursing Home*: "There are different meanings to be attached to the word 'rehearing'."[26] Of similar importance is May, LJ's statement in the English Court of Appeal case of *Dupont de Nemours v Dupont*,[27] that re-hearing has a range of meanings. Where therefore a particular statute provides for an appeal by way of a re-hearing, there is no *a priori* form of proceeding. That must be ascertained by a proper interpretation of the statute in question.[28]

Appeals against the exercise of a discretion by a lower court may be viewed as an exception to the general rule that appeals in Barbados are by way of review. Where the appeal is against the decision of a lower court whose decision is reached by the exercise of discretion, the nature of the appellate function may involve a review as well as a re-hearing. In numerous decisions of the Court

---

25. Ibid.
26. *Powell v Streatham Manor Nursing Home* [1935] AC 243 at 249.
27. *Dupont de Nemours v Dupont* [2006] 1 WLR 2793 at 94.
28. See *Phillips v The Commonwealth* (1964) 110 CLR 347 (HCA).

of Appeal, that court has held that, in appeals against the exercise
of a discretion by a trial judge, its function is to first of all to see
whether the judge's use of discretion is based on a misunderstanding
or misapplication of either the law or the evidence. If it is, then the
court is entitled to set aside the judge's discretion, and to exercise
its independent discretion in considering what decision should have
been reached. That may involve a re-hearing in the sense that the
appellate court will be required to consider anew all relevant facts
and circumstances of the case as disclosed in the trial records.

Part II

With the foregoing analysis of the purpose of the appellate function
firmly in mind, observations on how an appellate attorney in
Barbados can be of most assistance to the appellate Court may
now be explored.

1. The Notice of Appeal

It goes without saying that the foundation of an appeal is the
notice of appeal. It is in this document that the issues in the appeal
are framed. From the perspective of an appellate judge, the most
helpful notice of appeal is one which does not contain a multitude
of grounds in which the most persuasive grounds get buried in
thickets of dense weak grounds. The most helpful notice of appeal
is one which identifies only those errors of ultimate fact or law
which affect the result of the appeal.[29]

In many appeals the Court of Appeal has said in its written
judgment something like: "Twenty grounds of appeal are listed in
the notice of appeal. However, reduced to their essentials, the issues
raised in these grounds are encapsulated in two issues which are
dispositive of this case."

Justice Branson's explanation in *Sydneywide Distributors
Property Ltd. & Anor v Red Bull Australia Property Ltd. &
Anor* (2002) as to how an appellate attorney should approach the
drafting of a notice of appeal worth repeating here. Justice Branson

---

29.   A good example of such a notice of appeal is that filed in *Munroe Haywood v The
      Queen* (unreported) (Criminal Appeal No. 26 of 2010) (Barbados). *RBTT Bank
      Barbados Ltd v Fitzroy Davis and Lisa Davis* (unreported) Civil Appeal No. 2 of 2015 is
      another.

said there:

> In drafting a notice of appeal, the first question is, what is the nature of the error? Is it an error of fact or law or discretion? If the only error is one of fact, you have to carefully consider whether it is one which the Court of Appeal is likely to reverse. The prospect of reversal of a finding of fact which depends on the trial judge's assessment of the credibility of witnesses is poor. If the supposed error is one of law, the prospects of success in the appeal are enhanced. The appellate court is in the same position as the trial judge to determine that issue of law. Misapplication of legal principle and incorrect interpretation of statutory provision are usually the most fertile source of legal error. But they are not the only source of such error. The trial judge may have incorrectly formulated a legal proposition...If the error is one of an exercise of discretion, the difficulty of attacking the exercise is high. An appellate court will not interfere with an exercise of discretion unless the appellant can establish that the exercise of the discretion was based on a misunderstanding or misapplication of either the law or the evidence.[30]

Another matter of considerable importance in drafting the notice of appeal is the question of the orders which are sought.[31] This should be the subject of careful thought and should be drafted with precision. Judges have told of cases where attorneys have suffered embarrassment when the Court points out that the relief they were seeking was not in their notice of appeal. Worst of all are cases where the orders sought in a notice of appeal did not reflect what the successful party was seeking!

2. Checks Before Filing Notice of Appeal

As has already been pointed out, an appeal is not a common law right. The availability of an appeal depends on statute or rules of court. Many rights of appeal are limited by reference to subject matter, or the amount involved. Again, many appeals may only be brought by leave or special leave of the court as, for instance, is

---

30.   *Sydneywide Distributors Pty Ltd. & Anor v Red Bull Australia Pty Ltd. & Anor* (2002) 55 IPR 354 at 355–56.

31.   See Chief Justice French AC's presentation to the World Bar Conference, 29 June 2012, UKSC, London, titled "Appellate Advocacy in the High Court of Australia" (unpublished paper), 5.

the case with respect to interlocutory appeals. So, before filing a notice of appeal, it is of fundamental importance that appellate counsel ascertains what, if any, jurisdiction the court has to hear the intended appeal.[32]

3. The Written Submissions

In recent times, written submissions have become the most critical part of an appeal.[33] They are now acknowledged as being more important than oral argument. As Justice Kirby said in "The Future of Appellate Advocacy": "[a] good advocate ordinarily uses oral argument to complement and strengthen written submissions".[34] Accordingly, appellate counsel must have firmly in mind the old adage: "The pen is mightier than the sword."

Each appellate judge sitting on the case invariably reads the written submissions before the hearing commences.[35] So written submissions make the first impression on the appeal court. The judge when composing their judgment will frequently refer to written submissions to make sure that they have not missed any argument. Also, written submissions will invariably be looked at by the judge before finalizing their judgment.

The written submissions in some cases have been declared by judges to be of inestimable assistance in the writing of the judgment. What went into making the written submissions in those cases stand out?

First, the submissions in those cases demonstrated extensive preparation by counsel before they were written and filed.[36] It is obvious from them that counsel mastered the trial transcript and the judgment of the trial court which was the subject of appeal. It was

---

32. Ibid.
33. For a good discussion of this see Perry, "The Art of Persuasion Through the Written Word in Appellate Advocacy" (unpublished paper).
34. Justice Kirby, "The Future of Appellate Advocacy," *Australian Bar Review* 27 (2006): 141, 144.
35. But see Chester Porter, QC in "The Gentle Art of Persuasion," (230), where he states that written submissions are often not read and that he "was somewhat comforted by the amusement raised for me by the judges pretending they had read my submissions when they obviously had not, and were rapidly scanning them so as to be able to claim some knowledge of what I had written".
36. As to the importance of preparation see opening address by the Honourable Michael McHugh, AO, QC, at the Appellate Advocacy Course titled "The Essence of Appellate Advocacy" (unpublished paper), 2012, 1–2.

also clear that, as part of the preparation of the written submissions, counsel had thoroughly researched all statutory provisions, case authorities and secondary legal materials relevant to the appeal. Counsel explained these authorities in the submissions and exhibited copies of these authorities in appendices to the written submissions. It was also obvious that, as part of the preparation, counsel had read the relevant CPR rules concerning written submissions and had complied with the directions contained in the rules.

The written submissions in those cases exhibited the characteristics identified by the Honourable Michael McHugh AO, QC in his opening address to the 2012 Appellate Advocacy Course entitled "The Essence of Appellate Advocacy" (unpublished). The submissions were clear and concise. They "expounded a theory of the case that was based on the evidence"; that seemed "to produce a fair result"; that was logical and not "inconsistent with accepted law".

The argument which was being advanced in those written submissions was broken down with point headings and the error which was sought to be reversed was identified precisely, either by a verbatim quote or by a short summary with a reference to the page in the record of appeal.[37] This obviated the occasion for the judges having to ask: "Where do we find that?"

Last but not least, the submissions answered the arguments put forward by the other side and recognized weaknesses in the counsel's case. The submissions did not seek to rely on the assumed inherent strength of the case being advanced. This allowed the court to better appreciate the pros and cons of the appeal before it. Put simply, the submissions eschewed the trap identified by that esteemed Australian jurist, Sir Anthony Mason, in "The Role of Counsel and Appellate Advocacy", where he cautioned: "It is vital to make those points of the appellant's case which seems to have attracted the Court, and it is important to make those points without delay. There is an element of anti-climax in beginning with inconsequential matters and it may convey the impression that there is no real answer on the critical issues."[38]

---

37.   As to the importance of this, see also Perry, "The Art of Persuasion Through the Written Word in Appellate Advocacy," *Adelaide Law Review* 28, no. 133 (2007): 141–42.

38.   Sir Anthony Mason, "The Role of Counsel and Appellate Advocacy," *Australian Law*

The Oral Argument

From the court's perspective, oral argument before the court is next in importance to the written submissions.[39] The major value of oral argument before the court is that it gives the judges an opportunity to deal with issues raised (or not raised) in the written submissions that they may want to pursue. Consequently, Socratic dialogue can be an integral part of the dialogue between the bench and advocate as such dialogue promotes a clearer articulation of the error the appeal seeks to correct or the departure from the universal application of the law alleged in the appeal.

At the oral hearing, appellate counsel must expect, as a minimum, questions concerning the other side's case. Counsel should also anticipate and work out answers to difficulties and potential weaknesses in their argument.[40]

The most helpful appellate attorneys appearing before the appellate court are those who, before the hearing, have spent a good deal of time preparing answers to the questions they anticipate that that they will get from the bench.[41]

Conclusion

As acknowledged at the outset, the appellate counsel's ultimate role in an appeal is to seek to win the matter for his client. This article has sought to show that they also have a role in assisting the appellate court in its error correcting function and in its universal application of law function. It has also attempted to highlight that there is no necessary tension between these two roles. In fact, the aim of the article has been to expose to appellate counsel a deeper understanding of the fundamental importance of their role in the appellate function.

Journal (1984) 537 at 543.

39.   For a good discussion of this, see Renee Pomerance "Appellate Advocacy: Presenting the Oral Argument," Ministry of the Attorney General, Toronto, 2002, https://www.scai-ipcs.ca/pdf/Pomerance-PresentingtheOralArgument.pdf. And see generally Justice John Laskin, "A View from the Other Side: What I Would Have Done Differently if I Knew Then What I Know Now," *Advocates Society Journal 6* (1998).

40.   Ibid.

41.   For a fuller exploration of the challenges in oral arguments, see Justice Sackville, "Appellate Advocacy," *Australian Bar Review* 15, no. 99 (1996).

CHAPTER 4

Whose Say Holds Sway?
Consent to Medical Treatment for Children

Rose Cameron

Many of the cases involving children concern their medical treatment, in particular, the course to be taken.[1] This is necessarily the case because so many views contend when children fall ill – preservation of life, individual autonomy, parental rights – making the resolution of the contending views challenging. Intuitively, parents, because of their parental rights and responsibilities, may assume that they have the final say concerning their children's medical treatment. However, this is not an accurate representation of the law. It is important, therefore, to explore and clarify how these disputes are resolved by the law. The chapter will, from a Jamaican context and, where applicable, from the wider Commonwealth, look first at why consent is required and then at the rights of important stakeholders in this decision-making process: the child, the parents, the doctors and the courts. The rights that each has will guide whose consent prevails when there is a dispute. Of course, when they all agree to the course of treatment then no consent issues arise.

Why is the right to consent required? An individual has an absolute right not to have their bodily integrity/security violated. In other words, every person's body is inviolate.[2] When a person undergoes medical treatment, it is the provision of consent that prevents the doctor from being held liable for trespass to the person. A doctor may be guilty of unauthorised touching, a battery, when he does his medical procedures without the patient's consent. The doctor may even be sued in negligence for failing to advise the patient of procedures or medical information of which any prudent

---

1. Jonathan Herring, *Family Law* (Longman Law Series), 2nd ed. (Boston: Addison Wesley, 2004), 393.
2. *A (Children) (Conjoined Twins: Medical treatment) (No. 1), Re* 2000 WL 1274054 (2000) 27.

practitioner would have advised his patient. This is so because of
the existence of the doctrine of informed consent, wherein medical
personnel may not perform any medical procedures without
securing the patient's consent after providing sufficient information
to allow for a proper evaluation of its pros and cons. This doctrine
is enshrined in law.

The Jamaican constitution, the Charter of Fundamental Rights
and Freedoms, in section 13(3) (a) and (j) speaks to the right to life,
liberty and security of the person and the right not to be deprived
thereof, except in the execution of the sentence of a court in respect
of a criminal offence of which the person has been convicted, and
so on.

The inviolability of bodily integrity/security is also recognized in
the common law of Britain[3] and the Commonwealth. In Canada,[4]
Malette v Shulman et al. powerfully illustrates the point.[5] The
severely injured plaintiff was taken, unconscious, to the defendant
hospital, where she was examined in the emergency department by
the defendant physician who formed the opinion that the plaintiff
needed a blood transfusion to preserve her life. In the plaintiff's
purse was a card which identified her as a Jehovah's Witness
and requested that she not be given any blood transfusions. The
defendant physician administered transfusions to her and later
refused to comply with the request of the plaintiff's daughter, who
sought to terminate the transfusions.

A recovered Mrs Malette brought an action against the
physician and the hospital, alleging that the administration of
blood constituted negligence and assault and battery. The trial judge
awarded the plaintiff $20,000 by way of damages for battery. The
defendants appealed. The Court of Appeal dismissed the appeal on
the ground that Mrs Malette had a right to control her own body.

---

3.   In *Re F. (Mental Patient: Sterilisation)* [1990] 2 A.C. 1, 72E. at 71D Lord Goff opines: "It
     is a well-established principle that as a general rule, the performance of a medical
     operation upon a person without his consent is unlawful, as constituting both the
     crime of battery and the tort of trespass to the person." Lord Reid makes the point in
     S. v McC., W. v W. [1972] A.C. 24, 43, that "there is no doubt that a person of full age
     and capacity cannot be ordered to undergo a blood test against his will...".
4.   Section 7 of the Canadian Charter of Rights and Freedoms states: "Everyone has the
     right to life, liberty and security of the person and the right not to be deprived thereof
     except in accordance with the principles of fundamental justice."
5.   (Ont. C.A.) [1990] O.J. No. 450.

With the law clearly protecting a person's right to bodily integrity, including children's, it means that the law has to contemplate at which stage of their development children earn the legal right to consent to their medical treatment. The United Nations Convention on the Rights of a Child led the way in giving children rights and made allowance for the rights they could exercise, depending on their "evolving capacities",[6] or the "age and maturity of the child".[7]

Legislation

By the time the child attains the age of sixteen, they would enjoy significant rights in the area of consent to medical treatment by virtue of the Law Reform (Age of Majority Act), Jamaica, or similar legislation in other jurisdictions. Section 8(1) states:

> Where a minor has attained the age of sixteen, his consent in respect of any surgical, medical or dental treatment to himself shall be as effective as it would have been if he were of full age; and where a minor has, by virtue of the provisions of this section given an effective consent in respect of any such treatment, it shall not be necessary for consent to be obtained from the parent or guardian.

The legislation allows the child the opportunity to make his own decisions at sixteen, notwithstanding that a parent's right to the custody of a child ends on their eighteenth birthday.

Common Law

The common law makes even more drastic inroads into the erosion of parental authority. Parental right, according to the common law, is a dwindling right which the courts will hesitate to enforce against the wishes of the child.[8] *Gillick v West Norfolk and Wisbech Area Health Authority* makes this fundamental change in the decision-making structure for children under sixteen.[9] Lord Scarman puts it thus: "I would hold that as a matter of law the parental right to determine whether or not their minor child below the age of 16 will

---

6. Article 5 and Article 14 of the Convention on the Rights of the Child.
7. Article 12 of the CRC.
8. This was a generally accepted view in *Gillick v West Norfolk and Wisbech Area Health Authority* [1986] AC 112.
9. *Gillick* [1986] AC 112.

have medical treatment terminates if and when the child achieves a sufficient understanding and intelligence to enable him or her to understand fully what is proposed."[10] The doctor would make the assessment if the child has achieved this level of understanding. If the child has, he is regarded as Gillick competent.

Lord Scarman acknowledged that the decision could be criticized for leading to uncertainty and, moreover, for leaving the law in the hands of the doctors. However, he felt that "the uncertainty is the price which has to be paid to keep the law in line with social experience, which is that many girls are fully able to make sensible decisions about many matters before they reach the age of 16".[11] In cases where the child lacks the capacity to consent (age, illness, immaturity) then the parents or *de facto* parents would supply the requisite consent.

Parent vs Parent

The dispute may instead be between parents regarding the course of treatment for the child. In *Re C. (Welfare of Child: Immunisation)*, two fathers who had parental responsibility orders from the court disagreed with the mothers of the children on immunizing their children. The Court of Appeal, in upholding the decision of the lower court, ordered the immunization of the children.

The court decided that neither parent could singly make the decision and held: Where parents were in dispute about the immunization of a child against infectious disease, neither parent had the right to make the decision alone and immunization should be carried out only where a court decided that this was in the best interests of the child.[12]

In any scenario where a parent denies a child medical care, that parent can be held criminally responsible for the death of or harm to the child because of their failure to seek and obtain medical help. The criminal responsibility would apply to both parents if they were in agreement to withhold the medical treatment, even if the denial was for religious reasons. *In Re S. (A Minor) (Medical Treatment)*, the court ordered blood transfusions as a necessary

---

10. *Gillick* [1986] AC 112, 188–89.
11. *Gillick* [1986] AC 112, 191.
12. *Re C. (Welfare of Child: Immunisation)* [2003] EWHC 137 (Fam).

part of treatment for leukemia to a four-year-old child whose parents opposed blood transfusion because they were Jehovah's Witnesses.[13] The parents supported medical treatment, provided it did not infringe upon their religious beliefs. The attending physicians testified that treatment would not be possible without these transfusions. The court ordered the transfusions because the welfare of the child must take precedent over all other concerns.

Doctors vs Parents

How do doctors proceed in the face of disagreement with the parents? In *R. v Portsmouth Hospitals NHS Trust ex parte Glass*, the disagreement centered on the withdrawal, without parental consent, of life-sustaining treatment for a severely disabled twelve-year-old boy with a very limited lifespan.[14] The doctors were of the opinion that the child should receive only palliative care, while the mother felt he should receive care to prolong his life as much as possible. The mother applied for judicial review and an anticipatory declaration from the court on the course to be followed if the family and the medical authorities disagreed. Her appeal to the Court of Appeal and the European Court of Human Rights was dismissed (ECtHR).[15] The courts were not prepared to rule in advance on the course to be followed, but felt those decisions should be made as the circumstances arose.

The ECtHR accepted, based on Article 8 of the European Convention on Human Rights (ECHR),[16] that a doctor's pursuance of a course of medical treatment to which parents objected was a violation of the child's right to bodily integrity. The resolution of the disagreement was the responsibility of the court, and the medical authorities had the responsibility of making the application. The court did not rule out the parents making the application as well. The court is never going to ask the medical authorities to act against their professional judgement. The process of adjudication

---

13. [1993] 1 FLR 376.
14. [1999] 2 FLR 905, *Glass v United Kingdom* [2004] 1 FLR 1019 – A parent, as the child's legal proxy, had the authority to act on his behalf and defend his interests. A decision to impose treatment against the parent's objection violated the child's right to respect for his private life. The hospital had an obligation to bring serious disagreements before the court.
15. *Glass v United Kingdom*.
16. European Convention on Human Rights.

will bring the contending stakeholders together and in arriving at a decision, the court will be compelled to act in the best interest of the child.

Doctors vs Doctors

In the case of baby J.,[17] the doctors disagreed on whether it would be medically appropriate for them to administer intensive therapeutic measures such as artificial ventilation if J. were to suffer a life-threatening event. One set of doctors treating J. posited that it would be unkind to put the child through such a procedure. Another consultant, Dr R., did not express a view concerning the appropriateness of the artificial ventilator. J.'s mother supported the local authority, who applied to the court for an order that J. be given intensive therapeutic measures, if necessary, contrary to the opinion of the doctors treating him. The court so ordered. The order was set aside by the Court of Appeal, citing the undesirability of having a doctor administer treatment which he thinks is not in the best interest of the child, but faced with contempt of court if he does not. The court was of the view that a court should never order a doctor to treat a patient contrary to the doctor's professional judgement.

Doctors Acting Without Consent

The common law doctrine of necessity could operate to allow the medical staff to waive the consent rights of the relevant stakeholder – be it the patient or the parents. This defence is well recognized.[18] The first obvious need for the application of the doctrine is in cases where the patient lacks capacity to weigh the risks and benefits of the proposed medical treatment then some other person, permissible by law would provide the consent.[19] The House of Lords criticized the unbridled power it gives to doctors: "It places effective and unqualified control in the hands of the hospital psychiatrist and other health care professionals."[20] Of course the Law Lords

---

17.   J (A Minor) (Child in Care: Medical Treatment), Re 1992 WL 895619 (1992).
18.   In Canada – Kent Roach et al., Criminal Law and Procedure (Toronto: Emond, 2015), 961. In England – A (Children) (Conjoined Twins: Medical Treatment) (No. 1), Re 2000 WL 1274054 (2000), 83–91, and the Commonwealth.
19.   In Re F [1990] 2 A.C. 1.
20.   HL v United Kingdom 35 EHRR CD, CD 293–313 at 298.

acknowledged that the common law principle which requires the medical staff to always act in the best interest of the patient would limit their power.

In *Re A (Children) (Conjoined Twins: Medical Treatment) (No.1)* the doctrine of necessity[21] loomed large. A thirty-four-year-old woman gave birth for the first time to conjoined twins, Jodie and Mary. Each had their own brain, heart, lungs, arms and legs, but shared an abdomen. The doctors were certain that the babies could be separated, but the weaker one, Mary, would not survive the separation. If they were not separated, both would die within three to six months. The parents refused to consent to the operation. The doctors "could not allay a collective medical conscience and see the children in their care die when they know one was capable of being saved".[22]

The doctors argued the doctrine of necessity. The requirements to be met are: the act is needed to avoid inevitable and irreparable evil; no more should be done than is reasonably necessary for the purpose to be achieved; and the evil inflicted must not be disproportionate to the evil avoided.[23] The doctors sought and were granted the requisite order from the court to separate the twins by Johnson J, who was persuaded it is in the best interest of both babies for the separation to occur. The parents appealed against the order. The Court of Appeal, on the ground of necessity, dismissed the appeal. Lord Justice Ward said all the requirements for the application of the doctrine of necessity were met in this case. The separation order was granted.

The State

The responsibilities of the Children's Advocate are outlined in the First Schedule to the Child Care and Protection Act, 2004. They are important and far-reaching and therefore those affecting a child's right to consent to medical treatment are shared in this section to show their breadth and scope. In Jamaica, the state, by way of the Office of the Children's Advocate (OCA), may represent the child

---

21. It is "acting reasonably and proportionately in order to avoid a threat of death or serious injury". *A (Children) (Conjoined Twins: Medical Treatment) (No. 1), Re* 2000 WL 1274054 (2000), 86.
22. Ibid., 25.
23. *A (Children) (Conjoined Twins: Medical Treatment) (No. 1)*, 92.

in court. The Child Care and Protection Act, which was passed into law in 2004, was a direct by-product of Jamaica's ratification of the 1989 United Nations Convention on the Rights of the Child (UNCRC). That legislation ushered in a rights-based approach to all matters impacting children, and provided for the creation of new institutions in line with Jamaica's commitments under the convention. The Office of the Children's Advocate, established in 2006, was given the statutory mandate to act as the independent commission of parliament that ensures all actions taken by persons and entities who interact with children (including state actors, such as the Child Protection and Family Services, medical practitioners and teachers, among others) are in line with the UNCRC and children's best interests in every applicable set of circumstances.

It is the OCA that has the over-arching responsibility to ensure that the rights of children, as articulated under the UNCRC, are observed and pursued by all actors across all sectors, and where there are identifiable and actionable failures, the OCA has been vested with the legal authority to institute proceedings against the offending party to hold them accountable and secure remedies on behalf of the aggrieved child, or in medical matters, on behalf of a child in any disagreement over what course of treatment ought to be taken. The actions pursued by the OCA are in line with its statutory responsibility for all children in Jamaica, whether they are in institutional care facilities, at home with their parents, in juvenile correctional institutions, whether they permanently reside in Jamaica or are merely visiting, or whether they are designated as being in need of care and protection or not. These actions are all guided by a consideration of the rights of the child, as well as their best interests.

The independence of the OCA is also a characteristic that has been internationally recognized as a positive attribute. It is critical that the OCA is unfettered in its ability to initiate steps against individuals (including parents) and institutions (including the government), who breach the rights of a child or act contrary to their best interests. One key responsibility is to conduct investigations into alleged instances of child rights violations and to pursue steps to seek any necessary redress on behalf of the affected children. These investigations are triggered by complaints that may be referred to the office or by the OCA becoming aware of a situation and acting upon its own volition to pursue the necessary action in keeping with the dictates of the CRC. The violation at any level – by parents, caregivers, guardians or any person – would give the Children's Advocate the right to intervene. This broad right allows for the provision of legal representation for children and also general legal services to ensure that their rights and best interests are promoted and preserved. This includes making applications to the court on behalf of medical institutions or practitioners for medical treatment to be given or procedures to be done, in the absence of parental consent. This responsibility also includes appearing for children in court proceedings (both civil and criminal); providing legal opinions for judges who have to determine court matters that involve children; appearing for children before any tribunal or panel involved in making decisions pertinent to the child in question; instituting proceedings against anyone or any institution (including state agencies) to seek redress on behalf of children where identifiable rights have been breached; appearing for children who are in conflict with the law and for those who are victims of crime or any other violation.

When the Children's Advocate intervenes by way of representation of the child, they are vested with the powers of a judge of the Supreme Court for the purposes of presiding over quasi-judicial hearings for the taking of evidence in matters concerning the rights of children as outlined in the CRC, and the preservation of their best interests. Upon the conclusion of such a hearing, the Children's Advocate determines how to proceed in order to address rights-based issues and best interests matters arising from the circumstances. Some of the timely interventions of the Children's Advocate made on account of the exercise of the state-bestowed rights to ensure they represent the child's rights and interests are discussed next.

Towards the end of 2018 and continuing into 2019 the story of baby F., a critically ill baby, grabbed Jamaica's attention. The hospital diagnosed the child as having cancer and recommended chemotherapy. The parents refused to have the baby treated and demanded that the child be released into their care. The hospital was of the view that the parents' consent was necessary for the treatment to be administered. When it was not forthcoming, the hospital correctly contacted the Office of the Children's Advocate, which sought and was granted a court order to permit the hospital to administer the chemotherapy.[24] This was but one of the cases in which the OCA filed applications in the Supreme Court seeking to have medical treatment and/or procedures done on the basis that this course was in the best interests of the children.

In the case of N.C., a girl born on 3 September 2004, and diagnosed with leukaemia, the doctors' best clinical judgement was that N.C. needed a blood transfusion as part of her treatment, without which she would very likely die. Her parents, Jehovah's Witnesses, objected to the treatment on religious grounds. N.C.'s parents received strong support from the elders of their faith. The OCA successfully intervened, after which N.C.'s parents eventually agreed to give consent.

Another case requiring the OCA's intervention involved A.Y., a girl born on 15 February 2018. The baby was admitted to hospital with watery, bloody stools and extreme dehydration. Her case was one that required close medical monitoring because her condition showed signs of becoming critical very quickly. The doctors determined that the cause of her health condition was an allergy to breast milk and infant formula. Her father wanted to remove the baby from the hospital, despite the advice of the medical staff against her discharge. The OCA's intervention involved seeking and obtaining an ex parte injunction to prohibit the child's removal by the parents. Despite the court order, the hospital under much pressure, subsequently discharged the child into the parents' care. After the hospital informed the OCA of the baby's discharge to her parents, the latter filed a notice of discontinuance. The child died after being discharged by the hospital and whilst in her parents' care. The final case which will be shared, and which demonstrates the interventionist role of the OCA in consent to medical treatment occurred in 2014. It involved a gravely ill male child who was suspected of having cancer. The child was admitted to the Bustamante Hospital for Children for treatment. His mother refused to consent to tests being conducted in order that a diagnosis could be confirmed. Her consent was necessary to facilitate the

24.   University Hospital of the West Indies, "Statement issued by the UHWI," Jamaica Observer, 24 January 2019.

doctors' deciding upon and pursuing a course of treatment. It was noted that the mother expressed a preference for treatment from an Obeah man. The OCA sought and obtained an injunction to prevent any release of the baby from the hospital. This successful intervention resulted in the hospital being able to administer an appropriate course of treatment to improve the child's chances of survival.

While each case turned on its own merit, the common thread involved a parent unreasonably withholding consent to a procedure that the medical opinion saw as necessary to preserve the child's life. In these applications, Article 18 of the CRC is greatly relied upon. Article 18 states that parents have a joint and primary responsibility to secure the best interests of their child; but this must be done within the confines of the rights of the child. If the parents are not able to manage this, the state must step in to secure the child's rights and needs. It also speaks to the legal responsibility of parents to act in the best interests of their children.

The Courts

The role of the court can be misunderstood, as the authorities reveal. In 2000, in the famous English case regarding the separation of conjoined twins, Jodie and Mary, Lord Justice Ward felt compelled to comment on the public's concern "as to why the court is involved at all".[25] He reminded the public that when judges examine the consent rights involved in the medical treatment of children, it is by no means the case that the court is trying to occupy itself by finding something to do. Instead, the court had an obligation, "to decide what parties with a proper interest ask us to decide".[26] In 2016, the famous Charlie Gard case gripped the world and evoked responses from the president of the United States, the pope, doctors, the media,[27] protesters angry with the hospital staff for recommending

25.   *A (Children) (Conjoined Twins: Medical treatment) (No. 1)*.
26.   Ibid., 24.
27.   Dan Bilefsky, "Charlie Gard Dies, Leaving a Legacy of Thorny Ethics Questions." *New York Times,* 28 July 2017, https://www.nytimes.com/2017/07/28/world/europe/charlie-gard-dead.html?mcubz=0 (accessed 6 August 2019). In the article, Charlie's mother lamented: "We've had no control over our son's life and no control over our son's death." The BBC reported in 2017 on death threats made to hospital staff who treated the baby and asked for the court to withdraw life support to allow the baby to die with dignity and not prolong his vegetative, incurable state. It reported also that

the removal of the baby's life support, and protesters objecting to the court's decision. None seemed to appreciate the important role of the court. The attorney for the parents, Richard Gordon, KC, did not seem to appreciate the role of the court either. In amplifying his position, he pointed out that the court's decision to intervene was really an example of the wrongful intrusion of the state in the private and family life of the parents of little Charlie Gard. Counsel failed to appreciate that the state by way of the courts possesses the inherent jurisdiction to grant orders for treatment of the child – even when the parents and other authorities do not agree with it. Amply illustrating the court's role was the case of dangerously ill baby, CW.[28] The parents objected to the doctor's advice to administer morphine to relieve the pain the child was experiencing. The hospital had to make and an out-of-hours emergency telephone application to the judge for an order to administer the morphine.[29]

Limiting the Influence of the Common Law Decision in *Gillick*

In the case of all disagreements concerning the medical treatment of the child, the court is obliged to decide in the child's best interest.[30] That posture has caused the court to take action in limiting the child's consent rights if it is of the view that the child's exercise of its right is not in its best interest. It is not surprising that *Gillick* has been circumscribed by subsequent cases, the effect of which is to let the best interest of the child prevail over any exercise of rights contrary to this position. In 1991, Lord Donaldson, in *Re R.*,[31] examined Lord Scarman's judgment in *Gillick* and made clear that the child's right was not unbridled. He said: "I see no reason whatsoever why it (the court) should not be able, and in an appropriate case willing, to override decisions of 'Gillick competent' children who

thousands of abusive and menacing messages had been received. (https://www.bbc.com/news/uk-england-london-40691478).

28. *Portsmouth NHS Trust v W*, 2005 WL 2706869 (2005).
29. Ibid., 4.
30. Article 3, UNCRC.
31. *(A Minor) (Wardship: Medical Treatment)* [1991] 4 All ER177.

are its wards or in respect of whom applications are made."[32] Other similar decisions followed. In *Re W*[33] Lord Donaldson held that there can be no doubt that the court "has power to override the refusal of a minor, whether over the age of 16 or under that age but 'Gillick competent'".[34]

The court's wardship jurisdiction is wider than any jurisdiction the parents can exercise over their children. The authority is derived from the state, or Crown, which has delegated the duty of ongoing protection of vulnerable children to the court.[35] In its wardship jurisdiction the court is able to give consent for medical treatment of a *Gillick*-competent or incompetent minor who has refused consent.[36] In *Re B. (A Minor) (Wardship: Sterilisation)*,[37] the House of Lords affirmed on appeal a lower court decision authorizing sterilization of a mentally retarded, epileptic seventeen-year-old girl. The House held that sterilization was for her welfare and in her best interests because she had no understanding of the connection between sexual intercourse and pregnancy. There was evidence that she could not be placed on a regimen of contraceptive drugs because of her mental capacity would not allow her to administer the medication to herself. The court gave leave for the operation to be carried out.

Parens Patriae Jurisdiction (Common Law)

It is an "essentially protective" jurisdiction which empowers the court with the right to suspend or supersede parental rights when judicially satisfied that the welfare of the child requires it.[38] *Parens patriae* is different from wardship in that the former is exercised to "resolve a single issue relating to the child".[39] In *Re M.*, a fifteen-year-old girl refused to consent to the heart transplant needed to save her life.[40] She did not want to have someone else's heart and

---

32.   Ibid., 186 [e].
33.   *(A Minor) (Medical Treatment: Court's Jurisdiction)* [1992] 3 WLR 758.
34.   Ibid., 783.
35.   *Re R. (A Minor) (Wardship: Medical Treatment)* [1991] 4 All ER177, 186, para. g–h; and Jonathan Herring, "Family Law," in *Family Law*, 488.
36.   *Re R. (A minor) (Wardship: Medical Treatment)*, 188, para. a–b.
37.   [1988] AC 199.
38.   *X. v Sydney Children's Hospitals Network* [2013] NSWCA 320 (2013) 3.
39.   Herring, "Family Law," 488.
40.   [1999] 2 FLR 1097 and 52 BMLR, 124.

did not wish to take medication for the rest of her life. The hospital, which had obtained the mother's consent to the treatment, sought leave from the court to carry out the heart transplant. Johnson J authorized the hospital to give treatment according to the doctor's clinical judgement, including a heart transplant. He relied heavily on Lord Donaldson's statement in *Re W. (A Minor) (Consent to Medical Treatment)*: "There is ample authority for the proposition that the inherent powers of the court under its *parens patriae* jurisdiction are theoretically limitless."[41]

The court found the child to be Gillick-competent, but overrode her refusal of medical treatment and acted in her best interest, according to the doctors' clinical judgement. The court uses this jurisdiction to settle ethical issues. The *New York Times* reported that the Charlie Gard case raised the following issues: Should parents or doctors or the courts have the final say in irreconcilable disputes over the treatment of sick children? And at what point should the limits of medicine be recognized, and the parents of an infant be compelled to let go?[42] The court, as was illustrated throughout this case, will definitely override all other stakeholder interests as it resolves all matters in the best interest of the child.

As the case law confirms, the best interest of a child espouses the preservation of life. The general purpose of this standard is to provide courts with a focus and perspective through which to act on behalf of those who are vulnerable. C illustrates: The parents (the mother is HIV-positive) appealed against the decision of Wilson J when he directed that the five-month-old infant should undergo an HIV test.[43] Lady Justice Butler-Sloss of the Court of Appeal reminded the court that "at the end of the day it is the child who matters. Whether or not the child should or should not be tested is a matter for the welfare of the child". The court ordered that the infant be tested on the ground that the HIV status of the child should be known so that the appropriate care can be designed and administered.

In rare instances, the court in acting in the best interest of the

---

41.   *Re M. (Child: Refusal of Medical Treatment)* 52 BMLR, 1999, 124 at 125.
42.   Dan Bilefsky, "Charlie Gard Dies, Leaving a Legacy of Thorny Ethics Questions," *New York Times*, 28 July 2017, https://www.nytimes.com/2017/07/28/world/europe/charlie-gard-dead.html?mcubz=0 (accessed 6 August 2019).
43.   *C (A Child)* [1999] EWCA Civ 3007.

child may override the doctors' advice. In *Re T.*, a child born with a grave liver defect, underwent an unsuccessful operation at age three and a half weeks which left him in great pain and distress.[44] The medical prognosis was that he needed a liver transplant, or he would die in a couple of years. Three medical experts opined that the child was suitable for a liver transplant which if successful would allow him to live a normal life for many years. The mother refused to give her consent to the operation because she was not willing to permit the child to undergo the pain and distress of invasive surgery. The mother later moved out of the jurisdiction to join the child's father. The local authority, at the specialist's insistence, applied to the court for permission to carry out the operation. The judge held that it was in the child's best interest to undergo a liver transplant. The mother appealed. In determining whether permission should be granted to carry out the invasive surgery, the paramount consideration was the welfare of the child and not the reasonableness of the parent's refusal of consent. However, since in the instant case the welfare of the child depended on the mother, who would be expected to care for him through surgery and for many years after, her views were relevant, and the judge had erred in deciding that her decision was unreasonable in the light of the unchallenged clinical opinion in favour of the operation. The court ruled that it would not be in the best interests of the child to give consent for him to be returned to the jurisdiction to undergo a liver transplantation. The decision was influenced by the fact that the mother, who did not agree with the proposed complicated surgery which offered no guarantee of success, would be required to return to the jurisdiction, possibly without the father, to manage the years of complex care unaided.

Conclusion

So many persons have exercisable rights in the decision-making process when children become ill, resulting in the potential for disagreements to arise at each phase of the treatment. But because the child is a vulnerable little person with rights that should not be ignored, yet balanced against the rights of the parents, the doctors and the courts, the last will always have an important role to

---

44.   *Re T. (A Minor) (Wardship: Medical Treatment)* Court of Appeal (Civil Division) [1997] 1 WLR 242.

perform when there is disagreement on the course of treatment. In the exercise of its wardship or *parens patriae* jurisdiction, the courts are focused on acting in the best interest of the child. To achieve that goal, judges rely ultimately on medical advice and not solely on the child's or parental opinion. The medical advice given may be fraught with complications. The doctors may differ but before they can act, they have to have the consent of someone or some entity with the authority to give it. It is only under the doctrine of necessity the doctors may act without consent. Although the court order carries sanctions for its disobedience, it never requires doctors to act against the dictates of their professional judgement.

In every instance, it is clear that none of the decision-making stakeholders can act alone in resolving the contending views. The checks and balances that present themselves ensure that a participatory approach is utilized. Even the court, the most powerful stakeholder in the matter of consent rights to determine medical treatment for children, cannot decide without considering the views of the other stakeholders. *Re T.*, a rare case of the court honouring the mother's wishes over the doctors', confirms that the court is the ultimate decision-maker, but it, too, must adopt a participatory approach as it acts in the best interest of the child, its paramount objective.

CHAPTER 5

Corporate Governance and the Evolving Law on the Fiduciary Duties of Directors in the Commonwealth Caribbean

Suzanne Ffolkes-Goldson

Corporate governance is one of the most important topics in corporate law internationally, regionally and locally. It is arguable that since the 1990s, the United Kingdom started a movement after the spectacular collapse of the Maxwell empire[1] and the attendant introduction of corporate governance codes and increased scrutiny of boards of directors. Before this, a movement to overhaul the archaic corporate laws of the Commonwealth, led by Canada in the late 1970s, sought to increase the duties of directors and officers of companies. The Enron debacle[2] further cemented the movement in the United States, which was followed by the introduction of new legislation to address corporate governance failures.[3] Much of the emphasis was on increasing the standard of the duties of directors and officers of companies, and increasing their exposure to liability through greater stakeholder access to derivative actions, the oppression remedy and director disqualification.

As the corporate governance movement has grown, so have corporate laws in the Commonwealth, which have moved from a shareholder primacy model to that of a stakeholder model, where directors and officers need to consider the interests of the company and its shareholders as well as a wide range of stakeholder interests, such as the environment, employees, and the community in which

---

1. Thomas Clarke, "Case Study: Master of Corporate Malfeasance," *Corporate Governance: An International Review* 1, no. 3 (1993): 141.
2. Gerald Vinten, "The Corporate Governance Lessons of Enron," *Corporate Governance* 2, no. 4 (2002): 4–9; report by the Permanent Subcommittee on Investigations of the Committee on Governmental Affairs, US Senate, *The Role of the Board of Directors in Enron's Collapse* (Washington, DC: US Government Printing Office, 2002), https://www.govinfo.gov/content/pkg/CPRT-107SPRT80393/pdf/CPRT-107SPRT80393.pdf accessed 7 July 2022.
3. For example, the Sarbanes-Oxley Act of 2002.

the company operates. The corporate governance imperative of environmental, social and governance (ESG) standards, which is currently developing through various standards and measurements, takes the stakeholder model to another level, as companies now need to ensure that these three pillars of corporate governance are met at the risk of loss of investment and exposure to liability. Directors are therefore under greater pressure to ensure that ESG imperatives are introduced, as a part of their fiduciary duties to act in the best interest of the company.

A director's two main obligations are fiduciary duty, and duty of care, diligence and skill. The latter was traditionally neglected; the director was judged according to a subjective standard and was not required to give constant attention to the business. It was stated by Romer, J in *Re City Equitable Fire Insurance Co.*, that "a director need not exhibit in the performance of his duties a greater degree of skill than may reasonably be expected from a person of his knowledge and experience".[4] The common law on the duty of care, diligence and skill was described by Professor Bruce Welling in the following terms: "...as with many other areas of common law, ignorance may be no defence, but stupidity often is".[5]

It has been substantially raised through statute in much of the Commonwealth and now is variously interpreted as an objective standard,[6] or at the least, an objective/subjective standard[7] to "exercise the care, diligence and skill that a reasonably prudent person would exercise in comparable circumstances"[8]. Some Commonwealth territories have also established due diligence

---

4.   [1925] 1 Ch 407 (CA) 428.
5.   Bruce Welling, *Corporate Law in Canada: The Governing Principles,* 3rd ed. (London: Scribblers Publishing, 2006), 326.
6.   *Peoples Department Stores Ltd. (1992) Inc. (sub nom Peoples Department Stores Inc. (Trustees of) v Wise* [2004] 3 SCR 461 SCC.
7.   Suzanne Ffolkes-Goldson, *Corporate Business Principles: A Guide to the Jamaica Companies Act* (Kingston: Caribbean Law Publishing, 2020), 63; Andrew Burgess, *Commonwealth Caribbean Company Law* (Oxford: Routledge Taylor and Francis, 2013), 271.
8.   For example, the Companies Act, 1985 of Barbados, sec. 95(1)(b); the Companies Act, 1995 of Trinidad and Tobago, sec. 99(1)(b); the Canada Business Corporations Act, 1985, sec. 122(1)(b); and the Companies Act, 2005 of Jamaica, sec. 174 (1) (b) adds the words "including, but not limited to the knowledge, skill and experience of the director or officer"; and the Companies Act, 2006 of the UK, sec. 174 (2) (b) adds the words "the general knowledge, skill and experience that the director has", which appear to reintroduce a subjective element to the duty of care, diligence and skill.

defences to the duty of care diligence and skill.[9] Due diligence defences include reliance on financial statements by officers of the company or professional reports (Canada and Jamaica); or belief in the existence of facts, that if true, would render the conduct of the director, reasonably prudent. Also of note is that the duty of care, diligence and skill may not be limited to the company alone, but may be extended to other stakeholders depending on the wording of the statute.[10]

The fiduciary duty of directors on the other hand, has its genesis in the law of trusts, where at common law, the fiduciary duty is akin to that of a trustee, where it was made clear in the seminal House of Lords case of *Regal (Hastings) Ltd. v Gulliver*,[11] that regardless of honest motive and the benefit to the company, directors could not benefit from a contract made with the company.

Traditionally, the fiduciary duties of directors have been expressed as the following:

- The duty not to have a conflict of duty and interest.[12]
- The duty not to make a secret profit.[13]
- The duty to act bona fide and in the best interest of the company and not for an improper purpose.[14]

The Canadian corporate law model has informed much of the statutory development of the fiduciary duty of directors in the Commonwealth, and most territories have adopted the following wording: "…act honestly and in good faith with a view to the best interests of the company", which, it is arguable, encompasses the three duties articulated at common law, (the duty not to have a conflict of duty and interest, the duty not to make a secret profit, the duty to act bona fide in the best interest of the company and not for an improper purpose).[15]

---

9.   Canada Business Corporations Act, sec. 122 (4) and (5); Jamaica Companies Act, sec. 174 (2) and (3).
10. Barbados Companies Act, sec. 95 and Trinidad and Tobago Companies Act, sec. 99; Canada Business Corporations Act, sec. 122; Jamaica Companies Act, sec. 174.
11. [1967] 2 AC 134n, Eng HL.
12. *Aberdeen v Blaikie* (1854) 1 Macq 461 HL Sc.
13. *Regal Hastings v Gulliver* (n 11).
14. *Punt v Symons* [1903] 2 Ch. 506 Eng Ch D, *Teck Corp. v Millar* 33 DLR (3d) 288 (B.C.S.C.), *Hogg v Cramphorn* [1967] Ch 254 Eng Ch D., *Howard* Smith Ltd v Ampol Petroleum Ltd. [1974] AC 821 PC.
15. Ffolkes-Goldson, *Principles*, 61; but see Burgess, *Caribbean Corporate Law*, 244–45, for an alternative view as to the applicability of the proper purpose test in statutory

The statutory statement of the fiduciary duty of officers and directors requires them to act honestly, in good faith and with a view to the best interests of the corporation. This duty is a recognition and codification of the common law fiduciary duties owed by directors and officers to the corporation.[16]

This chapter will highlight the evolving nature of the fiduciary duty and increased exposure of directors since the law has been codified in the Commonwealth by using examples in Commonwealth Caribbean legislation of the Barbados Companies Act, the Jamaica Companies Act, the Trinidad and Tobago Companies Act and from the wider Commonwealth, the Canada Business Corporations Act, and the UK Companies Act and the UK Company Directors Disqualification Act.

Types of Directors

The statutory definition of a director may be found in Commonwealth statutes and they typically and variously state that, "…in relation to a body corporate, means (includes) a (any) person occupying therein the position of a director by whatever name (title) called."[17] There are several types of directors – de jure, de facto and shadow directors – which begs the question as to whether there is one standard of fiduciary duty for all. In addition to the establishment of the type of director, other considerations, such as whether lack of authority gives rise to a breach of fiduciary duty and whether the rule in Turquand's case still applies in the wake of statutory provisions, are but some of the issues with which the courts have or may need to contend.

A de jure director is a director who has been duly (formally and validly) appointed whereas, a de facto director is "a person who has assumed the status and functions of a company director even though he has not been properly appointed."[18] The law has since further developed to hold that a director may be a de facto director

---

fiduciary duty.

16. Fasken LLP, *Canada Business Corporations Act & Commentary 2019–2020* (Toronto: Lexis Nexis Canada, 2020), 84.

17. Barbados Companies Act, sec. 448 (i); Jamaica Companies Act, sec. 2; Trinidad and Tobago Companies Act, sec. 4; Canada Business Corporations Act, sec. 2; UK Companies Act, sec. 250.

18. Explanatory Notes to the UK Companies Act.

without the need for the person to have been invalidly appointed.[19]

Arden, LJ, in *Smithton v Naggar*, developed and refined the factors established in previous case law by outlining some of the considerations for deciding if a person is a de facto director:[20]

1. A person may be a de facto director even if there was no valid appointment. The question is whether he has assumed responsibility to act as a director.

2. To answer that question, the court may have to determine in what capacity they were acting.

3. The court will, in general, also have to determine the corporate governance structure of the company to decide in relation to its business whether the defendant's actions were directorial in nature.

4. The court is required to look at what the director actually did and not any job title given to him.

5. A defendant does not avoid liability if he shows that he in good faith thought he was not acting as a director. The question of whether or not he acted as a director is to be determined objectively and irrespective of their motivation or belief.

6. The court must look at the cumulative effect of the activities relied on. It should look at all the circumstances "in the round" (per Jonathan Parker, J in *Secretary of State v Jones*).

7. It is also important to look at the actions in their context. A single action might lead to liability in an exceptional case.

8. Relevant factors include:
   i. whether the company considered the defendant to be a director and held them out as such;
   ii. whether third parties considered that they were a director.

9. The fact that a person is consulted about directorial decisions or their approval does not in general make them a director because they are not making the decision.

10. Actions taken outside the period when they are said to have been a de facto director may throw light on whether they

---

19. *Revenue and Customs Commissioners v Holland* [2010] UKSC 51.
20. Ibid.

were a de facto director during the relevant period.[21]

De facto directors are also held to the same standard of fiduciary duty and liability as de jure directors.[22] Whether either has exceeded their authority or has acted without the requisite authority is also a question with which the courts have had to grapple. Distinctions have been made between i) actual authority, which may be express (authority given through articles or in board minutes), or implied (arising from the position which the director holds); and ii) ostensible or apparent authority, where the courts look at factors, inter alia, as to whether the director was held out as having authority by someone with actual authority or whether the board was aware of the conduct and acquiesced in it.[23] If a director (de jure or de facto) acts without actual or ostensible authority, it may be argued that they may be found to have breached their fiduciary duty to act in the best interest of the company and not for an improper purpose. Put another way, a director would hardly have actual or implied authority to act in a way that is not in the best interest of the company.[24]

On the other hand, a shadow director is a creature of statute. The concept is found in the UK Companies Act[25] and the Jamaica Companies Act,[26] but appears to be absent from most Commonwealth Caribbean company law statutes. A shadow director is defined as a person in accordance with whose directions or instructions the directors of the company are accustomed to act. However, a person is not deemed a shadow director by reason only that the directors act on advice given by that person in a professional capacity.[27] The UK Companies Act makes very clear the circumstances where a

21.   [2013] EWHC 1961 (Ch.) [35–44]; see also *HMRC v Holland* [2010] 1 WLR 2793; see also *Revenue and Customs Commissioners v Holland; Re Paycheck Services 3 Ltd.; Re UKLI Ltd. Secretary of State for Business, Innovation and Skills v Chohan and others* [2013] EWHC 680 Ch.
22.   *David Ingram (Liquidator of MSD Cash & Carry plc) v Mohinder Singh & Others [2018] EWHC 1325 (Ch);* (1) J A Popely (2) A Popely v (1) R A Popely and others [2019] EWHC 1507 (Ch).
23.   *Hely-Hutchinson v Brayhead Ltd.* [1967] 3 All ER 98 CA; *Freeman and Lockyer v Buckhurst Park Properties (Mangal) Ltd.* [1964] 1 ALL ER 630 CA.
24.   *LNOC Ltd. v Watford Association Football Club Ltd.* [2013] EWHC 3615 (COMM).
25.   UKCA, sec. 251.
26.   JCA, sec. 2.
27.   Ibid.; UKCA, sec. 251.

person or a company will not be considered a shadow director.[28]

A person is not to be regarded as a shadow director by reason only that the directors act:

a. on advice given by that person in a professional capacity;
b. in accordance with instructions, a direction, guidance or advice given by that person in the exercise of a function conferred by or under an enactment;
c. in accordance with guidance or advice given by that person in that person's capacity as a Minister of the Crown (within the meaning of the Ministers of the Crown Act, 1975);

(3) A body corporate is not to be regarded as a shadow director of any of its subsidiary companies for the purposes of:

- Chapter 2 (general duties of directors);
- Chapter 4 (transactions requiring members' approval); or
- Chapter 6 (contract with sole member who is also a director);

by reason only that the directors of the subsidiary are accustomed to act in accordance with its directions or instructions.

The concept of shadow director addresses the mischief where a person may not be qualified to be a director (for example, they do not satisfy a "fit and proper" test where required or is otherwise disqualified), or where the person does not wish to be exposed to liability or be on the radar, but wishes to control the decision-making process of the board (such as a majority shareholder). An individual or a company (such as a parent company, unless otherwise excluded in the definition) may be a shadow director. Case law has evolved on the criteria for establishing whether a person fulfils the statutory definition of shadow director. Traditionally, shadow directors were distinguished from de facto directors based on the description that the former were "lurking" in the shadows.[29] More recent case law has, however, concluded that lurking in the shadows is not an essential ingredient,[30] and it has also established that a person can be both a shadow director and a de facto director, although this is difficult to envisage as the notion of "shadow" suggests that the shadow director does not want to be identified as a director,

---

28.   UKCA sec. 251 (2).
29.   *Re Hydrodam (Corby) Ltd.* [1994] 2 BCLC 180, 183 Eng.Ch D.
30.   *Secretary of State for Trade and Industry v Deverell* [2000] 2 BCLC 133, 146 Eng. CA.

whereas a de facto director holds themself out to be a director. Factually, however, it may not be deliberate but inadvertent, where a person or company finds themselves in the position of a shadow director, such as a parent company or a director or officer of a parent company, who wishes to direct and control decision-making in a subsidiary.

The question as to whether a shadow director owes the same fiduciary duty to the company as de jure and de facto directors has been settled in the United Kingdom in the affirmative.[31] However, it remains to be seen whether the same can be said in Jamaica, since the Companies Act speaks to shadow directors in specific contexts, such as particulars of directors in trade catalogues, circulars and so on; register of interests; and offences antecedent to or in the course of winding up. Recent Jamaican case law has suggested that shadow directors owe the same fiduciary duty as that of de jure directors. This was stated in the context of an application by a minority shareholder for leave to bring a derivative action, on behalf of the company against directors and an alleged shadow director (the parent company) for an alleged breach of fiduciary duty.[32] The Report of the Joint Select Committee on the Companies Bill, however, suggests that the definition of director does not include shadow director.[33]

Development of the Statutory Fiduciary Duty

As stated in the introduction, a breach of the common law fiduciary duty of directors occurs where they make a secret profit or has a conflict of duty and interest, or does not act in the best interest of the company and for an improper purpose. The common law fiduciary duty is owed to the company alone.[34]

In the seminal House of Lords case of *Regal Hastings v Gulliver* on the duty not to make a secret profit, Lord Russell stated:

> The rule of equity which insists on those, who by use of a fiduciary position make a profit, being liable to account for

31.   *Vivendi SA and another v Richards and another* [2013] EWHC 3006 (Ch.).
32.   *Jason Abrahams v Cable and Wireless Jamaica Ltd.* [2020] JMCC Comm 18.
33.   Jamaica Houses of Parliament Joint Select Committee, Report of the Joint Select Committee on the Bill Shortly Entitled the Companies Act, 1998; Ffolkes-Goldson, *Principles*, 57.
34.   *Percival v Wright* [1902] 2 Ch. 421 Eng Ch D.

that profit, in no way depends on fraud, or absence of bona fide; or upon such questions or considerations as whether the profit would or should otherwise have done gone to the plaintiff, or whether the profiteer was under a duty to obtain the source of the profit for the plaintiff, or whether he took a risk or acted as he did for the benefit of the plaintiff, or whether he the plaintiff has in fact been damaged or benefitted by his action. The liability arises from the mere fact of a profit having, in the stated circumstances, been made. The profiteer, however honest and well-intentioned, cannot escape the risk of being called upon to account.[35]

The common law duty not to have a conflict of duty and interest was articulated in another seminal House of Lords case, *Aberdeen v Blaikie Bros.*,[36] where a director of Aberdeen Railway was also a partner in Blaikie Bros., which sold a quantity of railway chairs to Aberdeen. The patent conflict rendered the transaction voidable at the option of the corporation, which appears to mean that the shareholders could ratify the transaction. No matter how small the conflict, any transaction involving a conflict of duty and interest is voidable at the instance of the company – "…the validity or invalidity of a transaction cannot depend upon the extent of the adverse interest of the fiduciary".[37]

The duty to act bona fide and in the best interest of the company and not for a collateral or improper purpose was established in *Re Smith & Fawcett Ltd.*[38] The qualification regarding the "collateral" or "improper purpose" forms the basis of the common law "proper purpose" doctrine, which has been applied in particular in cases where directors, in exercising their powers and discharging their duties, may have mixed motives. In order to establish whether a director had acted for an improper purpose, the courts looked at whether the defendant acted outside of the purpose for which the power was conferred.[39] The common law further developed by ascertaining the substantial purpose of the director's actions, where

---

35. *Regal Hastings v Gulliver;* see also *Keech v Sandford* (1726) Sel. Cas. King 61, a trust case where the rule was first established.
36. [1843–60] All ER Rep. 249, 2 Eq. Rep. 1281 (HL).
37. *Transvaal Lands Co. v New Belgium (Transvaal) Land and Development Co.* [1914] 2 Ch. 488, 84 L.J. Ch. 94 (CA).
38. [1942] Ch. 304 CA.
39. *Punt v Symons; Hogg v Cramphorn Ltd.*

they had mixed motives, in order to establish whether they acted for an improper purpose.[40] The watershed ruling in the Canadian case of *Teck Corp. v Millar*,[41] in rejecting the *Hogg v Cramphorn*[42] approach, which was the view previously espoused at common law, the court emphasized that the directors must act in good faith, and that there should be reasonable grounds for their belief that they are acting in good faith. In the absence of reasonable grounds, it may then be found that the directors were acting for an improper purpose.

The statutory fiduciary duty in Commonwealth territories is typically stated as a duty to act honestly and in good faith with a view to the best interest of the company.[43] It is accepted that this duty encompasses the three main fiduciary duties at common law, however there is some debate as to whether the proper purpose doctrine has survived. Andrew Burgess highlights some arguments as to why the proper purpose test does not qualify the statutory fiduciary duty:[44]

1. The test is complex and deflects attention from central statutory consideration.

2. Common law ratification of breach of the test is not restricted to breaches in the best interest of the company.

3. Drafters omitted the test because it was regarded as unnecessary.

It is notable, however, that the UK Companies Act modifies and restates the common law test to act bona fide as "a duty to act to promote the success of the company"[45] and retains the "proper purpose" test.[46] It is also notable that other Commonwealth countries' companies legislation, such as Australia and New Zealand, have also retained the proper purpose doctrine.[47] Case law in some

---

40.   *Howard Smith Ltd. v Ampol Petroleum Ltd.*
41.   *Teck Corp. v Millar.*
42.   *Hogg v Cramphorn Ltd.*
43.   BCA, sec. 95(1)(a); JCA, sec. 174 (1)(a); TTCA, sec. 99(1)(a); CBCA, sec. 122(1)(a); the UKCA differs in that, sections 171–77 stipulate a range of duties, considering the common law and equitable principles as stated in sec. 170.
44.   Burgess, *Caribbean Corporate Law*, 243–45.
45.   Brenda Hannigan, *Company Law* (Oxford: Oxford University Press, 2009), 205.
46.   UKCA, sec. 171.
47.   Australia Companies Act, 1961, sec. 181; New Zealand Companies Act, 1993, sec. 133.

Commonwealth territories still refer to it when considering whether the statutory fiduciary duty has been breached.[48] The question as to whether a director has acted for an improper or collateral purpose often arises in the context of takeover bids, where they may have mixed motives in either accepting the takeover bid or thwarting it, especially if it is hostile. Putting in defence mechanisms to thwart the last may be in the best interest of the company, considering the interests of shareholders, employees and so on, and maintaining the share price, or may be in the best interest of the directors and management, who "desire merely to retain their directorships and their control of the company."[49] It is in these cases that some references are still made to the proper purpose doctrine.

Some Canadian authorities, such as *Exco Corp. v Nova Scotia Savings & Loan Co.*[50] and *347883 Alberta Ltd. v Producers Pipelines Inc.*,[51] have adopted a proper purpose test, which is similar to enhanced scrutiny in that it shifts the burden of proof to the directors to show that their acts are consistent only with the best interests of the company and inconsistent with any other interests. These cases recognize that there may be a conflict between the directors who manage the company and the interests of certain groups of shareholders....[52]

Impact of the Stakeholder Theory and ESG

As stated earlier, it has long been established at common law that the fiduciary duty of directors is owed to the company alone.[53] This duty has oftentimes been conflated with a duty to shareholders under the shareholder primacy doctrine. However, as the law has evolved from that of a shareholder primacy model to that of a stakeholder model, there has been some debate as to whether, in acting in the best interest of the company, directors are required to take into account the interests of other stakeholders such as shareholders, employees, the environment and the community in

---

48. *Benkley Northover v Eric Northover and Rohan Northover and Godfrey Dixon and Winston G. Northover Associates Limited* [2014] JMCC Comm. 14 [69].
49. *Teck Corp. v Millar.*
50. (1987), 35, B.L.R. 149, 78 N.S.R.(2d) 91 (S.C.)
51. (1991), 80 D.L.R. (4th) 359, 92 Sask. R. 81 (C.A.)
52. *Pente Investment Management Ltd. v Schneider Corp.* (1998) 42 OR (3d) 177.
53. *Percival v Wright.*

which the company operates.

Some Commonwealth statutes include a provision which requires or permits directors to consider the interests of other stakeholders. This is consistent with the modern stakeholder theory. Company law legislation in some territories typically state, that in determining what are in the best interests of a company, a director shall or must or have regard for the interests of the employees in general as well as its shareholders.[54] Other Commonwealth Caribbean company legislation, on the other hand, provide that a director "may" have regard to the interests of the company's employees and shareholders,[55] and the community in which the company operates.[56]

The UK Companies Act goes further, to mandate that directors must act in good faith to promote the success of the company and in doing so, must take into account a wide range of stakeholders, including, but not limited to employees, suppliers, customers, the community, members of the company.[57]

There is some debate in Canada, in the absence of wording in the Canada Business Corporations Act, whether the Supreme Court of Canada has indicated that directors may (permissive) or must (mandatory) take into account, the interests of other stakeholders. In the case of *Peoples v Wise*, it was stated that: "We accept as an accurate statement of law that in determining whether they are acting with a view to the best interests of the corporation it may be legitimate, given all the circumstances of a given case, for the board of directors to consider, *inter alia*, the interests of shareholders, employees, suppliers, creditors, consumers, governments and the environment."[58]

On the other hand, in the case of *BCE Inc. v 1976 Debentureholders*, it was stated that: "There are no absolute rules and no principle that one set of interests should prevail over another. In each case, the question is whether, in all the circumstances, the directors acted in the best interests of the corporation, having regard to all relevant

54.   For example, the BCA, sec. 95(2); the TTCA, sec. 99(2).
55.   For example, the Antigua and Barbuda Companies Act, 1995 sec. 97 (2); the St Lucia Companies Act, 1997 sec. 97(2); the St Vincent and the Grenadines Companies Act, 1994 sec. 97 (2); and the Dominica Companies Act 1994, sec. 97 (2).
56.   Jamaica Companies Act, sec. 174 (4).
57.   UK Companies Act, sec. 172 (1).
58.   *Peoples Department Stores v Wise*.

considerations, including – but not confined to – the need to treat affected stakeholders in a fair manner, commensurate with the corporation's duties as a responsible corporate citizen."[59]

What is clear is that the fiduciary duty imposed on directors by the various company law statutes is owed to the company alone.[60] In other words, where there are competing interests, the duty to act in the best interest of the company trumps other considerations.

In the context of the modern stakeholder theory and the more recent ESG imperatives, this may pose a delicate balancing act for directors, especially where the duty to act in the best interests of the company requires that a host of other stakeholder interests be contemplated. This is more than a theoretical quandary, as ESG considerations may impact investment opportunities and share value. In addition, directors may be further exposed to liability if the considerations are not carefully managed. These challenges are highlighted especially in the context of takeover bids (especially where defensive tactics may be employed to avert a hostile takeover), or where the company is in the vicinity of insolvency or where a board may consist of "activist" directors.

Directors' Fiduciary Duties in the Vicinity of Insolvency
Common law vs statute

It appears that in common law the director's fiduciary duty to the company may be displaced by creditors where a company is in the vicinity of insolvency, or at least the interests of creditors are to be considered.[61] More recent UK cases suggest that a distinction might need to be made as to whether the company is nearing insolvency, at risk of insolvency, of doubtful solvency or in some financial predicament.[62] A mere risk of insolvency may not give rise to a

---

59. *BCE Inc. v. 1976 Debentureholders* [2008] 3 S.C.R. 560, 2008 SCC 69, [81–83].

60. JCA, sec. 174 (5); TTCA, sec. 99(3); BCA, sec. 95(3); CBCA, sec. 122(1)(a) (note also the Ontario Business Corporations Act 1990, sec. 134).

61. Suzanne Ffolkes-Goldson, "Directors' Duties to Creditors On or Near Insolvency and Duty of Care in the Commonwealth Caribbean: Should the Peoples Decision be Adopted?" *Oxford University Commonwealth Law Journal* 6, no.1 (2006): 61–75; *Kinsela v Russell Kinsela Property Ltd. (in liquidation)* (1986) 4 NSWLR 722, 730, which was cited with approval in *West Mercier Safetywear Ltd. (in liq.) v Dodd* [1988] BCLC 250 (CA). Also, *Nicholson v Permakraft* (NZ) Ltd. [1985] 1 N.Z.L.R. 242, and *Walker v Wimborne* (1975–1976) 137 C.L.R.

62. See *The Liquidator of Wendy Fair (Heritage) Ltd. v Hobday* [2006] EWHC 5803 [66];

fiduciary duty to creditors, however, "the duty to creditors may arise at a point short of actual, established insolvency where the directors know or should know that the company is or is likely to become insolvent".[63]

All members of the court agree that the creditor duty should be affirmed for the following reasons. First, the duty is supported by a long line of UK case law (as well as authority from Australia and New Zealand), which began in the mid-1980s [29]–[36]; [43]; [152]; [207]; [387]–[416]. Second, the majority hold that the duty is affirmed (per Lord Briggs [153] and Lord Hodge [209]; [224]), or its possible existence is preserved (per Lord Reed [69]–[71]; [76] and Lady Arden [344]) by section 172(3) of the 2006 Act. This makes the duty under section 172(1) "subject to any enactment or rule of law requiring directors, in certain circumstances, to consider or act in the interests of creditors of the company". Third, the duty has a coherent and principled justification. Creditors always have an economic interest in the company's assets, but the relative importance of that economic interest increases where the company is insolvent or nearing insolvency. In those circumstances, the directors should manage the company's affairs in a way which takes creditors' interests into account and seeks to avoid prejudicing them [12]; [45]; [83]; [147]–[148]; [246]; [256]. For the meaning of insolvency in this context see [88]; [120] and [307]–[310].[64]

In the context of the fiduciary duty of directors to promote the success of the company, it is interesting that the UK Companies Act also provides that the duty has effect, subject to any enactment or rule of law requiring directors, in certain circumstances, to consider or act in the interests of creditors of the company.[65]

The debate has raged for some time, however, since the advent

---

Eastford Ltd. v Gillespie, Airdrie North Ltd. [2010] CSOH 132 [22]; *Gwyer v London Wharf (Limehouse) Ltd.* [2002] EWHC 2748; [2003] BCC 885; *Kinsela v Russell Kinsela Property Ltd.; Winkworth v Edward Baron Development Ltd.* [1986] 1 WLR 1512 ; *Facia Footwear Ltd. (in administration) v Hincliffe* [1998] 1 BCLC 218 at 228; *Williams v Farrow* [2008] EWHC 3663 (Ch) at 21; *Linton v Telnet Property Ltd.* [1999] NSWCA 33; (1999) 30 ACSR 465 and *Re MDA Investment Management Ltd.* [2005] BCC 783 [70].

63. *Sequana SA v BAR Industries Plc and Others* [2019] EWCA Civ. 112.; https://www.supremecourt.uk/press-summary/uksc-2019-0046.html; BTI 2014 LLC (Appellant) v Sequana SA and others (Respondents) [2022] UKSC 25

64. https://www.supremecourt.uk/cases/uksc-2019-0046.html; BTI 2014 LLC *(Appellant) v Sequana SA and others (Respondents)* [2022] UKSC 25.

65. UKCA, sec. 172 (3).

of the statutory oppression remedy, which empowers complainants (who may include a wide range of stakeholders) to bring an action against directors, where a stated victim class (for example, directors, shareholders, creditors) can show that they have been the subject of oppression, or that their interests have been unfairly prejudiced or unfairly disregarded, there is no direct fiduciary duty, or even a duty to consider the interests of creditors in the vicinity of insolvency. The Supreme Court of Canada, in *Peoples v Wise*, stated: "The various shifts in interests that naturally occur as a corporation's fortunes rise and fall do not, however, affect the content of the fiduciary duty under section 122(1)(a) of the Canada Business Corporation Act. At all times, directors and officers owe their fiduciary obligation to the corporation. The interests of the corporation are not to be confused with the interests of the creditors or those of any other stakeholders..."[66]

Short of bankruptcy, as the corporation approaches the vicinity of insolvency, the residual claims of shareholders will be nearly exhausted. While shareholders might well prefer that the directors pursue high-risk alternatives with a high potential payoff to maximize the shareholders' expected residual claim, creditors in the same circumstances might prefer that the directors steer a safer course so as to maximize the value of their claims against the assets of the corporation.

The directors' fiduciary duty does not change when a corporation is in the nebulous vicinity of insolvency. That phrase has not been defined; moreover, it is incapable of definition and has no legal meaning. What it is obviously intended to convey is a deterioration in the corporation's financial stability. In assessing the actions of directors, it is evident that any honest and good faith attempt to redress the corporation's financial problems will, if successful, both retain value for shareholders and improve the position of creditors. If unsuccessful, it will not qualify as a breach of the statutory fiduciary duty.

Territories without the statutory oppression remedy, or at least a more restricted remedy in terms of scope and complainants, may still need to contend with the common law approach. UK cases have continued to hold to the view that directors may owe

---

66. *Peoples Department Stores Ltd. v Wise* [43], [45] and [46].

a duty to take into account the interest of creditors where the
company is of doubtful solvency or is in the vicinity of insolvency
etc.[67] It remains to be seen whether the courts in Commonwealth
Caribbean territories, such as Jamaica (where the oppression
remedy has a limited complainant class) will rely on the common
law and find that directors owe a fiduciary duty to creditors, or at
least are required to take the interests of creditors into account, in
the vicinity of insolvency.[68]

Expansion of the Duty not to have a Conflict of Interest

It has long been established that directors should not have a conflict
of duty and interest,[69] and that a potential breach of fiduciary
duty could only be cured through original disclosure by the
director, and approval at common law by the company in general
meeting. Further, at common law, the breach could be ratified by
the shareholders.[70] Failure to have the necessary disclosure and
approval or ratification would render any contract voidable at the
instance of the company.

More recently, legislation provides that where directors have an
interest in a "material" contract with the company, the conflict may
be "cured" by disclosure and in accordance with the legislation
and then approved by the board of directors.[71] It has been argued,
however, that ratification is not possible by the shareholders in
general meeting.

The question as to whether the common law rule that a conflict
of duty and interest and subsequent profit could be ratified in
general meeting has survived the legislation, is yet to be established.
In the absence of clear words in the Companies Act – here and in
Canada – the better view is that ratification of a conflict of duty
and interest by the shareholders in general meeting is not possible,
as the wrong can only be ratified by the company to whom the

---

67.   UKCA, sec. 172(3)(3). The duty imposed by this section has effect subject to any
      enactment or rule of law requiring directors, in certain circumstances, to consider or
      act in the interests of creditors of the company.
68.   Ffolkes-Goldson, "Directors' Duties".
69.   *Aberdeen v Blaikie Bros.*
70.   *North-West Transportation v Beatty* (1887) LR 12 App Cas 589.
71.   Bruce Welling, *Corporate Law*, 421; UKCA, sec. 239.

wrong was done.[72]

In addition, there is no definition as to what "material" is, probably because it depends on various factors peculiar to each company as to what is "material". In other words, "material" is relative. It is suggested, however, that when in doubt, directors should disclose to avoid liability.

More recently, the obligation not to have a conflict of interest and duty has been enlarged to include *avoiding* a conflict of interest and duty. It is arguable that this always existed at common law,[73] and was even referred to in SCC *Peoples v Wise;*[74] however, statutory amendments now include a duty for directors to avoid a conflict of interest, with specific rules, which appear to have much more restrictive requirements for disclosure and approval than the general conflict rules.[75]

1. Subject to subsection (9), it shall be the duty of the director of a company to avoid circumstances which, whether directly or indirectly, constitute a conflict of interest or may result in a conflict of interest with the interests of the company.

2. A director who is directly or indirectly interested in a matter which may constitute a conflict of interest or may result in a conflict of interest with the interests of the company –
   a. shall disclose the nature of his interest at a meeting of the directors;
   b. shall not take part in any deliberations at the meeting of the directors in respect of that matter.

3. The duty under subsection (1) applies in particular to the exploitation of any property, information or opportunity (and it is immaterial whether the company could take advantage of the property, information or opportunity).

4. The duty referred to in subsection (1) is not infringed –
   a. if the circumstances cannot reasonably be regarded as likely to give rise to a conflict of interest; or
   b. if the matter giving rise to the circumstances has been approved by the directors.

---

72. Ffolkes-Goldson, *Principles*, 61.
73. *Aberdeen v Blaikie Bros.*
74. *Peoples Department Stores v Wise* [42].
75. JCA, sec. 174A; see also UKCA, sec.175.

5. The approval referred to in subsection (4)(b) may be given by
    the directors, where –

    a. the company is a private company and nothing in the
        company's articles invalidates such approval, by the
        matter being proposed to and approved by the directors
        in accordance with the company's articles; or

    b. the company is a public company, and its articles include
        a provision enabling the directors to approve the matter,
        by the matter being proposed to and approved by them
        in accordance with the company's articles.

6. The approval of the directors is effective only if –

    a. any requirement as to the quorum at the meeting at
        which the matter is considered is met without counting
        the director in question or any other interested director;
        and

    b. the matter was agreed to without their voting or would
        have been agreed to if their votes had not been counted.

An example of this is where a director takes advantage of a
corporate opportunity that they have become aware of by virtue
of being a director of that company. Where the company has a
continuing interest in a corporate opportunity, the common law is
that the fiduciary duty is breached, if the director takes advantage
of that opportunity.[76] Common law suggests that a distinction
should be made where a director takes advantage of a corporate
opportunity where the company could not take advantage of the
opportunity, as opposed to where the company is not actively seeking
the opportunity or rejects it. The former would be considered a
conflict of interest and therefore a breach of the director's fiduciary
duty,[77] whereas the last two cases would not be considered a breach
of their fiduciary duty.[78] However, statutes which include the
provision on avoidance of conflicts now prohibit taking advantage
of corporate opportunities, whether the company could or would

---

76. *Cook v Deeks* [1916] AC 554 PC.
77. *Regal (Hastings) v Gulliver; Industrial Development Consultants v Cooley* [1972] 2 All
    ER 162; *Bhullar v Bhullar, Re Bhullar Bros. Ltd.* [2003] 2 BCLC 241 Eng CA.
78. *Canadian Aero Services Ltd. v O'Malley* [1974] S.C.R. 592, 40 D.L.R. (3d) 371; *Island
    Export Finance Ltd. v Umunna* [1986] BCLC 460; *In Plus Group Ltd. v Pyke* [2002] 2
    BCLC 201 Eng CA; *Foster Bryant Surveying Ltd. v Bryant* [2007] 2BCLC 239 Eng CA;
    Peso Silver Mines Ltd. v Cropper (1966)58 D.L.R. (2d) 1; [1966] S.C.R. 673.

take advantage of it or not. Further, a public company can only ratify a directors' conflict, after declaration of interest, if the articles so permit or, in the case of a private company, the articles do not prohibit the ratification. It is submitted that directors may also be found to be in breach of their fiduciary duty, where the ratification of such conflicts is challenged on the basis that it was not done in good faith in the best interest of the company.

A further question may arise as to whether directors have a duty to avoid competition as part of the duty not to have or to avoid a conflict of interest. It was held in *London v Mashonaland Exploration Co. v New Mashonaland Exploration Co.*[79] that, "there is no principle preventing a director from acting as a director of a rival company".[80] However, the more recent case of *In Plus Group Ltd. v Pyke* suggests that *Mashonoland* is fact-specific and does not lay down a general rule regarding directors' duties to avoid competition.[81]

Liability for Breach of Fiduciary Duties

The liability for breach of the fiduciary duties of directors under Commonwealth statutes has seemingly increased. Apart from the traditional liability to account, where there is a secret profit, joint and several liability for loss, voidability of contracts where there is a breach of a duty not to have a conflict of duty and interest, directors may be punished by court disqualification, where it appears to the court that the director is unfit to be concerned in the management of a public company.[82] The court may order that a person may not be a director or in any way, directly or indirectly, to be concerned in the management of the company for such period as may be specified in the order, not exceeding five years.[83] Consistent with the modern stakeholder theory of corporate governance,

---

79.   *London v Mashonaland Exploration co. v New Mashonaland Exploration Co.* [1891] WN 165.

80.   Burgess, *Caribbean Corporate Law*, 263; *London v Mashonaland Exploration Co. v New Mashonaland Exploration Co.*; followed by *Bell v Lever Bros.* [1932] AC 161 Eng HL.

81.   Burgess, *Caribbean Corporate Law*, 263; *In Plus Group Ltd. v Pyke.*

82.   BCA, sec. 64; TTCA, sec. 69; Company Directors Disqualification Act (CDDA) 1986, sec. 6 (UK).

83.   BCA, sec. 64(1)(b); TTCA, sec. 69(1)(b); JCA, sec. 180(6)(b); CDDA, sec. 6 states up to fifteen years.

stakeholders, such as the registrar[84] – or in the case of Jamaica, shareholders, creditors, trustee of the company or the trustee – may bring an action to have a director disqualified, and in the latter case, once a complaint is made to the registrar by a shareholder, director, creditor, trustee of the company or the trustee, and the registrar has investigated the complaint and is satisfied that there are sufficient grounds for a hearing of the matter by the court, the registrar may issue a certificate.[85] The requirements to involve the registrar act as a safeguard against the possibility of frivolous and vexatious suits.

Section 182 of the Jamaica Companies Act further provides that a person may be disqualified from being a director where it appears to the court that there are "persistent breaches" of the Companies Act. It is arguable that persistent breaches found in the Jamaica Companies Act and UK legislation are redundant, as those breaches could qualify under the heading of "unfit". Furthermore, there is no indication as to who may bring the action. However, it may be assumed that it is the same stakeholders, under the same conditions, as found in Section 180 of the Jamaica Companies Act.

The introduction of civil remedies increases the exposure of directors to actions by stakeholders against them for breach of fiduciary duty. The modern derivative action empowers stakeholders, described as complainants, to bring an action in the name of or on behalf of the company for wrongs done to it. Complainants may include shareholders, former shareholders, debenture holders, former debenture holders, director or officer, or former director or officer of the company, or any its affiliates, the registrar or any other person who, in the discretion of the court, is a proper person to make an application.[86] The complainant, however, must seek leave from the court to bring a derivative action and show that the

---

84. BCA, sec. 64(1); TTCA, sec. 69(1); CDDA, sec. 16 provides that the application to the court for disqualification may be made by a wide range of applicants, depending on the type of offence committed or is alleged to have been committed or other default. These may include the Secretary of State or the official receiver, or the liquidator or any past or present member or creditor of any company or overseas company in relation to which that person has committed or is alleged to have committed an offence or other default.
85. JCA, sec. 180.
86. BCA, sec. 225 (b); TTCA, sec. 239 (b); JCA, sec. 212 (3) (does not include Registrar or "any other person"); CBCA, sec. 239 (2) (does not include Registrar). Please note, the UKCA, sec. 261 limits derivative actions to members of the company.

director was given "reasonable" notice of the intention to apply to the court; that the complainant is acting in good faith; and that it appears to be in the interests of the company that the action is brought. Directors face a wide range of final, or in some territories interim, orders under these provisions, which include authorizing the complainant or registrar or any other person to control the conduct of the action; giving directions for the conduct of the action; directing that any amount adjudged payable by a defendant in the action be paid in whole or in part, directly to former and present shareholders or debenture holders of the company or is subsidiary, instead of to the company or its subsidiary; or require the company or its subsidiary to pay reasonable legal fees incurred by the complainant in connection with the action, or any order the court thinks fit.[87]

Directors may face additional exposure to liability as complainants may bring an action under the "oppression remedy", which is not for breach of fiduciary duty to the company, but a personal remedy for oppression, unfair prejudice or unfair disregard of a prescribed victim class, which typically includes shareholders, directors, debenture holders and creditors.[88] A very interesting issue that arises is that a derivative type action may be allowed to proceed under the oppression remedy. In these cases, a plaintiff would thereby avoid the procedural hurdles and safeguards where there is an application for a derivative action.

"I accept that the derivative action and the oppression remedy are not mutually exclusive. Cases like *Malata* and *Jabalee* make it clear that there are circumstances where the factual underpinning will give rise to both types of redress and in which a complainant will nonetheless be entitled to proceed by way of oppression remedy."[89]

In this case, the Ontario Court of Appeal found that there was no overlap between the derivative action and the oppression remedy on the facts as pleaded. The loophole, where there is an overlap, and thereby further exposing directors to actions for breach of fiduciary duty, under the guise of an action for oppression is even

---

87.   BCA, sec. 227; JCA, sec. 213; TTCA, sec. 241; CBCA, sec. 240.
88.   BCA, sec. 228; JCA, sec. 213A; TTCA, sec. 242; CBCA, sec. 241.
89.   *Rea v Wildeboer* 2015 ONCA 373, 2015 Carswell Ont 7602 (Ont. C.A.). See also *Malata Group (HK) Ltd. v Jung* 2008 ONCA 111, 2008 Carswell Ont 699 (Ont. C.A.).

more acute in the context of closely held/private companies, where "…the wrong that is formally a wrong to 'the company" is in fact simply symptomatic of a dispute between various parties in the corporation".[90]

The Jamaican courts have also acknowledged the possibility of an overlap. However, in *Debbian Dewar v Ervin Moo Young et al.*,[91] the Commercial Court, in refusing the claimant leave to bring a derivative action, stated that the appropriate action should have been under the oppression remedy. Further, in *Sally Ann Fulton v Chas E Ramson Ltd.*,[92] the Commercial Court confirmed that the same circumstance may give rise to both an oppression action and a derivative action. In deciding whether a claimant may bring a derivative action or an oppression action, the court is to focus on the nature of the complaint.

Conclusion

The fiduciary duties of directors in the Commonwealth are still owed to the company alone, but now there appears to be an expansion of the duty to include the interests of stakeholders. These considerations have taken on particular significance in situations where the company is the subject of a takeover bid or change of control or in the vicinity of insolvency. The introduction of a statutory avoidance of conflict provision in several Commonwealth territories has added another layer to the traditional rules regarding breach of fiduciary duty and conflict of interest. The exposure of directors for breach of fiduciary duty is further compounded by the ability of specific stakeholders to bring actions to disqualify directors or by way of derivative action on behalf of the company for breach of fiduciary duty to the company or indirectly through the mechanism of the oppression remedy.

Environmental, Social and Governance (ESG) imperatives, which now form part of the corporate landscape, may have serious implications for investment. These imperatives could well usher in another avenue where directors may find themselves liable

---

90.   Poonam Puri and others, *Cases, Materials and Notes on Partnerships and Canadian Business Corporations*, 6th ed. (London: Thomson Reuters, 2016), 850; *Diligenti v RWMD Operations Kelowna Ltd.* 1976 Carswell BC 3, 1 BCLR 36 (B.C.S.C.).
91.   *Debbian Dewar v Ervin Moo Young et al.* [2015] JMCC Comm. 23 [82].
92.   *Sally Ann Fulton v Chas E Ramson Ltd.* [2016] JMSC Comm. 14.

for breach of fiduciary duty, if found to have not fulfilled the requirements, which currently appear to be uncertain, given that there are different yardsticks worldwide. These imperatives may even encourage further breaches of the fiduciary duty of directors, in a bid to satisfy ESG requirements, through "greenwashing" or "blue washing".[93] Further, where there are "activist" directors or shareholders, there may be some uncertainty as to whether certain actions by directors are in the best interest of the company as opposed to a particular set of stakeholders. The question would be, what is in the best interest of the company and whether the director has acted for an improper purpose under the new rules for proper purpose.

There is no doubt that the fiduciary duties of directors have been expanded in the Commonwealth since the introduction of legislation and the emergence of ESG. Although there is some protection through the business judgment rule[94] (which directors may invoke where there is a question as to a breach of the duty of care), directors face a more daunting responsibility where it is alleged that they have breached their fiduciary duty to the companies on whose boards they sit, and indirectly to a broad range of stakeholders, whose interests are to be taken into account.

---

93. "Greenwashing" is described as the practice of inflating a company's commitment to the environment. "Blue washing" is where a company uses deceptive marketing to inflate its commitment to social responsibility.

94. In *Maple Leaf Foods Inc. v Schneider Corp.* (1998), 42 O.R. (3d) 177, 192 (Weiler JA) cited *Peoples Department Stores v Wise*, [65] – "The court looks to see that the directors made a *reasonable* decision *not a perfect* decision. Provided the decision taken is within a range of reasonableness, the court ought not to substitute its opinion for that of the board even though subsequent events may have cast doubt on the board's determination. As long as the directors have selected one of several reasonable alternatives, deference is accorded to the board's decision. This formulation of deference to the decision of the board is known as the "business judgment rule".

CHAPTER 6

Defamation Law as the Enforcement of Morals – The Case for Greater Use of the Moralist Approach

Gabrielle Elliott-Williams

Defamatory conduct has been variously defined – as that which "tends to lower a person in the estimation of right-thinking members of society generally";[1] exposes them to "hatred, contempt or ridicule";[2] causes other persons to "shun or avoid" them;[3] "discredits them in their trade, profession or calling";[4] or damages their credit. These definitions are but illustrations of the law of defamation's objective to afford redress, in some instances, for actual or presumed, but unjustified injury to reputation, in the sense of a claimant's standing in their community.[5]

The tort in all its dimensions is concerned with how a tribunal believes that a community will respond to the imputations made of the claimant by the defendant.[6] This community is represented by the "right-thinking" member of society. This person, as the writers of *Winfield and Jolowicz* put it, is "the personification of the judge's view of the state of public feelings and opinion".[7] For that reason, defamation law can reveal public morals (as seen through judges' eyes) and in fact entails the enforcement of morals in a

---

1.   *Sim v Stretch* [1936] 2 All ER 1237, at 1240 (Lord Atkin); the Court of Appeal of England and Wales in *Gillick v BBC* [1996] EMLR 267.
2.   *Parmiter v. Coupland* (1840) 6 M. & W. 105, 108 (Parke, B).
3.   *Youssoupoff v Metro-Goldwyn-Mayer Pictures Ltd.* (1934) 50 TLR 581 at 587, Slesser, LJ.
4.   *Drummond-Jackson v British Medical Association* [1970] 1 All ER 1094, [1970] 1 WLR 688.
5.   *Jameel v Wall Street Journal Europe SPRL* [2006] UKHL 44, [24]; *Berkoff v Burchill* [1996] 4 All ER 1008, 1018; Robert Post, "The Social Foundations of Defamation Law: Reputation and the Constitution," *California Law Review* 74, no. 3 (1986): 697.
6.   *Berkoff*; David Ardia, "Reputation in a Networked World: Revisiting the Social Foundations of Defamation Law," *Harvard Civil Rights-Civil Liberties Law Review* 45 (2010): 261, 283.
7.   John Jolowicz, Percy Winfield, and W. Rogers, *Winfield and Jolowicz on Tort*, 18th ed. (London: Sweet and Maxwell, 2010), 578.

context where various values, including fundamental rights, may be implicated.[8]

The law of defamation employs two distinct approaches to determining loss of standing in the community: the realist and the moralist approaches.[9] The example of an imputation that the claimant was a police informant is illustrative. On the moralist approach, that imputation would not be defamatory since the right-thinking member of society would think highly of someone who assists law enforcement.[10] Tribunals taking this approach necessarily form a view of what *right-thinking* members of the community should think, rather than what the majority will think.[11] In other words, the right-thinking person is imbued with a set of objective morals. This necessarily also involves evaluation of the morality of the community value that the claimant is seeking to protect, and the claimant is denied redress even though they may in fact have suffered reputational harm. In situations of this kind, the tribunal is withholding its protection from communities or community values that it believes are morally objectionable.[12] Thus, cases decided using the moralist approach can reveal a set of values which the courts think are objectively moral.

The moralist approach was applied by the majority in *Byrne v Deane*.[13] The court had to determine whether an imputation that the claimant had been guilty of disloyalty, having reported to the police unlawful conduct taking place in a club of which he was a member, was defamatory. The majority imbued the right-thinking member of society with a set of objective morals, such that, an imputation that he set law enforcement against wrongdoers could not be defamatory. As Slesser, LJ put it,

We have to consider in this connection the arbitrium boni,

---

8. Lawrence McNamara, *Reputation and Defamation* (Oxford: Oxford University Press, 2007), 46.
9. Leslie Treigar-Bar-Am, "Defamation Law in a Changing Society: The Case of *Youssoupoff v Metro-Goldwyn Mayer*," *Legal Studies* 20, no. 2 (2000): 291.
10. *Byrne v Deane* [1937] KB 818. In that case the majority considered the right-thinking member of society to be the good and worthy subject of the king and determined that that subject would think highly of an informer.
11. Roy Baker, "Defamation and the Moral Community," *Deakin Law Review* 13, no. 1 (2008): 1, 10.
12. Op cit. (n570), 714.
13. *Byrne* (n 575).

the view which would be taken by the ordinary good and worthy subject of the King, and I have assigned to myself no other criterion than what a good and worthy subject of the King would think of some person of whom it had been said that he had put the law into motion against wrongdoers, in considering that such a good and worthy subject would not consider such an allegation in itself to be defamatory.

And Slesser, LJ cited with approval Lawson, J, who said, "The very circumstances which will make a person be regarded with disfavour by the criminal classes will raise his character in the estimation of right-thinking men. We can only regard the estimation in which a man is held by society generally."

On the realist approach, however, the imputation that the claimant is an informer would be defamatory in a society with a strong anti-informer culture, whether generally or in relation to a specific maligned public authority. For instance, Lord Fullerton, speaking in *Graham v Roy*,[14] in the context of mid-nineteenth century Scotland, said in relation to a report that the claimant had given information to the officers of excise against a distiller: "If you publish on the streets of a town that a man is a common informer, is that not slander? It may be perfectly legitimate to give information, but an informer is by no means a popular character." Defamation on this approach is founded on the likely response of a majority of the members of the community, without consideration of the rationality or moral acceptability of the community's position.[15]

This paper uses cases emanating from the United States and the Caribbean on racial identification and gay mislabelling respectively to illustrate that defamation law involves the enforcement of morals, and that cases decided according to the realist approach can reveal the public morality (or at least the morality of the ruling classes) and with that, the majority's (or ruling classes') vision for the moral and social order.[16] I argue, that courts utilizing the realist approach sometimes uphold the right to reputation in circumstances which require the enforcement of exclusionary values. Thus, in the

---

14.   In *Graham v Roy* (1851) 13 D 634.
15.   Treigar-Bar-Am (n574) 307; McNamara (n573) 203; Baker (n576).
16.   In the racial misidentification cases, a white claimant asserts that the defendant defamed him by misidentifying him as being black, and in the gay mislabelling cases, the (presumably) heterosexual claimant asserts that the defendant defamed him by mislabelling him as a homosexual.

balancing exercise which defamation calls for, judges should not assume, even in cases where reputation is verifiably harmed, that the greater interest always lies in safeguarding reputation, since other important values may be at stake.[17] I argue that since the realist approach is concerned only with reflecting the presumed popular morality, regardless of whether the community's values are morally repugnant, Anglo-Caribbean courts ought to consider broadening use of the moralist approach. The latter approach allows courts to better reconcile or balance the competing values and thus presents an opportunity to better align the law of defamation with inclusive constitutional values, such as dignity, equality and non-discrimination, and thus with the decolonization project. Judges are, therefore, urged to consider broadening the types of cases in which they utilize the moralist approach if they wish to avoid being complicit in the enforcement of values which are difficult to justify in a constitutional democracy.

Defamation Law as a Reflection of and Enforcement of Morals

Robert Post theorized that there are three aspects of reputation protected by defamation law – defamation as property, honour and dignity.[18] The last two, I would suggest, are particularly useful for unveiling public morals, since morals undergird the concepts of honour and dignity. Where defamation is safeguarding reputation as property, its aim is "to protect individuals within the market by ensuring that their reputation is not wrongfully deprived of its proper market value".[19] Reputation as honour is based on shared social perceptions.[20] With reputation as honour, Post reasoned, the law safeguards the estimation the community accords to a person simply because it attaches a certain status to the social role occupied by the individual.[21] Defamation, safeguarding reputation as honour, supports and can reveal a non-egalitarian community

---

17. Defamation law requires judges to weigh the right to reputation as against freedom of expression. However, in the racial misidentification and gay mislabelling cases, rights to dignity and equality of black and gay people are implicated.

18. Op cit (n570).

19. Op cit (n570) 695.

20. Op cit (n570) 702.

21. Op cit (n570) 699-700.

since it assumes a hierarchical social structure.[22] Reputation as dignity acknowledges the connection between one's sense of self and self-worth, and the affirmation one receives from members of one's community.[23] Post posits that defamation as dignity protects the respect and self-respect that arises from full membership in society.[24] In so doing, defamation as dignity marks individuals for inclusion and exclusion from the community,[25] and in so doing does "the dirty work of boundary maintenance".[26]

Defamation law, then, is in part social control.[27] It entails the enforcement by the court of morals arrived at through a dialectic between itself and the relevant community.[28] To the extent that judges in the anglophone Caribbean enforce morals without reference to constitutional values, although fundamental rights are implicated, this enforcement is taking place in the absence of the strictures which ordinarily accompany the limitation of rights on the basis of public morality. On the realist approach, the community dictates its preferred social ordering, both in terms of its preferred composition and its preferred hierarchical structure. Then the law, through the work of the court, affirms and reinforces its view of the public morality, quite often, irrespective of the rationality or moral worthiness of the community's values.[29] Consequently, in some instances tribunals have been anxious to distance themselves from the values inherent in their finding of defamatory conduct.[30] For instance, the anxiety of the New York Southern District Court in *Gallo v Alitalia-Linee Aeree Italiane-Societa Per Azioni*, where the tribunal decided to include imputation of homosexuality in the slander per se category is palpable:[31]

---

22. Op cit (n570)700-702.
23. Op cit (n570) 710.
24. Op cit (n570) 711.
25. Op cit (n570) 711.
26. Adrian Favell, "To Belong or Not to Belong: The Postnational Question," in *The Politics of Belonging. Migrants and Minorities in Contemporary Europe*, eds. Adrian Favell and Andrew Geddes (Aldershot: Ashgate, 1999), 209–27.
27. McNamara (n573) 74.
28. Ibid.
29. John Watson, "Defamation by Racial Misidentification: A Study of the Social Tort," *Rutgers Race & Law Review* 4 (2002): 77.
30. *Gallo v Alitalia-Linee Aeree Italiane-Societa Per Azioni* (US District Court SD New York) (2008).
31. *Gallo* (n595) 549.

> This court's decision to include homosexuality in the slander
> per se category should not be interpreted as endorsing
> prejudicial views against gays and lesbians. Rather, this
> decision is based on the fact that the prejudice that gays and
> lesbians experience is real and sufficiently widespread so that
> it would be premature to declare victory. If the degree of this
> widespread prejudice disappears, this court welcomes the red
> flag that will attach to this decision.

On the realist approach, due to the absence of objectively moral
moorings, the law of defamation has been and is used to reinforce
abhorrent yet popular values, including exclusionary ones.[32] A
number of US cases on racial misidentification are illustrative.
In *Flood v News & Courier Co.*,[33] the Supreme Court of South
Carolina concluded that "to publish a white man to be negro, it
would not only be galling to his pride, but would tend to interfere
seriously with the social relation of the white man with his fellow
white men". Decades later, that same court affirmed the notion
that the imputation that "a white person is a Negro or mulatto,
or is tainted with Negro blood, is actionable per se" in *Bowen
v Independent Publishing Co.*[34] The judgment of the Court of
Appeals of Georgia in *Wolfe v Georgia Railway & Electric Co.*[35] is
particularly revolting. The court acknowledged the constitutional
amendments which recognized legal equality as between blacks
and whites, but determined that those provisions could not confer
social equality on the Negro and could not dislodge, in the court's
view, the God-ordained social hierarchy recognized in the Bible:

> It is a matter of common knowledge that, viewed from a
> social standpoint, the negro race is in mind and morals
> inferior to the Caucasian. The record of each from the
> dawn of historic time denies equality... The distinction and
> inequality is recognised in Holy Writ... Before the law, the
> Code of Georgia makes all citizens equal, without regard to
> race or color. But it does not create, nor does any law of any

---

32.   Baker (n576) 3. In *Youssoupoff v Metro-Goldwyn Mayer Pictures Ltd.* (1934) 50
      TLR 581, the English Court of Appeal found that right-thinking members of society
      would shun or avoid a woman said to be "defamed in her sexual purity", having been
      "despoiled in her innocence and purity" either by being seduced or raped.
33.   *Flood v News & Courier Co.* 71 SC 112, 50 SE 637 (1905) 639.
34.   *Bowen v Independent Publishing Co.* 96 SE2d 564, 230 SC 509 (1957) 513.
35.   *Wolfe v Georgia Railway & Electric Co.* 2 Ga App 499 (1907).

state attempt to enforce, moral or social equality between different races or citizens of the United States. Such equality does not in fact exist, and never can. The God of nature made it otherwise, and no human law can produce it, and no tribunal enforce it…The fortunes of war have compelled us to yield to the freedman the legal rights above mentioned; but we have never authorised or legalised the marriage relation between the races, nor have we enacted laws regulating the social status, so as to compel our people to meet the colored people on terms of social equality. Such a state of things could never be desired by the thoughtful and reflecting portion of either race. It could never promote peace, quiet, or social order in any state or community.

The morality of the ruling classes in the relevant communities affirmed a social structure which both subordinated and excluded blacks, contrary to their rights to dignity, equality and non-discrimination. Appeals to the Divine and natural law were a part of the technique employed to justify the popular morality and that morality was enforced through the protection of reputation as honour and dignity of whites.[36]

Subsequent cases signalled shifts in the public morality, which emboldened tribunals to refuse to give effect to prejudices through the law of defamation. In *Thomason v Times-Journal*,[37] the Court of Appeals of Georgia dismissed as "indecorous" the claim that an obituary that falsely indicated that the appellant had died and that her funeral arrangements had been handled by a funeral home typically used by blacks was defamatory. In *Polygram Records, Inc. v Superior Court*,[38] the Court of Appeals of California rejected the assertion that an imputation which associated the petitioner's wine with blacks was defamatory. The court in the latter case, while acknowledging the persistence of prejudice, concluded that the "Courts will not condone theories of recovery which promote or

---

36. See Michael Graziano, "Race, the Law, and Religion in America," in *Oxford Research Encyclopedia of Religion* (Oxford: Oxford University Press, 2017) for a brief history of the role religion has played in US society as both an instrument of oppression and as a driving force behind the march towards freedom. Retrieved from https://oxfordre.com/religion/view/10.1093/acrefore/9780199340378.001.0001/acrefore-9780199340378-e-501 on 25 February 2020.

37. *Thomason v Times-Journal* 190 Ga App 601, 603 (1989).

38. *Polygram Records, Inc. v Superior Court* 170 Cal App 3d 543 (1985).

effectuate discriminatory conduct."[39]

Gay Labelling as Defamation in the Anglophone Caribbean

Contemporary anglophone Caribbean cases on gay labelling as defamation echo the US racial misidentification as defamation cases of yesteryear in their enforcement of morals through the safeguarding of reputation as honour and dignity. As M. Jacqui Alexander states: "To be moral is to be asexual, (hetero)sexual, or sexual in ways that presumably carry the weight of the 'natural'."[40] As with the racial misidentification cases, the protected social order and composition are rooted in religiously derived morals.[41] *Aaron v Abel JNO Baptiste,*[42] *Lowe v Ricketts*[43] and *Welch v PBCT Ltd.*[44] are three cases in which anglophone Caribbean courts found gay mislabelling to be defamatory.[45] The court in each case did not find defamation established on the basis that the claimant imputed the commission of a crime without more. In each case, the gay mislabelling was injurious to the claimant's reputation as honour and dignity because it imputed that the claimant engaged in a sinful/immoral/unacceptable sexuality.

The judgments read, to borrow Post's description, as status rehabilitation ceremonies.[46] The gay labelling sullies the claimant's reputation.[47] In order for his reputation as honour and dignity to be restored, he must first avow his heterosexuality. Having done so, his right to full membership in the community, positioned atop the hierarchy, is restored through the court's concurrence in

---

39. *Polygram Records* (n603) 557.
40. M. Jacqui Alexander, "Redrafting Morality: The Postcolonial State and the Sexual Offences Bill of Trinidad and Tobago," in *Third World Women and the Politics of Feminism*, eds. Chandra Mohanty et al. (Bloomington: Indiana University Press, 1991).
41. Mahalia Jackman, "They Called it the 'Abominable Crime': An Analysis of Heterosexual Support for Anti-gay Laws in Barbados, Guyana and Trinidad and Tobago," *Sexuality Research and Social Policy* 2 (2016): 130; *Jason Jones v AG of Trinidad and Tobago* TT 2018 HC 191 (Carilaw TT HC).
42. *Aaron v Baptiste* DM 2014 HC 13 (Carilaw, Eastern Caribbean Supreme Court).
43. *Lowe v Ricketts* [2022] JMSC Civ 1.
44. *Welch v PBCT Ltd. and others* TT 2017 HC 64 (Carilaw, HC TT).
45. See also *Rajkumar v Ali and T&T News Centre Ltd.* TT 2010 HC 146 (Carilaw TT HC) where the Trinidad and Tobago High Court found that an imputation that the claimant is a lesbian would lower her in the estimation of right-thinking members of society.
46. Op cit (n570) 704. See *Lowe v Ricketts* [2022] JMSC Civ 1 [46] where the court determined that the gay mislabelling was injurious to the claimant's honour.
47. See, for example, *Lowe v Ricketts* [2022] JMSC Civ 1 [28].

the denunciation of gays by the community.[48] "If it is defamatory to impute to a claimant a particular act or condition, then only those who are not 'guilty' of that act or condition can claim full membership of the society the law exists to serve. Those who are 'guilty' may still be members of the society, but in not quite the same way, or not quite to the same extent."[49]

In *Aaron v Baptiste*, the claimant was a public figure who held significant positions in diplomatic circles, including being Dominica's ambassador to Venezuela. The defendant wrote a calypso entitled "Bug Her", which was published in various ways. The claimant claimed and the court accepted that "Bug Her" was a reference to buggery, which is a crime in Dominica, punishable by imprisonment and still viewed by society in general as immoral or sinful. Buggery, of course, can refer to heterosexual anal intercourse. The thrust of the evidence and discussion, however, indicates that the conduct is objectionable because of its association with gays. Witnesses testified that they understood the song to mean that the claimant was either a homosexual or bisexual, and guilty of committing the offence of buggery. In order to demonstrate the defamatory character of the imputation, the claimant had to aver that same-sex intercourse is regarded by the society as immoral and sinful; that he is not a homosexual, and that he did nothing to deserve such an ugly attack on his reputation.[50] The court then restores his honour and with it, his dignity, in the sense of his place in the community, by concluding that the insulting imputation of homosexuality was one falsely made.

Lowe v Ricketts is a gay mislabelling case from Jamaica, a place which is often castigated as being exceptionally homophobic. Among other things, the defendant in this case said that the claimant had an "unacceptable sexuality". The Supreme Court determined that this amounted to an imputation that the claimant is gay. Mott Tulloch-Reid, J noted that homosexuality is frowned upon. No doubt referring to Jamaica's anti-buggery law, she asserted that, "in fact, it is against the law". Additionally, the judge determined that "to insinuate that a Jamaican man is a homosexual in the Jamaican

48.　Op cit (n570) 704.
49.　Baker (n576) 11.
50.　*Aaron v Baptiste* DM 2014 HC 13, [7], [26].

environment will put a stain on his reputation and could put him in jeopardy of being harmed",[51] and that the defendant's statements caused damage to the claimant's honour.[52] Those passages highlight two chief risks which the court in *Lowe* is determined to address by awarding damages for defamation: (1) the risk of physical injury to those mislabelled; and (2) the risk of injury to reputation as honour and dignity, given the strong antipathy in some spheres toward gays. Here, too, the judge performed a status rehabilitation ceremony, washing away the sodomy stain; the ceremony having been necessitated by the defendant's failure to personally atone by way of public apology.

In *Welch v PBCT Ltd.*, the claimant was a well-known media personality who used "Emperor" and "Gladiator" as his sobriquets. A few of the defendants referred to him as "Empress" and "Gladys", and made references to "his boyfriend" and to his "riding the back of Gemini", which was the sobriquet used by a man known to the parties involved. The court accepted that the statements imputed that the claimant is gay.[53] It went on to note that:

> [W]hether or not words are defamatory ought to be considered in the context of both the society and the era in which they were uttered. The Court can take judicial notice of worldwide trends towards increased tolerance for persons of non-traditional sexual orientations. These trends are manifest in human rights activism, striving to de-stigmatise persons of non-traditional sexual orientation...It is clear that in our jurisdiction, there is no equivalent legislative acceptance of alternative lifestyles.

Before rehabilitating the claimant's status, the court highlights the depths from which it must be lifted. It does so by referring to two bits of evidence which illustrate the subaltern position of gays at the time in Trinidad and Tobago: (1) the societal "revulsion" towards homosexual advances; and (2) the prohibition of entry

---

51.   *Lowe*, 28.
52.   *Lowe*, 46.
53.   However, see the later case of *Liburn v Pierre* TT 2019 HC 257 16] identifying the *Welch* matter as something other than a gay mislabelling case: "In that matter the word 'gay' was recognized also as not in itself being defamatory but that the label might import or connote infidelity, dishonesty or unfitness when applied to certain circumstances." That characterization, however, is not borne out by the *Welch* judgment. See in particular para. 48.

of homosexuals under Trinidad and Tobago's Immigration Act.[54] In relation to the first, the court invokes *Marcano v The State*,[55] one of a number of cases in the anglophone Caribbean in which a court made the provocation defence available to a man who has killed in response to an unwanted homosexual advance.[56] In *Marcano*, Sharma, CJ refers to approaches made by the deceased to the appellant and his friend "to have unnatural, [and] to perform unnatural acts which the youngsters rejected outright". Sharma opined that this was "a case where ...the acts themselves were so unnatural as to create in the minds of any right-thinking person that they would have caused serious reaction as indeed these boys had reacted". The significant societal value communicated is that a homosexual's life is so insignificant that an unwanted advance, without more, justifiably renders it forfeit. Second, T&T's Immigration Act, which was modelled on the Canadian Immigration Act of 1952, targeted a class typical of colonial-era laws,[57] in that members of the prohibited class were undesirable, useless or dangerous in some sense.[58] The prohibited class includes persons who are likely to be a charge on the public funds, those afflicted with infectious diseases, convicted criminals and suspected traitors[59] – persons who pose a threat of some kind to a perceived vital state interest. Rather than benefitting the economy and the life of the state, they will likely harm either or both. In the case

---

54.   *Welch*, 47. See *Tomlinson v State of Trinidad and Tobago* [2016] CCJ 1 (OJ), in which the CCJ concluded that the prohibition no longer applies to CARICOM national homosexuals; and *Jason Jones v AG of Trinidad and Tobago*, where the High Court struck down the state's anti-sodomy law. I do not mean to suggest here that gays no longer occupy a subaltern status in the society. I mean only to signal that shifts have occurred in the direction of equality.

55.   *Marcano v The State* Cr App No 2 of 2002 (26 July 2002) (CA, Trinidad and Tobago).

56.   Se-shauna Wheatle, "The Constitutionality of the 'Homosexual Advance Defence' in the Commonwealth Caribbean," https://www.equalrightstrust. org/ertdocumentbank/The%20Constitutionality%20of%20the%20 Homosexual%20Advance%20Defence%20in%20the%20Commonwealth%20 Caribbean.pdf.

57.   Alison Bashford and Catie Gilchrist, "The Colonial History of the 1905 Aliens Act," *Journal of Imperial and Commonwealth History* 40, no. 3 (2012): 409; Richard Green, "'Give Me Your Tired, Your Poor, Your Huddled Masses' (of Heterosexuals): An Analysis of American and Canadian immigration policy," *Anglo-American Law Review* 16, no. 2 (1987): 139; T&T's Immigration Act, Section 8(1)(e) is almost identical to the Canada Immigration Act, 1952, Section 5(e).

58.   Philip Girard, "From Subversion to Liberation: Homosexuals and the Immigration Act 1952–1977," *Canadian Journal of Law and Society* 2, no. 1 (1987).

59.   Trinidad and Tobago Immigration Act, 1969, Section 8.

of homosexuals, the law is undoubtedly intended to safeguard the state's "moral ecology".[60] Laws of this kind are notoriously difficult to enforce.[61] They stand, nevertheless, as the "incarnation of policy",[62] meant to signal physical and metaphysical unbelonging by affirming a social order in which homosexuals reside both below and outside.[63]

Having thus established the depths from which the claimant's reputation must be pulled, the court then concludes that although "the degree of revulsion" experienced by right-thinking members of society may have abated over the years, the shifts are not enough for false allegations of homosexuality to no longer be defamatory per se.[64] While decisions like *Welch*, *Aaron* and *Lowe* may reflect existing prejudices, they also lend legal legitimacy to the demeaning and exclusion of gays from the community.[65] "Whether the plaintiff wins or loses, the concept of reputation as dignity will require the court to affirm the community's identity as one that excludes homosexuals."[66]

Significantly, *Welch* confirms the intimate connection between Caribbean homophobia and misogyny.[67] Some of the defendants, in portraying Welch as gay, used words which effeminized him.[68] Since he depended on the projection of "an image that was authoritative, outspoken and robust" – a presumably masculine and thus heterosexual image – imputations which effectively styled

---

60.   See Immigration Act, 1969, Section 9(4); Howard Lesnick, *Religion in Legal Thought and Practice* (Cambridge: Cambridge University Press, 2010), chapter 11, on the long-held presumption of the immorality of homosexuality; Robert George, *Making Men Moral: Civil Liberties and Public Morality* (Oxford: Oxford Scholarship Online, 2012) on a state's duty and right to safeguard "moral ecology".

61.   Girard, "From Subversion," 11.

62.   *Welch*, 48.

63.   Holly Miller, "Homosexuality as Defamation: A Proposal for the Use of the 'Right-Thinking Minds' Approach in the Development of Modern Jurisprudence," *Communication Law & Policy* 18 (2013): 349, 363; Gabrielle Elliott-Williams, "Who Belongs?: The Caribbean Court of Justice Reveals Caribbean Identity's Inclusive Potentiality," *Social and Economic Studies* 69, nos. 1&2 (2020): 73.

64.   *Welch*, 48.

65.   *Albright v Morton* on, 321 F Supp 2d 130, 136 (D Mass 2004).

66.   Post (n570) 737; Baker (n576) 11.

67.   *Welch* (n609) [38], [49-50]; Tara Atluri, "When the Closet is a Region: Homophobia, Heterosexism and Nationalism in the Commonwealth Caribbean," Centre for Gender and Development Studies, the UWI, Cave Hill Campus Working Paper No. 5, March 2001, https://sta.uwi.edu/crgs/september2015/journals/CRGS_9_Pgs287-326_When theClosetisaRegion_TAtluri.pdf.

68.   *Welch* (n609) [32].

him as a "gender traitor"[69] weakened his image and subjected
him impermissibly to ridicule.[70] Thus the defamation ceremony in
Welch, while reaffirming the claimant's status as a member of the
commander class, also reaffirmed the positioning of women in the
anglophone Caribbean as inferior to men.[71]

Promotion of Inclusive Constitutional Values

Aaron, Lowe and *Welch* take the realist approach in that they
capture what is thought to be the prevailing, religiously derived,
public morals. In the process, the courts are protecting communities
which value the subordination and exclusion of gays, and endorsing
those values.[72] Unlike the court in *Gallo,* which at least expressed
anxiety that its decision should be taken as endorsement of such
values, the courts in *Aaron, Lowe* and *Welch* were not similarly
taxed. As explained above, since the courts had the moralist
approach available to them, this was not an inevitable result. I
argue that courts should consider taking the moralist approach in
gay labelling cases for two reasons: First, the moralist approach
allows courts to better align the common law of defamation with
constitutional values of dignity, equality and non-discrimination.
Second, and relatedly, the moralist approach provides the potential
for the law to be used positively as a tool of social change.

Since morals are being enforced, defamation law is helping
to shape society and thus necessarily has implications for rights
realization. For instance, in *Aaron, Welch* and *Lowe,* the society
being both reflected and shaped is one to which gays do not fully
belong. The impact of laws which communicate those ideas is
well documented.[73] Such laws conduce to the stigmatization of

69.   "Gender traitor" is the label assigned to homosexuals in Margaret Atwood's dystopic
      novel, *The Handmaid's Tale,* which was set in Gilead.
70.   *Welch* (n609) [10].
71.   Atluri (n632).
72.   72. Baker (n576).
73.   See Mahalia Jackman, "They Called it the 'Abominable Crime': An Analysis of
      Heterosexual Support for Anti-gay Laws in Barbados, Guyana and Trinidad and
      Tobago," *Sexuality Research and Social Policy* 2 (2016): 130; Ryan Goodman, "Beyond
      the Enforcement Principle: Sodomy Laws, Social Norms, and Social Panoptics,"
      California Law Review 89, no. 3 (2001): 643; Chan Tov McNamarah, "Silent, Spoken,
      Written, and Enforced: The Role of Law in the Construction of the Post-Colonial
      Queerphobic State," *Cornell International Law Journal* 51, no. 6 (2018): 495; *Dudgeon
      v United Kingdom* App No 7525/76 (Official Case No), [1981] ECHR 5.

its targets who are marked for exclusion from belonging within their communities as equals vis-à-vis the non-targeted analogue. Inequality then begets and justifies itself.[74]

Ordinarily, where public morality is being enforced, the state must justify its enforcement by demonstrating the rationality and proportionality of the measure(s) it has employed.[75] But where morals are being enforced via defamation laws, those strictures are absent, potentially leaving defamation law out of step with the rights claims of gays and lesbians, which have been affirmed in recent times by some Anglo-Caribbean courts. In *Orozco*,[76] *Jones*,[77] *David*[78] and *Jeffers*,[79] from Belize, Trinidad and Tobago, Antigua and Barbuda, and St Kitts and Nevis respectively, first instance courts affirmed sexual autonomy rights by repudiating colonial era anti-sodomy laws.[80] The decisions exclude the enforcement of purely religiously derived morals and the will of the majority without more, as public morals. The presumed popular morality had to give way to the right to privacy (among other things), of individuals traditionally marginalized based on sexual orientation. For, without anti-majoritarian constraints, the traditionally marginalized have been, and continue to be, vulnerable to the tyranny of the majority.[81] In each case, the courts preferred the enforcement of *constitutional*, rather than popular, morality.[82] And the constitutional morality determined in each case was premised

---

74. Elliott-Williams, "Who Belongs?," 78. See Jackman, "Abominable Crime," 130, 131, noting that anti-gay laws imposed during colonialism are now seen as representative of local culture.
75. *de Freitas v Permanent Secretary of Ministry of Agriculture, Fisheries, Lands and Housing* [1999] 1 AC 69; *Julian Robinson v Attorney General of Jamaica* [2019] JMFC Full 04; Elliott-Williams (n657).
76. *Orozco v Attorney General of Belize* 10 August 2016 (Supreme Court, Belize,).
77. *Jones v Attorney General of Trinidad and Tobago* TT 2018 HC 191 (High Court, Trinidad and Tobago – Carilaw).
78. *David v Attorney General of Antigua and Barbuda* 5 July 2022 (High Court, Antigua and Barbuda).
79. *Jeffers v Attorney General of St Christopher and Nevis* 29 August 2022 (High Court, St Kitts and Nevis).
80. See also *Holder-McClean-Ramirez v Attorney General of Barbados* 25 November 2023 (High Court, Barbados).
81. Gabrielle Elliott-Williams, "Public Morals and the 'Civilizing Mission': Anglophone Caribbean Jurisprudence: New Redemption Songs," Global Meeting on Law and Society, Lisbon, July 2022.
82. Ibid.

on inclusionary values, rather than exclusionary ones.[83]

As Thoreson explains, "[T]he concept of constitutional morality defines the morals that matter in law as those that derive from and reflect the values of the constitution, and not the popular morality of any particular moment."[84] Assuming that the approach to discerning constitutional morality necessarily embraces a liberatory ethic, constitutional rather than popular morality offers the more ethical approach to using morals as a basis for determining the scope of individual rights, given the tension between rights and public morality understood simply as the will of the majority. The assumption becomes material in places like Jamaica where a constitutional reform process yielded bad faith provisions, such as sections 13(12)[85] and 18,[86] which obviously impact traditionally marginalized groups. This approach to deriving the constitutional morality jibes with Rawls' notion of justice-as-fairness. He arrived at his conception of justice-as-fairness in part through the development of a thought experiment for the crafting of a just society. In his experiment, participants could not know their positions in society and so operated from behind a veil of ignorance. Unaware of where they will fall when there are lines of inclusion/exclusion or privilege/disadvantage, decision-makers would default to egalitarianism.

---

83.   Ibid.
84.   Ryan Thoreson, "The Limits of Moral Limitations: Reconceptualizing 'Morals' in Human Rights Law," *Harvard International Law Journal* 59, no. 1 (2018): 197, 225.
85.   Section 13(12) provides as follows:
        Nothing contained in or done under the authority of any law in force immediately before the commencement of the Charter of Fundamental Rights and Freedoms (Constitutional Amendment) Act, 2011, relating to ¬
        a.   sexual offences;
        b.   obscene publications; or
        c.   offences regarding the life of the unborn,
        shall be held to be inconsistent with or III contravention of the provisions of this Chapter.
86.   Section 18 provides as follows:
        (1) Nothing contained in or done under any law in so far as it restricts
           (a) marriage; or
           (b) any other relationship in respect of which any rights and obligations similar to those pertaining to marriage are conferred upon persons as if they were husband and wife, to one man and one woman shall be regarded as being inconsistent with or in contravention of the provisions of this Chapter.
        (2) No form of marriage or other relationship referred to in subsection (1), other than the voluntary union of one man and one woman may be contracted or legally recognized in Jamaica.

This idea that the common law of defamation should be developed in harmony with the constitutional morality finds support in the judgment of Wit JCCJ in *Lucas v Attorney General of Belize*.[87] There he indicates that even though the Belize constitution does not expressly mandate that the common law should be developed to bring it in line with constitutional standards, it does not prohibit this. Further, Wit JCCJ suggests that constitutional supremacy should mean that courts have an inherent duty to mould and develop the common law in order to make it more just, fair and consistent with constitutional standards.[88] In other words, rather than siloing human rights principles to human rights claims, those values should inform (perhaps dictate) courts' development and articulation of the common law. Here, I am suggesting that in order to do just that, when judges approach various classes of defamation cases, they should weigh the societal interest in safeguarding a claimant's right to reputation as honour and dignity against other implicated societal interests, such as fundamental rights to dignity and equality and non-discrimination with no *a priori* assumption that the greater interest lies in vindicating reputation. Applying the moralist approach, a court might imbue the "right-thinking" or "ordinary, reasonable" person with inclusive values which affirm the rights to dignity, equality and non-discrimination of marginalized groups which pose no harm to society.[89] In that way, a false imputation of homosexuality would not be defamatory even in a community which currently ostracizes lesbians and gays.[90]

Defamation law, with its quest for the reaction of the community as represented by the right-thinking person or the ordinary reasonable person, represents an opportunity to rethink and reshape community values; to help craft a more egalitarian society.[91] In taking the moralist approach described above, courts would be seeking to exploit law's ability to effect or contribute to social engineering non-coercively by providing a framework for social relations and by modelling and teaching a set of values.

---

87.   [2015] CCJ 6 (AJ).
88.   [2015] CCJ 6 (AJ), (2015) 86 WIR 100 [180].
89.   See McNamara (n573) Ch 8. McNamara suggests that the community be imbued with liberal values and that recognition of exclusionary values should require ethical justification by the tribunal.
90.   See also Roy Baker (n576) 10.
91.   McNamara (n573).

Thus, whereas the Appellate Division of the Supreme Court of New York, resigned itself in *Matherson v Marchello* to finding the gay mislabelling defamatory,[92] on the moralist approach, the court would engage with the question of the right- or wrongness of the community value. It would ask itself whether a "right-thinking person" would lower the claimant in his estimation or shun or avoid him on the basis of sexual orientation – an innate characteristic.[93]

Morality shifts.[94] While the court in *Youssoupoff v Metro-Goldwyn-Mayer Pictures Ltd.*[95] concluded that it would be defamatory (in the sense that others would shun or avoid her) to say of a woman that she had been raped, that case would almost certainly be decided differently now. Given the shifts in British society away from the strict puritanism which characterized the period, Slesser, LJ's view that it did not matter the precise manner in which the woman was "despoiled of her innocence and virginity" now appears incredibly anachronistic.[96] Even if some contemporary British communities continue to value chastity as sexual purity, it is highly unlikely that the imputation that a woman was raped would be one likely to cause her to be shunned or avoided by reasonable persons, given the lack of moral blameworthiness on her part.[97]

Future generations will likely largely view bigotry in relation to gays and other groups which are traditionally marginalized as impermissible. If courts in the region are to avoid being complicit in the enforcement of unjust values, the categories for recognition of loss of community standing must be rooted in some conception of justice or objective morality.[98] This idea of concepts such as justice, fairness and morality driving decision-making is not foreign to the common law. Defamation law, as is, does not provide redress for all reputational harms. Public policy decisions are taken in this and

92. In *Matherson v Marchello* 100 AD 2d 233, 242 (NY Appellate Division 1984) the court said: "It cannot be said that social opprobrium of homosexuality does not remain with us today. Rightly or wrongly, many individuals still view homosexuality as immoral."
93. McNamara (n573) notes that the primary definition (lowered in estimation) and the "shun or avoid" test are both linked to this idea of the right-thinking person.
94. *Jason Jones v AG of Trinidad and Tobago*; Gabrielle Elliott-Williams, "The Public Morality Limit in the Commonwealth Caribbean Conventional Model Constitution," 23 January 2010, *UWI Cave Hill Student Law Review*. Available at SSRN: https://ssrn.com/abstract=3550499.
95. (1934) 50 TLR 581 at 587.
96. Treigar-Bar-Am (n574).
97. Ibid.
98. McNamara (n573), 218.

other areas of law, regarding which harms the state wishes to guard against, since, not every misfortune can sound in a remedy.[99] Even where there is reputational loss in the police informant defamation cases, no redress is available because the policy decision is taken that the greater interest lies in upholding the rule of law.[100] In a similar vein, I argue that with the gay mislabelling cases, the greater interest may well not lie with vindicating reputation but may lie instead with communicating egalitarian rather than exclusionary values.

The benefit in the realist approach is that it likely acknowledges the reality of things,[101] whereas the moralist approach, Richards argues, risks "creating legal fictions of society having reached some aspirational level of tolerance" by taking decisions which are arguably not contextually or culturally appropriate.[102] Persons who typically face discrimination on the basis of sexual orientation continue to face violence and discrimination in many forms. And as I mentioned above, this was a significant factor in *Lowe*. Thus, while a moralist approach may signal to gays that the state machinery, through the courts, is not positioned against them, it does not, Arend argues, protect individuals ruined by false gay labelling.[103] Furthermore, so the argument goes, social change will not be effected quickly via this medium.[104] Additionally, Richards points out the irony that taking imputations of this kind out of the realm of defamation law has as its consequence the fact that homophobic invectives go unpunished.[105] Those arguments, however, ignore the law's significant pedagogical function and thus its capacity and effect as a social engineering tool.[106] Additionally, I would argue that the authors' insistence on state protection for mislabelled heterosexual men, in contexts where the state withholds its protection from,

---

99. *Gorringe v Calderdale MBC* [2004] UKHL 15.

100. Daniel More, "Informers Defamation and Public Policy," *Georgia Journal of International and Comparative Law* 19 (1989): 503, 527.

101. Robert Richards, "Gay Labelling and Defamation Law: Have Attitudes Toward Homosexuality Changed Enough to Modify Reputational Torts?" *CommLaw Conspectus* 18 (2010): 349.

102. Richards (n664) 368.

103. Patrice Arend, "Defamation in an Age of Political Correctness: Should a False Public Statement that a Person is Gay be Defamatory?" *Northern Illinois University Law Review* 18 (1997): 99, 112.

104. Ibid.

105. Richards (n664) 369.

106. Lee Potts, "Law as a Tool of Social Engineering: The Case of the Republic of South Africa," *Boston College International and Comparative Law Review* 5, no. 1 (1982): 1, 4.

and in some instances is itself the author of violence against those who are "guilty", simply serves to underscore the latter's subaltern status. The protection of heterosexual Jamaican men in *Lowe* is obligatory even as the state excludes gays from the protection of the law.[107]

Here, too, Caribbean judges should begin to ask themselves whether the enforcement of such morals is justifiable in democratic, postcolonial societies. They should ask themselves whether gay mislabelling cases, like the early US racial misidentification cases, immorally affirm oppression, while invocations of natural and divine law help to obscure the coloniality of power.[108]

Conclusion

Defamation law entails the enforcement of morals. The US racial misidentification and the Caribbean gay mislabelling cases illustrate that those values are sometimes subordinating and exclusionary ones. While the morals enforced by a court employing the realist approach may well reflect the public morality, judges should contemplate whether they wish to be complicit in their enforcement. In time, as with *Youssoupoff*, cases like *Aaron*, *Lowe* and *Welch* will appear anachronistic. Judges will recognize the importance of competing interests and determine that the greater societal interest lies in safeguarding the rights to dignity, equality and non-discrimination of groups, which have been traditionally marginalized based on their orientation by declining to enforce values aimed at their exclusion. The moralist approach would allow judges to do just that. *Jones*, *Orozco*, *David Jeffers* and *Holder-McClean-Ramirez* are evidence of shifting winds. In each case, a first instance court in the region eschewed exclusionary values (notwithstanding presumably popular support for them), in favour of egalitarian ones in circumstances where adults were exercising autonomy without harming others. The moralist approach provides an opportunity for defamation law to be aligned with those new winds.

---

107.   See *Gareth Henry & Simone Carline Edwards v Jamaica*, IACHR Report No. 400/20 Case 13.637, *Report on the Merits*, 31 December 2021.

108.   Anibal Quijano, "Coloniality of Power, Eurocentrism, and Latin America," *Nepantla: Views of South* 1, no. 3 (2000): 533; Shannon Gilreath, "Feminism and Gay Liberation: Together in Struggle," 4 September 2014, Wake Forest University, Legal Studies Paper No. 2491606. Available at https://ssrn.com/abstract=2491606 or http://dx.doi.org/10.2139/ssrn.2491606; *Wolfe* (n600).

CHAPTER 7

"Puss an daag nuh ave de same luck"*
– An Intersectional Approach to Fairness in Sport

Jason Haynes

No serious conversation can be had about sport without considering the question of fairness.[1] The notion of fairness (whether substantive or procedural) is a philosophical, ethical, and practical issue which is typically defined by its synonyms – justice, equity, impartiality, integrity, legitimacy, propriety, and rationality. Fairness is not, of course, unique to the sporting world, as it permeates domestic constitutional concepts like the rule of law,[2] as well as in philosophical narratives like John Rawls' *Justice as Fairness*.[3] Rawls' distinguished work explains that justice involves the "elimination of arbitrary distinctions and the establishment, within the structure of a practice, of a proper balance between competing claims".[4] In his view, first, each person participating in a practice, or affected by it, has an equal right to the most extensive liberty compatible with a like liberty for all; and second, inequalities are arbitrary unless it is reasonable to expect that they will work out to everyone's advantage, and provided the positions and offices to which they attach, or from which they may be gained, are open to all. These principles express justice as a complex of three ideas: liberty, equality and reward for services contributing to the common good.[5]

In the sporting context, fairness has been described in similar

---

1. Thomas Murray, "Making Sense of Fairness in Sports," in *The Ethics of Sports Technologies and Human Enhancement*, eds. Thomas Murray and Voo Teck Chuan (London: Routledge, 2020), 91.
2. Lord Bingham, "The Rule of Law," *Cambridge Law Journal* 66, no. 1 (2007): 67.
3. John Rawls, *Justice as Fairness: A Restatement* (Cambridge, MA and London: Belknap Press of Harvard University Press, 2001).
4. John Rawls, "Justice as Fairness," *Philosophical Review* 67, no. 2 (1958): 164–65.
5. Ibid., 165–66.

*This is a Caribbean idiom that means life is not fair and not everyone has the same luck.

terms.[6] In fact, fairness is viewed by sports law scholars as indispensable to the legitimacy of sporting rules, institutions and procedures. In this connection, fairness in sport has traditionally been judged by (1) the fairness of outcomes; (2) policies and procedures used to determine outcomes; (3) interpersonal treatment; and (4) decision justifications.[7] Without adherence to fairness, it has been argued that there would be no legitimate sport, as doping would become widespread,[8] manipulation of competitions would become rampant,[9] and women and other marginalized groups would be pushed to the sidelines.[10] Against this backdrop, reference to fairness can be found in the governing instruments of almost all sporting bodies, including the International Olympic Committee (IOC),[11] the Federation Internationale de Football Association (FIFA),[12] the International Cricket Council (ICC),[13] and the World Anti-Doping Agency (WADA),[14] among others.

While fairness in sport is axiomatic, it is the assumption that, in practice, fairness operates in an immutable manner that is problematic. Indeed, as this chapter will illustrate, whether fairness is applied in its strictest and most unadulterated form is highly contingent upon the subject in issue. More particularly, there have been cases when fairness appears to operate as a malleable concept that affords luck to "puss" (Caucasian athletes), but no such luck is afforded "daag" (athletes of colour). Although, admittedly, myriad temporal and spatial considerations may have impacted the

---

6.   Francis Keenan, "Justice and Sport," *Journal of the Philosophy of Sport* 2, no. 1 (1975): 111.
7.   Jeremy Jordan, John Gillentine, and Barry Hunt, "The Influence of Fairness: The Application of Organizational Justice in a Team Sport Setting," *International Sports Journal* 8, no. 1 (2004): 139.
8.   Christof Breitsameter, "How to Justify a Ban on Doping?" *Journal of Medical Ethics* 43, no. 5 (2017): 287.
9.   Minhyeok Tak, Michael Sam, and Steven Jackson, "The Politics of Countermeasures against Match-Fixing in Sport: A Political Sociology Approach to Policy Instruments," *International Review for the Sociology of Sport* 53, no. 1 (2018): 30.
10. Warren Whisenant, Debbiesiu Lee, and Windy Dees, "Role Congruity Theory: Perceptions of Fairness and Sexism in Sport Management," *Public Organization Review* 15, no. 4 (2015): 475.
11. IOC Olympic Charter (in force from 8 August 2021) Fundamental Principles of Olympism, Principle 4.
12. FIFA Statutes (April 2016 edition), Article 2(g).
13. ICC Amended and Restated Memorandum of Association and Articles of Association (15 December 2020), Article 5(F).
14. World Anti-Doping Code (2021), Preamble.

reasoning of the sporting bodies that decided the cases discussed below, the objective of this chapter is to problematize how fairness is impacted by the intersectionality of race and gender.

An Intersectional Approach to Fairness in Sport

The intersectional approach to problematizing the law's application to persons of colour was first articulated in the 1980s by leading black scholars, such as Kimberle Crenshaw,[15] and later by Patricia Hill Collins,[16] and, in the Caribbean context, by Tracy Robinson.[17] The intersectional approach, an essentially critical legal theory, is grounded in the view that the experiences of people of colour, and, in particular, women of colour, are not fully reflected in mainstream feminist and anti-racist discourses. It argues that the experiences of people of colour are frequently the product of intersecting patterns of racism and sexism, and that these experiences are qualitatively different from their white counterparts.[18] Race, gender and nationality, intersectional academics such as Crenshaw argue, shape the structural, political and representational aspects of society, and these axes need to be accounted for when we are describing how the social world is constructed.

In her work in the anti-discrimination field, Crenshaw argues that the value of the intersectionality approach lies in its concrete focus on how people of colour, and, in particular, women of colour, are subordinated.[19] This point has since been taken up by more contemporary scholars (for example, Doyin Atewologun), who argue that to combat multiple forms of intersecting subordination against people of colour, we must examine the crossing, juxtaposition and meeting points of the various axes of power, dominance and oppression that confront this particular group.[20]

15. Kimberlé Crenshaw, "Demarginalizing the Intersection of Race and Sex: A Black Feminist Critique of Anti-discrimination Doctrine, Feminist Theory and Antiracist Politics," University of Chicago Legal Forum, 139.
16. Patricia Hill Collins, *Black Feminist Thought: Knowledge, Consciousness, and The Politics of Empowerment* (New York and London: Routledge, 2002).
17. Tracy Robinson, "The Properties of Citizens: A Caribbean Grammar of Conjugal Categories," *Du Bois Review: Social Science Research on Race* 10, no. 2 (2013): 425.
18. Kimberle Crenshaw, "Mapping the Margins: Intersectionality, Identity Politics, and Violence against Women of Color," *Stanford Law Review* 43, no. 6 (1991): 1241, 1245.
19. Crenshaw, "Demarginalizing," 139.
20. Atewologun, "Intersectionality".

Atewologun's work is principally concerned with identifying the ways in which heterogenous members of specific groups, namely women of colour, experience the workplace very differently than their counterparts based on their race and sex. She argues that racism and patriarchy, economic disadvantages and other discriminatory systems contribute to layers of inequality that structure the relative position of women vis-a-vis men, white people vis-a-vis back people, and so on.[21]

One of the more insightful aspects of Atewologun's work is her focus on how nuanced and complex within-group differences can also operate to disadvantage certain categories of people. More pointedly, although both men and women of colour experience intersecting axes of discrimination and oppression, women experience them in qualitatively different ways than men.[22] In this regard, she challenges assumptions about within-group homogeneity, and foregrounds the experience of marginalized women of colour in her work. This form of intersectionality studies she refers to as "content specialization".[23]

Sami Cho and Leslie McCall, contemporary intersectional scholars, share Crenshaw's and Atewologun's sentiments, exposing in their work the weaknesses of single-axis thinking, which they claim undermines the struggle for social justice of oppressed peoples.[24] Their goal is to capture and engage with the contextual dynamics of power by employing open-ended investigations into the overlapping and conflicting elements of race, gender, class, sexuality and nationality, as well as other inequalities. Apart from uncovering the rationalizations that reinforce social power against persons of colour, they call for the adoption of strategies to "dismantle the violent capacities of racialized gendered systems that operate under the pretense of neutrality".[25] Citing David Spade, they argue that "race and gender neutral legal and administrative systems fundamentally produce and maintain race and gender

---

21.   Ibid., 2.
22.   Ibid., 5.
23.   Ibid.
24.   Sumi Cho, Kimberlé Crenshaw, and Leslie McCall, "Toward a Field of Intersectionality Studies: Theory, Applications, And Praxis," *Signs: Journal of Women in Culture and Society* 38, no. 4 (2013): 785.
25.   Ibid., 798.

categories that ultimately distribute inequitable life choices".[26]

This chapter illustrates, through examination of several case studies, how the intersecting praxes of race, gender and nationality in the realm of sport sometimes operate to systematically oppress and subordinate athletes of colour, and, in particular, the women. It contends that, under the guise of the supposedly neutral and immutable concept of "fairness", sporting systems, rules, institutions, personnel, and procedures collectively conspire to marginalize and disempower athletes of colour in ways that their white, middle-class, Western counterparts do not experience the sporting world. It also advances the argument, relying on Atewologun's notion of "content specialization", that, in as much as there is some truth to the argument about the subordination of people of colour in sport, black female athletes' experiences of oppression in sport are qualitatively different from their black male counterparts.

The sections below illustrate, from an intersectional perspective, the ways in which the supposedly neutral and immutable concept of fairness sometimes operates in a qualitative different manner in its application to puss and daag.

Seemingly Neutral Uniform Requirements

Most professional sporting bodies prescribe uniform requirements for athletes wishing to participate in their events. While, in principle, these uniform requirements are not objectionable as they ensure visual consistency and, in some cases, may be closely connected to concerns about fairness, there have been occasions on which these requirements have operated to disempower, frustrate, and discriminate against athletes of colour, and, in particular, women of colour, under the guise of fairness.

In November 2021, the International Handball Federation (IHF) reversed a rule in its uniform regulations that required female athletes to wear bikini bottoms in official competitions. This change of heart came after the organization received intense criticism in response to its decision in July 2021 at the European Handball Championships in Bulgaria to impose a fine on Norwegian handball players who opted to wear shorts instead. Although they

---

26.   Ibid.

were fined, they were still allowed to participate.[27]

By contrast, in the weeks preceding the postponed 2020 Tokyo Olympic Games, the International Swimming Federation (FINA) did not approve UK-based manufacturer Soul Cap's request for their swimming caps to be worn by players of colour at official FINA swimming matches held around the world, including the Olympics.[28] The IOC persisted with the ban, despite intense lobbying by a number of black athletes and anti-racist campaigners.

From an intersectional perspective, FINA's ban of soul caps was problematic for several reasons. First, the ban presumed, without scientific evidence or empirical validation, the illegitimacy of the caps, which were designed by persons of colour for swimmers of colour, while simultaneously privileging competing caps manufactured by white-owned companies, like Speedo. FINA's heavy-handed and paternalistic approach, in this connection, was methodologically and ideologically indefensible and undoubtedly contributed to the 'othering' of sports entrepreneurs of colour and, indeed, athletes of colour.

Second, the ban assumed a certain degree of homogeneity among swimmers, without fully accounting for obvious phenotypical differences. FINA's hackneyed explanation that only caps that "follow the natural form of the head"[29] were permitted could not possibly account for the thick, curly and voluminous hair that characterizes the typical woman of colour, and which accordingly necessitated the manufacture of soul caps in the first place.

Third, FINA's blanket ban on the wearing of soul caps without fulsome consideration of how such a ban could adversely affect athletes of colour was disproportionate, and not rationally connected to the objective of fairness, which it claimed to be seeking to achieve. Proportionality would require that the measure

27.	"International Handball Federation reverses decision to force women's beach handball players to wear bikini bottoms," *ABC News*, Washington, 1 November 2021, https://www.abc.net.au/news/2021-11-01/beach-handball-scraps-bikini-rule-after-outcry/100586216.

28.	Sudiksha Kochi, "Soul Cap, designed for swimmers with natural Black hair, banned from Tokyo Olympics," *USA Today*, 2 June 2021, https://www.usatoday.com/story/sports/olympics/2021/07/02/tokyo-olympics-soul-cap-swimming-black-afro-hair/7845369002/.

29.	Alice Evans, "Soul Cap: Afro swim cap Olympic rejection 'heartbreaking' for black swimmers," *BBC News*, 2 July 2021, https://www.bbc.com/news/newsbeat-57688380.

taken was the least restrictive in the circumstances; certainly, an outright ban on the caps, without robust scientific evidence of the so-called "competitive advantage" it conferred, was arguably not the least restrictive measure in these circumstances. It is ironic that the elusive concept of fairness was touted by FINA as the reason for the ban, but, in the same breath, the ban entrenched unfairness by operating in a disproportionately unfair manner against a historically marginalized group of persons, namely, women of colour.

Fourth, the ban policed black bodies by prescribing a dominant mode of dress, while ignoring how their immutable characteristic – their race – informs their wearing of dreadlocks, afros, weaves, hair extensions, braids, and thick and curly hair. Regrettably, the policing of black hair is nothing new. In other spheres, black hair has been policed for many years, and has in fact been the subject of court decisions,[30] policy intervention,[31] and, more recently, juridification.[32] More pointedly, the ban did not effectively countenance the reality that the chlorine found in swimming pools would inevitably damage the natural oils and overall texture of black hair. The use of the soul caps, in this connection, was not merely for cultural or aesthetic purposes; they were intended to serve a purely functional purpose. Sadly, the ban robbed affected athletes of their autonomy to determine the type of cap that best exemplified their desire to protect their hair.

Fifth, the ban was paternalistic and may even be described as racist in nature in that it privileged Eurocentric ideals about what conferred a competitive advantage, even in the absence of empirical evidence to support such a finding. It also indirectly celebrated dominant discourses about what works best to ensure FINA's fanciful idea of "fair competition", which was neither measurable nor sensible.

---

30. Alaa Elassar, "Jamaica's high court ruled a school was legally right in banning a child with dreadlocks," *CNN*, 4 August 2020, https://edition.cnn.com/2020/08/04/world/jamaica-dreadlocks-ban-student-trnd/index.html#:~:text=A%20school%20that%20said%20a,Court%20of%20Jamaica%20ruled%20Friday.

31. Janelle Griffith, "New York is second state to ban discrimination based on natural hairstyles," *NBC News*, 15 July 2019, https://www.nbcnews.com/news/nbcblk/new-york-second-state-ban-discrimination-based-natural-hairstyles-n1029931?msclkid=1d1ce4ccb31111ecba0588f47a58c9a6.

32. Leah Rodriguez, "8 States Across the US That Have Banned Black Hair Discrimination," *Global Citizen*, 5 March 2021, https://www.globalcitizen.org/en/content/hair-discrimination-crown-act-states/?template=next.

At the same time, it failed to engage properly with alternative approaches to headwear, and, in so doing, alienated black athletes who wished to participate in swimming by subtly articulating that their opposition to the ban did not matter. Interestingly, the FINA's official release, which indicated that soul caps were appropriate for "recreational and teaching purposes",[33] yet simultaneously banned them from the Olympic Games for potentially conferring a competitive advantage, not only comes across as hypocritical, but also demonstrates the malleability of FINA's concept of fairness. Indeed, a strict and immutable conception of fairness was applied here to exclude athletes of colour who wished to wear soul caps, but the Norwegian handball players were allowed to compete in their shorts. Clearly, puss and daag did not have the same luck.

The Variable Application of the 'No Disrepute Clause'

The 'no disrepute' clause is one of the most controversial clauses that may be found in sports contracts, and, indeed, the governing instruments of most sporting bodies. A typical clause of this nature reads: "The Athlete shall not, by [his] acts or omissions, engage or participate in … conduct which, if publicly known, would bring [or would likely bring] … [him] and/or [the sport] into disrepute."

At the international level, Rule 50(2) of the Olympic Charter stipulates, "No kind of demonstration or political, religious or racial propaganda is permitted in any Olympic sites, venues or other areas." Although there is a dearth of jurisprudence on the interpretation of this clause, the Byelaw to Article 50 warns that should there be a violation of this rule, the person so acting in violation (or his delegation) may, *inter alia*, be disqualified or have his accreditation withdrawn.

Despite the seemingly strict nature of Rule 50, however, Vladyslav Heraskevych, a Ukrainian skeleton racer who participated in the 2022 Winter Olympic Games, escaped sanction when he flashed a sign that read "No War in Ukraine" after his third run.[34] The IOC,

---

33. FINA, Media statement, 2 July 2021, https://www.fina.org/news/2183443/fina-media-statement.

34. Ashley Collman, "The Ukrainian athlete who staged an anti-war protest at the Beijing Olympics was forced to flee Kyiv after the Russian invasion," 25 February 2022, https://www.insider.com/ukrainian-olympian-vladyslav-hareskevych-on-russian-invasion-2022-2.

in response, simply noted that, "We have spoken with the athlete. This was a general call for peace ... For the IOC the matter is closed."[35]

Heraskevych's apparent "puss" luck was not what was meted out to "daag" athletes of colour. In fact, Wayne Collett and Vince Matthews were immediately banned for life from participating in IOC-sanctioned events because during the playing of the US national anthem at the 1972 Munich Olympics, they stood casually on the podium – one barefoot, hands on his hips; the other in thoughtful repose, right hand stroking his chin.[36] At the time, they were collecting the silver and gold medals in the 400-metre sprint. They were protesting racial injustice, like the cases of Tommie Smith and John Carlos, who, four years earlier in Mexico City, were banned from participating in the Olympics. While accepting their medals for the 200-metre race, they raised their black-gloved fists in the air in the Black Power salute, expressing their anger at the state of race relations in the United States.[37]

Several decades later, history repeated itself. In the wake of George Floyd's murder at the hands of US police officers, Colin Kaepernick,[38] while representing the San Francisco 49ers, a professional American football team, kneeled during the playing of the US national anthem to protest police brutality, and generalized racial injustices in the United States. The 49ers later released Kaepernick, and the National Football League (NFL) and Donald Trump strongly condemned his act as unruly and effectively

35. Carlie Porterfield, "IOC Will Not Punish Ukrainian Olympian Over 'No War In Ukraine' Sign," *Forbes*, 11 February 2022, https://www.forbes.com/sites/carlieporterfield/2022/02/11/ioc-will-not-punish-ukrainian-olympian-over-no-war-in-ukraine-sign/?sh=1d1ebdac662a.

36. David Wiggins, "Vince Matthews, Wayne Collett, and the Forgotten Disruption in Munich," *Journal of African American History* 106, no. 2 (2021): 278.

37. Jason Peterson, "A 'Race' for Equality," in *From Jack Johnson to Lebron James: Sports, Media, and the Color Line*, ed. James Lamb (Lincoln: University of Nebraska Press, 2016).

38. Steve Marston, "The Revival of Athlete Activism(s): Divergent Black Politics in the 2016 Presidential Election Engagements of LeBron James and Colin Kaepernick," *FairPlay, Revista de Filosofia, Ética y Derecho del Deporte* no. 10 (2017): 45; Daniel Kane and Bonnie Tiell, "Application of Normative Ethics to Explain Colin Kaepernick's Silent Protest in the NFL," *Sport Journal* (2017), https://thesportjournal.org/article/application-of-normative-ethics-to-explain-colin-kaepernicks-silent-protest-in-the-nfl/.

bringing the sport of American football into disrepute.[39] In 2023, outlooks have seemingly changed. However, at the time of writing, Kaepernick still had not been drafted by another NFL team.

While it is clear that certain conduct – namely violent and reckless behaviour, corruption and doping – should always be met with a robust approach to the invocation of the no disrepute clause, it must be appreciated that the clause is typically drafted in such broad terms that it can be invoked in circumstances where athletes engage in conduct that challenges and addresses, in a public manner, social justice issues, such as structural and institutionalized racism and sexism. The effect of this clause, then, is to silence athletes' voices.

The interpretation and application of the no disrepute clause by sporting bodies must take account of the fact that although robust, intense and potentially offensive to some sections of the public, protest action, such as kneeling and the wearing of armbands in support of a social justice movement, is both necessary and desirable. The long-cherished false dichotomy between sport and society cannot continue to go unchallenged. Sport, while in principle a neutral activity, is undoubtedly also a microcosm of society; the structural and institutional inequities found in society are also found in sport, particularly as it relates to discrimination on the basis of race and sex against minorities, especially women of colour. Sporting associations can no longer adopt a fortress mentality when confronted with the legitimate plight of its black constituents, who wish to challenge structural inequalities that invariably affect their lives and livelihoods in real ways.

In the final analysis, having regard to the differential treatment of Vladyslav Heraskevych, a Caucasian male, compared to Tommie Smith, John Carlos, Vince Matthews, Wayne Collet and Colin Kaepernick, all black men, it is clear that the application of the no disrepute clause to achieve the notional concept of fairness is problematic. As has been illustrated above, when it comes to issues of race and other systemic inequalities that affect persons of colour ("daag"), international sporting federations are far more

---

39.   Lori Latrice Martin, "The Politics of Sports and Protest: Colin Kaepernick and the Practice of Leadership," *American Studies Journal* no. 64: 645. *The Stacks* (2018), http://www.asjournal.org/64-2018/the-politics-of-sports-and-protest-colin-kaepernick-and-the-practice-of-leadership/.

inflexible in their application of the no disrepute clause. However, when it concerns issues that touch and concern Caucasian athletes, considerably more leniency is shown. Clearly, puss and daag nuh 'ave the same luck.

Inequitable Treatment of DSD Women of Colour

Differences of sex development (DSD) is a condition in which a person's chromosomes may not match their reproductive organs or genitalia. Under the guise of fairness, women of colour with DSD, like Caster Semenya, Francine Niyonsaba, Beatrice Masilingi, Christine Mboma and Dutee Chand, have been systematically alienated, marginalized and treated with utter contempt by international sporting federations.[40] By contrast, Caucasian transgender women have been embraced by the rules and administrators. At no point have these rules or administrators called white transgender women's femininity into question, even though Laura Hubbard, a New Zealand weightlifter, for example, competed in male categories before coming out as transgender, setting the New Zealand junior records in 1998 in the M105+ division in both lifts (snatch 135 kg, clean and jerk 170 kg), as well as total (300 kg).[41] Similarly, another Caucasian athlete, Lia Thomas, began swimming on the men's team at the University of Pennsylvania in 2017, and during her freshman year, ranked as the sixth-fastest national men's time. On the men's swim team (2018–2019), Thomas finished second in the men's 500, 1,000, and 1,650-yard freestyle at the Ivy League championships. She then transitioned in 2019, and in March 2022, became the first openly transgender athlete to win a NCAA (National Collegiate Athletics Association) Division I national championship in any sport, after winning the women's 500-yard freestyle with a time of 4:33.24.[42]

---

40.   Vikki Krane, Emma Calow, and Brandy Panunti, "Female Testosterone: Contested Terrain," *Kinesiology Review* 11 no. 1 (2021).

41.   Tariq Panja and Ken Belson, "Olympics' First Openly Transgender Woman Stokes Debate on Fairness," *New York Times*, 4 August 2021, https://www.nytimes.com/2021/07/31/sports/laurel-hubbard-trans-weight-lifting.html#:~:text=TOKYO%20%E2%80%94%20When%20Laurel%20Hubbard%2C%20a, at%20the%20Games%20at%20all.

42.   Azeen Ghorayshi, "Trans Swimmer Revives an Old Debate in Elite Sports: What Defines a Woman?," *New York Times*, 18 February 2022, https://www.nytimes.com/2022/02/16/science/lia-thomas-testosterone-womens-sports.html?action=click&pgtype=Article&state=default&module=styln-transgender-

DSD women of colour, by contrast, have been under the microscope for many years.[43] In fact, the IAAF (International Amateur Athletic Federation), now known as World Athletics, in what appeared to be an act of systematic aggression against DSD athletes of colour, adopted the Eligibility Regulations for the Female Classification (Athletes with Differences of Sex Development) in November 2018. The regulations restrict the eligibility of DSD females with levels of endogenous testosterone above 5 nmol/L from participating in select events at international competitions, namely the 400m, 800m and 1,500m events, unless they reduce their testosterone to below 5 nmol/L.

In 2018, in the matter of *Caster Semenya v International Association of Athletics Federations*,[44] the legality of these regulations was challenged by the leading South African 800m athlete, who argued that they were unfair, discriminatory, arbitrary and disproportionate in that they only applied to female athletes having certain physiological traits, namely DSD. Although the Court of Arbitration for Sport found that the regulations were *prima facie* discriminatory, the majority ultimately ruled that they were necessary to ensure fair competition, and that they were also proportionate. Interestingly, the dissenting arbitrator, Justice Hugh Fraser, who is Jamaican-born, disagreed with the majority, finding that the regulations were disproportionate.

On the question of necessity, the CAS considered that the regulations were an objective, fair and effective means of ensuring the legitimate objective of ensuring fairness among female athletes competing in the restricted events in question. It found evidence that androgen-sensitive women with elevated testosterone levels enjoy a significant performance advantage over other female athletes. More pointedly, it noted that androgen-sensitive female athletes consistently beat women who do not have 46 XY DSD, and that this performance advantage could not be fairly characterized as marginal or minimal. In this context, the majority felt constrained

---

general&variant=show&region=MAIN_CONTENT_1&block=storyline_top_links_recirc.
43. Sigmund Loland, "Caster Semenya, Athlete Classification, and Fair Equality of Opportunity in Sport," *Journal of Medical Ethics* 46, no. 9 (2020): 584; Cheryl Cooky and Shari Dworkin, "Policing the Boundaries of Sex: A Critical Examination of Gender Verification and the Caster Semenya Controversy," *Journal of Sex Research* 50, no. 2 (2013): 103.
44. CAS 2018/0/5794.

to rule that: "The IAAF discharged its burden of establishing that regulations governing the ability of female athletes with 46XY DSD to participate in certain events are necessary to maintain fair competition in female athletics by ensuring that female athletes who do not enjoy the significant performance advantage caused by exposure to levels of circulating testosterone in the adult male range do not have to compete against female athletes who do enjoy that performance advantage."[45]

Meanwhile, with respect to the question of proportionality, the majority considered the effect of the DSD regulations on society generally. They found, in this connection, that the DSD regulations are necessary and reflect a rational resolution of conflicting human rights.

The majority also considered the effects of testosterone-suppressing medical treatment as part of its proportionality analysis. In this context, they noted that because oral contraceptives could achieve the result of maintaining the level of testosterone below 5 nmol/L, this was a proportionate response by the IAAF. Interestingly, the CAS rejected Semenya's argument that the use of oral contraceptives to reduce testosterone levels can cause a range of unwanted side effects, including decreased bone density, significant weight gain, hypotension, renal dysfunction, electrolyte abnormalities and venous thromboembolism. In this regard, the CAS found that these effects were not shown to be attributable simply and exclusively to the use of oral contraceptives, and that, in any event, "requiring 46 XY DSD athletes to take oral contraceptives to lower testosterone in order to compete in the female category in Restricted Events at International Competitions is not, of itself, disproportionate".[46]

In other words, "the side effects that may be experienced by such athletes [...] as a result of taking an oral contraceptive do not outweigh the need to give effect to the DSD Regulations in order to attain the legitimate objective of protecting and facilitating fair competition in the female category".[47]

Notwithstanding the foregoing, however, the majority considered

---

45.   Ibid., 580.
46.   Ibid., 599.
47.   Ibid.

that if the affected athletes were required to use Gonadotropin-releasing hormone (GnRH) agonists or gonadectomy to compete, "a different analysis of proportionality would need to be undertaken".[48]

Another interesting question that arose in the context of the majority's proportionality analysis was the effect of requiring athletes like Semenya to undergo intimate medical examinations and assessments of virilization. While the majority accepted that examinations for virilization may be unwelcome and distressing, even when conducted with due care and sensitivity, the benefits of such examinations outweigh the cost in that "[such examinations] may in some cases yield the discovery of medical information that is capable of assisting athletes to reach informed decisions about possible necessary medical treatments and of exonerating them from any erroneous finding that they have taken exogenous testosterone".[49]

Another important point of contention was the question of the proportionality of the 5 nmol/L threshold used as the basis of eligibility to participate in restricted events. In the majority's estimation, the IAAF's decision to reduce the testosterone threshold from 10 nmol/L to 5 nmol/L was not arbitrary, since 5 nmol/L was rationally selected because it represents the highest level well above the normal female range. In their view, testosterone above the 5 nmol/L threshold increases muscle mass and strength, and hemoglobin, and thus confers a competitive advantage.

Notwithstanding this, the panel was concerned about the ability to maintain a level of testosterone below 5 nmol/L, namely, unintentional fluctuations. More pointedly, the concern was that spikes could result in an athlete inadvertently breaching the 5 nmol/L maximum level under the DSD regulations, even if the treatment regime of oral contraceptives was followed diligently. In this regard, they explained, an athlete risked disqualification despite attempting to comply conscientiously with the regulations, highlighting "concerns as to the maximum level of 5 nmol/L and the practical ability of female athletes with 46 XY DSD to ensure that their levels of testosterone do not exceed that level. These

48.   Ibid.
49.   Ibid., 601.

matters will necessarily require oversight by the IAAF to ensure that this requirement is workable in practice."[50]

Having regard to the many issues raised at the hearing, the panel noted that it had:

> "some grave concerns as to the future practical application of the DSD Regulations. While the evidence has not established that those concerns are justified, or that they negate the conclusion of ex facie proportionality, this may change in the future unless constant attention is paid to the fairness of how they are implemented.[51]
>
> ... There are difficulties of implementation of the DSD Regulations and the significance of those difficulties in the context of a maximum permitted level of testosterone of 5 nmol/L rather than 10 nmol/L. The Panel notes the strict liability aspect of the DSD Regulations and repeats its concern as to an athlete's potential inability to remain in compliance with the DSD Regulations in periods of full compliance with treatment protocols, and, more specifically, the resulting consequences of unintentional and unavoidable non-compliance.[52]

Moreover, the panel expressed concerns regarding the strength of the IAAF evidence that was used to support the disqualification of DSD athletes with levels of testosterone above 5 nmol/L who wished to participate in certain events. It noted that "the evidence of actual (in contrast to theoretical) significant athletic advantage by a sufficient number of 46 XY DSD athletes in the 1500m and 1-mile events could be described as sparse. The IAAF may consider deferring the application of the DSD Regulations to these events until more evidence is available[53].... The Panel strongly encourages the IAAF to address the Panel's concerns in its implementation of the DSD Regulations."[54]

In the final analysis, however, notwithstanding the foregoing concerns, the majority's view was that female athletes with 5-ARD, like Semenya, with high levels of circulating testosterone in the male

---

50.   Ibid., 617.
51.   Ibid., 620.
52.   Ibid., 622.
53.   Ibid., 623.
54.   Ibid., 624.

range, have a significant competitive/performance advantage over other women in respect of the restricted events in question. The majority, in this connection, agreed with the IAAF that, in order to qualify to participate in the restricted events, Semenya and similarly placed athletes had to take medication, including contraceptives, to lower their testosterone levels.

Interestingly, despite scathing attacks on the legitimacy and accuracy of Bermon and Garnier's 2017 study ('BG17'), the majority of the CAS panel ultimately concluded that "while BG17 cannot, alone, establish a causal relationship and has a number of shortcomings identified by the Claimants' experts, this does not disprove the IAAF' s case concerning the connection between 46 XY DSD, testosterone and athletic performance. Rather, BG17 (even as an observational study) provides empirical data which demonstrate that the IAAF's scientific evidence concerning the physiological effects of increased testosterone levels translates, in a real world competitive context, to a significant and often determinative performance advantage."[55]

The majority also took note of the "limitation on the conclusions in BG17 and the methodological and statistical criticisms advanced by the Claimants in respect of that study. The majority of the Panel nevertheless considers that BG17 provides a degree of further evidential support for the IAAF's position."[56]

Invariably, Semenya, being unsatisfied with the outcome of the CAS ruling, petitioned the Swiss Federal Supreme Court, which dismissed the appeal on the basis that there was no evidence of a violation by the CAS decision of fundamental and widely recognized principles of public order (ordre public). The Federal Supreme Court[57] agreed with the CAS ruling, ultimately finding that the CAS had issued a binding decision based on the "unanimous opinion of the experts who were consulted that testosterone is the main factor for the different performance levels of the sexes in athletics".[58] It found that the CAS decision, in this context, was compatible with public order in that Semenya's personality and

---

55.   Ibid., 99.
56.   Ibid., 573.
57.   Judgment of 25 August 2020 (4A_248/2019, 4A_398/2019).
58.   Press release of the Federal Supreme Court (Lausanne, 8 September 2020) 4A_248_2019_yyyy_mm_dd_T_e_18_18_10.pdf (bger.ch).

human dignity, and the principle of non-discrimination had not been violated. It considered that the recommendation for the drug-induced lowering of affected athletes' testosterone levels because it was carried out by qualified doctors and under no circumstances against the will of any female athletes, justified this limitation on their right to their personality, and that, in any event, their dignity was not implicated because they were free to refuse treatment to lower their testosterone levels.

Dissatisfied with the CAS ruling and the decision of the Swiss Federal Supreme Court, Semenya lodged a complaint in February 2021 before the European Court on Human Rights (ECtHR),[59] alleging that her rights had been violated under Articles 3 (prohibition of inhumane or degrading treatment) and 8 (right to respect for private life), taken alone and in conjunction with Article 14 (prohibition of discrimination), and also a breach of Articles 6 (right to a fair hearing) and 13 (right to an effective remedy) of the European Convention of Human Rights (ECHR).

Then came, in August 2021, the Tokyo 2020 Olympic Games, at which Semenya did not participate, despite attempting to qualify in the 3,000m event, for which she did not meet the qualifying time. [60]

Interestingly, just mere days after the conclusion of the Olympic Games, a proverbial bombshell dropped. The *British Journal of Sports Medicine* published a correction to Bermon and Garnier's 2017 article,[61] in which Stephane Bermon, the current Director of World Athletics' Health and Science Department, noted that the 2017 paper "could have been misleading".[62] He explained that there is no confirmatory evidence for causality in the observed relationships reported in the 2017 study since it was merely exploratory. He considered that the statement on which the CAS had extensively relied, namely "Female athletes with high T

---

59. *Semenya v Switzerland* (application no. 10934/21).

60. "Tokyo 2020: Caster Semenya fails to meet Olympic qualifying time for 5,000m as deadline passes," Sky Sports, London, 20 July 2021, https://www.skysports.com/more-sports/athletics/news/29175/12345997/tokyo-2020-caster-semenya-fails-to-meet-olympic-qualifying-time-for-5000m-as-deadline-passes.

61. Stéphane Bermon and Pierre-Yves Garnier, "Correction: Serum androgen levels and their relation to performance in track and field: mass spectrometry results from 2127 observations in male and female elite athletes," *British Journal of Sports Medicine* (2021), http://dx.doi.org/10.1136/bjsports-2017-097792corr1.

62. Ibid.

[testosterone] levels have a significant competitive advantage over those with low T in 400 m, 400 m hurdles, 800 m, hammer throw, and pole vault"[63] was misleading as it suggested a causal link between DSD and enhanced athletic performance. He then sought to amend his previous statement to now read, "High T levels in female athletes were associated with higher athletic performance over those with low T in 400 m, 400 m hurdles, 800 m, hammer throw, and pole vault."[64]

This latest development in the Semenya saga illustrates, in no uncertain terms, "the danger of a single story", the title of novelist Chimamanda Adichie's 2009 TEDx talk.[65] More pointedly, despite numerous inherent flaws in BG17, the majority of the CAS panel was prepared to turn a blind eye and embrace a purely exploratory study as gospel, thereby excluding one of the most dedicated women in sport from obtaining a potential place on the podium at the Tokyo 2020 Olympic Games.

That said, the recent correction to the 2017 study should not come as a surprise since the CAS hearing of Semenya's case was characterized by a patent failure by the majority to properly countenance anything but a single story. The majority ignored the countervailing views of several leading scientists that no causal relationship existed between DSD and athletic performance. Their embrace of a single story led them to either overlook or partially ignore several problematic features of the study on which they heavily relied.

Yet still, despite Bermon's own acknowledgement of the shortcomings of his study and the CAS panel's recognition that the study alone could not establish a causal relationship, the majority accepted the single story, ignoring all other contending voices, to legitimize the discriminatory regulations. How could the legitimacy of the controversial regulation, whose adverse effects on Semenya and similar athletes were devastating, have been principally supported by a mere observational study with so many flaws? The majority's constant need to reiterate "the limitation on

---

63.   Ibid.
64.   Ibid.
65.   Chimamanda Adichie, "The Danger of a Single Story," TEDGlobal, July 2009, https://www.ted.com/talks/chimamanda_ngozi_adichie_the_danger_of_a_single_story?language=en.

the conclusions in BG17 and the methodological and statistical criticisms advanced by the Claimants"[66] should have alerted them that they could not base the legitimacy of the regulations principally on such a flawed study.

Apart from that, from an intersectional perspective, the DSD regulations themselves can, on the face of it, arguably be described as fundamentally discriminatory, sexist and racist in their orientation. More pointedly, the regulations, enacted under the cloak of fairness, by design, unfairly target an already historically marginalized group of women for exclusion from sporting disciplines in which they invested considerable time and energy, while mischaracterizing endogenous testosterone as if it were a performance-enhancing drug. At the same time, other athletes, who have natural gifts, such as long legs and big hands, or who have decided to transition from men to women, are celebrated and revered. The regulations are also sexist because they create a false dichotomy between 'real' and 'artificial' women, the former apparently deserving of a place in sport, while the latter, notwithstanding the fact that hyperandrogenism is no fault of their own, are treated as outcasts. It also creates racial hierarchies that privileges and protects non-black women who, comparatively speaking, tend to have lower levels of endogenous testosterone, while alienating and outright excluding women of colour, like Semenya, who naturally have higher levels of testosterone.

The regulations are also misogynistic because they reinforce harmful stereotypes about the static and binary nature of sex and gender, without fully accounting for natural genetic diversity, as in DSD. Moreover, the regulations reinforce the toxic view that only women who fall on one end of the spectrum, namely those with lower levels of endogenous testosterone, are worthy of participating in sport. The regulations are, by their very nature, dangerous for women with DSD because they create a deeply problematic impression that their natural diversity is to be hidden, and that they ought to be ashamed of their unique, unaltered bodies. The regulations treat these talented women as commodities to be poked and prodded, and modified, as appropriate, with contraceptives, if they wish to participate in their sporting disciplines. The regulations

---

66. CAS 2018/O/5794, 573.

are crude in that they offer no sympathy for the agony that these already targeted women experience because of societal pressures and invasive treatments. The regulations also strip these women of their inherent dignity as human beings, and their basic right to privacy.

The regulations are fundamentally paternalistic in nature in that they prescribe specific targets that women with DSD must satisfy, while ignoring natural advantages and disadvantages that exist in male sporting disciplines. At no point has the conversation been about whether certain men enjoy, because of their higher testosterone levels, greater athletic performance advantage over other men with lower testosterone levels. How then does it make practical sense for women with DSD to be constantly policed, when male bodies are not policed for endogenous advantages? In addition, because the management and administration of sport is dominated by men, it was they who orchestrated the drafting of these discriminatory regulations. It is principally men who police their enforcement; and it is principally men that benefit from their enforcement. This paternalistic approach, while reflective of broader societal concerns regarding the proper role of women in society, is not new to sport, however. Indeed, traditionally, women have had to work harder than their male counterparts and have had to expose themselves to a greater level of scrutiny and invasive treatment to obtain a seat at the table, a basic right which, by virtue of being human, they should be entitled to exercise.

Finally, the DSD regulations are duplicitous in nature. They presuppose that World Athletics and the IOC are concerned with fairness in sport, but yet, they reflect only a superficial understanding of fairness that privileges only a select category of persons while ignoring the legitimate plight of others. How can female transgender athletes, such as Laurel Hubbard,[67] be allowed to freely compete with women and this does not raise alarm bells? Yet Semenya and others, who were not born 'male' and have always identified as women, be excluded from competing with females when a person, born male, who has transitioned to female,

---

67.   "First openly transgender Olympians are competing in Tokyo," *NBC News*, 26 July 2021, https://www.nbcnews.com/nbc-out/out-news/first-openly-transgender-olympians-are-competing-tokyo-rcna1507.

is allowed to? The dubious causative link between endogenous testosterone and athletic performance aside, are the regulations implicitly advocating that DSD females are lesser women than female transgender athletes?

While our attention is now turned to the ECtHR, which might very well rule in Semenya's favour in light of the recently published correction to BG17, one cannot help but think that Semenya and similarly placed athletes have received the dirty end of the stick. After serving the sporting world with much enthusiasm, sweat and tears, and after World Athletics and various cognate institutions have benefitted tangibly and otherwise from their athletic prowess, they have been thrown like sheep to the slaughter. In Semenya's case, she lost the opportunity to defend her gold medal at the 2020 Tokyo Olympics, as well as numerous opportunities to ply her trade and earn a decent living all because of a single story, unsupported by evidence, of a causal connection between endogenous testosterone and enhanced athletic performance. Clearly, Semenya and fellow DSD athletes of colour – "daag" – do not have the same luck of their white counterparts, "puss".

Unequal Application of Anti-doping Regulations

Under the cloak of fairness, WADA's doping rules have sometimes operated to oppress and disempower athletes of colour, in particular, women of colour. These rules, principally in the form of the World Anti-Doping Code and its associated International Standards, are grounded in an apparently immutable conception of fairness. However, as will soon become evident, in practice, it appears that the application of these rules to people of colour is highly malleable.

Perhaps a useful starting point in this context is the recent saga involving Russian teenage figure skater, Kamila Valieva.[68] In early 2022, the Court of Arbitration for Sport (CAS), which is often cited as the bastion of justice in the adjudication of sporting disputes,[69] lifted a provisional ban imposed on Valieva at the 2022

---

68.   David Close, Jacob Lev, and Jeevan Ravindran, "Kamila Valieva saga set to run and run as blame game breaks out over Russian skater's positive drugs test," *CNN*, 18 February 2022, https://edition.cnn.com/2022/02/18/sport/olympics-beijing-kamila-valieva-russia-skating-doping-spt-intl/index.html.

69.   Richard McLaren, "The Court of Arbitration for Sport: An Independent Arena for

Winter Olympics in Beijing after her 'A' sample returned an adverse analytical finding in a pre-Olympic doping test.[70] The effect of lifting the ban was that Valieva was allowed to compete in the games. Although she placed fourth in the individual event, the team – of which she was a member – placed first. Months after the conclusion of the Olympics, however, the medal ceremony was postponed, as a determination as to her 'B' sample results took an inordinately long time to be completed. In fact, one sports law scholar, Professor Steve Cornelius, described the postponement of the ceremony as having "set new world records for the longest delay in announcing the final result and for holding the medal ceremony".[71]

In stark contrast, a black US athlete, Sha'Carri Richardson, then twenty-one, whose sample returned an adverse analytical finding for tetrahydrocannabinol (THC), a banned substance, was immediately suspended for thirty days from participating in the 100-metre sprint.[72] In fact, even though Richardson had won the 100-metre event in June 2021 US Olympic team trials in Eugene, Oregon, her ban, which came on the heels of the postponed 2020 Olympics, prevented her from participating in the games.[73] Valieva's age was used as a defence to offer her "protected status" under the World Anti-Doping Code, at least against provisional suspension, and much deference was shown to her in this regard by the CAS. (Incidentally, the Russian Anti-Doping Committee, which has a terrible track record, had imposed the ban initially. It was later reversed.) But no such sympathy was afforded a young black woman

the World's Sports Disputes," *Valparaiso University Law Review* no. 35 (2000): 379; Darren Kane, "Twenty years on: An Examination of the Court of Arbitration for Sport," *Melbourne Journal of International Law* 4, no. 2 (2003): 611; Lorenzo Casini, "The Making of a Lex Sportiva by the Court of Arbitration for Sport," *German Law Journal* 12, no. 5 (2011): 1317.

70.   CAS OG 22/08 *IOC v RUSADA* / CAS OG 22/09 *WADA v RUSADA & Kamila Valieva* / CAS OG 22/10 *ISU v RUSADA, Kamila Valieva & ROC*.

71.   Steve Cornelius, "Beijing 2022 Winter Olympic Games: Valieva Case – Doping Control and the Result Conundrum," *Sport and Taxation*, 28 March 2022, https://sportslawandtaxation.com/news/1779-beijing-2022-winter-olympic-games-valieva-case-doping-control-and-the-result-conundrum.

72.   Marlene Lenthang, "Sha'Carri Richardson questions Kamila Valieva decision, says being Black is 'only difference I see'," *NBC News*, 15 February 2022, https://www.nbcnews.com/news/world/shacarri-richardson-questions-kamila-valieva-decision-says-black-only-rcna16261.

73.   Elisha Fieldstadt, "U.S. sprinter Sha'Carri Richardson suspended for one month after failed drug test," *NBC News*, 2 July 2021, https://www.nbcnews.com/news/sports/sha-carri-richardson-could-miss-olympics-after-failed-drug-test-n1272960.

who used marijuana after her biological mother passed away, in a bid to calm her "emotional panic". Notwithstanding the fact that marijuana is legal in Oregon as well as several other US states, Richardson received very little concession from the World Anti-Doping Agency (WADA). Justice, however construed by WADA, was swift and robust to protect the immutable concept of fairness in sport, and no derogation was countenanced, even though WADA later indicated that marijuana's place on the Prohibited List was being reviewed.[74] Had she appealed to the CAS, it is likely that it, too, would have afforded her very little sympathy and would likely have been swift to condemn her. Clearly, Richardson (the daag) did not have the same luck as Valieva (the puss).

The malleability of the concept of fairness in the context of the application of doping rules not only operates to disenfranchise people of colour as a group, but more particularly women of colour, even in circumstances where men of colour are involved. In fact, by reference to Atewologun's content specialization in the intersectional theoretical context, it can be argued that although both men and women of colour do not have the same luck as their white counterparts, the females, qualitatively speaking, are often adjudged more harshly, and face more dire consequences than the males in the doping arena. This inter-group differentiation is best illustrated by reference to the *NAAATT v Kelly-Ann Baptiste* doping case.[75] Here, Trinidad and Tobago's athlete, Kelly-Ann Baptiste, searched for a replacement nutritionist after her former nutritionist could not continue to work with her for personal reasons. On the advice of her training partner and friend, Tyson Gay, she was introduced to a doctor, who assured her that all of his products were natural, food-based and did not contain any prohibited substances. Contrary to these assurances, however, the Trinidadian athlete tested positive for an anabolic steroid after she received and used a batch of products from the doctor, which included two creams, the labels for which indicated the presence

---

74.   Tom Schad, "Three months after Sha'Carri Richardson's DQ, WADA announces it will re-examine marijuana as banned substance," *USA Today*, 14 September 2021, https://www.usatoday.com/story/sports/olympics/2021/09/14/wada-review-marijuana-banned-substances-sha-carri-richardson/8339486002/.

75.   Kwame Laurence, "Baptiste free to compete after doping ban lifted," *Trinidad Express*, 27 January 2015, https://ttnaaa.org/archive/news/article/2015/01/2015_01_27_back_on_track_baptiste_doping_ban.html.

of dehydroepiandrosterone (DHEA) and human growth hormone (HGH).

Shortly after being notified of the adverse analytical finding, the athlete agreed to meet with USADA to provide them with a full and true account relating to the doctor, his creams, her use of the creams and her training relationship with Tyson Gay. In addition, she sent USADA all of the electronic communications she had exchanged with the doctor. Further, she signed a medical release form, requesting that the doctor release to USADA any and all records and information pertaining to treatments she received. USADA subsequently prepared a draft affidavit on behalf of the athlete, based on the information she provided. USADA was able to use the athlete's information to corroborate Gay's version of events; build a case against the doctor; and initiate disciplinary proceedings against Jon Drummond, a high-profile coach. The athlete accordingly submitted that she had provided substantial assistance within the meaning of Article 10.6 of the then applicable WADA Code, and thus entitled to a suspension of at least part of the otherwise applicable sanction of two years' ineligibility.

The IAAF Doping Review Board agreed with the athlete, finding that the assistance which she provided could be regarded as substantial assistance, but left it up to the National Association of Athletics Administration of Trinidad and Tobago (NAAATT) to decide upon the sanction that would apply to the athlete. The NAAATT concluded that the sanction to be applied to the athlete, by virtue of the substantial assistance which she provided, was that of suspension for half of the two-year period of ineligibility otherwise applicable. Interestingly, however, the IAAF appealed against the suspension of the twelve-month period imposed by the NAAATT, arguing that no more than three months of the two-year period of ineligibility should have been suspended. Ultimately, after about sixteen months of ineligibility, the NAAATT finally confirmed that Baptiste was free to return to competition "with immediate effect".[76]

Although the confidentiality provisions applicable to the proceedings meant that the award of the CAS was never made

---

76.   "Baptiste free to resume competition, federation says," *Reuters*, 31 January 2015, https://www.reuters.com/article/uk-athletics-baptiste-idUKKBN0L40VI20150131.

public, the question invariably remains as to whether the female Trinidadian athlete in this case was treated fairly. This question is particularly apposite in light of the fact that, in a case bearing the same facts involving her training partner, Tyson Gay, the US athlete was subject to a twelve-month period of ineligibility,[77] while Baptiste, an athlete of colour, was, in effect, handed a sixteen-month ban. While it can be argued that there is no guarantee that like cases will inevitably be treated alike in the absence of *de jure stare decisis* in the context of sports arbitration, one cannot help but consider this argument to be both superficial and devoid of a basic understanding of the principle of fairness, which, according to John Rawls, requires that, among other things, like situations be treated alike. What distinguishes the differential treatment of these similar cases remains a mystery, particularly in light of the fact that both athletes' assistance contributed to the institution of proceedings against a high-profile coach, namely Jon Drummond, and the subsequent imposition of an eight-year period of ineligibility. The *Baptiste* case, in this context, suggests that the rules regarding substantial assistance do not always work fairly for all athletes, in particular female athletes of colour, which is, of course, problematic, from an intersectional perspective.

A similar argument can be advanced in respect of the difference of treatment between two Jamaican athletes, Simone Forbes and Ricardo Cunningham. *Simone Forbes v JADCO*[78] was a case in which the athlete, a seasoned netballer, tested positive for Clomiphene metabolites, a prohibited substance, in circumstances where she took a fertility drug to treat a medical condition that was incapacitating on a monthly basis. The Jamaica Anti-Doping Appeal Tribunal, while acknowledging the lack of intention to enhance performance on the athlete's part, nonetheless found that she had been negligent in not informing her team physician and in not asking her doctor about the drug's suitability for use as a national athlete. More fundamentally, for an elite athlete who was

---

77.   Nick Zaccardi, "Jon Drummond banned 8 years after assisting Tyson Gay's doping," 17 December 2014, https://olympics.nbcsports.com/2014/12/17/jon-drummond-banned-tyson-gay-doping-usada-track-and-field/#:~:text=Gay%20said%20he%20began%20taking,decision%20regarding%20Drummond's%20ban%20here._

78.   Disciplinary Hearing of the Independent Anti-Doping Disciplinary Panel, 28 March 2011.

tested several times in the past, she had a responsibility to apply for a Therapeutic Use Exemption (TUE) certificate before using the drug.

By contrast, in *JADCO v Ricardo Cunningham*,[79] he tested positive for pseudoephedrine, a prohibited substance, in circumstances where he had taken Panadol, Cetamol Cold and Flu, and DPH Cough and Cold medicine to treat a persistent cold. The athlete wrongly believed that TUEs were given to athletes who suffered from asthma. It was held that because the athlete did not intend to enhance performance, and given that it was his first violation, a reprimand and no period of ineligibility was appropriate. The Independent Anti-Doping Disciplinary Panel went on to caution that educational opportunities should be provided to ensure that athletes are properly informed of the anti-doping rules, and, in particular, the use of the TUE facility, in situations where medication may be required for illnesses.

Having regard to the glaring similarities between the *Simone Forbes* case and the *Cunningham* case, it is hard to rationalize how the panel could have arrived at the decision that Forbes should be subject to a three-month period of ineligibility, while Cunningham received only a reprimand. In both cases, the athletes had taken prescribed drugs which contained prohibited substances; both had been negligent to some degree in not ascertaining whether the prescribed drugs in fact contained prohibited substances; it was their first violation; and, fundamentally, both misunderstood the true nature of the TUE. For this reason, it appears that the *Forbes* case, but not the *Cunningham* case, was correctly decided, since the circumstances in both cases warranted the imposition of a period of ineligibility, as opposed to a mere reprimand. Given the inconsistency between the two decisions, however, one is left to wonder whether Forbes' monthly incapacitating pains, inherent to her femininity, was viewed as less worthy of being countenanced for sanctioning purposes than a man's temporary struggle with the cold. Clearly, Forbes ('daag') did not have the same luck as Cunningham ('puss').

---

79.   Disciplinary Hearing of the Independent Anti-Doping Disciplinary Panel, 30 January 2013.

Conclusion

This chapter demonstrated that whether fairness is applied in its strictest and most unadulterated form is highly contingent upon the subject in issue through analysis of several case studies. In some cases, fairness appears to operate as a malleable concept that affords luck to 'puss' (Caucasian athletes), but no such luck is afforded 'daag' – athletes of colour. Although the cases mentioned cannot be treated as representative of the status of fairness in sport in all disciplines across all timespans, given the disparate temporal and spatial considerations applicable to each of those cases, the lived experience of the athletes of colour in question strongly suggests that fairness is not as immutable as one would think. From an intersectional perspective, the differential and often less favourable treatment of athletes of colour on the basis of immutable characteristics, like their race and gender, is deeply problematic because it is often insidious and systematic. Indeed, the disparate application of the principle of fairness, as described above, to athletes of colour betrays John Rawls' characterization of fairness as justice, and flies in the face of the hard work that intersectional scholars, like Kimberle Crenshaw and others, have been doing over many years to rid social structures of intersecting forms of discrimination against people of colour. What is even more concerning is the fact that female athletes of colour – as a distinct category within the larger grouping of people of colour – often experience the notional concept of fairness very differently from their white, and even black, male counterparts. While this is, of course, not unique to the sporting realm, it is nonetheless no less problematic. Regrettably, until sporting bodies come to a realization of how their rules, procedures and institutions marginalize, oppress, and disempower people of colour, and especially women of colour, we will continue having the same conversation about puss and daag not having the same luck.

CHAPTER 8

Tort Liability in the Hospitality Sector
Gilbert Kodilinye

The advent of COVID-19 in early 2020 cast a long shadow over hospitality and tourism around the world, ravaging the industry. It is only now appearing to recover. With the availability of vaccines and other tools to control the spread of the disease, a return to something like normalcy is expected. Hotels and resorts have become experienced in compliance with the necessary Covid-related protocols and attention may now turn to traditional risks arising from the expected surge in visitors, whose pent-up exuberance may lead to an increase in incidents resulting in personal injury. Compensation for such injury is most often settled out of court, but should a visitor need to obtain redress through litigation, a decision will have to be made as to where the action should be brought. If, for instance, a US visitor to Jamaica sustains an injury from slipping and falling at their hotel, which they believe is attributable to the hotel's negligence, they would have to decide whether to sue the hotel in the Jamaican courts or bring an action in the United States, whether against the hotel or against the tour operator with which they booked the vacation. In legal terms, the choice will be one of jurisdiction, and the court that accepts jurisdiction will decide the issue of the choice of law, that is, which rules of substantive and procedural law the court should apply in deciding the case.

Choice of jurisdiction and choice of law are matters that are subject to principles derived from legal precedent but, in so far as they have a choice in the matter, the visitor who has suffered an injury during a Caribbean vacation would most likely prefer to sue in a court in her home jurisdiction, which will typically be in the United Kingdom, Canada or the United States. There are at least four reasons for this: (i) the additional expense, inconvenience and stress involved in instructing an attorney and suing in a foreign country; (ii) the fact that, unlike in North America, most attorneys in the Caribbean do not act on a contingency-fee basis; (iii) unlike North America, there are no jury trials of negligence and personal injury cases in the Caribbean, as a consequence of which awards of damages are generally much lower in the region; (iv) whereas in North America each party to litigation bears their own costs, in Caribbean jurisdictions the party who loses the action is generally required to pay the winner's costs, so a claimant whose action fails will have to pay their own legal costs and those of the defendant. On the other hand, a hotel or resort that is a defendant in a personal injury claim might prefer the action to be brought in the local courts, for at least two reasons: (i) in the event that the claim succeeds, damages would most probably be much lower than if the action were brought in a North American court; (ii) in North America, personal injury cases can take from five to eight years, during which time the defendant could be faced with huge legal fees, which might be twice or three times the cost of legal representation in the Caribbean courts.

Forum non conveniens

Where a claimant brings a personal injury action in a North American court, for instance, against a Caribbean resort, which they allege is responsible for the damage, the resort may seek to have the action dismissed on the ground of *forum non conveniens*, under which a court may dismiss an action over which it has jurisdiction when it appears that the convenience of the parties and the interest of justice weigh in favour of adjudicating the action abroad.[1] In the US case *Van Hoy v Sandals Resorts International Ltd.*,[2] Judge Seitz said:

> The touchstone of the doctrine is convenience. Dismissal for *forum non conveniens* is appropriate where:
>
> 1. The trial court finds that an adequate alternate forum exists which possesses jurisdiction over the whole case, including all of the parties;

---

1.   *Piper Aircraft Co v Reyno* 454 U.S. 235, 241.
2.   2013 U.S.Dist.Lexis 40352.

2. The trial court finds that all relevant factors of private
    interest favour the alternate forum, weighing in the
    balance a strong presumption against disturbing
    plaintiffs' initial forum choice;

3. If the balance of private interests is at or near equipoise,
    the court further finds that factors of public interest tip
    the balance in favor of trial in the alternate forum; and

4. The trial judge ensures that plaintiffs can reinstate their
    suit in the alternate forum without undue inconvenience
    or prejudice.

An adequate forum is one that is "capable of providing some
relief for a plaintiff's claims",[3] and such relief does not need to
be perfect, "so long as the forum offers some relief". It is only in
rare circumstances, where the remedy offered by the other forum is
clearly unsatisfactory, that the alternative forum may be regarded as
inadequate. The "private interest" factor entails a consideration of
such matters as: (a) the relative ease of access to sources of proof; (b)
the ability to obtain witnesses; (c) the ability to view the premises
where the accident occurred, if necessary; (d) the availability of
compulsory process for attendance of unwilling witnesses, and
associated costs; and (e) all other practical problems that make trial
of a case easy, expeditious and inexpensive. In weighing the private
interests, a court should examine the contacts between the case and
the United States as a whole, and not just contacts with the state in
which the action had been brought.

The Canadian approach to *forum non conveniens* is somewhat
different. The basic principle is that jurisdiction will be assumed by
a Canadian court where:

a. The foreign defendant is physically present in the
    Canadian jurisdiction at the time of service of the claim; or

b. The defendant attorns either by agreement or by taking steps
    to defend the action; or

c. The Court finds that there is a 'real and substantial
    connection' between the subject matter of the claim and a
    Canadian jurisdiction.

The Supreme Court of Canada has pointed out that a court
should refrain from leaning too instinctively in favour of its

---

3.   *Pinder v Moscetti*, 666 F. Supp. 2d 1313, 1318 (S.D. Fla.2008).

own jurisdiction and, in deciding whether to apply *forum non conveniens*, should consider factors such as (i) the locations of parties and witnesses; (ii) the cost of transferring the case to another jurisdiction or of declining the stay; (iii) the impact of a transfer on the conduct of the litigation or on related or parallel proceedings; (iv) the possibility of conflicting judgments; (v) problems related to the recognition and enforcement of judgments; and (vi) the relative strengths of the connections of the two parties.[4] Ultimately, such decisions come within the reasoned discretion of the trial court, which should not be disturbed by a higher court, absent an error of law or a clear and serious error in the determination of relevant facts occurring at an interlocutory or preliminary stage.

It is common for hotels and resorts in the Caribbean to insert a clause in the contract between the hotel and a visitor to the effect that all disputes between the parties shall be (i) adjudicated exclusively by the local courts and (ii) governed by the laws of the local jurisdiction. For example: "I agree that any claims I may have against the Resort Parties resulting from any events occurring in the Bahamas shall be governed by and construed in accordance with the laws of the Commonwealth of the Bahamas, and further irrevocably agree to the Supreme Court of the Bahamas as the exclusive venue for any such proceedings whatsoever."

The principle established in *M/S Bremen v Zapata Off-Shore Co.*[5] and *Carnival Cruise Lines, Inc. v Shute*,[6] and followed in *Sun Trust Bank v Sun International Hotels Ltd.*,[7] is that a forum selection clause is prima facie valid and should be specifically enforced, unless (i) it was induced by fraud or overreaching; or (ii) there is evidence that the forum was selected to discourage legitimate claims; or (iii) the consumer was not given adequate notice of the forum selection clause; or (iv) the consumer did not have the option of rejecting the forum selection clause without penalty.

Regarding reasonable notice, a forum selection clause will not be held invalid merely because it is contained in a pre-printed form. However, taking into account the concept of inequality of bargaining power between hotel and consumer, the concern, in settings where

---

4.   *Club Resorts Ltd v Van Breda* and *Club Resorts Ltd v Charron* [2012] 1 SCR 572.
5.   407 U.S. 1,9-1015, 92 S. Ct. 1907, and 32 L. Ed. 2d 513 (1972).
6.   499 U.S. 585, 111 S. Ct. 1522, 113 L. Ed. 2d 622 (1991).
7.   184 F. Supp. 2d 1246 S.D. Fla. 2001.

a guest is asked to sign a forum selection clause immediately on arrival and presumably before being given a room key, is whether the terms of the clause were reasonably communicated to them, and whether they realistically had the opportunity to reject those terms without penalty. Thus, in *Son v Kerzner International Resorts Inc.*,[8] it was held that sufficient notice of the forum selection clause had been given to the plaintiff, since the defendant resort had advised her by e-mail sent to her in the United States prior to her arrival in the Bahamas. Further, the plaintiff had stayed at the resort on a previous occasion and had signed an almost identical forum selection clause.

A court in the USA or Canada which accepts jurisdiction over a claim arising out of an accident that has occurred in a Caribbean country will, in adjudicating on liability, most often apply the substantive law of the country in which the alleged tort was committed (the *lex loci delicti*). Thus, for instance, if a Canadian citizen vacationing at a resort in Jamaica sustains injuries in a road accident allegedly caused by the negligent driving of the resort's shuttle bus, an Ontario court that accepts jurisdiction in the matter will normally apply the Jamaican law of negligence. Similarly, if a US citizen suffers a 'slip and fall' accident in a hotel in the Bahamas and brings an action for damages in a court in Florida, the court may apply the Bahamian law of negligence. The application of foreign rules of substantive law in a North American court will require the testimony of an expert in those rules, in order to comply with procedural requirements, but, in any event, a US or Canadian court, including counsel for the litigants, should have little difficulty in interpreting and applying the substantive laws of Commonwealth Caribbean jurisdictions, in view of their mutual common law origins. As was stated by Judge Huck in *Sun Trust Bank v Sun International Hotels Ltd.*,[9] "Courts are often required to decide issues of foreign law. Here, there are no language barriers to the court's understanding of Bahamian law, and Bahamian law is derived from English common law and... recognizes theories of negligence... It has many similarities to Florida law."

In Canada, the application of the *lex loci delicti* in negligence

---

8.   2008 U.S. Dist.Lexis 67482.
9.   Fn 7, supra.

cases was authoritatively established by the Supreme Court in *Tolofson v Jensen,*[10] where La Forest, J stated that, in tort cases with an international element, an important argument in favour of applying the *lex loci delicti,* rather than the *lex fori,* was that: "Ordinary people expect their activities to be governed by the law of the place where they happen to be, and expect that concomitant legal benefits and responsibilities will be defined accordingly... In our modern world of easy travel and with the emergence of a global economic order, chaotic situations would often result if the principle of territorial jurisdiction were not, at least generally, respected."

Liability and Assessment of Damages

Where a North American court applies a foreign law (such as the law of the Bahamas or Jamaica) in adjudicating a tort case over which the court has accepted jurisdiction, it is established that whereas *liability* may be decided according to the foreign law, the *assessment of damages* is a procedural matter and, as such, should be decided according to the law and practice of the forum (the *lex fori*).[11] This is subject to two qualifications: (i) any statutory ceiling on damages is not a procedural but a substantive issue governed by the applicable foreign law; and (ii) although the assessment or quantification of damages is a procedural matter and to be carried out according to the *lex fori,* the applicable *heads* of damage, such as pain and suffering, loss of amenities and loss of earnings, is a substantive issue governed by the applicable foreign law. It is well known that, in Caribbean jurisdictions, the formulation of heads of damage made by Wooding, CJ in *Cornilliac v St Louis*[12] is the one most often relied upon by the courts.

The majority of claims brought in the local courts against hotels and resorts in the Caribbean by persons who have suffered personal injury while staying as guests in such establishments are founded on principles of occupiers' liability. In Jamaica and Barbados, the liability of occupiers of premises to lawful visitors is governed

---

10. (1995) 120 DLR (4th).
11. See Hon. Justice W. Anderson, *Caribbean Private International Law,* 2nd ed. (London: Sweet and Maxwell, 2014), para 12-014; *Harding v Wealands* [2006] UKHL 32, para 51, per Lord Hoffmann.
12. 1965) 7 WIR 491.

by the respective Occupiers' Liability Acts (OLAs), and a similar statute, the Occupiers' and Highway Authorities' Liability Act 1978, is in force in Bermuda. In other Commonwealth Caribbean jurisdictions, such as Antigua and Barbuda, the Bahamas, St Kitts and Nevis, and Trinidad and Tobago, the liability of occupiers is governed by common law negligence principles. St Lucia is a special case, in that liability for civil wrongs is based partly on the St Lucian Civil Code and partly on English common law. St Lucian case law has established that any issue as to whether an occupier, such as a hotel, is in breach of its duty of care to a visitor, such as a hotel guest, will be decided by applying the provisions of the Occupiers' Liability Act, 1957, an English statute which applies in St Lucia by virtue of article 917A of the St Lucian Civil Code, which imported into St Lucia "the Law of England for the time being", including the law of torts.[13]

Both the Jamaican and the Barbadian statutes are closely modelled on the English OLA 1957. Under the Acts, "an occupier of premises owes the same duty, the common duty of care, to all his lawful visitors, except in so far as he is free to and does extend, restrict, modify, or exclude his duty to any visitor by agreement or otherwise" – OLA (Barbados), section 4(1); OLA (Jamaica), section 3(1).

The duty under the Acts is a duty to take such care as in all the circumstances of the case is reasonable to see that the visitor will be reasonably safe in using the premises for the purposes for which he is invited or permitted by the occupier to be there: OLA (Barbados), section 4(2); OLA (Jamaica), section 3(2). Thus, there was a breach of the duty where, for example, a slippery substance left on a shop floor caused a customer to slip and fall; there was no proper system for removing spillages or any warning notices;[14] and where the management of a sports club failed to prevent spectators from sitting on a dangerous wall, with the result that a visitor fell off and sustained injuries from which he died.[15]

'Slip and fall' incidents are by far the most common causes of

---

13.   *Cools v St Lucia Agriculturalists Association Ltd.* (1974) High Court, West Indies Associated States, Petition No. 105 of 1972, per Peterkin, J.

14.   *Gibbs v Cave Shepherd & Co. Ltd.* (1998) High Court, Barbados, No. 35 of 1989.

15.   *Morris v National Sports Club* (1993) Court of Appeal, Bermuda, Civ. App. No. 25 of 1992.

personal injury in the hospitality sector in the Caribbean, and are the most likely to be litigated in local jurisdictions. Many cases in Commonwealth Caribbean courts involve guests who have relied on occupiers' liability principles in order to establish liability for personal injuries suffered through slip and fall incidents at hotels and resorts. Whether an occupier is to be held liable will ultimately depend on the court's assessment of the facts in the individual case, and these are infinitely variable. It seems also that some judges are more inclined to impose liability than others, and are willing to discount actions on the part of claimants, which other judges might regard either as contributory negligence or as conduct sufficient to justify the conclusion that the claimant was solely responsible for their own misfortune.

In Jamaica, the responsibility for slip and fall and similar incidents in hotels and other public places is invariably measured by reference to the Occupiers' Liability Act. As we have seen, under section 3(1) of the OLA, the occupier of premises (that is, the person having possession or control of the premises) owes "the common duty of care" to its lawful visitors, and under section 3(2) that duty is "to take such care as in all the circumstances of the case is reasonable to see that the visitor will be reasonably safe in using the premises for the purposes for which he is invited or permitted by the occupier to be there".

Such a case that occurred in a guest room in a Jamaican hotel is *Thompson v Renmote Mews Ltd.*[16] Jones, J categorized the case as a perfect example of Sod's Law, a maxim reflecting the cynical aspects of life, which he interpreted thus: "If anything can possibly go wrong, it will, and it will happen at the worst possible moment." The defendant had just completed the refurbishing and addition of a new wing at its hotel in New Kingston. The claimant guest slipped and fell while using a bathtub in one of the newly constructed rooms. She had stayed in the old wing of the hotel many times before, without complaint or incident. In an action for negligence and breach of statutory duty under the OLA, the claimant contended that the injury she suffered was due to the defendant's failure to take reasonable care to ensure that anyone using the premises was reasonably safe. Jones, J found for the

---

16.   (2006) Supreme Court, Jamaica, No. CLT-138 of 2001.

claimant. The most crucial evidence was that the bathtub was not constructed with an abrasive or non-slip surface; a non-skid mat was not provided; neither a grab handle at the side. The hotel was held to be in breach of its duty under Section 3 of the Act. Further, there was no evidence of contributory negligence on the claimant's part, and the *volenti non fit injuria* defence under Section 3(7) and (8) was inapplicable.

A similar case, with a similar result, was *Sanfarraro v Bay Roc Ltd.*,[17] where the claimant, a visitor from the United States, slipped and fell inside the bathing area of her hotel room and injured her wrist. Although there was a grab bar, the floor was not fitted with non-slip tiles. This, in the view of Sykes, J, amounted to a failure to take reasonable care to see that the claimant would be reasonably safe in using the shower. He considered that the combination of a grab bar and non-slip tiles was "the minimum necessary to meet the required standard".

Typically, beachfront hotels in the Caribbean have predominantly outdoor settings, unlike the city hotels (as, for example, those in New Kingston or Port of Spain), which may resemble urban establishments in North America and Europe. Caribbean resorts can often be described as sprawling, with extensive grounds which guests must traverse on foot when going from bedroom to reception area, restaurant, bar or swimming pool, and back. Potential hazards may confront guests when negotiating the long pathways and occasional stairs that separate the various resort facilities, particularly after dark.[18] It is of paramount importance that, in order to keep guests safe, stairs and pathways should be well maintained with adequate lighting in perfect working order throughout the establishment.

A path in the grounds of a hotel or resort may be in perfect condition and yet be dangerous if made slippery by rainfall, which many judges in the Caribbean have recognized as a normal state of affairs. Where such an external path has become slippery through rainwater, it may, unless the presence of water is obvious, be incumbent on the occupier to place warning signs to alert visitors

---

17.   (2011) Supreme Court, Jamaica, No. 220 of 2004.
18.   See *Sullivan v Jack Tar Village Management Co.* (2002) High Court, St Kitts/Nevis, No. 203 of 1995

as to the danger. Where such notices are placed, it will be difficult for a visitor who nonetheless slips and falls to succeed in an action against the resort.[19]

When hotel guests fall ill

The 'eggshell skull' principle in negligence applies in the hospitality arena. According to this rule, a tortfeasor "takes its victim as it finds him" , and will be fully liable for the consequences of negligence, notwithstanding that the extent of the claimant's injury was greater than could have been foreseen, owing to some pre-existing weakness or medical condition in the claimant.[20] A Jamaican example is *Crandall v Jamaica Folly Resorts Ltd.*[21] Here, C., a guest at the defendant's hotel, fell from an unstable chair in the hotel bar and sustained injuries which necessitated two operations. C. was obese and, after the second operation, he suffered a heart attack. Ellis, J held that the defendant was in breach of its duty of care under the Occupiers' Liability Act and was fully liable for the consequences, including the heart attack, which was not too remote an injury. The learned judge expressly stated that a defendant must "take his victim as he finds him".

On the other hand, where there has been no negligence or fault on the part of a hotel, the question may arise as to whether such hotel is under any duty to render assistance to a guest who happens to encounter a medical emergency while staying there. This issue does not appear to have arisen in the jurisprudence of England or, by extension, any of the Caribbean jurisdictions in which English-derived tort law is applied. It was, however, considered in *Abramson v Ritz-Carlton Hotel Co.*,[22] a case before the District Court in New Jersey, in which a visitor from the United States suffered a fatal heart attack while dining in a restaurant at the defendant's hotel in Jamaica. The deceased's widow, as executrix of his estate and on her own behalf, brought a wrongful death action against the hotel, asserting that it breached a duty of care owed to her husband

19.   See *Hepburn v Hutchison Lucaya Ltd.* (2012) Supreme Court, The Bahamas, No. FP 34 of 2006.

20.   *Smith v Leech Brain & Co. Ltd.* [1962] 2 QB 405.

21.   (1997) Supreme Court, Jamaica, No. 1988/C204; (1999) Court of Appeal, Jamaica, Civ. App No. 102 of 1998.

22.   D.C. Civil No. 09-cv-03264 (2012).

by failing to properly maintain the medical equipment it provided during this emergency.

The District Court considered that a hotel's duty to a guest in need is limited to summoning medical help and, until it arrives, providing basic first aid. This limited duty was set out in the *Restatement (Second) of Torts* § 314A, which provides that an innkeeper is under a duty to its guests to "take reasonable action … to give them first aid after it knows or has reason to know that they are ill or injured, and to care for them until they can be cared for by others", and the commentary to § 314A states: "The defendant will seldom be required to do more than give such first aid as he reasonably can, and take reasonable steps to turn the sick man over to a physician, or to those who will look after him and see that medical assistance is obtained."

In this case, there had been no breach of that duty, since the undisputed evidence showed that the hotel discharged its duty by immediately calling the medical centre for an ambulance and providing basic first aid until help arrived.

Further, the court rejected Mrs A.'s claim that she booked her room in reliance on the understanding that the hotel had state-of-the-art medical services in case of emergency. The court pointed out that the plaintiff had not asserted any breach of contract or fraud: rather, her contention seemed to be that the hotel created a reasonable expectation that such equipment would be available, resulting in an alleged legal duty to maintain it in good working order. However, Mrs A. had "cited neither case law nor evidence to support her claim".

Loss of guests' property

Exclusion clauses are commonly inserted in written contracts in order to absolve a party from liability for certain types of harm. They may also be effectively incorporated into a contract by way of notice, for example, by a sign in a hotel car park, "All cars parked at owners' risk."[23] However, such incorporation must take place before or contemporaneously with the making of the contract. Where a prospective customer turns up at a hotel without a reservation, looking for accommodation, the reception clerk will check the

---

23.   See *Thornton v Shoe Lane Parking Ltd.* [1971] 1 All ER 686.

room availability chart and inform the customer whether or not they have a vacancy. If the visitor responds by saying they will take the room, this is an acceptance, and a contract for accommodation will have been formed. Certain registration formalities will then follow. Thereafter, any attempt to include further terms in the contract by means of a notice displayed in the guest's room will be ineffective.

In the well-known case of *Olley v Marlborough Court Ltd.*,[24] a married couple arrived at a hotel. They paid for the accommodation and went to their room. On the wall there was a notice: "The proprietors will not hold themselves responsible for articles lost or stolen unless handed to the manager for safe custody." When they decided to go out, the wife closed and locked the door, taking the key to reception. A thief took the key and stole some of the wife's property from the room. The couple sued the hotel for damages with regard to the stolen property. The hotel tried to rely on the notice in the room as a term of the booking contract that exempted it from liability. It was held that the contract was completed at the reception desk and no subsequent notice could affect the claimants' rights. The notice was not sufficient to incorporate the exclusion clause in the booking contract.

The contractual position must be seen in the light of the common law rule that a hotel is strictly liable for the loss of property brought to the hotel by a guest, unless the hotel can prove that the loss was caused as a result of the negligence of the guest. This rule has been modified by legislation in some Caribbean jurisdictions, such as Jamaica, Barbados, Antigua and Barbuda, and Trinidad and Tobago. This legislation is modelled on an English statute, the Hotel Proprietors' Act 1956.

The duty of hoteliers is set out in the various Hotel Proprietors Acts,[25] (in Jamaica, by the Hotelkeepers Liability Act). In England, a hotel's liability is restricted to those guests who have purchased sleeping accommodation, but in the Caribbean legislation liability is towards all guests, including those coming only for food and

---

24. [1949] 1 KB 532.
25. See, for example, Hotel Proprietors Act, Cap. 309 (Barbados); HPA, Cap. 203 (Antigua and Barbuda); HPA, Cap. 15:21 (St Lucia); HPA, Chap. 87:55 (Trinidad and Tobago); Hotelkeeper's Liability Act, 1950 (Jamaica).

drink. An important provision of the Acts is that the hotel's liability is limited to relatively small amounts: for example, in Antigua and Barbuda, to $500 for a single item and $1,000 on aggregate.

Hotels must display a prominent sign confirming the extent of their duty held under the Acts in order to benefit from the low payment limits. A difficulty for hotel proprietors arises (i) if it is proved that the loss of a guest's property was caused by the negligence of the hotel proprietor or its employees; or (ii) where the property is lost after being deposited with the hotel for safekeeping; or (iii) where the hotel refuses to accept the property for safekeeping. Such circumstances are problematic for hotel proprietors since, where a guest's property is lost in these circumstances, they are not entitled to the protection of the payment limits set down in the Acts, and they would be liable for the full value of any property lost. This would be particularly concerning should very valuable items go missing.

Hotel proprietors may seek to limit their statutory exposure, first, by ensuring high standards of security; second, by refusing the safekeeping of items of "exceptional character". In the latter case, the proprietors need to ascertain whether they have a reasonable excuse for refusing to accept valuable items for safekeeping. If an item is so valuable that to accept it would be to leave the hotel exposed to a high degree of expenditure in the event of its loss, the hotel should be entitled to refuse to accept the item.

Hotel proprietors may also seek to exclude their liability under the Act by inserting a limitation clause into the booking contract (as the hotel tried and failed to do in the *Marlborough Court* case). This would limit their liability to make good the loss of high-value items caused by negligence of the hotel staff. However, in some jurisdictions a contractual clause limiting a hotel's liability will be subject to consumer protection legislation, such as the Consumer Protection Act (Jamaica), section 37 (2), which provides that a service provider may exclude or restrict its liability for negligence only where the term is "reasonable", as defined by section 43.

Package Tours

Visitors to Caribbean destinations may make their travel and accommodation bookings independently, that is, by making both flight and hotel reservations online through one of the many online booking sites, or they may book flights online and make their hotel reservations separately by fax, email or telephone. Such independent booking is particularly convenient for the business traveller, but the vacationer, especially one who is travelling with a family, may find it cheaper and more convenient to purchase a package holiday. Tour operator is the term used to describe a company that organizes package holidays, which are advertised in the company's brochure and sold to consumers, often through travel agents.

In a package holiday contract, the tour operator will agree to provide air transportation, transfers to and from the hotel or resort, and accommodation (with or without meals) at the chosen resort for one or two weeks, as advertised in the tour operator's printed or website brochure. Typically, package holidays will be sold subject to the booking conditions set out on the tour operator's website. In addition to provisions relating to matters such as travel and health documents, holiday insurance and cancellation charges, the booking conditions will normally contain a term to the effect that the tour operator accepts no responsibility for services or facilities which do not form part of the holiday agreement or are not advertised on the tour operator's website. In particular, excursions, tours, activities or other events that the customer may book or pay for through the tour operator's concierge service or otherwise will not form part of the package holiday provided by the tour operator, and the tour operator will not be responsible for anything that happens during the course of such activities. Lastly, the services and facilities included in the package holiday will be deemed to be provided with reasonable skill and care if they comply with any applicable local regulations or local standards.

A tour operator contemplating the inclusion of a new destination or tour in its brochure should, wherever possible, arrange a site visit, so as to assess the potential risks that could be faced by customers purchasing package holidays at the particular resort. This is because a tour operator may be held liable for injury suffered by a customer through some dangerous feature or state of affairs at a resort which ought to have been observed by the tour operator's representative and remedied by management before customers were sent there. In the absence of a site visit, in some instances the reports and recommendations of third parties may be sufficient, provided the third parties' standards and expectations are on a similar level to those of the tour operator.

A tour operator, when offering a package tour for sale, should ensure that the whole package measures up to the details given to the customer at the pre-booking stage. If the package falls short of the standards the customer was promised, the tour operator could be liable for breach of contract.

Any risk assessment undertaken by a tour operator should be documented, retained on file, and checked regularly to ensure that it is kept up to date. Such documentation is commonly requested by groups such as school parties or sports teams. Another advantage of documented risk assessment is that it may be vital evidence in defending claims brought by customers against the tour operator, and it may be demanded by insurers or by third party representatives.

Risk assessment headings in the Caribbean may include such matters as the safety of local transport, the safety of beaches and adjacent ocean, the likelihood of contracting disease, the quality and security of accommodation, security and crime prevention, and the provision of wholesome food and drink.

The question of beach and ocean safety came to the fore in *Jones v Sunworld Ltd.*,[26] in which a visitor to the Maldives drowned close to shore when he stepped into an unseen depression in the sea bed and, being a poor swimmer, was unable to swim back to the surface. The holiday destination in this case was a tiny island surrounded by a lagoon, and one of the issues in the case was whether the beach and lagoon, and the use of them, was within the holiday package. The court accepted evidence that the answer to the question ultimately depended on the wording of the tour operator's brochure and the terms and conditions referred to therein, but that the practice of the tour operators' industry was to regard beaches and the sea as outside a package, even where it was foreseeable that purchasers of the package would spend much of their time on a particular beach. However, the present case was unusual in that there was no swimming pool on the island and the holiday brochure had emphasized the attractions of the lagoon, which was accepted by both parties to have been a major selling

---

26.   [2003] EWHC 591.

point for the resort. Moreover, although the lagoon was a natural phenomenon, it was an integral part of the resort over which the resort's owners had legal control by virtue of a lease from the Maldivian government. As Field, J commented, it was "virtually inconceivable that a holiday maker would stay on Fun Island and not go into the lagoon to enjoy the coolness and clarity of the water". The resort management knew that at certain places in the otherwise shallow lagoon there were "pools" of deeper water up to ten feet deep. Given that the lagoon was to be treated as an integral part of the resort over which the owners had control, the further question was whether the defendant tour operator was under a duty to assess the lagoon's safety before sending its customers to the resort. Field, J took the view that the defendant was not obliged to assess the safety of the lagoon in the same way as it would have to assess the safety of the buildings and paved areas on the island, which could relatively easily be inspected for fire safety and other risks of physical harm. However, the defendant ought to have undertaken a visual inspection of the lagoon, to enquire of the resort's management whether they were aware of any particular features of the lagoon that might have a bearing on safety, and to inspect the records kept by the resort pertaining to any accidents reported to have occurred in the lagoon. A visual inspection of the lagoon would have revealed areas where the water was a much darker blue than the surrounding water, which would indicate pools of deeper water. However, Field, J took the view that there would have been no duty to warn the claimant about the pools, as adult holidaymakers must be taken to know that the sea bed is not even, and that there is nothing unusual about changes in depth. Further, it was significant that in the preceding ten years no guest had reported to management any difficulty with any of the pools. In the result, the defendant was held not liable for the guest's death.

Building Code Infractions

In this type of case, a visitor suffers injury because of a defective fixture in a hotel or resort. A notable example is *Japp v Virgin Holidays*,[27] where an English visitor to Barbados came into contact with the glass balcony door in her hotel room. The glass shattered,

---

27.   [2013] EWCA Civ 1371.

causing her severe injury. She brought a successful action in the
county court in England against the tour operator for damages for
personal injury, and the Court of Appeal upheld that decision.

The main issue in the case was whether the hotel had complied
with local standards in Barbados in relation to the type of glass
used for the balcony doors. If the answer to that question was in
the negative, then the tour operator would be liable for the harm
suffered by the claimant by virtue of reg 15 of the Package Tours
Regulations, 1992 (UK), which provided that a tour operator "is
liable to the consumer for the proper performance of the obligations
under the contract, irrespective of whether such obligations are to
be performed by that other party or by other suppliers of services".
Evidence as to local standards was given by reference to the
Barbados Building Code, 1993 edition, published by the Barbados
National Standards Institution. This code set out "technical
requirements and standards for the design and construction of
buildings in respect of issues concerning structural sufficiency and
durability, fire safety, health and amenity, which are regarded as
essential minimum provisions in the public interest". With respect
to doors, section 6.5 of the code provided that "measures shall be
taken to reduce the hazards of human impact on glass panels and
glazed doors by...the use of laminated or toughened safety glass,
organic-coated safety glass or wired safety glass". It was further
provided that safety glass should be installed in all doors with a
glass area exceeding 0.5 m and in all unframed glass doors.

It was accepted that the balcony doors in the *Japp* case fell within
the above characteristics, and that they did not comply with the
Code, as the glass used was not safety glass but annealed float glass,
the dangers of which, according to the county court judge, had
been known for many years. There was therefore non-compliance
with local standards, for which the defendant tour operator was
liable.[28]

---

28.   It was also held in this case that compliance with local standards is to be assessed at
      the date of construction of the building and not at the date of the accident. Therefore,
      it will be sufficient for a hotel to show that it complied with the building code that
      was current at the date of design and construction, and there is no duty to retrofit,
      or "to engage in a constant process of updating existing buildings, by building or
      refurbishment, so as to reflect changes in standards".

Conclusion

Varying aspects must be considered when applying negligence principles to the hospitality industry in the Caribbean, some of which have a contractual element, and the fact that most visitors to Caribbean hotels and resorts are overseas residents adds to the uncertainties surrounding legal liability. Personal injury is by far the most likely type of harm, giving rise to tort actions in hospitality and tourism. Loss of property is another potential source of liability. Claims brought by package holiday tourists who suffer injury are likely to be settled out of court, or be decided according to the terms of the package holiday agreement between tour operator and customer, as determined by courts overseas, and subject to statutory regulations governing such agreements. The result is that most claims in the hospitality sector will not come before Caribbean courts; accordingly, it should not be assumed that the paucity of cases decided in the local courts is an indication of the rarity of incidents and accidents causing injury.

CHAPTER 9

Harm to Reputation is a 'Serious' Thing: Lessons for Jamaica from Recent Developments in Defamation Laws in Australia and in England and Wales

Coleen B. Lewis

Within the last year the defamation laws of England and Wales, and Australia have undergone siginifcant developments, which address their approach to the common law principle of presumption of harm and its impact on the threshold for initiating actions. This reflects an effort to achieving a more reasonable approach to balancing the competing interests of protecting one's right to freedom of expression with another's right to a protection of their reputation. How to properly address the presumption of harm and actionability of defamation claims were among the issues debated during the revision of the Jamaican defamation law framework, which culminated with the proclamation of the Jamaica Defamation Act, 2013.[1] This article argues that it would be worthwhile for the Jamaican legislature to take into consideration the developments in the defamation laws of England and Wales, and in Australia when next the revision of the Jamaica Defamation Act (JDA) is being undertaken. This would auger well in achieving one of its aims of ensuring that unreasonable limits are not imposed on the right to freedom of expression.

Low Threshold: Problem of the Presumption of Harm

The JDA, 2013 was enacted after a period of review and critique of previous defamation laws, and pursuant to, inter alia, the findings and recommendations arising from and as condensed mainly in two government commissioned reports namely the Small Committee's *Review of Jamaica's Defamation Laws*[2] and Mark Stephens'

---

1. A bill entitled an "Act to Repeal the Defamation Act and the Libel and Slander Act and make new provisions relating to the tort of defamation".
2. The Small Committee Report was specifically commissioned by Prime Minister Bruce Golding and chaired by Justice Hugh Small, 29 February 2008.

Reform of Jamaican Libel Law,[3] (together referred to as the Commissioned Reports).[4] The Commissioned Reports highlighted aspects of the pre-2013 Jamaican defamation framework which were deemed as problematic because they adversely affected and exerted a disproportionate chilling effect on the right to freedom of expression. Those aspects included the common law principle of presumption of harm. Despite the aim of the tort of defamation being to strike a balance between a person's right to freedom of expression and the protection of reputation, the common law principle of presumption of harm was identified as one of the ways in which the tort of defamation reflected an imbalance in favour of the protection of reputation.

The common law principle of presumption of harm arose from the fact that in order to bring an action for the tort of defamation, the claimant only had the burden to prove:

- a defamatory expression was published;[5]
- the defamatory expression was "of and concerning" the claimant; and[6]
- the defamatory expression was published to a third person by the defendant.[7]

Proof of harm by the claimant was therefore generally not required for a publication to be actionable as defamatory but harm to reputation, in general, was presumed.[8] English scholar

3. Mark Stephens, *Reform of Jamaican Libel Law: Briefing Prepared for the Joint Select Legislative Committee of the House of Parliament* (20 September 2010).
4. Also influencing the final provisions of the JDA, 2013 were the stakeholders' responses to the Commissioned Reports and the Joint Select Legislative Committee submissions to Parliament.
5. *Sim v Stretch* [1936] 2 All ER 1237, 1240. (Lord Atkin).
6. *Knupffer v London Express Newspaper Ltd.* [1944] AC 116.
7. See for example *Reynolds v Times Newspapers Ltd. and others* [1998] 3 WLR 862.
8. The issue of presumption of harm is linked to the classification of the types of defamatory publications. As noted in the Commissioned Reports, in both Jamaica and England there were two main categories of defamation present in the law. Defamatory expressions which were in a permanent form, for example in writing, were classified as a libel. In respect of this type of defamatory expression, a claimant was able to bring an action without having to prove any harm to his reputation was caused by its publication. There was, therefore, a presumption of harm. Proof of actual harm or special damage was only required where the defamatory expression was classified as a slander. Slander refers to defamatory expressions which were in a transient form, for example where the expressions are made orally. For this category of expression to be actionable, generally there was no presumption of harm. However, in a limited number of prescribed special instances, slander was actionable per se, and proof of harm by the claimant was also not required.

Jones noted that this presumption proved to be problematic as it represented a shifting of the legal burden of proof in a civil action from the claimant to the defendant and this amounted to "reversal of the natural laws of justice".[9] This presumption contributed to the scale being tipped adversely against the defendant, shifting the burden of proof to the defendant in claims of defamation.

The Commissioned Reports also noted that an effect of the operation of the presumption of harm principle was to create a low threshold for claims of defamation to be made. Accordingly, this significantly attributed for a prevalence of frivolous, trivial, and unjustified claims being brought, especially by those who wished to silence any defendant from criticising or questioning their actions. In particular, the threat of defamation proceedings was noted as having the effect of deterring the press from performing their role of reporting on public officials' discharge of their public duties to ensure and demand accountability and transparency. This view was expressed by the Press Association of Jamaica, which explained that this low threshold had caused the press to engage in excessive self-censoring in fear of the threat of a defamation claim.[10]

Despite the range of recommendations made regarding the approaches that could be taken to address this issue, no mechanism to address the issue of presumption of harm and the low threshold for the actionability of claims of defamation was included in the JDA.[11] This has meant that persons remain vulnerable to frivolous, trivial claims being brought against them. The possibility for such claims means the balance/scale remains tilted in favour of the protection of the right to reputation in defamation proceedings in Jamaica. The prevalence of such types of claims would be even more harmful in this era where persons are able to express themselves more than before, for example by utilizing various media, internet

---

9.   Mariette Jones, "The Defamation Act 2013: A Free Speech Perspective" (2019) 7–8.
10.   http://pressassociationjamaica.org/wp-content/uploads/2010/08/02.-Submission-to-Joint-Select-Committee-MAJ-PAJ-Defamation-Laws.pdf.
11.   Such recommendations may be found notably in the Commissioned Reports, a joint letter of response by the Press Association of Jamaica and the Media Association of Jamaica during the reform process. Among the recommendations made was the adoption of a defence of triviality as existed in Australia's National Uniformed Defamation Laws. The Special Joint Select Committee of the Jamaican parliament, however, rejected the recommendation that there be a defence of triviality as it posited that issue of triviality of harm went to the issue of damages.

applications and platforms. Accordingly, and arguably, persons are even more susceptible to frivolous, baseless, unmeritorious, or trivial claims of defamation being brought against them in relation to statements "made in jocular circumstances to a few people".[12]

Shared Problem: England and Wales, and Australia

The problem of the presumption of harm is not unique to Jamaica's defamation law framework. Notably, as part of the process of deliberating on an appropriate approach to address those problematic aspects of the pre-2013 Jamaican defamation laws, the approaches adopted in the defamation laws of England and Wales, and Australia, inter alia, were examined. This was because, as the Commissioned Reports acknowledged, as a former colony of England, Jamaica's defamation framework (as well as Australia's) stemmed from the English defamation laws. This shared common law origins meant that the principles of defamation laws of Australia and England and Wales were largely the same and consequently shared many of the same problems.[13] Accordingly, as explained in the Stephens Report, "the colonial legacy ... of such laws means that...criticisms [of the pre-2013 English defamation laws] can be fairly said to be Commonwealth-wide'.[14] Despite the fact that, as Australian academic Rolph similarly noted, the problems faced in Australia's and England's defamation laws were analogous,[15] varying approaches were taken within their respective defamation laws to address the shared similar issue of the presumption of harm and low threshold for actionability of claims of defamation. Specifically, as at the date of enactment of the JDA, the approach adopted in the Australia was the triviality defence as set out in section 33 of the Defamation Act, 2005, while in England and Wales, the serious harm threshold was introduced by section 1 of their Defamation Act, 2013. Recently, these approaches underwent significant developments in the respective Australian and English defamation laws. The article, therefore, examines the development

---

12.   *Morosi v Mirror Newspapers Ltd.* [1977] 2 NSWLR 749, 800.
13.   Mark Stephens, "Reform of Jamaican Libel Law," Briefing prepared for the Joint Select Legislative Committee of the House of Parliament, 20 September 2010, 3–5.
14.   Stephens, *Reform of Jamaican Libel Law* 3.
15.   David Rolph, "A Critique of the Defamation Act 2013: Lessons for and from Australian Defamation Law Reform," *Communications Law* 21, no. 4 (2016): 129.

of the approach taken in the respective defamation laws of Australia and England to address the common law principle of presumption of harm and the actionability of defamatory publications and trivial defamation claims. Section 35(2) of the JDA, the first review of the Act, should be conducted no less than five years after its commencement. However, more than five years have passed, and no review has been done. Accordingly, the following sections will examine what lessons may be gleaned from these developments in England and Australia and whether they may provide a road map for any revision that could be made to the JDA.

The English Approach and the Presumption of Harm

The recent Supreme Court decision in *Lachaux v AOL (UK), Independent Print Ltd. & Evening Standard Ltd.*[16] represents the latest and an important development in England's approach to addressing the issue of presumption of harm and the actionability of claims of defamation. The justices were tasked with interpreting section 1 of England's Defamation Act, 2013 and settling the dispute of whether it abolished the presumption of harm and the actionability of claims of defamation. According to section 1:

1. A statement is not defamatory unless its publication has caused or is likely to cause serious harm to the reputation of the claimant.

2. For the purposes of this section, harm to the reputation of a body that trades for profit is not "serious harm" unless it has caused or is likely to cause the body serious financial loss.

In order to appreciate the significance of this current development in the Supreme Court decision in *Lachaux*, it is useful to examine the approach to addressing the issue of presumption of harm, which paved the way to the inclusion section 1 in England's Defamation Act, 2013.

Background to Recent Development of English Approach

Two common law cases, namely *Jameel (Yousef) v Dow Jones & Co. Inc.*,[17] and *Thornton v Telegraph Media Group Ltd.*,[18] became

---

16.   [2019] UKSC 27, [2020] AC 612.
17.   [2005] EWCA Civ 75, [2005] QB 946.
18.   [2010] EWHC 1414 (QB), [2011] 1 WLR 1985.

seminal for paving the way to the current English approach to the issue of harm and its impact on the actionability of publications. In *Jameel*, the English court's approach was to assess the usefulness of the remedy sought for the harm suffered to reputation and consider what would be best in the interest of better administration of justice. Here a claim of defamation was brought against Dow Jones, as publishers, in relation to an article posted online. In response, Dow Jones applied for the matter to be struck out as an abuse of process and opined that the action had no reasonable prospect of success. The Court of Appeal stated that to determine whether to strike out an action the court must take into consideration the benefits of proceeding with the trial and the remedy sought for the harm inflicted to their reputation versus the cost of the proceedings. The Court of Appeal concluded that the action would not bring about the remedy of vindication to the claimant for the harm inflicted to their reputation in other jurisdictions, such as Saudi Arabia, and that any judgment given by the court was likely to be unenforceable in Saudi Arabia. Such a judgment, therefore, would not amount to a "declaration to all the world that the allegation was false".[19] In light of this, the action was struck out.

Thornton was the next seminal case which devised principles that were applied to the issue of harm and actionability of claims of defamation. Here, the court introduced the threshold of substantiality. In the *Thornton* case, a claim of defamation was brought in relation to the publication of a review of the claimant's book in *The Daily Telegraph* as well as on the *Telegraph's* website. The claimant alleged that she was defamed by the assertions that she had engaged in the practice of "copy approval" in interviews. Dr Thornton also claimed that it was also defamatory of the reviewer to have asserted that she falsely stated in her book that she conducted an interview with the reviewer as part of her research for her book.

In determining whether the statements were actionable as defamatory, High Court judge Tugendhat, J revisited the various tests established in past cases of what constituted a defamatory statement[20] and concluded that these tests always incorporated a

---

19.   *Jameel* [67] per Lord Phillips.
20.   For example, *Sim v Stretch* [1936] 2 All ER 1237 per Lord Atkin, *Youssoupoff v Metro-*

threshold of seriousness.[21] He stated that "whatever the definition of 'defamatory' is adopted, it must include a qualification or threshold of seriousness, so as to exclude trivial claims".[22] He asserted that it would be an unjustified infringement of the right to freedom of expression to impose liability in cases where the expression had inflicted minimal or no damage upon the claimant's reputation.[23] To impose liability in such circumstances would therefore be contrary to the right to freedom of expression, protected under the European Convention on Human Rights Article 10.2.[24] In light of this, Tugendhat, J asserted that in order for an expression to be actionable as defamatory, it must be one that "substantially affects in an adverse manner the attitude of other people towards him or has a tendency to do so".[25] This judgment introduced a threshold of substantiality to be met before a claim could be actionable.[26] This was significant considering the pre-existing common law presumption that harm had been suffered upon publication.

It was against the background of these principles developed in the cases of *Jameel* and *Thornton* that the current English legislative approach to the issue of presumption of harm and the actionability of claims of defamation was formulated and included in section 1 of the 2013 Act. According to the Explanatory Notes to the Act, section 1 "builds on" addressing "the question of what is sufficient to establish that a statement is defamatory".[27] Additionally, the revised approach built on and followed through on the recommendations which were outlined in the Joint Parliamentary Committee 2011 Report on the Draft Defamation Bill.[28] In this report, it was stated that the new legislation's focus was to modernize the English defamation laws and, in the end, to strike the correct balance between the conflicting interests of protecting freedom of expression

---

     Goldwyn-Mayer Pictures Ltd. (1934) 50 TLR 581,587, per Slesser, LJ; *Berkoff v Burchill* [1996] 4 All ER 1008 per Neill, LJ and *Ecclestone v Telegraph Media Group* [2009] EWHC 2779 (QB) per Sharp, J.

21.   *Thornton*, 89.
22.   Ibid.
23.   Ibid.
24.   Ibid., 90.
25.   Ibid., 96.
26.   Ibid.
27.   Explanatory Notes to the Defamation Act, 2013 (England).
28.   Joint Committee on the Defamation Bill, *First Report: Draft Defamation Bill* [2010–12] HL Paper 203 /HC930.

and protecting reputation, whether offline or online.[29] In pursuance of this goal, the minister with responsibility for the bill, the Rt Hon Lord McNally, indicated that the first step to discourage frivolous trivial claims was to raise the threshold for a statement to be considered defamatory.[30] This would dispose of claims which take up the courts' and parties' time and resources in a trial and which ultimately only serve to adversely and unjustifiably put a chill on the exercise of the right to freedom of expression.[31] Additionally, in the UK government's response to the Joint Committee on the Draft Defamation Bill, which was presented to parliament by the Lord Chancellor and Secretary of State for Justice, it was reiterated that the "Government's intention in introducing a 'substantial harm test' was to reflect the current law as articulated by the courts [and] have the effect of strengthening the law…to discourage trivial and unfounded claims."[32] However, after much consultation with the interested stakeholders, parties, the public, and the government, instead of a substantial harm test, the section 1 "serious harm" test was crafted and included in the Defamation Act of England.[33]

Recent Development in English Approach

Since the enactment of section 1, there have been contrasting views on its impact on the presumption of harm and the actionability of claims of defamation. The UK Supreme Court's decision in *Lachaux,* delivered in 2019, settled this debate and its judgment represents a most significant development for defamation actions. This case arose in respect of the publication of five articles that contained allegations against the claimant that, inter alia, he subjected his ex-wife to abuse; he exploited the legal system to discriminate against her; and he falsely brought prosecution proceedings against her for kidnapping their son. The claimant asserted that these statements/ articles were defamatory of him. In the trial court,[34] Warby, J

---

29. Ibid., 4.
30. HL Deb 9 October 2012. Vol. 739 col. 934.
31. Ibid.
32. Ministry of Justice, *Government's Response to the Report of the Joint Committee on the Draft Defamation Bill* Cm 8295 (2012) [41].
33. Among the stakeholders were newspaper journalists and editors; writers and publishers; libel lawyers; academics and interest groups; current and former government law officers.
34. [2015] EWHC 2242 (QB), [2016] QB 402.

construed that section 1(1) of the Act required claimants to provide proof of serious harm, as the presumption of harm which previously obtained at common law was abolished. Warby, J, delivering the decision, indicated, however, that in the appropriate case, likely serious harm may be inferred, having taken into consideration all the circumstances of the matter. Based on this interpretation, the High Court held that, in the circumstances of the case before it, the words "complained of" met the 'serious harm' threshold and, as such, was actionable.

The High Court's decision and its interpretation of the impact of the section 1 'serious harm' threshold, however, were appealed by the defendant. The Court of Appeal agreed that the section 1 serious harm requirement was more than 'substantial' harm threshold as developed in *Thornton*. However, the Court of Appeal did not concur with the High Court's construction that the common law presumption of harm was removed by section 1(1) of the Act and that positive proof of serious reputational harm was required. The Court of Appeal asserted that "the seriousness of the harm caused to the claimant's reputation by the publication depended on the inherent tendency of the words".[35] Nevertheless, the Court of Appeal concluded that the High Court's decision was correct in its findings that the statements published were defamatory, and serious reputational harm had been caused to Mr Lachaux by the publication of the statements.[36] The defendants appealed the Court of Appeal's findings. The Supreme Court was, therefore, tasked with determining the correct interpretation and significance of section 1 of Act in relation to actionability of claims of defamation.

The Supreme Court, on surveying the history of the presumption of harm principle and the decisions in *Jameel* and *Thornton*, disagreed with the Court of Appeal's conclusion that the common law presumption of harm was not removed by section 1(1) of the Act. While noting that "there is a presumption that a statute does not alter the common law unless it so provides, either expressly or by necessary implication", the Supreme Court explained that it was evident that it was parliament's intention to change the law.[37]

35.   *Lachaux* (SC) [20].
36.   *Lachaux* [2017] EWCA Civ 1334 [102].
37.   *Lachaux* (SC) [13].

To illustrate this point, the Supreme Court referred to the preamble of the Act, which expressly states it is "an Act to amend the law of defamation".[38] To further illustrate this conclusion, the Supreme Court pointed out that the presumption of harm to reputation principle, which existed at common law, did not include that the harm was also presumed to be 'serious'.[39] The Supreme Court further asserted that the Court of Appeal's interpretation that "the seriousness of the harm caused to the claimant's reputation by the publication depended on the inherent tendency of the words" gave "little or no effect to the language of section 1 and was contradictory".[40] Additionally, the Supreme Court pointed out that if the Court of Appeal construction was correct, the claimant would not have to provide "evidence of the actual impact of the publication", and that the common law rule survived.[41] The justices of the Supreme Court further explained the mischief in the law, which section 1 seeks to resolve, was attributable to the fact that harm to reputation was presumed from the words alone. That approach gave rise to liability even where the harm was less than 'serious' and very different from any harm to reputation which could be established in fact.[42] The Supreme Court expounded that, in order to ascertain the effect of the statement on another's reputation and whether the serious harm threshold is proved, among the factors that a court may take into consideration are the scale of the publications, specifically whether the statement was published to a small number of people; or to people who did not believe it; or possibly to people among whom the claimant had no reputation to be harmed.[43]

The Supreme Court noted that the trial judge, Warby, J, had based his finding of serious harm on the circumstances of publication which included:

1. the scale of the publications;
2. the fact that the statements complained of had come to the attention of at least one identifiable person in the United

---

38. Ibid.
39. ibid.
40. Ibid., 20.
41. Ibid.
42. Ibid., 16.
43. Ibid.

Kingdom who knew Mr Lachaux; and

3. that they were likely to have come to the attention of others who either knew him or would come to know him in future; and

4. the gravity of the statements themselves.[44]

Based on a "consideration of the combined effect of the meaning of the words, the situation of Mr Lachaux, the aforementioned circumstances of publication and the inherent probabilities",[45] the Supreme Court agreed with Justice Warby's decision that Lachaux had successfully established the threshold of serious harm to his reputation. The court also emphasized that the section 1 harm referred to harm to reputation and that injury to feelings was not covered in the section 1 harm.

Accordingly, from the Justices of the Supreme Court's judgment, that the lessons to be learnt is that section 1(1) of the Act:

1. introduced a new threshold of serious harm which did not exist before;

2. removed the common law presumption of harm;

3. meant that a statement could not be considered to be actionable as defamatory unless it "has caused or is likely to cause" harm which was serious;

4. reference to serious harm was not referring to the publication per se but rather to the consequences of the publication;

5. and serious harm is proved only by referring to the effect that the statement actually had on the reputation of the claimant.

This is a proposition of fact which is dependent on the "inherent tendency of the words", combined with the impact the defamatory statement actually had on the persons to whom the statement was published,[46] and the seriousness requirement "supplements the common law".[47]

This judgment thereby establishes that claims relating to statements which do not cause harm or is not likely to cause harm would be deemed trivial and not actionable as defamatory. Furthermore, the placing of this burden on the claimant to also

---

44.   Ibid., 21.
45.   Ibid.
46.   Ibid.
47.   Ibid., 19.

prove serious harm in order to bring an action contributes to stemming frivolous, trivial claims of defamation from being brought. As noted by Rolph, the inclusion of a requirement for serious harm was the "biggest balancing tool of the Defamation Act 2013 [of England and Wales] introduced to rebalance the rights of reputation and freedom of expression and, in doing so, make[s] it harder for claimants to bring frivolous unmeritorious defamation cases".[48]

Australian Approach and the Presumption of Harm

In 2020, the approach to the issue of the presumption of harm and the actionability of claims of defamation was also revised in the Australian defamation framework. To better appreciate what motivated the recent revision, it is useful to examine the approach previously employed to address the issue of presumption of harm.

At the time the Jamaica defamation framework was being reviewed and revised, the legislative approach employed in Australia to address the issue of harm that was most relevant was the triviality defence, as set out in section 33 of its Defamation Act: "It is a defence to the publication of defamatory matter if the defendant proves that the circumstances of publication were such that the plaintiff was unlikely to sustain any harm."

The triviality defence was adopted from and substantially based on the similarly termed defence found in section 13 of the Defamation Act, 1974 of New South Wales (now repealed). Section 13 of that Act provided that "it is a defence that the circumstances of the publication of the matter complained of were such that the person defamed was not likely to suffer harm".

As such, the purpose of the Australian 2005 section 33 triviality defence could be gleaned by reference to purpose of the 1974 section 13 triviality defence. According to the NSW Court of Appeal in *Chappell*, as explained by Moffit, president of the court: "The apparent purpose of section 13 and its predecessors, despite some difference in their terms and application, was to give a defence to and hence discourage actions for trivial defamation."[49]

Extrapolating therefrom, the purpose of the 2005 section 33

48.   Rolph, "Critique," 116, 122.
49.   *Chappell v Mirror Newspapers Ltd.*, 68, 647.

triviality defence and the success of this approach is therefore linked to the extent to which persons are discouraged from bringing defamation claims, where the victim was unlikely to sustain any harm to his reputation from the publication. As noted by leading Australian defamation law expert, David Rolph, this section 33 triviality defence approach did not yield much positive results or relief for the defendant in stemming the instances of frivolous and trivial claims. This was largely due to how strictly the requirements of section 33 were construed by the courts, as well as the stage of the proceedings at which the issue of harm was considered. This contributed to making the bar to be satisfied by the defendant very high.[50]

The high bar the defendant had to meet in order to successfully rely on the triviality defence could be gleaned from the decision of the Court of Appeal of Victoria in *Barrow v Bolt*.[51] *Barrow* was an appeal by the claimant from a Supreme Court of Victoria decision on the ground, inter alia, that the trial judge had erred in dismissing the claim of defamation by finding that the elements of the section 33 triviality defence had been satisfied. The second respondents, *Herald and Weekly Times*, were the employer of the first respondent, who was a journalist and the publisher of the "Bolt Blog". This blog was accessible on a website owned and operated by the second respondent. The applicant had been displeased with the content of the first respondent's blogs and made complaints to him and his employer. However, the first and second respondents failed to reply to the applicant and the applicant directed his complaints to the Australian Press Council. The Australian Press Council invited the respondents to reply to the applicant's complaints. The second respondent then forwarded the complaint to the first respondent who, in reply thereto, emailed the second respondent addressing the applicant's complaints. This emailed reply was then forwarded by the second respondent to the Australian Press Council. The email stated, inter alia, that "Mr Barrow [was] a vexatious litigant in many fora over a long time... who seeks not to promote debate but to close it down. The Press Council should declare his latest attempt vexatious and against

---

50.   Ibid., 37.
51.   [2015] VSCA 107.

the interest of debate."[52] The applicant claimed that this email was defamatory of him and initiated defamation proceedings against the first and second respondents.

To come to a construction of the section 33 triviality defence, heavy reliance was placed by the court on the judgments from other cases in which the 1974 triviality defence was raised. This impacted how strictly the court construed the elements of circumstances of publication and harm. For example, in terms of the test to determine what would encompass "circumstances of the publication", the court relied on the critical test stated in *Morosi v Mirror Newspapers Ltd.*[53] and the judgment in *Jones v Sutton.*[54] Accordingly, a court would need to consider whether, at the time of publication, the circumstances, such as "the content of the publication, the extent of the publication, the nature of the recipients and their relationship with the applicant" were such that "it was unlikely that the applicant would suffer harm".[55] The court noted that it was 'the quality of the circumstances of the publication that cause it to be unlikely that the person defamed will suffer harm".[56] Additionally, they pointed out that the circumstances were objective facts that were also linked to "the acts of publication".[57] Relying on *Jones*, the court further explained that the element in the triviality defence "unlikely to sustain any harm" meant that the defendant had to establish that there was "the absence of a real chance", or the "absence of a real possibility" of harm. It required more than simply demonstrating that it is "more probable than not" that the plaintiff will not suffer harm.[58] The court went on to explain that the defendant, therefore, had the high onus to prove that the plaintiff was unlikely to suffer "any" harm at the time of publication.[59]

Applying this construction to the facts of *Barrow,* the court found that it was relevant to note that:

---

52.   Ibid., 7.
53.   [1977] 2 NSWLR 749.
54.   (2004) 61 NSWLR 614, 618 [15] (Beazley JA).
55.   *Barrow,* 35.
56.   *Chappell,* 68-948.
57.   Ibid.
58.   Ibid., [16].
59.   Ibid.

... The impugned email went only to two persons. I consider that the tenor of the email makes it clear that the author was expressing his personal opinion, rather than saying that the plaintiff had been declared to be a vexatious litigant. Although the email did not contain the factual foundation for the opinion, its recipients, Mr Armsden and Mr Herman were aware of at least some of it, and I consider it likely they would have seen the opinion for what (in my view) it was. It is also clear that the defendants were responding to one of many complaints made by Mr Barrow to the APC. There is no evidence of any 'grapevine effect' or the likelihood of same at the time of publication. The only 'leakage' of the impugned email was caused by the plaintiff himself who published it on his website.[60]

The court further concluded that other "circumstances of publication" which impacted the finding of likely harm should include what is known to the defendant at the time of publication and the likelihood of the defamatory content being republished. However, the element of the circumstances of publication required for a defence of triviality was not wide enough to include a consideration of the applicant's previous bad reputation and previous education. Based on the above, what the court was willing to consider as constituting "the circumstances of publication" was very narrow and demonstrated the strictness of the court's construction.

The construction of the harm element was also very narrow. A distinction in the wording of the NSW 1974 section 13 triviality defence and the Australian Act's section 33 triviality defence contributed greatly to this. The Supreme Court of Victoria, in *Barrow*, noted that the NSW section 13 defence referred to "the harm", while section 33 of the Australian Act uses the word "any" to describe the harm.[61] The court held that, in respect of the section 33 defence, it therefore required a consideration of the quantum of the harm as well as the types of harm suffered.[62] Consequently, in terms of quantum, the "any harm" element of the section 33 defence was construed as meaning any "harm at all", as distinct from "great or substantial harm", which was required to satisfy the

---

60.   Ibid., [35].
61.   *Barrow v Bolt* [2014] VSC 599 [64].
62.   Ibid.

NSW section 13 triviality defence.[63] Furthermore, in terms of the types of harm covered, the court strictly construed that any harm referred only to injury to reputation and that injury to feelings did not fall within that definition of any harm.[64] Should injury to feelings be included within the definition of any harm pursuant to section 33, the court concluded this would have the effect of rendering the defence "virtually unworkable".[65]

Since the defendant was only able to successfully raise the defence particularly because the court found that the publication had been made to only two persons, it may be gleaned that based on the Court of Appeal's construction of the section 33, the triviality defence was likely to be successfully satisfied only in very limited circumstances. Additionally, because the court explained that the defence was not concerned with whether actual harm was inflicted, arguably, just the likelihood of harm would cancel the availability of the defence to the defendant. This demonstrated that the burden and standard of proof required of the defendant were, therefore, very high and onerous. This was evidenced by the fact that only in a few instances a defendant is recorded as being successful in availing themselves of this defence. Consequently, the statutory defence of triviality did not have a good track record as Australia's main approach to addressing the issue of harm and to eliminating or minimising trivial, "unworthy" defamation claims.[66] Section 33 of the Australian Act, when contrasted with section 1(1) of the English Act, placed a greater burden on defendants in defamation claims and consequently was less potent than the English approach in deterring and discouraging claims being brought where the harm caused was minimal or trivial. Accordingly, this served to motivate a review and ultimate revision of approach to the issue of harm and the actionability of trivial, 'unworthy' defamation claims.

Australia's New Approach to Presumption of Harm

In Australia, the adverse ramifications of the presumption of harm principle, such as facilitating trivial, 'unworthy' defamation

---

63. Ibid. [67].
64. Ibid. [68].
65. Ibid. [66].
66. Kim Gould, "Locating a 'Threshold of Seriousness' in the Australian Tests of Defamation," *Sydney Law Review* 39, no. 3 (2017): 333.

claims to be brought, was also acknowledged. Accordingly, Australian academic Kim Gould explained in her article, "Locating a 'Threshold of Seriousness' in the Australian Tests of Defamation", that where 'unworthy' claims are allowed to flourish without being curbed or discouraged, an unreasonable burden is also placed on the "administration of justice in terms of its resources, costs and delay".[67] Therefore, as Gould further noted, by referring to the High Court of Australia's decision in *Lange v Australian Broadcasting Corporation*,[68] the law's capacity to exclude 'unworthy' defamation claims is useful "for the purpose of maintaining the balance the law purports to strike between free speech and protection of reputation".[69] It is pursuant to these sentiments that, after a period of consultation and legislative review, Australia's National Uniformed Defamation Laws were revised and the Model Defamation Amendment Provisions, 2020 enacted in 2020. Pursuant to this, on 6 August 2020, the New South Wales parliament introduced the Defamation Amendment Bill, 2020. This revision had not been introduced by any of the other state or territory parliaments at the time of writing. However, all the Australian states and territories had indicated their commitment to enact the changes, as set out in the Model Defamation Amendment Provisions "as soon as possible".[70]

Among the revisions was the change in approach to addressing the issue of presumption of harm and deterring trivial unworthy claims of defamation.[71] This was set out in section 10A of the Model Defamation Amendment Provisions 2020 of Australia which provided that: "It is an element (the serious harm element) of a cause of action for defamation that the publication of defamatory matter about a person has caused, or is likely to cause, serious harm to the reputation of the person."[72]

---

67.   Ibid., 333, 334–35.
68.   [1997] HCA 25.
69.   Gould, "Threshold," 334–35.
70.   Council of Attorneys-General, Council of Attorneys-General communiqué – July 2020, https://www.ag.gov.au/about-us/publications/council-attorneys-general-communique-july-2020, last accessed 3 June 2021.
71.   The Model Defamation Amendment Provisions, 2020 revised both the Australian Uniformed Defamation Laws, 2005 and the Limitation Act, 1969.
72.   Section (2) of the EDA 201: For the purposes of subsection (1), harm to the reputation of an excluded corporation referred to in section 9 is not serious harm unless it has caused, or is likely to cause, the corporation serious financial loss.

In contrast to the triviality defence approach where the issue of harm is considered at the back end of the trial proceedings, section 10 gives the judge the task to determine whether serious harm was caused or likely to be caused to one's reputation at any time before the commencement of the trial proceedings or during the trial. This issue is to be considered "as soon as practicable before the trial commences". The judge, at that, point may dismiss the proceedings if satisfied the element of harm is not established.[73] This revised Australian approach is therefore very similar to the English section 1 approach, and the construction and application of the new approach to the issue of harm and the actionability of claims of defamation are likely to influenced by the construction given to the serious harm provision by the Supreme Court in *Lachaux*.

Conclusion

The removal of the presumption of harm principle from the revised legislation adopted in Australia and England and Wales demonstrates an appreciation that not every negative statement should give rise to a claim in defamation. It is not disputed that persons should not be allowed to recklessly make statements which are untrue and cause harm to another's reputation. However, the courts ought not to be inundated with baseless claims or otherwise frivolous cases. In an era where discourse is being encouraged and facilitated by access to mass media platforms such as the internet, the imposition of a 'serious harm' requirement represents, therefore, a significant development in the law of defamation, as it signals a positive move to achieving the aim of the tort of defamation of striking a fair balance between right to freedom of expression and the claimant's protection of reputation and thereby provides support to freedom of expression in a greater way than before. By requiring the claimant to satisfy a minimum threshold for commencing an action in defamation reduces the exposure and susceptibility of the potential defendants to frivolous claims where no serious harm to reputation has been suffered or is likely to be suffered from the exercise of the right to freedom of expression. It may be argued that in jurisdictions like Jamaica, where the presumption of harm continues to be a part of the defamation law,

---

73. Model Defamation Amendment Provisions, 2020, section 10A (4).

the claimant would be awarded a small quantum of damages in cases where it is proved that no or minimal harm to reputation was done. However, this article submits that with the implementation of the serious harm threshold, a defendant and the court would no longer have to endure lengthy and costly trial proceedings, and expend time and financial resources when no or minimal harm to reputation has been caused or was likely to be caused by the publication of the statement. Accordingly, persons may be less inclined to disproportionately chill their exercise of their right to freedom of expression in fear of a threat of defamation proceedings. This would be particularly meaningful to the press, who have had to contend with threats of defamation claim as they seek to execute their investigative and reporting functions and duties.

The Jamaican legislature failed to make good use of the opportunity in 2013 to level the playing field between the protection of reputation and the right to freedom of expression. Consequently, the issue of presumption of harm and the resulting low threshold to initiating frivolous trivial defamation claims continue to haunt the defamation framework in Jamaica. If, therefore, the issue of the presumption of harm is an indicator of an unreasonable limit being imposed on the right to freedom of expression, then a step forward requires that the Jamaican legislature consider removing the presumption of harm and introducing a minimum threshold to determine the actionability of claims of defamation. When Jamaica legislators, pursuant to section 35 of the Defamation Act, 2013, finally deliberate on and revise the defamation laws, it may be useful to take cues from the experience and development of the defamation law in Australia and England and Wales on the issue of presumption of harm. For a claim in defamation to arise, harm to reputation should be a *serious* thing!

CHAPTER 10

The Forgotten Exceptions of the Revised Treaty of Chaguaramas*

André Sheckleford

Rules are at the centre of legal systems. In any system of complex rules, there are exceptions, and these exceptions play an important role. The Caribbean Community (CARICOM) is a customs union comprised of fifteen member states – thirteen anglophone territories,[1] Haiti and Suriname. It was established by the Revised Treaty of Chaguaramas (RTC),[2] which covers a range of topics, including policies with respect to industry, agriculture, trade, transportation and competition. The most concretized norms, however, are those with respect to the free movement of goods, services, capital and labour, as well as those establishing a competition framework. As one would expect with any such complex legal system, there are several rules, and exceptions to the rules.

The Caribbean Court of Justice, sitting in its "original jurisdiction", where it considers matters pertaining to the interpretation and application of the treaty, has been called upon to resolve several disputes in its comparatively short history. In so doing, the court has been asked to measure certain activity by states against the RTC's norms. Unfortunately, the general exceptions have been scarcely discussed in cases where it has been appropriate to do so. The result has been some undesirable developments concerning the substantive norms of the treaty. This chapter highlights some of these cases and suggests a framework for the interpretation and application of the general exceptions.

* This chapter is current up to 2022.

---

1.   All the independent territories (Antigua and Barbuda, the Bahamas, Barbados, Belize, Dominica, Grenada, Guyana, Jamaica, St Kitts and Nevis, St Lucia, St Vincent and the Grenadines, and Trinidad and Tobago) and Monserrat. However, the status of the Bahamas and Monserrat allows participation, but does not subject them to all the rights and obligations of the RTC. They are not open for suit before the court.
2.   The Revised Treaty of Chaguaramas establishing the Caribbean Community including the CARICOM Single Market and Economy (entered into force 1 January 2006), 2259 UNTS 293.

Firstly, there is a broad, general discussion on exceptions in international economic law, and proposals of certain classifications for different exceptions (or exemptions, as the case may be). Suggestions are then offered as to how the general exceptions in the RTC ought to operate, and followed by a discussion instances where circumstances were apposite for consideration of the general exceptions, but no such consideration took place. In this part, the dangers of the syllogistic fallacies, which have taken different forms in certain disputes, are discussed.

Exceptions in International Economic Law

The role, function and conceptual underpinnings of exceptions in international law is beyond the scope of this chapter, and a discussion of exceptions within international economic law is in and of itself a gargantuan task. For the purposes of this section, without attempting to be exhaustive, two sets of exceptions will be explored; internal and external exceptions, and well as exceptions as-of-right and contingent exceptions.

Internal exceptions (or exemptions in some cases; the allocation of the burden of proof may play a role in the determination) are those which arise from the very norm in question, and flow from the act of interpreting the relevant rule. Article 4 of the Sanitary and Phytosanitary (SPS) Agreement,[3] for example, provides that a World Trade Organization member is to treat the SPS measures of another member as being equivalent, providing that the exporting member is able to objectively demonstrate that its SPS measures achieves importing member's standards. The importing member, therefore, need not treat the exporting member's measure as equivalent if they are not sufficient, and therefore will be exempted from the core obligation of the rule on the very basis of the rule itself. Some 'new generation' international investment agreements contain internal exceptions concerning rules pertaining to expropriation, providing that only in rare cases measures taken for the protection of public safety, health or the environment be treated as expropriation.[4]

---

3.   Agreement on the Application of Sanitary and Phytosanitary Measures (entered into force 1 January 1995), 1867 UNTS 493.

4.   See, for example, Annex 9-B of Chapter 9 of the Comprehensive and Progressive Agreement for Trans-Pacific Partnership (entered into force 30 December 2018); Annex 13-B of Chapter 13 of the Australia-United Kingdom Free Trade Agreement

Another type of internal exception may be seen in article 21 of the Treaty of the Functioning of the European Union, which guarantees freedom of movement to citizens of the European Union, subject to limitations and conditions in other EU treaties.[5] Here the normative basis for the exception, which flows from the text of the rule itself, points to external normative sources.

External exceptions are those which, though forming a part of the relevant agreement (or body of agreements which forms an *acquis*), exist outside of the specific rule, and may be invoked when there has been a finding of a breach of some primary treaty obligation. A well-known example is article XX of the General Agreement on Tariffs and Trade (GATT), which contains general exceptions to the obligations under the treaty.[6] Article 226 of the RTC, the focus of this chapter, is materially similar to article XX of the GATT. These exceptions provide excuses to subjects of international law obligations for conduct which, prima facie, abrogates some substantive norm.[7]

Exceptions as-of-right are those which a subject of the relevant international law norm may (sensibly) rely on without more, in that no decision of an organ, or an administrative or executive body, triggers a proper invocation of the exception. By contrast, contingent exceptions require some sort of decision before they may be properly relied upon. An example of a contingent exception in the RTC may be found in article 92(1) where, should a CARICOM member state face a significant decline in demand for a domestic good due to the importation of a good from another member state, that state, if approved by a certain CARICOM organ, is entitled to impose quantitative restrictions with respect to the imported product. The imposition of quantitative restrictions on community

---

(signed 17 December 2021). Though the exceptions are, as a matter of form, separate from the provision containing the primary obligation (not to expropriate the investment of a home state's investor unless certain conditions are met), being in an annex, the exception nevertheless attached to a specific rule.

5. Consolidated versions of the Treaty on European Union and the Treaty on the Functioning of the European Union (TFEU) [2016] OJ C202/1.

6. General Agreement on Tariffs and Trade, 1994 (entered into force 1 January 1995) 1867 UNTS 187.

7. Such exceptions have been described as "exceptions *strictu sensu*" by Jorge E. Viñuales, "Seven Ways of Escaping a Rule," in *Exceptions and Defences in International Law*, eds. Lorand Bartels and Federica Paddeu (Oxford: Oxford University Press, 2020).

goods is prohibited by article 91; however, article 92 allows such an imposition, with permission. Article 92 of the RTC is an internal, contingent exception. Article 226, which provides the general exceptions of the RTC, contains external exceptions as-of-right.

How the RTC's General Exceptions Should Operate

As noted above, the RTC provides exceptions which may operate as "excuses" for breaches of treaty obligations. The general exceptions may be found at article 226(1), which provides:

1. Nothing in this Chapter shall be construed as preventing the adoption or enforcement by any Member State of measures –
    a. to protect public morals or to maintain public order and safety;
    b. to protect human, animal or plant life or health;
    c. necessary to secure compliance with laws or regulations relating to customs enforcement, or to the classification, grading or marketing of goods, or to the operation of monopolies by means of state enterprises or enterprises given exclusive or special privileges;
    d. necessary to protect intellectual property or to prevent deceptive practices;
    e. relating to gold or silver;
    f. relating to the products of prison labour;
    g. relating to child labour;
    h. imposed for the protection of national treasures of artistic, historic or archaeological value;
    i. necessary to prevent or relieve critical food shortages in any exporting Member State;
    j. relating to the conservation of natural resources or the preservation of the environment;
    k. to secure compliance with laws or regulations which are not inconsistent with the provisions of this Treaty including those relating to:
        i.   the prevention of deceptive and fraudulent practices, and the effects of a default on contracts;
        ii. the protection of the privacy of individuals in relation to the processing and dissemination of personal data

and the protection of confidentiality of individual records and accounts; and

l. to give effect to international obligations including treaties on the avoidance of double taxation,

but only if such measures do not constitute arbitrary or unjustifiable discrimination between Member States where like conditions prevail, or a disguised restriction on trade within the Community.

Paragraph 2 of the article treats with the procedural requirement to notify the Council for Trade and Economic Development (COTED), an organ of CARICOM, of any such measures, and paragraph 3 places a coordination obligation on another organ (the Community Council) concerning certain free movement of capital provisions.

A possible argument against the use of article 226(1) as a general exception clause to the substantive provisions of the treaty is that it does not extend to the substantive provisions, as the paragraph opens with: "Nothing in this *Chapter*..." The relevant chapter is chapter 10, which contains no substantive provisions or obligations. It is, however, the chapter which states how the treaty comes into force. It can therefore be read, taking into account the context, as well as the object and purpose of the treaty and the chapter, as "[the entry into force of this treaty] shall [not] be construed as preventing the adoption or enforcement by any Member State of measures..." This, it is suggested, is the sensible reading, else the provision would be otiose. Alternatively, as has been stated by one author, the phraseology employed may be viewed as a textual error.[8]

Article 226(1) of the RTC is similar to article XX of the GATT, with a notable structural difference being that the chapeau of article XX takes the form of a proviso at the end of article 226(1). The GATT is a multi-national trade treaty, to which all members of the World Trade Organization are subject. The jurisprudence of the WTO's Appellate Body (with the exception of a few decisions) suggests that the justifications listed in the sub-paragraphs of article XX of the GATT are measured by reference to the trade restrictiveness of a measure and the chapeau addresses any

---

8. David Berry, *Caribbean Integration Law* (Oxford: Oxford University Press, 2014), 153–54.

discrimination present.[9] As discussed below, the approach of the WTO Appellate body in matters concerning the general exceptions of the GATT (and the General Agreement on Trade in Services) mirrors the general concept of proportionality used in various international and domestic forums, and it is suggested that a similar analysis is warranted under the RTC.[10]

Proportionality takes into account (1) whether the subject matter for consideration has a legitimate objective (in the case of enumerated general exceptions, as in article 226(1), the potential legitimate bases are explicitly provided in the sub-paragraphs); (2) whether the subject matter is rationally connected to the objective; (3) whether the subject matter is necessary to achieve the legitimate objective (often by interrogating whether there are less intrusive alternatives which could have been explored with less of an effect on the norm affected by the measure); and (4) proportionality *strictu sensu*, which usually arises where a tribunal finds the subject matter to be rationally connected to the objective and necessary. At this last stage, what is considered is whether the intrusion of the norm in question outweighs the benefit to be derived from the measure or action, or vice versa. Some tribunals, perhaps on a combination of "the necessity test" and proportionality *strictu sensu*, are highly prescriptive as to the contours of the derogation from some principal norm.[11]

An RTC-specific rubric for proportionality is considered below, after a discussion on WTO jurisprudence on the general exceptions in the GATT and the GATS.

---

9.   Lorand Bartels, "The Chapeau of the General Exceptions in the WTO GATT and GATS Agreements: A Reconstruction," *American Journal of International Law* 109, no. 1 (2015): 95, 109.

10.   See Emily Crawford, "Proportionality" in *Max Planck Encyclopedia of Public International Law*, ed. Rüdiger Wolfrum (online edition, May 2011) for a general discussion of proportionality in international law. Though the court has made reference to a concept of proportionality in some decisions (see, for example, *Trinidad Cement Ltd. v CARICOM* [2009] CCJ 4 (OJ) para. 78, where the importance of the concept was emphasized; *Myrie v Barbados* [2013] CCJ 3 (OJ) para. 70 and 71; *Trinidad Cement Limited v Trinidad & Tobago; Trinidad Cement Limited & Arawak Cement Limited v Barbados* [2019] CCJ 1 (OJ) para. 37), there has been no schema suggested for approaching the idea. At most, there seems to be a general notion that CARICOM organs must act "proportionately", with different approaches taken to the standard. A standard, more akin to "high level of deference", was espoused in *TCL v CARICOM (merits)* [2009] CCJ 4 (OJ) under the label of "proportionality" at para. 78.

11.   Some examples of this may be seen in CJEU privacy jurisprudence; see, for, example, Joined Cases C-203/15 & C-698/15, *Tele2 Sverige AB v Post-och telestyrelsen and Others*, 2016 ECR I-970, paras. 109–11, 116–23.

As noted above, article XX of the GATT and article 226(1) of the RTC are materially similar; both provisions contain listed bases upon which a state may rely to found the basis of side-stepping a treaty rule, and both require that measures which potentially abrogates a treaty rule do not amount to "arbitrary or unjustifiable discrimination" where like conditions prevail, or a disguised restriction on trade (this latter element being found in the proviso to article 226(1) of the RTC, and the chapeau to Article XX of the GATT). WTO tribunals conduct a two-step analysis with respect to article XX of the GATT – the first step involves an enquiry as to whether the measure in question may be provisionally justified under the listed paragraphs, followed by an analysis concerning discrimination or disguised trade restrictiveness under the chapeau.

The WTO Appellate Body, with respect to the listed bases which carry the words "necessary to" (such as article XX (a) and (b) of the GATT, and article XIV(a) and (b) of the GATS), typically focuses its analysis on the question of whether a WTO-consistent measure, or a less WTO-inconsistent measure, could reasonably be pursued.[12] This is similar to the necessity test at step (3) of the proportionality schema above. Though WTO jurisprudence focuses on the necessity test, in inquiry is also made as to whether the measure makes some contribution to the relevant objective, this being similar to step (2) above.[13]

For those bases which use the softer language of "relating to" (such as article XX(c), (e) and (g) of GATT), an enquiry is made as to whether there is a close and genuine relationship between the end sought and the means sought to achieve that end.[14] This, too, is similar to step (2) above.

---

12. WTO, *Korea – Measures Affecting Imports of Fresh, Chilled and Frozen Beef – Report of the Appellate Body* (adopted 10 January 2001), WT/DS161/AB/R and WT/DS169/AB/R, para. 166.

13. The question is only whether there is "some" contribution, and not whether there is a "material" contribution: WTO, *European Communities – Measures Prohibiting the Importation and Marketing of Seal Products – Report of the Appellate Body* (adopted on 18 June 2014), WT/DS400/AB/R and WT/DS401/AB/R, para. 5.215. In treating with the question of whether there is some contribution to the objective by the measure, a panel ought to consider the design of a measure, "including its content, structure, and expected operation" (*Colombia –Measures Relating to the Importation of Textiles, Apparel and Footwear – Report of the Appellate Body* (adopted on 22 June 2016) WT/DS461/AB/R, para. 5.69).

14. WTO, *China – Measures Related to the Exportation of Various Raw Materials – Report of the Appellate Body* (adopted on 22 February 2012), WT/DS394/AB/R, WT/DS395/AB/R and WT/DS398/AB/R, para. 355.

In addition to assessing an impugned measure against the relevant, enumerated, exception, the chapeau to article XX of the GATT, which is similar to the proviso to article 226(1), calls for an examination of whether the measure amounts to an "arbitrary or unjustifiable discrimination between [states] where the same conditions prevail". This has been recognized as a part of the general obligation of good faith in international law[15], and a safeguard to ensure that the exceptions are not misused and abused.[16] Though earlier WTO jurisprudence had suggested that the justification under the chapeau of article XX of the GATT had to be the related to (or at the very least not undermine) the justification relied upon in the enumerated paragraphs[17], the Appellate Body later expanded the scope for analysis under the chapeau to other normative bases.[18]

As the RTC, with respect to its general exceptions, draws heavily from article XX of the GATT, WTO jurisprudence serves as an appropriate guide to the interpretation and application of article 226(1). The Court has also recognised the importance of CARICOM being protected under the GATT, which may suggest that general WTO compliance is of some importance.[19]

The following is suggested as guidance for questions raised under the Treaty, where a prima facie breach of a Treaty obligation is established.

1. Consider Whether the Measure or Power Raises any of the Exceptions in Article 226(1)

It will be desirable if, sometime in the near future, the relevant parties (be it member states, CARICOM, or other possible respondents) routinely raise defence arguments by reference to the general exceptions where appropriate. As this does not yet seem to

---

15. WTO, *United States – Import Prohibition of Certain Shrimp and Shrimp Products – Report of the Appellate Body* (adopted on 6 November 1998), WT/DS58/AB/R ("*US – Shrimp*"), para. 158.
16. Ibid., para. 160.
17. WTO, *Brazil – Measures Affecting Imports of Retreaded Tyres – Report of the Appellate Body* (adopted 17 December 2007), WT/DS332/AB/R.
18. *European Communities – Measures Prohibiting the Importation and Marketing of Seal Products – Report of the Appellate Body* (adopted 18 June 2014) WT/DS400/AB/R, para. 5.321.
19. *Trinidad Cement Limited v Trinidad & Tobago; Trinidad Cement Limited & Arawak Cement Limited v Barbados* [2019] CCJ 01 (OJ), para. 34.

be the case, the Court ought to keep the general exceptions in mind when addressing the question of a breach of a substantive treaty obligation.

2. Consider Whether the Measure or Power is Rationally Connected to the Relevant Exception

In the WTO context, states bring claims related to their own interests, against other states whose actions may run at variance to that interest.[20] In this context, "measure" carries a wide connotation, the word signifying something which is systematic, or reflective of a state's policy. As noted above, WTO panels consider the design and structure of a measure in assessing its connection to an article XX objective. A similar approach ought to be adopted with respect to the RTC; i.e. an assessment of whether there is a minimum contribution or rational connection between a measure and the relevant paragraph.

In the CARICOM context, private parties have the right to bring actions against states. While the provisions concerning freedom of movement of goods, services and capital will typically raise concerns of a state doing, or failing to do something, in some systematic or policy driven way, freedom of movement provisions have raised issues of the actions of a particular state employee in their daily duties.[21] In these situations, there may be no "design and structure" to contemplate in a manner which one may associate with trade in goods and services; however the relevant officer may be exercising some power given to them, as a matter of domestic law. Here, the relevant question ought to be whether the relevant power, where the officer's conduct falls within the ambit of some power available as a matter of domestic law, makes some minimum contribution to the relevant objective.

For those objectives which are prefaced with "related to", such as those at article 226(e)-(g) and (j), the analysis should end here.

---

20.   As one author has stated, "It is quite clear that any country bringing an action [in WTO dispute settlement] is invariably the holder of *direct interests of its own*, since the asset to be protected is its *national economy* rather than one...undertaking or class of...undertakings," Alberto Santa Maria, *European Economic Law*, 2nd rev. ed. (Boston: Wolters Kluwer Law International, 2009), 283. (original emphasis)

21.   For example, *Myrie v Barbados* [2013] CCJ 3 (OJ), *Gilberts v Barbados* [2019] CCJ 2 (OJ) and *David Bain v Trinidad & Tobago* [2019] CCJ 3 (OJ).

If the measure or power is rationally connected to these objectives, measure should be treated as RTC-compliant, and non-compliant if not so rationally connected.

3. Consider Whether the Measure or Power is Necessary

The consideration at this "necessity" step, with respect to measures (as distinct to powers, which are discussed below), is whether there is a less RTC-incompatible, or an RTC compatible, route to achieving the objective at hand, to the level desired by the state. This "same level" qualification, which may be gleaned in the GATS context from *US – Gambling*, means that a measure or activity ought not to be found as disproportionate merely because there is another avenue which may be pursued, if a similar meeting of the relevant objective is not possible from that alternative. In *US – Gambling*, the panel's finding that certain laws prohibiting the provision of cross-border gambling services failed the "necessity" requirement was considered flawed by the Appellate Body, as the panel's proposed alternative of consultations was inherently uncertain, and unable to meet the level sought by the state for the protection of public morals or maintenance of public order.[22]

When considering the actions of an officer of a state, an appropriate question may be whether the powers granted to the officer or group of officers impair the relevant treaty right as minimally as possible. If questions of less treaty-infringing alternatives are too abstract for the matter under consideration, an appropriate question may be whether the power granted is a fair and reasonable.

Grounds with No Prefatory Words

While the question of "necessity" is certainly fitting for those grounds of justification which are prefaced by the words

---

22.   WTO, *United States – Measures Affecting the Cross-Border Supply of Gambling and Betting Services –Report of the Appellate Body* (adopted on 20 April 2005), WT/DS285/AB/R, paras. 315–17. However, the measures were found to be in breach of the GATS for a failure to comply with the chapeau article XIV of the GATS (which is materially similar to article XX of the GATT, and the proviso to article 216(1)).

"necessary to" (being article 216(1)(c)[23], (d)[24] and (i)[25]). Some grounds, however, are prefaced by neither "necessary to" nor "related to", and the question arises as to the type of analysis these grounds ought to attract.[26] Should the analysis stop at the "rational connection" question (a more restrictive interpretation of the treaty obligations, and a wider interpretation of the exception), or should the analysis go further to an enquiry into "necessity" (a more expansive interpretation of the treaty obligations, with a narrower interpretation of the exception), or ought there to be a different analytical framework altogether?

There are different interpretive avenues available in this respect, the starting point being article 31 of the Vienna Convention on the Law of Treaties. A one-size-fits-all approach should be shunned, with these grounds being treated as autonomous and subject to independent interpretation. The interpretation of such grounds should take into account the language of the relevant ground, in context, in light of the object and purpose, as well, inter alia, any relevant rules of international law relevant between the parties.

Article 226(1)(k)(ii) provides an exception (not prefaced by "related to" or "necessary") concerning laws aimed at the protection of personal data, and a justifiable interpretation may take into account the fact that all CARICOM states have agreed to put in place legal and administrative regimes with respect to the processing of data, in line with "high international standards", under the CARIFORUM-EU Economic Partnership Agreement (this agreement being a relevant rule of international law between the

---

23. Measures "necessary to secure compliance with laws or regulations relating to customs enforcement, or to the classification, grading or marketing of goods, or to the operation of monopolies by means of state enterprises or enterprises given exclusive or special privileges".

24. Measures "necessary to protect intellectual property or to prevent deceptive practices".

25. Measures "necessary to prevent or relieve critical food shortages in any exporting Member State".

26. Article 226(1)(a) [measures to to protect public morals or to maintain public order and safety]; (b) [measures to protect human, animal or plant life or health]; (h) [measures imposed for the protection of national treasures of artistic, historic or archaeological value]; (k) [to secure compliance with laws or regulations which are not inconsistent with the provisions of the RTC, including those relating to the prevention of fraud and data protection]; (l) [measures to give effect to international obligations, including treaties on the avoidance of double taxation].

parties).[27] This may point towards a wider reading of the exception, leading to the analysis of this ground stopping at the question of rational connection.

Article 226(1)(a) (protection of public morals) and 226(1)(b) (protection of human, animal or plant life or health), similarly, do not have prefatory words. A compelling factor which may point to a wider interpretation of the exceptions is the fact that these grounds employ less restrictive language that their GATT counterparts, which are prefaced by the word "necessary", demonstrating an express desire to move from a more stringent interpretation of the exceptions. Alternatively, the exceptions may be considered as reflective of police powers already held by states at customary international law, which, in the context of discussions on expropriation in investor-state dispute settlement (ISDS), have been recognized as attracting a proportionality analysis (inclusive of "necessity" considerations).[28] It may be noted that, within the context of ISDS, the question of how to treat with *lex specialis* provisions which cover similar ground to customary international law defences is unsettled; on the one hand, it has been held that the customary international law requirements must be met,[29] and on the other, that the specific phraseology of the express, external exception is the appropriate focus.[30] With respect to article 226(1) (a) and (b) of the RTC, it is suggested that the latter position is

---

27.   [2008] OJ L289/1, article 197.1.
28.   For example, *Philip Morris Brands Sàrl, Philip Morris Products SA and Abal Hermanos SA v Oriental Republic of Uruguay,* ICSID Case No. ARB/10/7, Award, 8 July 2016, paras. 287 et seq, *Casinos Austria International Gmbh and Casinos Austria Aktiengesellschaft v Argentine Republic,* ICSID Case No. ARB/14/32, Award, 5 November 2021, paras. 338 et seq., esp. para. 351.
29.   See, for example, *CMS Gas Transmission Company v Argentina*, ICSID Case No. ARB/01/8, Award, 12 May 2005; *Enron Corporation and Ponderosa Assets, LP v Argentine Republic,* ICSID Case No. ARB/01/3, Award, 22 May 2007 (*CMS*); and *Sempra Energy International v Argentine Republic,* ICSID Case No. ARB/02/16, Award, 28 September 2007, which both considered an external, as of right, security exception in the Argentina-US BIT, concluding that the same requirements for establishing the defence of necessity at customary international law were required for a successful reliance on the security exception.
30.   The ICSID ad hoc committee in *CMS* criticized the award of the tribunal for conflating and assimilating the customary international law and treaty concepts, and found that the tribunal made a manifest error of law: *CMS Gas Transmission Company v Argentina*, ICSID Case No. ARB/01/8, Decision of the ad hoc committee, 25 September 2007, para. 130. The question is described as "unsettled", as there is no system of appeals or binding precedent in the ISDS regime.

more compelling, and the interpretation should properly focus on the specific drafting choices.

As may be seen above, the approach to be taken to each paragraph may differ in light of its drafting, content, and international relations which CARICOM, and/or its constituent states, may have. Further, in interpreting each of the paragraphs as the need arises, the court may consider two potentially competing principles: *in dubio mitius* and the restrictive interpretation of exceptions.

The principle of *in dubio mitius* calls for a tribunal, in cases of ambiguity in the meaning of a provision, to construe the provision in a restrictive manner which places a less demanding obligation on the state. Though *in dubio mitius* has not found favour with many international tribunals,[31] the concept has been said to be "reignited"[32] by the Appellate Body's decision in *EC – Hormones*, where the Appellate Body found the principle to an "interpretative principle…widely recognized in international law as a 'supplementary means of interpretation'".[33] An application of *in dubio mitius*, in this context, may favour a reading of those grounds without prefatory words in such a manner to favour the state, which may result in ending the proportionality analysis at the "rational connection" stage.

Potentially competing with *in dubio mitius* is the principle that exceptions or limitations to treaty rights ought to be construed narrowly. While some WTO panels have endorsed this notion[34], the Appellate Body has shied away from this principle, preferring not to elevate the status of any section of the treaty text, unless the treaty so provides.[35] An application of this principle favours a

---

31. Johannes Fahner, "In Dubio Mitius: Advancing Clarity and Modesty in Treaty Interpretation," *European Journal of International Law* 32, no. 3 (2021): 835. Fahner argues for an enhanced role of *in dubio mitius* in contemporary international tribunals.

32. Christophe Larouer, "In the Name of Sovereignty? The Battle over In Dubio Mitius Inside and Outside the Courts," Cornell Law School Inter-University Graduate Student Conference Papers, 2009, 49.

33. WTO, *European Communities – EC Measures Concerning Meat and Meat Products (Hormones) – Report of the Appellate Body* (adopted on 13 February 1998), WT/DS26/AB/R; WT/DS48/AB/R, footnote 154. The footnote has, however, been subject to some measure of criticism for its editing of the reference relied upon in support of the statement: Larouer, "Sovereignty," 29–30.

34. WTO, *Canada – Import Restrictions on Ice Cream and Yoghurt – Report of the panel* (adopted on 5 December 1989), para. 59.

35. David Palmeter and Petros Mavroidis, "The WTO Legal System: Sources of Law," *American Journal of International Law* 92 (1998): 398, 408, citing WTO, *EC – Measures*

reading of those exceptions without prefatory words in a manner which make them more difficult to establish, and therefore subject to the entirety of the proportionality analysis.

As highlighted above, each of these grounds ought properly to be subject to an independent analysis in their interpretation, with different factors and principles assisting in this interpretation. The approach taken to these grounds will have consequences on the analytical framework to be employed, as well as the nature and cogency of evidence required to successfully rely on the ground.

4. Consider Whether the Impairment to the Treaty Right Outweighs the Pursuit of the Relevant Objective by the Activity or Measure

Should the assessment of a measure or power pass the three steps outlined above, the next question for the court is whether the relevant measure does such violence to the objectives of the common market created by the treaty as to warrant admonition. The court should be cautious at this stage of the analysis, as the inquiries may involve subjective value judgements, rather that the relatively objective scope for analysis provided by the other steps outlined.

After considering if a measure or action is justifiable under the enumerated paragraphs, the other relevant question is whether the measures or activities "constitute arbitrary or unjustifiable discrimination between Member States where like conditions prevail, or a disguised restriction on trade within the Community", as stated in the proviso. It has been noted with respect to the chapeau to article XX of the GATT, from which the proviso to article 226(1) draws inspiration, that the chapeau addresses the manner in which a measure is applied (as distinct from the paragraphs, which are assessed against the measure's design, structure and, if appropriate, contemplated invocation).[36]

As noted above, in the context of the WTO, earlier decisions indicated that any offending arbitrary or unjustifiable discrimination in a measure ought to be tied to the enumerated paragraph relied

---

Concerning Meat and Meat Products (Hormones).

36.   WTO, *United States – Standards for Reformulated and Conventional Gasoline – Report of the Appellate Body* (adopted on 20 May 1996), WT/DS2/AB/R, para. 22.

upon in article XX of the GATT, but later decisions have highlighted that is not the only relevant question. However, the question of "arbitrary or unjustifiable discrimination" in the context of the RTC is an interesting one, as article 7 of the treaty, found in the section headed "Principles", provides that "any discrimination on grounds of nationality only shall be prohibited". The court has rightly treated the provision as one which permeates the other treaty provisions, and it will naturally form an important part of the context, in interpreting the rest of the treaty.[37] Therefore, a restrictive (and not entirely unreasonable) reading of the proviso, given the context provided by article 7, would equate "arbitrary or unjustifiable discrimination between Member States" on grounds of nationality only, meaning that a justification which provisionally meets one of the enumerated paragraphs may only be impugned if the measure or activity causes, or involves, such nationality-based discrimination.

While such an interpretation may seem attractive, it is suggested that a broader reading ought to be taken. If we consider, for example, import restrictions instituted by a member state on certain agricultural products due to the outbreak of a disease affecting certain crops in other CARICOM states (and let us consider the import restrictions including a licencing regime by which exporting farmers in affected countries are required to be licensed in line with certain standards), such import restrictions may be provisionally justified on the ground of protection of human, animal or plant life or health (in article 226(1)(b)); or the conservation of natural resources or the preservation of the environment (in article 226(1) (j)). If, however, the import restriction is implemented poorly (such as the licensing requiring an unreasonably high level of

---

37. The court stated in *Cabral Douglas v Commonwealth of Dominica* [2017] CCJ 1 (OJ) at para. 16:
    "Furthermore, Article 7 is not a stand-alone provision but rather was adopted to ensure that the rights enuring expressly or by necessary implication upon persons of the Community, were not thwarted because of discrimination on basis of nationality. Article 7 therefore does not confer an inherent substantive right but rather provides the rule by which the framers of the Treaty intended to ensure that rights granted, whether expressly or impliedly, were not distorted by discriminatory actions by one Contracting Party against the nationals of another Contracting Party. This explains why the Article appears within the Chapter dealing with the principles against which the remainder of the Treaty is to be interpreted and understood; and that its application is restricted to the 'scope of application of [the] Treaty'."

cogency of evidence), or does not evolve as situations change (for example, scientific evidence showing that the risk of diseased crop is seasonal), the import restriction may result in discrimination which is not nationality based. In such circumstances, the measure ought not to pass merely because the source of the discrimination is not based in nationality, as its "arbitrariness" or "unjustifiability" may be seen in how the measure is implemented. A less restrictive reading would admit for the consideration of other grounds of arbitrariness or unjustifiability in any discrimination, including the normative sources of which may be found in other parts of the treaty (whether in the substantive obligations, the aspirational provisions, or the recitals to the treaty). In the example given, the poor implementation of such a policy would run against the grain of the many provisions for the advancement of agriculture in the region.

On the practical question of burdens of proof under article 226(1), the claimant ought to have the burden of demonstrating an interference or abrogation with a treaty right, and the defendant (be it a state, CARICOM itself or the Competition Commission) the burden of establishing that the measure or power under scrutiny is provisionally justified under the paragraphs.[38] With respect to the proviso, the burden ought to be on the defendant to preliminarily establish justifiability or an absence of arbitrariness in any discrimination present, and the burden on the complaining party to establish unjustifiability or arbitrariness.[39]

Opportunities for the Consideration of the General Exceptions
The Environmental Context

Some early opportunities for court to consider article 226 arose with respect to environmental matters. *Rudisa Beverages & Juices*

---

38. The terms "claimant" and "defendant" are used here as this is the nomenclature used by the Court when a matter is being considered at the merits stage. Under the RTC, private parties require special leave before bringing proceedings, where the parties are referred to as "applicant" and "respondent". As is discussed with respect to a specific case below, the general exceptions ought not to be considered with any great depth at the special leave stage.
39. In essence, an evidential burden on the part of the defendant, and a burden of proof on the part of the claimant. The formulation is suggested as it is a general principle of evidence that no party should be called upon to prove a negative, and a requirement for a defendant to prove that something is not arbitrary or unjustifiable may fall foul of this principle.

NV and Caribbean International Distributors Limited v Republic of Guyana[40] and *SM Jaleel & Co. Ltd. and Guyana Beverages Inc v Guyana*[41] concerned the same environmental tax imposed by Guyana with respect to non-returnable (disposable) beverage containers (GUY$10 per bottle). The court, finding the tax to be an impermissible import duty (as it did not apply to locally produced beverages), ordered the cessation of its imposition and awarded more than US$6 million to the claimants (that amount having been specifically pleaded and proven), together with any other amount collected over the relevant period (with interest). The cessation of the imposition of the tax will apparently result in a loss of approximately GUY$10 billion per year[42] for Guyana, while at the same time affecting the nation's environmental policy.[43]

Similar issues arose for consideration in *SM Jaleel*, where the court was called upon to analyse the same tax, which a different beverage manufacturer complained about. The court, recognizing that a precedent had been set in *Rudisa* (and no doubt cognizant that its previous decisions form a part of the applicable law before it by virtue of article 221 of the treaty, which embraces the concept of *stare decisis*) did not treat with many substantive issues, having concluded that the claimants were "prima facie entitled to the relief sought".[44] The general exceptions were not referenced in either decision.

The failure to address article 226(1)(j), which provides an exception for measures "to the conservation of natural resources or the preservation of the environment", is a significant omission. Far from recognizing that there is scope within the CARICOM treaty regime for matters which are contrary to the principal norms of the RTC where matters concerning the environment arise, the court in *Rudisa* reasoned that "[t]he noble purpose served by the environmental tax, as suggested by the Attorney-General, namely the protection of the environment and conservation, does not excuse the discriminatory impact of the tax."[45]

---

40. [2014] CCJ 1 (OJ) (*Rudisa*).
41. [2017] CCJ 2(OJ) (*SM Jaleel*).
42. Approximately US$48 million per year, at the time of writing.
43. iNews Guyana, "Guyana has until January 2016 to pay US$6M to Rudisa," accessible at   http://www.inewsguyana.com/guyana-has-until-january-2016-to-pay-us6m-to-rudisa/ (accessed 25 January 2020).
44. *SM Jaleel* [2017] CCJ 2(OJ), para. 5.
45. *Rudisa*, para. 22.

As discussed above, a proper analysis would involve asking if the trade restrictiveness of the measure is "related to" the protection of the environment (which is a lower threshold to establish than the question of whether a measure is "necessary" for the protection of a particular interest). Answering this question involves assessing whether the environmental tax makes some minimum contribution to, or at the very least is rationally connected to, the protection of the environment. It is very difficult to see how the answer to this question could be "no". The questions contained in the proviso to article 226(1), that is, whether the tax amounted to arbitrary or unjustifiable discrimination, or a disguised restriction on trade do, however, require further analysis. The court did note that the tax did not apply to locally produced beverages; this however, by itself, cannot qualify a measure as falling foul of the standards set out in the proviso, as there must be some facts capable of supporting such a finding. Useful questions include whether there is any meaningful beverage manufacturing sector in Guyana, whether there are any domestic taxes or restrictions which those manufacturers are subject to which do not affect imported beverages, and whether the import duty is having, is likely to have an effect on demand for domestically produced goods over imported goods. In other words, a measure cannot result in arbitrary or unjustifiable discrimination, or a disguised restriction on trade, merely because it is an import duty; there must be a causative link between the existence of the duty and such a finding. It is possible that the answer to the questions may have led to a finding that the tax was an impermissible one under the RTC; however, such questions were not asked, as the exceptions were never raised.

There is some similarity between the events surrounding *Rudisa* and *SM Jaleel*, and the events which led to the WTO dispute in *Brazil – Retreaded Tyres*. The background to *Brazil – Retreaded Tyres* involved a Mercusor tribunal interpreting and applying the Treaty of Montevideo, considering whether Brazil's import restriction on re-treaded tyres, the stated reason for the restriction being to address the breeding of mosquitos, was consistent with Brazil's Mercusor obligations.[46] The tribunal did not pay any regard to the human health and safety exception in the treaty. They found

---

46.   Mercusor is a South American trading bloc with full members comprising Argentina, Brazil, Paraguay and Uruguay (Venezuela's status as a full member having been suspended since 1 December 2016), with Bolivia, Chile, Colombia, Ecuador, Guyana, Peru and Suriname as associate members.

Brazil's measures contrary to its Mercusor obligations and, under the Mercusor legal regime, Brazil was required to allow imports of re-treaded tyres from other Mercusor countries. Brazil complied with the requirement, but maintained the ban on re-treaded tyres from other sources. The surviving ban (in relation to non-Mercusor states), after a challenge by the European Community before the WTO Dispute Settlement Body, was deemed an impermissible quantitative restriction and a breach of an anti-discrimination provision under the GATT. While the Appellate Body found the measure justifiable on the grounds of public health under the paragraphs of article XX of the GATT,[47] the Appellate Body found no justification under the chapeau.[48]

The Appellate Body noted there was no incompatibility between the GATT and the Treaty of Montevideo, but rather a non-deployment of the relevant exception by the tribunal under the Mercusor regime.[49] The absence of any consideration of the general exceptions in *Rudisa* and *SM Jaleel* bear some similarities to the problems with the decision of the Mercusor tribunal. Had Guyana continued the tax in relation to non-CARICOM goods, exempting goods of CARICOM origin from this environmental tax, it is likely that such a measure would have been inconsistent with its WTO obligations.

Freedom of Movement

One of the few times the court has mentioned the general exceptions in the treaty involved the use of article 226(1) as an interpretive tool, in seeking to interpret a decision from a CARICOM organ. The court in *Myrie (merits)* examined a 2007 decision of the Conference of the Heads of Government (the supreme organ of

---

47. As discussed above, under article XX of the GATT, the trade restrictiveness of a measure is weighed against the paragraphs, and the chapeau addresses questions of discrimination; and further, the proviso to article 226(1) of the RTC plays a similar role to the chapeau of article XX of the GATT.
48. As this was one of the earlier cases where the Appellate Body considered that the justification under the chapeau had to be related to the justification under paragraphs, it leaves the question as to whether a potentially erroneous decision by a tribunal *vis-à-vis* a preferential trade agreement is a suitable justification under the chapeau. It is doubtful, however, that this would be the case (especially in light of the language of the Appellate Body in *EC – Seals*, which opened the possibility for a wider class or potential justifications).
49. Paras. 224–34.

CARICOM), which gave an entitlement to nationals of member states to stay in other member states for up to six months, provided they are not "undesirable persons" or likely to "[become] a charge on public funds".[50] The decision represented an extension of a basic, aspirational, treaty right involving a commitment to the free movement of nationals (article 45), and another which provides freedom of movement for university graduates and certain classes of workers (article 46). For the court, these decisions of organs form a sort of secondary legislation within CARICOM.[51]

In its examination of the conference decision, the court used article 226(1) to provide context in finding the meaning of the phrase "undesirable persons". Article 226(1)(a) provides an exception regarding public morals, order and safety, and article 226(1)(b) contains an exception relating to the protection of human, animal or plant life or health. The court stated: "The concept of 'undesirable persons' in Community law must be understood and construed against the background of Article 226(1)(a) and (b) RTC. Undesirability is meant to be concerned with such matters as the protection of public morals, the maintenance of public order and safety and the protection of life and health."[52]

It is understandable to seek context for an ambiguous phrase and it is understandable that such context is sought within the general exceptions, as certain categories of individuals are being excepted from the extension of the basic treaty right. However, it is difficult to comprehend why the exceptions in article 226(1)(a)-(b) are the only relevant ones. Article 226(1)(g), for example, contains an exception for matters relating to child labour; why would such a provision not supply relevant context?

The reason for the court's narrow view of the relevant exceptions in this regard may be found in its importation of principles from European Court of Justice cases cited, without much contextualization.[53] The three cases cited, of vintage ranging from 1973 to 2003, discussed derogations from the basic right of the freedom of movement of workers in the EEC/EC setting. However, the limitations on freedom of movement set out in the relevant

---

50.   *Myrie v Barbados* [2013] CCJ 3 (OJ) (*Myrie (merits)*).
51.   Ibid., paras. 8 and 10.
52.   Ibid., para. 68.
53.   Ibid., para. 70, footnote 12.

European treaties (the EEC Treaty in the earlier cases and the EC Treaty in the lattermost) were required to be justified on grounds of public policy, public security or public health, and therefore the ECJ's judgments focused on these categories. The limitation of the consideration of what amounts to an "undesirable person" in the context of freedom of movement in the conference decision, on such similar bases (on the basis of public morality, order and safety, and the protection of life and public health) may be reflective of mere importation of EEC/EC norms, without taking into account the source of these norms.

Myrie (merits) involved a claim by a Jamaican national that on her arrival in Barbados, she was subject to interrogation, a strip search, cavity searches and degrading comments by Barbadian immigration officials and police officers, before being denied entry into the country, detained in a cell with poor conditions, and put on a return flight to Jamaica. The court found a breach of the freedom of movement guarantee under the conference decision, and awarded damages to Ms Myrie. Had the general exceptions been considered in the manner suggested, the court may have asked whether the power given to immigration and police officers (as the case may be) to interrogate, detain, and conduct strip and cavity searches of CARICOM nationals may be provisionally justified under article 226(1)(a) (measures to protect public morals or to maintain public order), to which the answer may be "yes".[54]

If the power if provisionally justified under paragraph 226(1)(a) (and therefore on the assumption of a broader phrasing of the power), the next question is whether, in the circumstances, the power was used in a manner which amounted to arbitrary or unjustifiable discrimination, to which the answer ought to be "yes", as the court found that there was no reasonable basis for the search.[55] This analysis will also lead to an outcome of a breach

---

54.   An analysis in this respect may turn on how widely the power is phrased; for example, if the power is phrased as one to "conduct a strip and cavity search upon reasonable suspicion that an entrant into the state is carrying contraband, such as illegal drugs or firearms", provisional justification would be difficult to establish as, in light of the facts as found by the court, there appeared to be no reasonable basis for the strip and cavity search (paras. 41 and 42). Generally, care should be taken in describing the measure/power in this analysis, so as to be an accurate reflection of the circumstances, while not being unduly wide or narrow.

55.   *Myrie (merits)*, paras. 41 and 42.

of the treaty. This analysis shows the danger of a narrow reading of equating arbitrary or unjustifiable discrimination to nationality-based discrimination, as the court in *Myrie (merits)* found that there was not enough evidence to demonstrate nationality-based discrimination.

Another opportunity for a direct discussion of the general exceptions arose in *Gilberts v Barbados*.[56] The Gilberts were a family of Grenadian nationals who visited Barbados to conduct business at the US embassy there. While visiting a store, the adult daughters were accused of theft by a store owner, an allegation they denied. The daughters were arrested by the Barbadian police, and they alleged that were subjected to strip and cavity searches, which they described as humiliating and embarrassing. They further alleged that they were not allowed to leave the police station unless they removed certain sections from their statements, which painted the actions of the Barbadian police in an unflattering light. Their case was that their ordeal at the police station lasted for approximately six and a half hours, after which they departed for Grenada.

The court was called upon to consider whether special leave should be granted to the Gilberts to pursue a claim against Barbados under the RTC.[57] Two key elements for an applicant for special leave to establish are that (i) they are entitled to rely on the right claimed; and (ii) that there is an arguable case that they have been prejudiced in the enjoyment of the right.[58] For the court, though the freedom of movement under the treaty does guarantee freedom of movement within a member state, the Gilberts were not prejudiced in this right as (i) the applicants could not show that the treatment they faced was as a result of their nationality;[59] and (ii) related to the above, it is normal that people, including locals, are taken into police custody for the purpose of investigation.[60] By way of examples of relevant evidence, the court stated that statistical evidence, evidence showing a pattern of conduct, or evidence of specific targeting based on nationality would assist in showing

---

56.   *Tamika Gilbert, Lynnel Gilbert, Royston Gilbert and Glennor Gilbert v Barbados* [2019] CCJ 2 (OJ) (*Gilberts*).
57.   As is required for private entities under article 222 of the treaty.
58.   RTC, article 222.
59.   *Gilberts*, paras. 24–29.
60.   Ibid., para. 23.

discrimination.[61] The application for special leave was dismissed.

This decision is problematic for a number of reasons. According to the court, the substantive freedom of movement obligation was not breached in the absence of discrimination. Articles 45 and 46 of the treaty, together with the 2007 conference decision, guarantee freedom of movement, which the court in *Gilberts* recognized to include freedom of movement within a member state.[62] Nothing, textually or conceptually, limits breaches of the guarantee to freedom of movement to matters involving nationality-based discrimination. Not every breach of the treaty's freedom of movement provisions needs to be tied to nationality-based discrimination.[63]

A better way of approaching *Gilberts*, bearing in mind that the court was at the special leave stage, would be to consider the detention of the applicants as a breach of the freedom of movement guarantees. This alone, it is suggested, ought to have been enough for the matter to pass the special leave stage, especially in the absence of a sizeable body of jurisprudence from the court on the powers or actions of police officers in member states in the context of freedom of movement.

At the trial of the matter, relevant questions would have been whether the existence of the powers exercised by the police officers fell within, and are provisionally justified under, the general exceptions, and whether the exercise of those powers amounted to arbitrary or unjustifiable discrimination. An assessment of discrimination, especially nationality-based discrimination, would likely involve an examination of material which would naturally be within the state's domain and control (for example records of complaints of police conduct), and the court's power of disclosure could have elicited these matters in a trial setting.[64] By denying special leave, the court denied the applicants the ability to consider material which the state may have had to establish the very nationality-based discrimination which the court considered to be so vital.

---

61.   Ibid., para. 28.
62.   Ibid., para. 22.
63.   As the court recognized in *Myrie (merits)*, where the court found a breach of the right to entry in the 2007 conference decision, despite not finding nationality-based discrimination.
64.   Rule 22.1 enables the court to require any documents and information it considers desirable.

Syllogistic Fallacies

Deductive legal reasoning often involves syllogistic arguments, by which a conclusion is drawn on the basis of accepted propositions. For the court in *Rudisa* and *SM Jaleel*, (1) import duties on goods of CARICOM origin are unlawful; (2) Guyana's measures amounted to import duties, which applied to goods of CARICOM origin (as well as extra-regional goods), and therefore the measure was unlawful. In *Gilberts*, the court's reasoning followed the line of (1) freedom of movement, which includes the freedom to move freely within member states, is guaranteed under the treaty and the conference decision; (2) however, the freedom of movement guarantees do not immunize foreign CARICOM nationals from the law enforcement procedures of member states, and an applicant is required to show discrimination on the basis of nationality only by law enforcement officials, and the applicants were therefore not prejudiced in the exercise of any treaty right in the absence of an ability to demonstrate nationality-based discrimination.

The syllogistic fallacies in *Rudisa* and *SM Jaleel*, on the one hand, and *Gilberts*, on the other, both stem from the general exceptions not being considered, and lead to fundamentally different deductive outcomes. In *Rudisa* and *SM Jaleel*, the treaty's provisions are treated like blunt instruments, with no room for external considerations once a principal norm is affected. As such, the "noble" nature of the tax was of no consequence, and the mere existence of the tax was considered to be a breach of the treaty. A fundamentally different approach is seen in *Gilberts*, where the content of the principal norm was considered to be affected, in a fundamental way, by the general, contextual provision prohibiting discrimination on the basis of nationality only, and the perceived need to protect activity considered necessary to the functioning of the state. The court, therefore, made a significant inroad into the nature and content of the principal norm, and the basis of external factors, such as the need for law enforcement to function. Here, a category of activity which the court recognizes as important to a state's function resulted in an apparent court-generated exception, and this exception was treated as the blunt instrument. In *Rudisa* and *SM Jaleel*, the substantive principal norm was treated as a blunt instrument, whereas in *Gilberts*, the court-generated exception to the principal norm was treated as a blunt instrument.

An argument has been made for the replacement of the syllogistic outlook of legal reasoning, particularly with respect to international law, with the dialogic practice, in light of exceptions and the burden of proof considerations which apply.[65] Whatever outlook, or approach, is taken to legal reasoning by the court, consideration of the general exceptions will be critical in any analysis going forward, else further syllogistic fallacies are likely to emerge.

Conclusion

The RTC, like many international instruments, provide various methods for the subjects of its obligations to fall outside of the ambit of a particular rule. Some of these, such as those in article 226(1) of the treaty, provide defence arguments to potential defendants.[66] It appears that defendants before the CCJ have not been placing reliance on article 226(1)'s content, and no substantial jurisprudence has developed in this respect. Given the similarities between article 226(1) and article XX of the GATT, in that the latter is the obvious inspiration for the former, a sizeable body of GATT (and GATS) jurisprudence can form the foundation of the analytical outlook for the RTC's general exceptions. However, in light of some of the different circumstances which arise in the CARICOM context, especially vis-à-vis freedom of movement, some differences in the interpretation and application of article 226(1) are to be expected.

The non-consideration of the general exceptions has led to some issues in the development of CARICOM law. Because of the syllogistic fallacies flowing from the non-deployment of these exceptions, the principal obligations have, on the one hand, been treated like immutable constructs, and on the other hand, malleable or amorphous ideas subject to the exigencies of a functioning state. Neither approach is desirable, or in keeping with the international instrument as negotiated. The general exceptions are present within the treaty to, very importantly, provide avenues for states to pursue measures not related to the common market. It is vital that these exceptions are recognized, and developed upon.

---

65. Jaap Hage, Antonia Waltermann, and Gustavo Arosemena, "Exceptions in International Law," in *Exceptions and Defences in International Law*, sec. 11.

66. "Defence arguments", rather than "defences", as the labelling of a line of analysis as a "defence" involves an acceptance of a prima facie breach of an international obligation.

CHAPTER 11

Shiprider Reconsidered – Jamaican Jurisdiction Over Maritime Drug Trafficking

Stephen Vasciannie

Twenty-five years ago, following months of public and private argumentation, Jamaica and the United States completed a bilateral maritime treaty designed to tackle the well-known and intractable problem of unlawful drug shipments in the Caribbean Sea. The treaty – formally denoted as the Agreement between Jamaica and the United States of America concerning Cooperation in Suppression of Illicit Maritime Drug Trafficking[1] – sets out rules that allow American naval officers to search both Jamaican vessels at sea and foreign vessels in Jamaica's waters.[2] Conversely, and at Jamaica's insistence, the maritime agreement also gives Jamaica the right to undertake searches of US vessels and foreign vessels in US waters.[3]

The treaty has come to be popularly described as "the Shiprider agreement" because, on one side, it is built on the premise that Jamaican nationals may join US naval officers on US ships as "shipriders".[4] While aboard the US ships, the Jamaican shipriders may authorize US officers to undertake searches of foreign vessels in Jamaican waters.[5] By the same token, US nationals acting as shipriders on Jamaican ships may authorize searches of vessels in US waters.[6] At its core then the Shiprider agreement establishes an agency relationship: the shiprider from one state may ask the other

---

1. US Department of State, *Treaties and Other International Acts Series, 98–310.*
2. The treaty also addresses certain overflight rights that may be exercised in efforts to combat drug trafficking; these rights are not considered in this article, which is concerned with maritime areas.
3. See, for example, Articles 3, 7 and 8 of the Shiprider agreement.
4. The agreement does not use the term "Shiprider", preferring instead the phrase "Law enforcement officials"; but "shiprider" has passed into general usage.
5. Article 7.
6. Article 8.

state to stop and search certain ships as a means of combatting the flow of illicit drugs. The agreement also provides for the possibility of search by US authorities of Jamaican ships in waters beyond the Jamaican territorial sea, and for the possibility of Jamaican searches of US ships beyond the territorial waters of the United States.[7]

The original negotiations pertaining to the Jamaica/US Shiprider agreement were mired in controversy.[8] For some critics, the agreement was part of a broad US plan to impose its hegemonic will in the Caribbean Sea, if not across the entire Caribbean and beyond.[9] As part of this analysis, it was suggested that the United States, while referring to the need to deter drug trafficking, was prepared to limit the sovereignty of smaller Caribbean states.[10] This perspective was given initial sustenance by the fact that the United States had sought to rely on a single model Shiprider agreement in its negotiations with all Caribbean states. The suggestion was that the US government did not acknowledge the individual features of discrete Caribbean countries on issues of drug-trafficking: the Americans were said to have presumed that one size, in the form of the model agreement, should fit all countries. In response, the US took the view that a single approach to Shiprider arrangements in the Caribbean Sea was desirable for operational reasons. A US naval effort involving maritime searches in the waters of, say, Jamaica and five other Caribbean states would be complicated if the US authorities were obliged to follow different pursuit, search and seizure approaches for each jurisdiction. Uniformity is valuable, especially in the emergency circumstances of crime-fighting.

---

7. Article 3.
8. For review, see Stephen Vasciannie, "Political and Policy Aspects of the Jamaica/US Shiprider Negotiations," *Caribbean Quarterly* 43, no. 3 (1997): 34; Suzette A. Haughton, *Drugged Out: Globalisation and Jamaica's Resilience to Drug Trafficking* (Lanham, MD: University Press of America, 2011), 186–97; Holger W. Henke, "The 'Shiprider' Controversy and the Question of Sovereignty," *European Review of Latin American and Caribbean Studies* 64 (1998): 27; Lloyd Williams, "The Shiprider Agreement: No Smooth Sailing," *The Gleaner*, 8 February 2004.
9. See, for example, Hilbourne Watson, "The 'Shiprider Solution' and Post-Cold War Imperialism: Beyond Ontologies of State Sovereignty in the Caribbean," in *Living at the Borderlines: Issues in Caribbean Sovereignty and Development*, eds. Cynthia Barrow-Giles and Don D. Marshall (Kingston: Ian Randle, 2003), 226.
10. Presentation by then Jamaican Prime Minister P.J. Patterson to the Friedrich Ebert Stiftung Seminar, 18 September 1996, reprinted in *A Jamaican Voice in Caribbean and World Politics: P.J. Patterson, Selected Speeches, 1992–2000*, ed. Delano Franklyn (2002), 129–31.

A second methodological complaint was that the United States may have applied divide-and-rule tactics. Rather than undertake negotiations with CARICOM countries as a group, the United States had transmitted its model Shiprider agreement to Jamaica and other Caribbean countries one by one. Given the stark power imbalance between the United States, on the one hand, and individual Caribbean countries on the other, the critics suggested that the latter could not realistically have opposed the terms in the model agreement. In the period leading up to the Shiprider negotiations, Elliott Abrams, writing from a US standpoint, had recommended that the United States should assume powers vis-à-vis the security of some smaller Caribbean jurisdictions in terms that seemed to minimize the sovereign prerogatives of these states.[11] Negotiations between the United States and individual Caribbean countries seemed to emphasize the disparity between the presumably dependent smaller state and the powerful hegemon intending to assume extensive powers. But to be fair, this was not a decisive argument against the US approach for, by negotiating with the individual states, the United States acknowledged the sovereignty of each.

Some elements of the controversy between Jamaica and the United States turned on points of substance. Jamaica put up early resistance to the idea of allowing US officials to undertake searches in Jamaican waters in any circumstances, but eventually adjusted its position: provided that a Jamaican shiprider on the US vessel made the request, the search of vessels in Jamaican waters could proceed. Eventually, the major obstacle to agreement concerned the question of what should happen when there was no Jamaican shiprider on board the US ship to make the request.

The United States proposed that, in the absence of a Jamaican shiprider to make the request, US naval officers could still proceed to search vessels in Jamaican waters. From the US standpoint, this approach would facilitate drug searches in situations of pursuit,

---

11.   Elliott Abrams, "The Shiprider Solution: Policing the Caribbean", *National Interest*, 1 March 1996, https://nationalinterest.org/article/the-shiprider-solution-policing-the-caribbean-487, last accessed 22 December 2021: "What might be tolerated in distant lands – a government run by merciless thugs or the corrupted allies of drug traffickers – is far less acceptable in our front-yard" (p.3). Not surprisingly, if negotiations are built on the premise that leaders on one side are "corrupted allies of drug traffickers", there may be acrimony across the negotiating table.

whether or not a Jamaican shiprider is available, and thereby give wide-ranging effect to the agreement as a tool of crime-fighting. The US position on the value of uniformity among regional maritime agreements was also relevant here; for all the Shiprider agreements accepted by the Commonwealth Caribbean states carried this approach (save Jamaica and Barbados, which were the outriders). For Jamaica, the country's sovereignty or national pride would have been seriously impugned if Americans were granted unrestricted discretion to search foreign vessels in Jamaican waters, where no Jamaican shiprider was available.[12]

In the end, a compromise was reached. Where there is no Jamaican shiprider available, the US authorities wishing to undertake a search in Jamaican waters are obliged to seek the authorization of a senior Jamaican official before a search may be undertaken. This approach – with permission being sought on a case-by-case basis – allows the United States to pursue and search suspected vessels with expedition, while Jamaica's interest in retaining its sovereignty or national pride is preserved as the United States is obliged to refrain from searches not expressly authorized by Jamaica.

This solution prompted questions: Was the request made to undertake searches merely a matter of form? What was the likelihood that the Jamaican senior official would deny permission to search when a shiprider was not present? And what consequences could follow for the Jamaican state if its authorities were prepared to deny permission for US officials to undertake searches? In the practice since the entry into force of the Shiprider agreement, these questions appear not to have taxed relations between Jamaica and the United States, so it is plausible to conclude that neither side believes that the arrangements for permission to search have been abused.

The original Jamaica/US Shiprider agreement was signed in Kingston on 6 May 1997.[13] In 1998, the Jamaican parliament passed the Maritime Drug Trafficking (Suppression) Act to give effect to the Shiprider agreement in domestic law.[14] On 6 February 2004,

---

12. For discussion on different meanings that may be attributed to the term "sovereignty" in the context of Shiprider issues, see Stephen Vasciannie, "Reflections on Jamaican Sovereignty," *Jamaica Observer*, 12 December 2015.
13. Department of State, *Treaties*.
14. Effective 28 February 1998.

the original agreement was amended by the parties to give effect to certain operational changes and to strengthen the means by which drug traffickers may be challenged. These changes did not affect the basic structure concerning Shiprider searches contemplated in the original agreement.

In 2016, the Jamaican parliament then passed a new set of amendments to the Maritime Drug Trafficking (Suppression) Act.[15] Under the Act as originally passed, where a person was detained by US officials pursuant to a Shiprider search, this person could normally be taken either to Jamaica or the United States for trial, sentencing and imprisonment, as appropriate. There was, however, a major exception to this approach. Specifically, where a Jamaican was detained by the United States, the Jamaican laws required – or seemed to require – the Jamaican to be surrendered to the Jamaican authorities. The 2016 amendments to the Maritime Drug Trafficking (Suppression) Act sought to change this situation, so that Jamaicans could in some circumstances be surrendered to the jurisdiction of US courts.[16] This amendment has generated strong disagreement in Jamaican on legal and political grounds.

This essay undertakes a technical review of aspects of the arrangements that have come to be associated with the Shiprider agreement between Jamaica and the United States, as well as Jamaican law in this area. The discussion will concentrate on the legal rules that are applicable to ships in different parts of the sea, with emphasis on Jamaican maritime zones and Jamaican-registered ships. In light of the 2016 amendments to the Maritime Drug Trafficking (Suppression) Act, the essay will also consider the factors which prompted Jamaica to accept the possibility that Jamaicans may be surrendered to the jurisdiction of the United States. In addition, the essay will assess the Jamaican state's legal capacity to board and search vessels in different parts of the sea and consider the application of the relevant rules on the waiver of jurisdiction with respect to Jamaican nationals accused of involvement in maritime drug trafficking.

---

15.   Act No. 3 – 2016, 12 February 2016.
16.   See the Maritime Drug Trafficking (Suppression) (Amendment) Act, 2016.

Searches in Jamaican Zones

Jamaica's maritime zones are defined in the country's Maritime Areas Act.[17] Under the Act, Jamaica has assumed the status of an archipelagic state. Its main zones are internal waters, archipelagic waters, the territorial sea, the contiguous zone and the Exclusive Economic Zone. In these zones, Jamaica may exercise different degrees of jurisdiction – and therefore powers of search – over local and foreign ships, with the degree of jurisdiction turning in large part on the proximity of the maritime zone to Jamaica's coastline. Beyond the outer limit of the Exclusive Economic Zone lie the high seas: Jamaica has very limited jurisdiction over foreign ships in this area. The international law rules concerning Jamaica's jurisdiction over ships in different parts of the sea are set out mainly in the Law of the Sea Convention,[18] to which Jamaica is a party,[19] and in customary international law. In the discussion which follows, emphasis will be placed on the Jamaican legislation which addresses the main zones of the sea in relation to maritime drug trafficking.

It should also be noted from the outset that for the purpose of searches in different zones of the sea, Jamaican and international law distinguish between Jamaican and foreign ships. As a general matter, Jamaican ships are subject to search and the exercise of jurisdiction by Jamaican authorities in all parts of the sea, irrespective of whether the waters are regarded as Jamaican. In contrast, Jamaica's right to search foreign vessels is normally exercisable only in Jamaican waters. This is exemplified by Section 325 of the Jamaican Shipping Act, which draws this distinction between ships for the purpose of search by Jamaican maritime inspectors.[20] With respect to drug searches, the applicable rules follow this pattern. Ships flying the Jamaican flag, wherever they may be, are subject to Jamaican jurisdiction; whether foreign ships

---

17.   Act No. 25 of 1996; entered into force on 28 November 1996.
18.   United Nations, *Treaty Series* 1833 (1994): 3.
19.   Jamaica became a party to the Law of the Sea Convention on 21 March 1983: United Nations Treaty Collection (Law of the Sea), https://treaties.un.org/pages/Treaties. aspx?id=21&subid=A&clang=_en.
20.   Compare Section 325(2) on Jamaican ships with Section 325(1) on foreign ships: Shipping Act (1999). See also Section 21(1) of the Maritime Drug Trafficking (Suppression) Act which stipulates: "The laws of Jamaica extend to any offence committed outside of Jamaican waters on a vessel or aircraft registered in Jamaica."

are subject to Jamaican jurisdiction depends on the location of the ship at the time of the search.

Ports and Internal Waters

A Jamaican ship is in a Jamaican port. This ship will be subject to the exclusive jurisdiction of the Jamaican authorities. Thus, as long as the authorities show due regard for Jamaican law, they may detain the ship, board and search it, and arrest members of the crew, if they find illegal drugs. When a ship is in port, it is to be regarded as being in Jamaica. The Port Authority Act treats ports as part of the country and authorizes the responsible minister to declare any of the country's harbours to be a port.[21] Similarly, article 11 of the Law of the Sea Convention indicates in part that: "For the purpose of delimiting the territorial sea, the outermost permanent harbour works which form an integral part of the harbour system are regarded as forming part of the coast."

This, then, is clear: Jamaican authorities may search Jamaican vessels in Jamaican ports for illegal drugs in the same manner that they may search premises in other parts of the land territory of Jamaica. But what if, by reference to the Shiprider agreement, the Jamaican authorities ask US officials to undertake a search of the Jamaican ship in the Jamaican port – on behalf of Jamaica? Is this search lawful? This question was considered by Batts, J in the 2013 Jamaican Supreme Court case of *David Chin v Attorney General of Jamaica*.[22]

The claimant maintained that Jamaican authorities acted in breach of local law when they invited US Coast Guard personnel to join in the search of a vessel owned by the claimant while it was docked in Kingston Harbour.[23] The vessel in question, *Lady Lawla,* was suspected of having cocaine on board, but this was not substantiated. On the facts, the Jamaica Defence Force, Jamaica Customs officials and the police all searched the vessel to no avail. Jamaican officials then invited the US Coast Guard to assist in searching the vessel, bearing in mind that the Coast Guard had the

---

21. Section 3, Port Authority Act. By virtue of the Port Authority (Declaration of Ports) Order, 1974, Kingston Harbour and various other harbours in different parts of the country have been declared to be ports.
22. (2014) JMSC Civil 20.
23. Ibid., especially at paras. 5 to 16.

necessary experience and expertise to search spaces in the vessel not properly accounted for. The request for this search was expressly said to be pursuant to a "Shiprider operation". Justice Batts found that this search in Kingston Harbour was unlawful as it was not authorized by Jamaica's Maritime Drug Trafficking (Suppression) Act.[24]

Justice Batts based his conclusion primarily on two considerations. First, he found that the circumstances of the case did not fall within the scope of the Shiprider arrangements because the Jamaican officials were not aboard a US vessel when they requested US assistance.[25] Accordingly, the Jamaican officials had not satisfied an essential precondition for a Shiprider search, as stipulated in Section 8 of the Maritime Drug Trafficking (Suppression) Act: embarkation by the Jamaican making the request is necessary if a valid search is to be undertaken by US officials. This strict textual approach is justifiable. Unauthorized maritime searches undermine the freedoms of the individual and so the state's right to search should be narrowly construed. This approach is consistent with an underlying purpose of the Shiprider agreement with the United States, which is to allow the lawful operation of US officials within Jamaican waters. At the time of the request for the search of *Lady Lawla*, it is difficult to suggest that the US officers were operating in Jamaican waters.

The second point taken by Justice Batts concerns the legal status of a Jamaican ship located in Kingston Harbour. Justice Batts held that the search of *Lady Lawla* did not, in fact, take place in "Jamaican waters", as defined in the Maritime Areas Act, and for this reason, it was not a valid search pursuant to the Shiprider arrangements. As noted by Justice Batts, under the Maritime Areas Act, "Jamaican waters" are defined as internal waters, archipelagic waters, and the territorial sea. The Act does not incorporate ports or jetties in the definition of Jamaican waters; nor does it indicate that "when a ship is docked in a harbour, port or jetty, it is in the internal waters or the territorial sea".[26] For Justice Batts, therefore, the provisions of the Maritime Drug (Suppression) Act authorizing

---

24. At para. 26.
25. At para. 27.
26. At para. 32.

Shiprider searches in Jamaican waters do not apply to a vessel which is safely docked in a port or harbour and is therefore no longer at sea in territorial or inland waterways. The search of *The Lady Lawla* was therefore unlawful because, having been undertaken in port, it did not take place in "Jamaican waters".[27]

Justice Batts' reasoning on Jamaican waters is not entirely convincing. Article 11 of the Law of the Sea Convention, quoted above, specifies that the outermost part of the harbour works represent a country's coastline; *a contrario*, points in the sea beyond the harbour works constitute internal waters. Also, Batts' approach carries the implication that waters beyond harbour works are to be regarded as land territory. This is an implausible position. The fact that a vessel docked in the harbour is accessible from the land does not mean that the vessel is on the land. The better view, then, is that the water in port is to be regarded as internal waters. On this point, the definition of internal waters in the Maritime Areas Act may provide guidance. Section 4 of the Act stipulates that for Jamaica: "The internal waters comprise the areas of the sea which are on the landward side of the closing lines within the archipelagic waters which may be prescribed for the purposes of defining internal waters."

In effect, this definition – which takes its origins from the 1958 Geneva Territorial Sea Convention[28] and the Law of the Sea Convention – confirms that the *areas of sea* on the landward side of the closing lines for internal waters are internal waters. The idea that the waters within a port are internal waters is further reinforced by customary international law. Thus, Colombos expressly includes a state's ports as part of its "interior", "inland" or "national" waters,[29] while Jennings and Watts,[30] O'Connell[31] and Churchill

27.   Ibid.

28.   Convention on the Territorial Sea and the Contiguous Zone, United Nations, *Treaty Series*, 516 (1964): 205.

29.   Constantine John Colombos, *The International Law of the Sea*, 6th ed. (London: Longman, 1967), 175.

30.   Robert Jennings and Arthur Watts, *Oppenheim's International Law Vol. II* (Harlow: Longman, 1993), 606. ("The waters of ports have always been internal waters.")

31.   Daniel Patrick O'Connell, *The International Law of the Sea Vol. 1* (Oxford: Clarendon Press, 1982), 338.

and Lowe,[32] all proceed on the assumption that ports are part of a country's internal waters.

Also, as a matter of policy, if ports are distinguished from other internal waters for purposes of Shiprider searches, this could create a problem of enforcement for Jamaica. Specifically, if the distinction prevails, a foreign ship being pursued by a US vessel with a Jamaican shiprider on board would be inclined to race to the Jamaican port in order to avoid search by the American authorities; for, if detained in the internal waters, as construed by Batts, the foreign vessel could be subject to search. But, if it is detained in port, then, it could not legally be searched by US law enforcement officers. As this would appear to be a counter-intuitive result for a scheme designed to combat illegal drug trafficking in Jamaican waters, it is a conclusion that should be drawn only with reference to clear and compelling words.

The *David Chin* decision is therefore justifiable on the basis that the language in the Maritime Drug (Suppression) Act requires a Shiprider search to be initiated by a Jamaican shiprider "embarked" upon a US ship. The decision is consistent with the formulation in the Shiprider agreement to which the Act gives force in Jamaican law. On the other hand, the court's approach to the question of the status of ships in Jamaican ports may be vulnerable to challenge.

More generally, it should be noted that if ports and other internal waters are subsumed under the same heading, the Shiprider regime for internal waters as a whole is coherently structured. Under this regime, Shiprider searches may be conducted on the instruction of Jamaican shipriders on US vessels and persons detained pursuant to such searches will be subject to the jurisdiction of the Jamaican authorities and will be triable in Jamaican courts, in keeping with Jamaica's sovereignty over its internal waters. As the Shiprider agreement operates on the basis of reciprocity, US courts will have jurisdiction in respect of vessels searched in US waters by Jamaican law enforcement officials at the behest of US shipriders. The possibility of searches in US waters from Jamaican vessels has remained remote, but the reciprocal arrangement shows deference to Jamaica's sovereign will.

---

32. Robin Churchill and Vaughan Lowe, *The Law of the Sea* (Manchester: Manchester University Press, 1988), 51.

Archipelagic Waters

Jamaica assumed the status of an archipelagic state pursuant to Section 3 of the Maritime Areas Act. For the country, archipelagic status is justified by reference to the terms of Part IV of the Law of the Sea Convention, which allows the state to draw straight baselines around the islands that are part of it.[33] In the case of Jamaica, the main island carries a number of base points, with others for the archipelagic system placed on the Morant Cays, Southwest Rock, Blower Rock and on other small islands off the south coast of the main island.[34] The straight baselines that connect the base points have enclosed Jamaica's archipelagic waters, a significant maritime area extending in a southerly direction into the Caribbean Sea.[35]

Jamaica's archipelagic waters constitute a zone of sovereignty, declared in Section 5 of the Maritime Areas Act.[36] Foreign vessels have defined rights of access through Jamaican archipelagic waters: as specified in the Maritime Areas Act, foreign vessels have the right of innocent passage in general[37] and may enjoy the right of archipelagic sea lanes passage in specially designated parts of the zone.[38]

Where a foreign vessel is exercising innocent passage in Jamaica's archipelagic waters, local authorities have the right to search the vessels as an appurtenant of domestic sovereignty. This right to search also takes legislative authority from the interplay among sections 8, 13 and 14(2) of the Maritime Areas Act. Section 8 provides for the right of innocent passage in archipelagic waters and indicates that the right is enjoyed "in accordance with the provisions of Section 13". Section 13 indicates how the right of innocent passage is to be exercised in the territorial sea. And then section 14(2) provides, inter alia, that measures of criminal jurisdiction may be undertaken in respect of vessels in innocent

33. Article 47, Law of the Sea Convention.
34. United States Department of State, Bureau of Oceans and International Environmental Affairs, *Limits in the Seas, No. 125: Jamaica's Maritime Claims and Boundaries* (5 February 2004), 4.
35. Jamaica's archipelagic waters cover an area of approximately 22,200 square kilometres, in comparison with a land area of 10,990 square kilometres: Ibid., 6–7.
36. This position reflects the approach set out in article 49, Law of the Sea Convention.
37. Sections 8 and 13, Maritime Areas Act.
38. Sections 8, 9 and 26, Maritime Areas Act.

passage if they are "necessary for the suppression of illicit traffic in narcotic drugs and psychotropic substances".[39] Taken together, these provisions affirm the right of Jamaican authorities to search foreign ships enjoying innocent passage in the country's archipelagic waters. This interpretation is consistent, too, with the language of article 52 of the Law of the Sea Convention, the relevant portion of which provides that ships of all states "enjoy the right of innocent passage through archipelagic waters, in accordance with Part II, section 3 [of the Convention]". Section 3 includes the legal rule authorizing the coastal state to exercise criminal jurisdiction in drug trafficking matters.

Pursuant to the Maritime Areas Act, Jamaica may designate archipelagic sea lanes for the passage of vessels through the country's archipelagic waters. Passage through these sea lanes – denoted as archipelagic sea lanes passage – shall be continuous, expeditious and unobstructed for vessels. If Jamaica does not designate sea lanes, ships shall have the right to exercise archipelagic sea lanes passage "through the routes normally used for international navigation" in the archipelagic waters. May Jamaica exercise the right to search foreign vessels as they undertake archipelagic sea lanes passage?

One response to this question could possibly be that the rules pertaining to innocent passage in Jamaica's archipelagic waters also apply to archipelagic sea lanes passage in the same waters. This is doubtful. Section 8 of the Maritime Areas Act provides support for the idea that searches may be undertaken with respect to ships in innocent passage, but the rule in Section 8 is expressly said to be "subject to" the power of the Jamaican state to designate archipelagic sea lanes passage. This suggests that the regimes of innocent passage and archipelagic sea lanes passage differ from each other. Section 9 of the Act reinforces this interpretation, by stipulating distinct rules on archipelagic sea lanes passage in general. On the specific question of the right to search, Section 9(3)(b)(iii) of the Act offers helpful guidance. It states that: "A foreign vessel shall, in exercising the right of archipelagic sea lanes passage comply with the provisions of any enactment having effect with regard to the archipelagic waters in relation to customs, excise,

---

39. Section 14(2)(iv), Maritime Areas Act.

immigration or sanitation controls in respect of the loading or unloading of any commodity, currency or person."

This provision, it is submitted, allows local authorities to undertake searches of vessels exercising archipelagic sea lanes passage, on the grounds that searches are necessary to give force to Jamaica rules on customs that prohibit the loading and unloading of illicit drugs.

In sum, therefore, all foreign vessels in Jamaican archipelagic waters – whether exercising innocent passage or archipelagic sea lanes passage – are subject to search by Jamaican law enforcement officers. On this foundation, and having regard to the agency relationship established by the Shiprider arrangements, Jamaica may thus authorize US law enforcement officers to search foreign vessels in Jamaica's archipelagic waters.

Territorial Waters

The main rules concerning the Jamaican territorial sea are set out in the Maritime Areas Act. In brief, the Act provides that the territorial sea is a zone of Jamaican sovereignty which extends for twelve nautical miles from the archipelagic baselines around the country.[40] Foreign ships enjoy the right of innocent passage through the Jamaican territorial sea. While exercising innocent passage here, foreign ships are subject to rules of criminal jurisdiction set out in Section 14 of the Maritime Areas Act. With respect to search of foreign vessels, Section 14(2) provides, inter alia, that:

> (2) No person shall be arrested on board a foreign vessel which is passing through the territorial sea nor shall any investigation be conducted into any crime committed on board such foreign vessel:
> - during such passage except where –
> - the consequences of the crime extend to Jamaica; or
> - the crime is of a kind which disturbs the peace of Jamaica or good order of the territorial sea; or ...
> - the assistance of a Marine Officer has been requested by the master of the foreign vessel or by a diplomatic or

---

40. Jamaica's territorial sea incorporates an area of 17,995 square kilometres: *Limits in the Seas*, 6–7.

consular representative of the State of registration of the
foreign vessel; or

- such measures are necessary for the suppression of
the illicit traffic in narcotic drugs and psychotropic
substances.

Section 14(2) also addresses the situation in which a foreign
ship has been involved in a crime before entering the Jamaican
territorial sea, has travelled from a foreign port, and has not entered
Jamaican internal waters. In this situation, criminal jurisdiction
shall not normally be exercised over the vessel, save in certain cases
of pollution.

Two further points may be noted by way of clarification. First,
where a foreign vessel is passing through the Jamaican territorial
sea, it shall always be subject to search if it is passing through
the territorial sea, after having left Jamaica's internal waters.
Secondly, section 14(3) of the Act stipulates: "All offences under
the Dangerous Drugs Act, whether or not they are only summary
offences, shall be treated as if they are punishable on indictment."
This latter provision affirms that Jamaican criminal jurisdiction
over the territorial sea applies to all offences relating to illicit drug
movement through the territorial sea.

Thus, the provisions on criminal jurisdiction in the territorial
sea, as set out in the Maritime Areas Act – including search and
seizure – place responsibility for tackling illicit drug trafficking by
foreign ships in the hands of Jamaican law enforcement officers.
This approach gives effect in Jamaican law to the Law of the Sea
Convention and to article 19 of the Territorial Sea Convention,
1958.

The language used in article 19 of the Territorial Sea Convention
was given judicial consideration by the Privy Council in *Pianka
and Hylton v R.* in 1977.[41] In this case, a US vessel, *The Star Baby*,
was detained within the Jamaican territorial sea[42] by local officials
approximately 3.8 miles from the baseline of the zone.[43] *The Star
Baby* was carrying 3,277 pounds of marijuana at the time of its
detention.[44] One issue in the case concerned whether the relevant

41. (1977) 15 J.L.R. 175.
42. Jamaica adopted a 12-mile territorial sea on 19 July 1971: *Limits in the Seas,* 6.
43. (1977) 15 J.L.R. 175 at p. 176.
44. Ibid.

Jamaican legislation authorized trial of the defendants in the resident magistrates' court. This issue arose because one piece of legislation – the Territorial Sea Act, 1971 – authorized jurisdiction in respect of cases brought on indictment. This did not include cases triable before the resident magistrates' court. Another legislative act – the Resident Magistrates Act, 1887 – appeared, however, to extend jurisdiction to that court. The Privy Council held that the latter Act was applicable in the case, and so, the resident magistrates' court had jurisdiction.[45]

A second issue was whether the language of article 19 of the Territorial Sea Convention was applicable based on the facts. The Privy Council held that although article 19 was stated in hortatory terms, it assumed binding force in Jamaica when the country ratified the Territorial Sea Convention in 1971.[46] Criminal jurisdiction was confirmed by the Privy Council on the grounds that the drug activity of *The Star Baby* in the territorial sea had consequences for Jamaica, affected the good order of the country or the territorial sea, and was necessary to counter illicit trafficking in drugs.[47] In other words, the drug activity in this case was subject to local jurisdiction on three of the four grounds contemplated in article 19 of the Territorial Sea Convention, the precursor to article 27 of the Law of the Sea Convention and section 14(2) of the Maritime Areas Act, which currently apply vis-a-vis Jamaica. In *Pianka,* at the Court of Appeal level in Jamaica,[48] Luckhoo, P (acting), writing for the court, held that the drug activity involving *The Star Baby* had consequences for Jamaica and affected the good order of the territorial sea.[49] Luckhoo did not, however, refer to the possibility that criminal jurisdiction in this case could also have turned on the idea that it was necessary to suppress drug trafficking. It is not clear why the Jamaican Court of Appeal opted not to rely on this ground for jurisdiction set out in article 19 of the Territorial Sea Convention.

45.   Ibid., 180–83.
46.   Ibid., 183.
47.   Ibid.
48.   *R. v Bernard Pianka and Terry Hilton* (1975) J.L.R. 195.
49.   Ibid., 203–4.

In *R. v Thomas Dakin*,[50] the Jamaican Court of Appeal upheld the jurisdiction of the Jamaican authorities in respect of two Caymanian vessels, *The Peters* and *Zion,* which were in Jamaica's territorial sea. *The Peters* was towing the *Zion* at the time the ships were intercepted by local officials. Dakin went on board the *Zion* and threw overboard four to six parcels.[51] Only one parcel was recovered, and it was found to contain about two ounces of marijuana.[52] Some of the other parcels – unrecovered – were twenty-pound bags with vegetable matter resembling the item recovered.[53] So, only a very small quantity of marijuana came into the state's possession. The appellant argued, inter alia, that article 19(1)(d) of the Territorial Sea Convention did not justify Jamaica's exercise of jurisdiction because the total amount of marijuana in question was insufficient to support a finding that the ships were engaged in the illicit traffic of narcotic drugs.[54] The Court of Appeal rejected this argument and found jurisdiction on the basis of the need to tackle drug trafficking: "Although [the magistrate] did not expressly state that the ships were engaged in illicit traffic in narcotics, ... such a finding is implicit and reasonable. That there is considerable traffic in ganja in and through the Caribbean Sea and the territorial waters of Jamaica is notorious. From the evidence generally it is clear that the action of the [Jamaican authorities] was concerned with the suppression of illicit traffic in narcotics."[55]

The Court of Appeal, in *R. v Dakin,* was apparently more willing to rely on article 19(1)(d) of the Territorial Sea Act than its counterpart court had been in *Pianka. Dakin* expressly drew inspiration from the Privy Council's approach in *Pianka,* and it is noticeable that the Court of Appeal in *Dakin* did not link Jamaica's exercise of jurisdiction to the view that the passage of the foreign vessels had consequences in Jamaica or undermined the good order of the territorial sea. Reliance on the necessity to tackle drug trafficking – through article 19(1)(d) – is a more direct route to jurisdiction in drug cases than the other reference points in article 19(1)(a) and (b) of the Territorial Sea Convention.

---

50.   (1978) 15 J.L.R. 302
51.   Ibid., 302.
52.   Ibid.
53.   Ibid.
54.   Ibid., 304.
55.   Ibid., 305–6.

The Maritime Drug Trafficking (Suppression) Act and the Shiprider agreement both build on the rules of criminal jurisdiction applicable to the territorial sea, which may be traced back to article 19 of the Territorial Sea Convention. A Jamaican shiprider aboard a US vessel is authorized to request US assistance to undertake searches for illegal drugs in the Jamaican territorial sea.

The Contiguous Zone

The Jamaican contiguous zone lies immediately beyond the territorial sea and extends seaward from the territorial sea for twelve nautical miles.[56] The contiguous zone is not sovereign territory. Rather, it is an area over which Jamaica exercises jurisdiction with respect to particular matters. Section 20(1) of the Maritime Area Act identifies these matters. It states: "There is vested in the Crown authority in the contiguous zone to take such measures as are necessary to prevent in Jamaica, the archipelagic waters or the territorial sea, the infringement by any person or vessel of the provisions of any enactment relating to customs, fiscal matters, immigration or sanitation and to arrest any person who or vessel which, contravenes such laws and regulations."

Section 20(2) then indicates that local law enforcement officials shall have the power of arrest for any infringement of customs, fiscal matters, immigration and sanitation laws in the contiguous zone. On the assumption that the enforcement of customs rules includes jurisdiction over drug-trafficking offences, Jamaican law enforcement officials may, therefore, search foreign vessels to tackle drug trafficking in Jamaica's contiguous zone.

The question arises whether Jamaica's right to search foreign vessels in the contiguous zone for drugs may be applied to Shiprider searches. In other words, is a Jamaican Shiprider aboard a US ship entitled to conduct searches of foreign vessels in the Jamaican continuous zone? Or may Jamaica authorize US law enforcement officers to undertake searches of foreign vessels in the Jamaican contiguous zone? This issue is not expressly addressed in the provisions of the Jamaican Maritime Drug Trafficking (Suppression) Act. As regards "Jamaican waters" – namely, internal

---

56.   The area covered by the contiguous zone is approximately 21,055 square kilometres: *Limits in the Seas*, 6–7.

waters, archipelagic waters and the territorial sea – the Maritime Drug Trafficking Suppression Act expressly authorizes Shiprider searches. In contrast, no provisions of the Act expressly permit such searches in the contiguous zone. The formulation in the Act suggests, by implication, that Shiprider searches may not take place in the contiguous zone.

But the matter does not end there, for it is possible that Shiprider searches in the Jamaican contiguous zone are justified by means other than express provisions in the Maritime Drug Trafficking (Suppression) Act. In this regard, section 8(2)(a) of the Act requires consideration. Section 8(2)(a) reads as follows: "The [Jamaican] law enforcement officials may, while embarked on law enforcement vessels belonging to a treaty state [the USA], enforce the laws of Jamaica in Jamaican waters and seaward therefrom in the exercise of the right of hot pursuit, or otherwise, in accordance with international law."

A pertinent observation is that Shiprider searches under this provision are justified in the Jamaican contiguous zone if these searches are related to hot pursuit. As hot pursuit may indeed take place in a coastal state's contiguous zone, the right to exercise Shiprider searches in the Jamaican contiguous zone is confirmed for this situation. Secondly, section 8(2)(a) authorizes Shiprider searches "otherwise, in accordance with international law". The scope of this authorization may be unclear; but, in all likelihood, it supports Shiprider searches in the contiguous zone. Specifically, it may be assumed that Jamaican law enforcement officials are authorized to undertake Shiprider searches, as noted above. And if Jamaican officials have this right, then, "in accordance with international law", they may exercise it while aboard US ships or allow US officials to act as their agents in searching foreign ships. International law does not prohibit joint, cooperative efforts at law enforcement in a state's contiguous zone; nor does it bar agency relationships between states in this zone. The main argument against this interpretation is that it is somewhat circuitous: Jamaica could have authorized Shiprider searches in the contiguous zone by direct reference to rights in the zone; but it did not. This argument, though, is not decisive. The better view is that section 8(2)(a) allows

Shiprider searches in the contiguous zone as long as they are in accordance with international law.

The Exclusive Economic Zone

Under international law, the contiguous zone of a state overlaps with the first twelve nautical miles of the Exclusive Economic Zone (the EEZ) of the state.[57] This is true for Jamaica, so that Shiprider searches authorized in the contiguous zone would apply to searches in the first twelve nautical miles of the EEZ. Beyond the twelve-mile limit, however, a different set of rules is applicable. References in this sub-section to the EEZ pertain to that part of the EEZ beyond the inner twelve miles of the EEZ that constitute the contiguous zone. This is not to say that the inner twelve miles of the EEZ are not part of the EEZ; it is to acknowledge that different rules apply in the two parts of the EEZ.

With respect to foreign ships in the EEZ, the Jamaican Exclusive Economic Act[58] proceeds on the assumption that Jamaica may exercise criminal jurisdiction over drug trafficking as the coastal state. This possibility is supported by sections 10 and 19(2) of the Act. Section 10 stipulates that: "For the purpose of giving effect to this Act the jurisdiction and powers of the courts of Jamaica and officers thereof and of any constable or other person authorized to perform the duties of a constable shall extend to the zone in like manner as if the zone constituted the territorial sea of Jamaica."

This provision could be interpreted to mean that the offences subject to criminal jurisdiction in the Jamaican territorial sea, including drug trafficking, are also to be regarded as criminal offences in the Jamaican EEZ. Section 19(2) lends support to this reading for, in addressing the question of indictable offences for the purposes of the Act, it states that: "For the purposes of this section all offences under the Dangerous Drugs Act whether or not they are only summary offences shall be treated as if they are offences punishable on indictment."

---

57.   The Jamaican Exclusive Economic Zone is approximately 181,190 square kilometres. This figure does not include a joint area for sharing of resources between Jamaica and Colombia (52,036 square kilometres): *Limits in the Seas*, 6–7.

58.   Act No. 33 of 1991.

This latter provision uses the same language as that carried in the Maritime Areas Act with respect to jurisdiction over drug offences in the territorial sea. The upshot is that the Jamaican Exclusive Economic Zone Act apparently applies territorial sea rules of jurisdiction to foreign ships in the EEZ beyond the contiguous zone.

Jamaica's inclination to equate EEZ jurisdiction with that of the territorial sea was also evident in the country's declaration made upon accession to the United Nations Convention against Illicit Trafficking in Narcotic Drugs and Psychotropic Substances,[59] on 29 December 1995.[60] Article 17 of this convention provides generally that the states shall cooperate in the suppression of illicit drug trafficking by sea; and in article 17(11) it indicates that action under this article should not interfere with the rights and obligations and exercise of jurisdiction of coastal states in accordance with the international law of the sea. Jamaica, in response, declared that article 17(11) required the consent of the coastal state as a precondition for taking measures of cooperation in its EEZ. According to the Jamaican declaration, the coastal state has jurisdiction and control over ships undertaking drug activity in its EEZ. Jamaica, in effect, reserved the right to search foreign ships for drugs in its EEZ. By logical extension, Jamaica also claimed the power to authorize other states to undertake searches in its EEZ. Overall, therefore, the Jamaican declaration affirmed the view that, as far as the regulation of drug trafficking is concerned, the EEZ is subject to coastal state jurisdiction akin to territorial sea sovereignty.

Since its 1995 declaration, Jamaica seems to have revised its perspective. Perhaps most significantly for international law purposes, Jamaica withdrew its declaration on article 17(11) of the UN Convention on Illicit Trafficking of Narcotic Drugs and Psychotropic Substances on 10 December 1996. This withdrawal coincided with the period during which Jamaica negotiated with the United States on the original Shiprider agreement. Jamaica, may, therefore have changed its position when it was viewed through the prism of a countervailing approach.

---

59.   United Nations, *Treaty Series* 1582 (1990): 95.
60.   United Nations Convention against Illicit Traffic in Narcotic Drugs and Psychotropic Substances, Objections, https://treaties.un.org/Pages/showActionDetails.aspx?objid =08000002800082b4&clang=_en.

Secondly, Jamaica may have concluded that the approach taken in its declaration was incompatible with the terms of the Law of the Sea Convention. Article 58 of the Law of the Sea Convention acknowledges that in the EEZ, all states have high seas freedoms, including freedom of navigation;[61] it then adds that articles 88 to 115 of the convention (on high seas rights) and other pertinent rules of international law shall apply to the EEZ "in so far as they are not incompatible" with EEZ rules.[62] Thus, high seas rules on freedom of navigation are deemed applicable in the EEZ, subject to the question of compatibility. On the high seas, article 92 of the convention provides for exclusive jurisdiction of the flag state of a ship – save in exceptional circumstances expressly provided for in other treaties or in the Law of the Sea Convention itself. And, at the same time, article 108 of the convention specifies that the flag state of a ship may "request cooperation of other States" where the flag state has reasonable grounds for suspecting that one of its ships is involved in drug trafficking. Broadly speaking, therefore, the regime in the Law of the Sea Convention leaves exclusive control over drug trafficking in the EEZ to the flag state. In its EEZ, the coastal state has "sovereign rights" and "jurisdiction" over defined matters,[63] but these matters do not include drug trafficking. Jamaican legislation which departs from this approach would be incompatible with the Law of the Sea Convention.

Thirdly, Jamaica may have come to the realization that its initial approach was open to challenge by several powerful maritime powers. At the time of its signing the UN Convention against the Illicit Trafficking in Narcotic Drugs and Psychotropic Substances, Brazil declared, in terms similar to Jamaica, that flag state jurisdiction in the EEZ could be subject to coastal state authorization.[64] In response to the Brazilian stance, twelve European Community

---

61. Article 58 refers to the right of navigation on the high seas in article 87 in terms described by Churchill and Lowe as "rather oblique and ambiguous": Churchill and Lowe, *Law of the Sea*, 141.
62. See article 108(2) of the Law of the Sea Convention.
63. The coastal state has sovereign rights to explore and exploit, conserve and manage living and non-living resources in its EEZ, and with regard to other activities for economic exploration and exploitation of the zone: article 56(1)(a), Law of the Sea Convention. It has jurisdiction with regard to artificial islands, marine scientific research, maritime pollution: article 56(1)(b).
64. Brazilian declaration, 20 December 1988: UN Convention against Illicit Traffic in Narcotic Drugs and Psychotropic Substances, Objections.

states,[65] acting individually, issued objections, maintaining that the Brazilian approach "went further than the rights accorded to coastal States by international law".[66] Similarly, in response to a Colombian declaration which could have the effect of limiting flag state jurisdiction over drug trafficking only to the high seas,[67] the United States objected to Colombia's approach: "To the extent that it purports to restrict the right of other states to freedom of navigation and other internationally lawful uses of the sea related to that freedom seaward of the outer limits of any state's territorial sea, determined in accordance with the International Law of the Sea, as reflected in the United Nations Convention on the Law of the Sea."[68]

Major maritime powers have publicly been opposed to Jamaica's initial position that coastal states have powers to authorize or prohibit searches of foreign vessels in the coastal state's EEZ on matters concerning drug trafficking.[69]

The Shiprider arrangements formulated in the Maritime Drug Trafficking (Suppression) Act do not reflect Jamaica's initial perspective on jurisdiction in the EEZ. Section 5(1) of the Act, addressing Shiprider searches of foreign vessels by Jamaica, "seaward of any State's territorial sea", requires Jamaica to seek authorization from the flag state as a precondition for searching the vessel. In other words, Jamaica needs to obtain permission to search foreign vessels for drugs in the Jamaican EEZ, as a zone which is, by definition, seaward of Jamaica's territorial sea. This conclusion is reinforced by section 8(2)(a) of the Maritime Drug Trafficking (Suppression) Act, which concerns embarkation by the Jamaican shiprider on US ships. As noted above, this provision

---

65. *Viz.* Belgium, Denmark, France, Germany, Greece, Ireland, Italy, Luxembourg, the Netherlands, Portugal, Spain, the United Kingdom: Ibid.

66. Quoted in United Nations, Division for Ocean Affairs and the Law of the Sea, Office of Legal Affairs, *The Law of the Sea: Practice of States at the Time of Entry into Force of the United Nations Convention on the Law of the Sea* (1994), 178.

67. Colombia: 7th Declaration upon Ratification, 10 June 1994, UN Convention against Illicit Traffic in Narcotic Drugs and Psychotropic Substances, Objections.

68. Ibid. See also J. Astley and Robert W. Smith, *United States Responses to Excessive Maritime Claims,* 2nd ed. (Leiden: Brill, 1996), 416–17.

69. US resistance on this point was also evident in the negotiations on the formulation of Article 17 of the Convention: see UN Conference for the Adoption of a Convention against Illicit Traffic in Narcotic and Psychotropic Substances, *Official Records,* Vol. II, 35, para. 80 (7th Plenary Meeting, 19 December 1988).

allows the Jamaican shiprider to enforce Jamaican law from vessels in hot pursuit or "otherwise in accordance with international law". The right of hot pursuit is applicable as an exception to the general rule about searches in the EEZ. On the other hand, as international law does not support other searches in the EEZ, Jamaica will not have the right to undertake EEZ searches in its EEZ, aside from hot pursuit searches. Nor is Jamaica empowered to transfer the right to search vessels in its EEZ to the United States.

Searches Outside Jamaican Waters

The rules pertaining to Jamaican Shiprider searches on the high seas may be briefly stated. The governing rule concerning jurisdiction on the high seas is set out in Article 92 of the Law of the Sea Convention. It states in part: "Ships shall sail under the flag of one state only and, save in exceptional cases expressly provided for in international treaties or in this convention, shall be subject to its exclusive jurisdiction on the high seas."

This governing rule, which reiterates the approach adumbrated in the 1958 High Seas Convention,[70] represents the codification of customary international law.[71] When read with article 108 of the Law of the Sea Convention,[72] it provides clear guidance on how Jamaica should proceed with searches on the high seas. Jamaica may request the right to search US vessels on the high seas for drugs interdiction and other purposes. This right may be granted by the United States, acting in the capacity of the flag state. By the same token, Jamaica, as the flag state, has the right to search Jamaican vessels on the high seas, as well as the right to authorize US searches of Jamaican vessels. More generally, Jamaica may undertake drug searches of foreign vessels on the high seas with the permission of the relevant flag states.

Given the EEZ rules in the Law of the Sea Convention considered above, it is further posited that Jamaica may only search foreign vessels for drugs in the EEZs of foreign states with the permission of the flag state of the vessel, and not with reference to the coastal state in whose zone the vessel is travelling. On this point,

---

70.   United Nations, *Treaty Series*, Vol. 450 (1963): 11.
71.   Preamble to the High Seas Convention.
72.   See article 108(2) of the Law of the Sea Convention.

it is acknowledged that the EEZ is a *sui generis* zone which, for navigational purposes, has the character of the high seas.

National Zones of Foreign States

As far as national waters of foreign states are concerned, the rules in the Law of the Sea Convention are directly applicable to any searches undertaken by Jamaica. So, for example, Jamaica needs express permission to undertake searches in the territorial seas, archipelagic waters and internal waters of foreign states. At the domestic level, the Maritime Drug Trafficking (Suppression) Act retains the position that the laws of Jamaica extend to any offence committed outside of Jamaican waters on Jamaican vessels. Accordingly, if there are, for example, drugs on a Jamaican ship in the territorial waters of another state, Jamaica will have prescriptive jurisdiction, but it will not have the right to enforce Jamaican law while the ship is in the foreign territorial waters. Where the offence of illicit trafficking is committed on a Jamaican vessel and the offender is present in Jamaica or is a Jamaican national, then the offender shall be liable to tried in Jamaica.

Searches in foreign waters may give rise to problems concerning information. If, for example, a Jamaican ship is searched outside Jamaican waters by US authorities pursuant to the Shiprider agreement, Jamaica may not be entirely certain about the location of the ship at the time of its interception by US officials. In the case of a 2017 search of a Jamaican ship, *The Josette*, the vessel was said to be in Haitian waters, but reports did not clarify whether the interception took place in the Haitian EEZ or its territorial sea. As different rules for searching are applicable to the two maritime zones, the location of *The Josette* was a matter of analytical significance to the case. *The Josette* was reportedly destroyed by the US Coast Guard authorities.[73] Legal responsibility for the destruction of the vessel may turn in part on the location of the vessel at the time of its destruction, as well as the source of authorization for the destruction.[74]

---

73. Thomas Dresslar, "No Human Rights on the High Seas," American Civil Liberties Union, 25 June 2019, https://www.aclu.org/issues/human-rights/no-human-rights-high-seas, last accessed 22 December 2021.
74. For jurisdiction over detained vessels in the Haitian waters – internal waters and territorial sea – see article 16, Agreement concerning Cooperation to Suppress Illicit

A similar problem seems to have arisen with respect to *Lady Lawla* and its demise in 2020. *Lady Lawla* was reportedly destroyed by US Coast Guard authorities, based on the allegation that it was involved in drug trafficking.[75] The Jamaicans accused of involvement in drug trafficking were tried in the United States and found not guilty. In the circumstances, questions were raised by Senator Peter Bunting, Opposition spokesman on national security, about responsibility for the destruction of the ship. Foreign Minister Kamina Johnson-Smith declined to address the matter directly, suggesting that she was not under a duty to give legal advice. She argued, though, that it was international practice to destroy some vessels on the high seas if they cannot be towed or be left stranded. This presumes that the vessel was, in fact, on the high seas. But what if *Lady Lawla* was, for argument's sake, in the Haitian EEZ or in the archipelagic waters of another Caribbean state? The analytical challenge cannot be summarily dismissed by referring to all waters beyond Jamaica's territorial sea as the high seas.

Waiver of Jurisdiction

In a variety of instances, the Shiprider arrangements allow the United States to undertake searches in lieu of Jamaican authorities. Where such searches occur, persons suspected of drug trafficking are detained and need to be taken either to Jamaica or the United States for trial. The question is whether and to what extent Jamaica may waive its enforcement jurisdiction and thus permit the surrender of detained persons to US authorities.

Between 1999 and 2015, the answer to this question in Jamaican law distinguished between Jamaican and foreign nationals. For this period, section 20(2) of the Maritime Drug Trafficking (Suppression) Act read as follows: "Where pursuant to Section 13,[76] a Jamaican vessel is detained seaward of any State's territorial sea by a treaty State, the Minister may waive Jamaica's right to exercise

Maritime Drug Traffic, signed at Port au Prince, 17 October 1997, entered into force on 5 September 2002, US State Department, 1997 UST LEXIS 128.

75. For criticism of the action of destroying the vessel, see, for example, Hardley Lewin, "No Defect in Shiprider Agreement," *Gleaner*, 31 January 2021. The Jamaican government has denied that it gave permission for the destruction: "Minister Says Gov't Not Responsible for Destruction of Lady Lawla," *Gleaner*, 16 January 2021.
76. Section 13 searches are undertaken outside the territorial waters of any state.

jurisdiction over the vessel and authorize the relevant treaty State to enforce its laws against that vessel, its cargo and persons found on board other than Jamaican nationals."

On the plain meaning of the words, the minister was empowered to waive Jamaica's right to exercise jurisdiction over Jamaican vessels in waters beyond the territorial sea. The minister could authorize the United States to enforce its laws against Jamaican vessels, their cargo and non-Jamaicans on board.

It was also strongly arguable, *a contrario*, that the minister was not empowered to authorize US enforcement of its laws against Jamaican nationals. This interpretation was supportable on policy grounds: the Jamaican state wished to protect its nationals from the hazards of a foreign justice system and emphasize its right to bring its nationals to trial. This interpretation – which barred the minister from surrendering Jamaican nationals to US courts – was bolstered by the legislative history of Section 20(2) of the Maritime Drug Trafficking (Suppression) Act, in its pre-2015 formulation. The following are the main points from the legislative history:

1. Minister of Foreign Affairs Seymour Mullings introduced the Bill with clause 20(2) (later section 20(2)) not having any express reference to "other than Jamaican nationals".[77]

2. MP Ronald Thwaites argued strongly that the Minister of National Security should not have the power to authorize a foreign state to try a Jamaican national in the circumstances of clause 20(2).[78] He said, among other things:

   The essence of sovereignty is the liberty of the subject. And in this instance, why should it be left to the Minister's discretion, whether Jamaican law applies in any circumstance over a Jamaican national? I do not know of any circumstance in law. Maybe I can be corrected – where it lies to Ministerial discretion to determine whether our law, our jurisdiction applies over our citizens? The more I think of it, the more it disturbs me, ma'am.[79]

3. It was suggested by MP Delroy Chuck that clause 20(3) would

---

77. Jamaica Hansard, *Parliamentary Proceedings of the House of Representatives*, Session 1998–1999 23, No. 3 (New Series), 15 January 1998–26 March 1998: 44.

78. Ibid., 47 and 51.

79. Ibid., 51.

have the effect of preventing Jamaicans from being tried by the foreign state, a view that appears to have been supported by Minister of National Security K.D. Knight.[80]

Clause 20(2) went to the Senate and then to a committee of the House. It was amended with the inclusion of the words "other than Jamaican nationals" at the end of the provision. The clear intention of the amendment, as stated by Minister Mullings in response to Mr Thwaites, and on the advice of the Attorney General's Chambers, was to make it clear that the minister could not authorize the foreign state to exercise jurisdiction over Jamaican nationals.[81]

Mr Thwaites, in supporting the change, said: "May I commend the amendments that are proposed to section 20 to preserve the rights of Jamaican citizens to the obligation and protection of Jamaican law from the vagary of anybody's discretion, Madam Speaker."[82]

Parliamentary intention was, therefore, to ensure that the Jamaican minister could not surrender Jamaican nationals to US authorities for trial. This was to be achieved by the insertion of the phrase "other than Jamaican nationals" in language that became section 20(2) of the Maritime Drug Trafficking (Suppression) Act.

In 2016, the Jamaican parliament amended section 20(2) of the Act with the express purpose of granting the minister "the power to waive Jamaica's right to exercise jurisdiction over Jamaican nationals who are detained on a Jamaican vessel by the law enforcement authorities of a treaty State (*viz. the USA*) seaward of any State's territorial sea". In effect, the amendment confirms that, prior to 2016, Jamaican nationals held by US officials in Shiprider searches beyond the territorial sea were required to be handed over to Jamaican authorities; they could not be taken to the United States for legal process. The amendment changed this basic fact: following 2016, Jamaicans may be surrendered to the United States for trial, on the discretion of the minister.

The amended section 20 sets out the circumstances in which the minister may exercise discretion to waive exercise of jurisdiction over Jamaican nationals. According to a new provision – section

---

80.   Ibid.., 51 and 52.
81.   Ibid., 110*ff.*
82.   Ibid., 116.

20(4) – before waiving jurisdiction over a Jamaican national, the minister is obliged to consider whether the waiver is in the interests of the security, defence, international relations[83] or other essential pubic interest of Jamaica or in the interests of justice.[84] Before making a decision on waiver, the minister is also required to obtain an opinion from the Attorney General that the Jamaican's rights pertaining to a fair trial[85] and non-discrimination[86] will be preserved. The Attorney General is also called upon to certify that the Jamaican national will not have his constitutional[87] or other rights[88] compromised and would have no impediments to trial in Jamaica.[89] It is provided, too, that, waiver shall not be granted for an offence where the offence is subject to the death penalty in the United States but not in Jamaica; in this case the United States is obliged to give assurances that the death penalty will not be carried out.[90]

With these safeguards in place, ministerial discretion ought not to be applied in an arbitrary manner, and it should preserve some of the basic rights of the individual. Even so, however, the ministerial power to waive rights has become a highly contentious feature of the Shiprider arrangements. For a start, it is vulnerable to the criticism that the United States may abuse Jamaicans in detention, believing that Jamaica is not likely to seek redress for any such abuse. Whether this criticism is reasonable or not, it reflects the fear of some Jamaicans that the asymmetrical power relations between both countries may work against individual Jamaicans who become entangled in the US court system, an alien, unfamiliar place.[91] In

---

83. Section 20(4)(a).
84. Section 20(4)(b).
85. Section 20(5)(a).
86. Section 20(5)(b); grounds for non-discrimination expressly listed include: race, place of origin, social class, colour, religion and political opinion.
87. Section 20(5)(c).
88. Ibid.
89. Section 20(5)(d). There is a good case – in the public interest – that the opinion of the Attorney General given pursuant to this provision should be made public, or at least reported to parliament, and not be shielded by attorney-client privilege: see reference to attorney-client privilege in the context of a request to waive jurisdiction, see, for example, "Golding Questions Waiver Process in Fishermen's Case", *Gleaner*, 28 June 2019; see also Gordon Robinson, "When the Shiprider Hits the Fan," *Gleaner*, 7 July 2019.
90. Section 20(6).
91. In the case of *The Jossette*, three of the claimants have argued that their convictions

some cases, too, the alleged drug offence may have occurred in the Caribbean Sea (quite far removed from the United States), and the accused have no links to the United States, save that they have been intercepted by US authorities. The complaint is heard that Jamaicans in this position should not be subject to US jurisdiction, as they have no real connections to the United States.

On the treatment question, the case of *The Josette* has received media attention in Jamaica. In this case, five Jamaican fishermen were intercepted in 2017 and detained by the US Coast Guard for thirty-two days. The fishermen maintain that, during this period, they were subjected to inhuman treatment on four different US Coast Guard ships. Specifically, the American Civil Liberties Union has filed suit on behalf of four of the fishermen claiming, inter alia, that they were stripped naked, chained by their ankles to metal cables, left largely exposed to the wind, rain and sun, and denied contact with their families and medical treatment for injuries sustained in detention.[92] No drug-related charges were sustained against them.[93] The United States, in denying the fishermen's claim, has maintained that it treated the men in keeping with standards in international and US domestic law. On the extended maritime detention, the US authorities have noted that the exigencies of Hurricane Maria restricted their ability to transport the accused to the United States promptly.[94] The matter is yet to be resolved, but it may be envisaged that the circumstances of detention at sea and transportation to a foreign jurisdiction will generate allegations of ill treatment that are difficult to prove or to refute in the public domain.[95] It is also to be expected, though, that basic human

in the United States should be vacated because the claimants believed that guilty pleas "presented them with the fastest possible path back to Jamaica": *Weir et al. v USA*, Civil Case No. 1:19-cv-23420; Criminal Case No. 1:17-cr-20877-UNGARO, Petition for Issuance of Writs of Error Coram Nobis Vacating Convictions and Incorporated Memorandum of Facts and Law in Support.

92.   *Weir et al. v US and Another*, United States District for the District of Columbia, Admiralty, Case 1:19-cv-01708, Complaint for Damages and Injunctive Relief (US Coast Guard Mistreatment of Civilian Fishermen), filed 12 June 2019; Dresslar, "No Human Rights," 5; *Weir v US*, https://www.aclu.org/cases/weir-v-us, last accessed 22 December 2021; "US Coast Guard Denies Abusing Fishermen", *Gleaner*, 24 June 2019.

93.   Dresslar, "No Human Rights," 12.

94.   Ibid.

95.   For an authoritative view that typical coast guard vessels are not intended for use as places of detention, see Hardley Lewin, "No Defect in Shiprider Agreement".

rights standards, as incorporated, for instance, in the International Covenant on Civil and Political Rights (the ICCPR),[96] will govern the judicial assessment of treatment issues,[97] including the time between capture and trial proceedings.[98]

Should Jamaican law be amended to prevent ministerial waiver of Jamaica's jurisdiction? The current procedure contemplated in Section 20 of the Maritime Drug Trafficking (Suppression) Act has given rise to practical problems and may be opposed on grounds that it gives inordinate and potentially arbitrary power to the responsible minister.[99] But this is not the entire picture. The strongest argument in support of waiving Jamaican jurisdiction is based on efficiency. Where trials of Jamaicans may take place in the United States, the main witnesses from a Shiprider search undertaken by the United States are apt to be available to the US courts, while they are not likely to be present in Jamaica for a local trial – a trial which may take place some years following the time of the putative offence. Similarly, where the accused in a given case are charged in one court together, the harnessing of evidence is more straightforward than if some of the accused (non-Jamaicans) are tried in the United States, while others (Jamaicans) are tried in local courts. Sometimes the accused are released without trial essentially because the evidence is not readily available in the local jurisdiction.[100] Having trials in the United States also ensures that

---

96.   United Nations *Treaty Series* 999 (1976): 171.
97.   Both Jamaica and the United States are parties to the International Covenant on Civil and Political Rights (ICCPR), the former ratified this treaty in 1975 and the latter in 1992: *United Nations Treaty Collection* (ICCPR), https://treaties.un.org/doc/treaties/1976/03/19760323%2006-17%20am/ch_iv_04.pdf. Article 10(2) of the ICCPR states that persons deprived of liberty shall be treated "with humanity and with respect for the inherent dignity of the human person".
98.   In the context of piracy, the European Court of Human Rights has supported the release and compensation of persons found guilty in national courts with reference to delay in bringing the accused before a judicial officer: see, for example, *Ali Samatar and Others v France (Judgment)*, App. No. 17110/10 and 17301/10, Eru 2014, Eur. Ct. H.R.; *Hassan and Others v. France (Judgment)*, App. No. 466/95/10 and 54588/10, Eru. 2014, Eur. Ct. H.R. For discussion, see Barry Hart Dubner and Brian Otero, "The Human Rights of Sea Pirates: Will the European Court of Human Rights Decisions Get More Killed?", *Washington University Global Studies Law Review*, 15, no. 2 (2016): 215.
99.   Editorial: "Outsourcing Sovereignty," *Gleaner*, 9 December 2015.
100. Jamaica Information Service, "Gov't Ensures Jamaicans Obtain Fair Trials in Treaty Countries – Golding", 8 December 2015, https://jis.gov.jm/govt-ensures-jamaicans-get-fair-trials-in-treaty-countries-golding/, last accessed 22 December 2021. See also "Golding Question Waiver Process in Fishermen's Case", *loc. cit.*, note 89 (comments of Peter Bunting).

the community most likely to be affected by the influx of illicit drugs – the United States – is involved in the prosecution of the drug-trafficking offences.[101] In addition, because the system of waiving jurisdiction does not apply to areas of Jamaican territory, it does not undermine the integrity of Jamaica's Extradition Act, which accords certain rights and procedures to persons "found in Jamaica".[102] Nor does the possibility of waiving jurisdiction compromise Jamaican sovereignty or national pride, for ultimately the decision on waiver rests with the Jamaican state.[103] These considerations all point towards retaining the system of waivers now sanctioned by Jamaican law.

At the same time, however, the Jamaican authorities would be well-advised to give due publicity to the protocols that are applicable to the treatment of Jamaican nationals who are taken to the United States for trial pursuant to Shiprider searches.[104] A system that is perceived to exist in secrecy may generate protest among human rights advocates, and ultimately undermine the legitimacy of the arrangements between Jamaica and the United States. The new protocols must ensure that human rights are respected and that the government of Jamaica is kept informed of all aspects of treatment concerning Jamaicans in detention.[105] Moreover, it should be recalled that the Jamaican state is not obliged to accede to every waiver request: in some cases, the logistical situation will suggest that the exercise of US jurisdiction would provide the most suitable solution, but this will not always be best.[106]

Finally, at the international law level, the waiver approach is not inconsistent with the terms of the Jamaica/US Shiprider agreement. Article 3(5) of the agreement is set out as follows:

> Where a vessel of one Party is detained seaward of any State's territorial sea, that Party shall have the right to exercise

---

101. In 2002, Jamaican constabulary sources estimated that only two to three per cent of drugs transshipped through Jamaica remained in the country: "Jamaica Main Transshipment Port for Colombian Drugs – Narcotics Chief", *Gleaner*, 31 January 2002.
102. Section 6, Extradition Act.
103. For the view, however, that the waiver approach "redefines sovereignty", see Bert Samuels, "Jamaica Taken for a Ride?" *Gleaner*, 21 July 2019.
104. Editorial, "Shiprider Needs Review", *Gleaner*, 23 June 2019.
105. Editorial, "Shocking Ignorance by Ministers," *Gleaner*, 18 June 2019.
106. Lewin, "No Defect in Shiprider agreement".

> jurisdiction over the vessel, its cargo and persons on board, but that Party may, subject to its Constitution and laws, waive its right to exercise jurisdiction and authorize the other Party to enforce its laws against the vessel, its cargo and persons on board. Nothing in this Agreement shall be construed as a waiver by a Party of its right to exercise jurisdiction over its nationals.

The last sentence of this provision should be noted. It indicates that nothing in the Shiprider agreement *itself* amounts to an automatic waiver of Jamaica's right to exercise jurisdiction; for a waiver of jurisdiction to be granted, there needs to be a distinct act on the part of the relevant authorities. The first sentence of Article 3(5) also needs to be considered. This allows Jamaica to waive its right to exercise jurisdiction over persons detained following Shiprider interception beyond the territorial sea, but it is expressly subject to the Jamaican constitution and laws. So, where Jamaica's Maritime Drug (Suppression) Act prohibits waiver of the country's jurisdiction, this prohibition would be decisive; but where there is no prohibition, waiver may be contemplated.

Concluding Remarks

The Shiprider arrangements between Jamaica and the United States emerged out of controversy in 1997. In that year both countries reached agreement on ways to protect themselves from illicit drug-trafficking efforts in the Caribbean Sea and beyond. These drug-trafficking efforts generally originate in South America and, using the Caribbean Sea as a major transshipment area, approach destinations primarily in the United States. Jamaica and other Caribbean states lack the proper means to deter transshipment through the region and have, therefore, been willing to accept measures by which the United States may help to reduce the flow of drugs from South America.

Although the negotiations on their Shiprider agreement were contentious, Jamaica and the United States established rules which have worked largely to the advantage of both countries. Jamaica has implemented the terms of the agreement in domestic law by means of the Maritime Drug Trafficking (Suppression) Act of 1999. This Act, together with the Maritime Areas Act and the

Exclusive Economic Zone Act, represents the foundation of the legal regime which governs Jamaica's maritime zones and, more generally, Jamaica's operations in all parts of the sea. At the same time, Jamaican law has been influenced significantly by multilateral treaties that govern the sea. These include mainly the Law of the Sea Convention, the Territorial Sea Convention and the High Seas Convention, but it also embraces the United Nations Convention against Illicit Trafficking of Narcotic Drugs and Psychotropic Substances, a treaty which encourages co-operation in the suppression of drug activity in respect of the sea and elsewhere.

In determining the rules applicable to Shiprider activities, therefore, reference has to be made to a variety of legal sources. These sources provide a somewhat coherent picture according to which Jamaican officials may act as shipriders on US vessels as a means of seizing ships involved in drug trafficking. At the same time, where a Jamaican shiprider is not available, US officials may undertake searches of Jamaican vessels, and foreign vessels in Jamaican waters with the permission of the Jamaican authorities. The rules on Shiprider searches – though formulated in technical terms – provide effective guidance on the means of tackling drug transshipment through the Caribbean Sea.

The latest version of the Maritime Drug Trafficking (Suppression) Act empowers the responsible Jamaican minister with the right to waive jurisdiction over Jamaican nationals in cases arising from Shiprider searches beyond the territorial sea. The effect of waiving jurisdiction is that Jamaica may lawfully surrender its nationals to the United States for prosecution in US courts. This facility has given rise to renewed controversy and there are still undecided cases concerning the standard of treatment to be meted out to Jamaicans in detention and en route to the US court system. It is important for Jamaica to maintain transparency and clarity in its relationship with the United States *vis-à-vis* maritime anti-drug trafficking efforts in the Caribbean region.

CHAPTER 12

The Juridification of Good Governance in CARICOM Law

Neto Waite

The Caribbean Court of Justice (CCJ) is the central dispute resolution body for the Caribbean Community (CARICOM), including the CARICOM Single Market and Economy (CSME) with a "compulsory and exclusive"[1] jurisdiction for interpreting and applying the Revised Treaty of Chaguaramas (RTC), the constitutive treaty. In discharging its duty, the CCJ, in its Original Jurisdiction,[2] reviews the actions of the Community and Member States for compliance with the RTC. In so doing, the CCJ is positioned to determine the standards and courses of behaviour required of public actors within CARICOM. To put it another way, the CCJ's dispute resolution duty enables it to define the quality of governance called for in the RTC. Taken in totality, the Original Jurisdiction jurisprudence of the CCJ defines good governance in CARICOM. Given that the CCJ's Original Jurisdiction decisions bind all CARICOM Member States, it follows that this good governance as defined by the court is not just a matter of good public policy, but also a legal requirement.

This chapter argues that the work of the CCJ in its original jurisdiction defines the concept of good governance in community law, leading to the juridification of good governance in CARICOM. Part I briefly describes the position and jurisdiction of the CCJ in

---

1. Article 211(1), Revised Treaty of Chaguaramas Establishing the Caribbean Community, Including the CARICOM Single Market and Economy (adopted 5 July 2001, entered into force on 1 January 2006), 2259 UNTS 293.
2. The Caribbean Court of Justice is established with an Appellate Jurisdiction and an Original Jurisdiction. In the Appellate Jurisdiction, the court is the final appellate court for those Member States that have amended their constitutions and judicature laws to allow for final appeals to the CCJ. In the Original Jurisdiction, the court has the compulsory and exclusive jurisdiction to interpret and apply the Revised Treaty of Chaguaramas.

the CARICOM eco-system. Part II discusses the working definition of good governance, while Part III builds on the discourse in Part II by delving into the CCJ's case law in order to piece together the court's definition of good governance so far. The chapter closes with Part IV, briefly discussing the implications of the argument made throughout.

Part I: The CCJ in CARICOM's Eco-system

In the preamble to the RTC, the Member States considered that "an efficient, transparent, and authoritative system of disputes settlement in the Community will enhance the economic, social and other forms of activity in the CSME leading to confidence in the investment climate…".[3] With that in mind, they established the CCJ as the apex dispute settlement body in the Community, having supervisory jurisdiction over all other modes of judicial dispute resolution that touches and concerns the RTC.[4] The Member States further disclosed their vision for the court in the preamble to the agreement establishing the CCJ,[5] that the court represents a deepening of the integration process and would play "a determinative role in the further development of Caribbean jurisprudence through the judicial process". In the words of Justice Kokaram of the High Court of Trinidad and Tobago:

> The CCJ therefore plays a critical role in the development of [C]ommunity law inclusive of the rights envisioned for [C]ommunity nationals to enjoy in this expanded economic space. It represents the jurisprudential underpinnings fashioning a Caribbean identity and reinforces the Caribbean legal framework in which our CARICOM nations are to give reality to the concept of a single market economy, a single space and a more influential seat at the global table.[6]

The CCJ has already embodied the envisioned role by declaring:

> The Member States transformed the erstwhile voluntary arrangements in CARICOM into a rule-based system, thus

---

3.   See final exhortation in RTC's preamble.
4.   See article 214, RTC.
5.   Agreement Establishing the Caribbean Court of Justice (adopted 14 February 2001, entered into force 23 July 2002), 2255 UNTS 319.
6.   *Hadeed v AG of Trinidad & Tobago et al.*, High Court of Justice, CV2018-02726, Judgment of 18 June 2019, at [4] (unreported).

creating and accepting a regional system under the rule of law. [...] The rule of law brings with it legal certainty and protection of rights of states and individuals alike, but at the same time of necessity it creates legal accountability.[7]

In addition, solidifying its determinative role in regional integration, the court has adopted the role of custodian[8] and guardian[9] of the RTC. The substantive provisions of the RTC seems to align with the court's declaration, having elevated it to a supervisory role to ensure that the exercise of public power that implicates the CSME are consistent with its rules, objectives and purpose. In particular, Article 211, RTC determines that the CCJ has a "compulsory and exclusive jurisdiction to hear and determine disputes concerning the interpretation and application of the Treaty", including disputes between and among Members States, the Community and persons coming within the scope of article 222 of the RTC. Article 187 sets out the types of disputes to come before the court: (1) whether actual or proposed national measures are inconsistent with the objectives of the RTC; (2) whether rights or benefits to be derived from the CSME are being or likely to be impaired or nullified; (3) whether actions of Community bodies or organs are ultra vires; and (4) whether the purpose or objective of the RTC is being frustrated. These two provisions together empower the CCJ to review a very large part of public governance activity in the region. In the context of freedom of movement in the RTC, the court made it clear that it had a role to play in the shaping of public policy insofar as the RTC is implicated:

> The scope of public policy and particularly that of the concept of "undesirable persons," which is used as a justification for derogation from the fundamental principle of freedom of movement and hassle-free travel of Community nationals, cannot wholly or unilaterally be determined by each Member State without being subject to control by the

---

7.   *Trinidad Cement Ltd. v Caribbean Community,* Judgment [2009] CCJ 2 (OJ), 5 February 2009 [Special Leave] at [32].

8.   *Trinidad Cement Ltd. v Competition Commission,* Judgment [2012] CCJ 4 (OJ), 12 November 2012 [Judgment], at [18]

9.   *Shanique Myrie v Barbados,* Judgment [2013] CCJ 3 (OJ), 3 October 2013 [Judgment] at [68].

major Community Organs, in particular the Conference, and ultimately by the Court as the Guardian of the RTC.[10]

In this judicial review capacity, the CCJ is vested with considerable power to shape the space of legality for Member States and the Community to exercise public power. The court's decisions in turn create general guidance to all participants in CARICOM, including foreign investors and partners, as to what is the lawful exercise of governance. The conclusion follows naturally that the power of the CCJ exists in a proportional relationship with the pace and breadth of regional integration. That is to say, as regional integration becomes more active and deepens, the power and influence of the CCJ in our lives increases.

Part II – A Working Definition of Good Governance

The concept of good governance, the quality of governance engaged in by a government or public actor, in international development and international relations practice and literature is bound to a neo-liberal democratic ideology.[11] The underlying concept is that governance pursued in a particular way, at a particular standard, will lead to development. Former United Nations (UN) Secretary General Kofi Annan said, "…good governance is perhaps the single most important factor in eradicating poverty and promoting development".[12] It is this idea that undergirds the currency that the concept has among stakeholders in the international fight against poverty and underdevelopment. It has become one of the many benchmarks used by international donors.[13]

Good governance has been described as a "normative principle of administrative law, which obliges the State to perform its functions in a manner that promotes the values of efficiency, non-

---

10. Ibid., 68.
11. *See* N. Chowdhury and C. E. Skarstedt, *The Principle of Good Governance* (Center for International Sustainable Development Law, Draft Working Paper, 2005); Klaus Frey, "Development, Good Governance, and Local Democracy," *Brazilian Political Science Review* 2, no. 2 (2008): 39.
12. Kofi Annan, *Partnership for Global Community: Annual Report on the Work of the Organization, 1998*, UN Doc DPI/1997.
13. Per Chowdhury and Skarstedt, *Good Governance*, 11: "The concept of good governance as developed in the World Bank is essentially a touchstone upon which the prevailing administrative structure of a given country can be measured."

corruptibility, and responsiveness to civil society".[14] However, while the concept is widely used, it remains without a single definition around which support has coalesced.[15] As a consequence, there may be nearly as many working definitions of good governance as there are international agencies. Each agency tends to adopt a definition that is in keeping with (or emphasizes) its mandate or objectives. The International Monetary Fund (IMF) defines good governance to include "transparency of government accounts, the effectiveness of public resource management, the stability and transparency of the economic and regulatory environment for private sector activity".[16] The European Commission said five principles underpin good governance: openness, participation, accountability, effectiveness and coherence.[17] And the UN says that "[g]ood governance promotes equity, participation, pluralism, transparency, accountability and the rule of law in a manner that is effective, efficient and enduring."[18] While the World Bank says that "[i]t is essentially the combination of transparent and accountable institutions, strong skills and competence, and a full willingness to do the right thing".[19] Fully aware of the ideological leanings of some definitions and surely influenced by the ideological pluralism among Asian States, the Asian Development Bank's working approach to good governance is this:

> Although policy aspects are important for development, the Bank's concept of good governance focuses essentially on the ingredients for effective management. In other words, irrespective of the precise set of economic policies that find favour with a government, good governance is required to ensure that those policies have their desired effect. In essence, it concerns norms of behaviour that help to ensure that governments actually deliver to their citizens what they say

---

14.   Ibid., *Good Governance*, 4.
15.   Phillip Keeper, "Governance," in *The Sage Handbook of Comparative Politics,* eds. Todd Landman and Neil Robinson (Thousand Oaks, CA: Sage Publications, 2009), 439.
16.   Michel Camdessus, IMF Managing Director, Address to the United Nations Economic and Social Council, 2 July 1997.
17.   European Commission, "European Governance: A White Paper," Brussels, COMM (2001) 428, 8 (25 July 2001).
18.   United Nations, *Governance,* 4 March 2016, http://www.un.org/en/globalissues/governance.
19.   World Bank, *Strengthening the World Bank Group Engagement on Governance and Anticorruption* 1, 21 March 2007.

they will deliver.... [I]n formulating an analytical framework for addressing governance issues, the Bank prefers to draw a distinction between, on the one hand, elements of good governance, and on the other, the specific areas of actions (e.g. public sector management) in which they could be promoted or their existence enhanced. In line with this reasoning, and building upon the approach of the World Bank, the Bank has identified four basic elements of good governance: (i) accountability, (ii) participation, (iii) predictability, and (iv) transparency.[20] (emphasis added)

Good governance has also been considered as "the proper use of government's power in a transparent and participative way..." that is primarily concerned with guaranteeing security of persons/society, effective public sector management and the promotion of economic and social aims.[21] The Office of the UN High Commissioner for Human Rights refers to good governance as the "exercise of authority through political and institutional processes that are transparent and accountable, and encourage public participation".[22]

These working definitions support the conclusion that good governance is "largely associated with statecraft."[23] They are concerned with mechanisms, processes and institutions through which public power is exercised so as to meet public aims. While it touches and concerns the substantive issue of the organization (or institutional design) for the discharge or exercise of public power and deployment of public resources, the concept is more procedurally oriented, geared at guaranteeing effective governance.[24] Good governance is a set of normative prescriptions in pursuit of some other goal, for example, protection of human rights[25] or securing economic development.

---

20.   Asian Development Bank, *Governance: Sound Development Management*, 3, 4, 8 (Asian Development Bank, 1995).

21.   Henk Addink et al., "HUGO European Asian Network on Human Rights and Good Governance," in *Human Rights and Good Governance*, eds. Gordon Anthony et al. (SIM Special 34, Utrecht University, 2010), 19.

22.   UN Office of the High Commissioner for Human Rights, *Good Governance Practices for the Protection of Human Rights*, 2, HR/PUB/07/4 (2007).

23.   Chowdhury and Skarstedt, *Good Governance*, 4.

24.   Ibid., 11: "Good governance is therefore chiefly envisaged as a set of procedural tools to guarantee efficacious improvement of the donor identified subject."

25.   UN Office of the High Commissioner for Human Rights, *Good Governance*, 1, "... human rights principles inform the content of good governance efforts..."

In light of these many working definitions, the substantive coherence of the concept has been called into question.[26] The observation has also been made that "[m]ost studies simply proceed by selecting one definition among the many..."[27] Stripped of any policy-choice or ideological discourse, these working definitions reveal many points of convergence. Rachel M. Gisselquist's study of these definitions and of the practical effect of the substantive incoherence in the field identified these procedural and substantive 'core components' of the good governance concept: (1) democracy and representation, (2) human rights, (3) the rule of law, (4) efficient and effective public management, (5) transparency and accountability, (6) developmentalist objectives, and (7) a varying range of specific economic and political policies, programmes, and institutions.[28] She proceeded to convincingly argue that the concept has been poorly specified[29] and further research and analysis is needed. She contended that it would be a more fruitful exercise to focus on the disaggregated components rather than the whole concept. Like Professor Francis N. Botchway, whose article "Good Governance: The Old, The New, The Principle and the Elements" predates Gisselquist's study, it is agreed that this disaggregated approach will give more traction to the goal of locking onto an adequately understood and defined concept.

So as to avoid the possible failing of choosing one among the many working definitions, the argument made here takes the disaggregated approach and focuses on the points of convergence or core components. This approach is sufficient to meet the objective in this argument, which is to show how the CCJ's Original Jurisdiction case law contributes to the improved practical specification and application of good governance in CARICOM. The aim here is to show that the legal duties elaborated by the court are core components of good governance. The argument is captured well in this statement by the Office of the UN High Commissioner

26. Francis N. Botchway, "Good Governance: The Old, the New, the Principle and the Elements," *Florida Journal of International Law* 13 (2001): 159, 180; Rachel M. Gisselquist, *Good Governance as a Concept, and Why This Matters for Development Policy*, 17 (UN University for World Institute for Development Economics Research, Working Paper No. 2012/30, 2012).
27. See Gisselquist, *Good Governance*.
28. Ibid., 2.
29. Ibid., 11.

for Human Rights: "human rights principles inform the content of good governance efforts: they inform the development of legislative framework, policies, programmes, budgetary allocations and other measures."[30]

In this Part, I do not make a normative argument for a substantive conception of good governance or responsible government. Rather, its value here stems from its wide acceptance in international politics and development and its growing use in international law. Therefore, the working definitions most aligned to this argument's aim are those of the Asian Development Bank and the HUGO European Asian Network on Human Rights and Good Governance. These two definitions are concerned more with responsible and effective government rather than a government's specific policy choices. Effective and efficient delivery of a government's policy aim is a *conditio sine qua non* to good governance. Good governance necessarily includes a responsible government. One component of responsible governance is the compliance with international obligations;[31] and, where such obligations are about the responsible husbandry of the exercise of public power, they are aligned with the good governance concept.[32]

Part III – The CCJ's Definition of Good Governance

The court's case law to date disclosed some of the core components of good governance as discussed above: (a) respect for the rule law, (b) duty of transparency and efficiency, including duty to give reasons, (c) duty to give reasonable and adequate notice, and (d) duty to provide independent and effective review system. These will be dealt in turn in the paragraphs to follow.

A Duty to Respect the Rule of Law

The rule of law concept is very broad and varied. It requires the enactment of appropriate known laws and regulations, which

---

30.   UN Office of the High Commissioner for Human Rights. *Good Governance*, 2.
31.   In *Tomlinson v Belize and Trinidad & Tobago*, Judgment [2016] CCJ 1 (OJ), 10 June 2016 [Judgment], at [56] the CCJ stated, "In principle, national legislation should expressly be harmonized with Community law."
32.   For example, in relation to international human rights legal obligations, the UN Office of the Commissioner on Human Rights, in *Good Governance*, rightly said, "Good governance and human rights are mutually reinforcing, and the former was a precondition for the realization of the latter."

are fairly and consistently applied and effectively enforced.[33] The central importance in its application to the broad notion of good governance is the predictability that flows from it. The World Bank considers the rule of law to contain five critical elements: "(a) there is a set of rules known in advance, (b) the rules are actually in force, (c) there are mechanisms ensuring application of the rules, (d) conflicts are resolved through binding decisions of an independent judicial body, and (e) there are procedures for amending the rules when they no longer serve their purpose."[34] These elements together have the effect of creating a stable legal environment that guides peoples' and governments' courses of action.

A prominent and possibly troublesome trait about the good governance concept is that it does not set out the specifically required norms of behaviour. The rule of law, like other core components, removes a layer of abstraction from the good governance concept. The State's compliance policy should be reflected in appropriate laws and regulations. Such rules communicate to private and public actors the types of activities that are regulated by the government and the standards and procedures that must be met by public actors. For example, through laws and regulations, the State informs CARICOM nationals of the requirements for enjoying the freedom of movement and the available legal recourses in the event of challenges along the way. In the main, the rule of law requires the enactment of clear laws that are communicated to public and private actors, which are effectively enforced. Not only is the operation of the rule of law necessary for the proper functioning of good governance, but good governance shows how a government of laws is expected to conduct its affairs. To put it another way, without rule of law compliance, it is hard to see how a State can make the case that it meets good governance standards.

The CCJ has made a few pronouncements already on the role of the rule of law in CARICOM law. Beginning with *Trinidad Cement Ltd. v Caribbean Community*,[35] where TCL challenged the lawfulness of two Community decisions to suspend the

---

33.   Lon Fuller, *The Inner Morality of Law*, rev. ed. (New Haven: Yale University Press, 1969), 33–91.
34.   World Bank, *Governance and Development*, 30 (Washington, DC: World Bank, 1992).
35.   *Trinidad Cement Ltd. v Caribbean Community*, Judgment [2009] CCJ 2 (OJ), 5 February 2009 [Special Leave].

Common External Tariff (CET), the CCJ determined that the RTC transformed the CARICOM into a rule-based regional system under the rule of law.[36] The court went on to say, "[t]he rule of law brings with it legal certainty and protection of rights of states and individuals alike, but at the same time of necessity it creates legal accountability."[37] In the exercise of its power of judicial review, a limb of legal accountability,[38] which is a natural consequence of the rule of law,[39] the court indicated that it would scrutinize the actions of the Community for their predictability, consistency, transparency and fidelity to the established rules and procedures to ensure that it does not undermine legitimate expectations that flowed from its actions and undertakings.[40] Further, the court stated that "applications for suspensions [of the CET] must be dealt with in a principled, procedurally appropriate manner"[41] and that "private entities should be provided with appropriate information regarding the operation of the CET and in particular the suspension of the tariff."[42]

The Court further developed the rule of law requirements that flowed from the RTC in *Tomlinson v Belize and Trinidad & Tobago*,[43] a case concerning the freedom of movement for LGBT CARICOM nationals. In respect of the rule of law and governance, there are two important issues in this case; first, whether domestic laws should always be consistent with a State's international obligations; and second, whether it is appropriate for procedures and practices, though beneficial to marginalized persons, to be inconsistent with written laws and regulations. The court resorted to the rule of law in commenting on both issues. First, that the rule of law requires Member States to ensure that their laws, subsidiary legislations and administrative practices are transparent in their

---

36. Ibid., 32.
37. Ibid.
38. In *Trinidad Cement Ltd. v Caribbean Community*, Judgment [2009] CCJ 4 (OJ), 10 August 2009, [Judgment] at [38] the court said: "...the Court has the power to scrutinise the acts of the Member States and the Community to determine whether they are in accordance with the rule of law which is a fundamental principle accepted by all the Member States of the Caribbean Community."
39. Ibid., 32.
40. Ibid., 39–40.
41. Ibid., 41.
42. Ibid., 46.
43. *Tomlinson v Belize and Trinidad & Tobago*, Judgment.

compliance with Community law. Second, since the rule of law requires clarity and certainty, administrative practices should align with the literal reading of legislation so that persons can guided appropriately.[44]

More recently in *Rock Hard Cement Ltd v Barbados and Caribbean Community*,[45] a case also concerning whether the community and a member state acted lawfully in the suspension of the CET for cement, the court clarified and advanced the implication of its earlier determination that the RTC's legal system is underpinned by the rule of law. The court said:

> The grounds upon which the Court will engage in such [judicial] review are not confined to such common law grounds as illegality, irrationality, improper purpose or procedural impropriety. The Court's remit is broader. The Court's overarching concern is to maintain and foster the rule of law. As a basis for review the rule of law may be utilised (i) as an interpretative tool; (ii) as a procedural lens, to assess fundamental requirements of governance such as good faith, fairness, predictability, consistency, transparency and fidelity to established rules and procedures, and (iii) as a substantive normative principle by which to judge Community acts.[46]

What is now clear in CARICOM law is that good governance is inextricably tied to the rule of law. While the rule of law is a core component of good governance, it is also the benchmark by which the court will assess the public actions within CARICOM, whether by the community or member states. Even more, based on the court's resort to the rule of law thus far, it appears very possible that claims before the court can be grounded in the rule of law and good governance together and are not limited to the express terms of the RTC.

At this point, certain observations can be made about the governance standard that public actors must meet within the Community. These are:

1. Member States should modify laws, subsidiary legislations and administrative practices to bring them into full and express compliance with Community law;

---

44. *Tomlinson v Belize and Trinidad & Tobago*, [56].
45. *Rock Hard Cement Ltd. v Barbados and Caribbean Community*, Judgment [2020] CCJ 2 (OJ), 10 June 2020 [Judgment].
46. Ibid., 61.

2. Administrative practices should align with the written law, be promulgated in official documents and published;
3. The Community should publish the procedure and requirements of its decision-making insofar as it directly affects other participants in the integration process, so as to not disappoint their legitimate expectation;
4. Community decisions and decisions of Member States in pursuit of the RTC requirements must be principled and procedurally correct, and must maintain fidelity to established rules and procedures;
5. Principled decision-making aligns with good faith, fairness, predictability, consistency, transparency and fidelity to established rules and procedures.

A Duty of Transparency and Efficiency

Transparency is closely connected to and complemented by the rule of law. A good government acts openly with the amendment of its laws. Transparency also addresses the procedure, which the State adopts to amend laws that are on the books. Following enactment, a government should communicate to actors (both private and public) the necessary rules and regulations to which they are bound. In addition, the basis for public decision-making should be publicly available, in some cases the information ought to be released (volunteered) by the government and in other cases it should be provided in a timely manner when requested.

Article 26, RTC enjoins the Community Council and the Secretary-General to "establish and maintain an efficient system of consultations at the national and regional levels" to enhance the decision-making of the Community. In *Rock Hard Cement Ltd. v Barbados and Caribbean Community*, the court observed that a key purpose of this consultative process is transparency and to ensure that affected stakeholders' inputs are considered in decision-making.[47] Critical to transparency is the flow of information to and from decision-makers and affected stakeholders; that is to say, transparency demands a two-way communicative process. This facilitates better decision-making by the Community (and States),

---

47.   Ibid., 41.

the full enjoyment of Community rights and benefits, and the ability of all Community actors to better plan their courses of actions.

The Court's decisions to date have disclosed three sets of duties that are corollaries of the transparency principle. First, in *Shanique Myrie*, the court recalled that the conference requested Member States to provide data and statistics on the free movement of skills and denial of entry to CARICOM nationals.[48] Given the critical role of CARICOM nationals in the freedom of movement, the court held that the Secretariat should "periodically publish these statistics and make them freely available to the general public".[49] This duty to publish the relevant data and statistics, complements the rule of law duty to publish laws and regulations. The effect of transparency, as understood by the court, is that CARICOM nationals should not only be privy to the Community's legal framework, but they should also be privy to data that discloses trends including its successes and failures. It is only then will such nationals be able to fully and strategically manoeuvre the system to reap its promises.

Second, the efficiency requirement in Article 26 RTC breeds additional duties. In *Trinidad Cement Ltd. v Caribbean Community*, in relation to the Article 26, RTC duty, the court said:

> The duty [of the Community Council in collaboration with the Secretary-General] to maintain an efficient system of consultation would include a duty to monitor the operation of that system once it has been established, as well as a duty to try and correct any weaknesses[50] that emerge in the system and to ensure as far as possible scrupulous adherence to that system.[51]

The court went further to articulate other duties that enjoin the Member States and the Secretary-General. Since the consultation

---

48. *Shanique Myrie v Barbados*, 86.
49. Ibid.
50. In *Rock Hard Cement*, the court restated the duty to rectify deficiencies in the consultative process at [56].
51. *Trinidad Cement Ltd. v Caribbean Community* [68]. It is important to note that in the later case of *Rock Hard Cement*, the court pinned the duty to rectify deficiencies to the both good governance and the rule of law. Specifically, in relation to the procedures for handling applications for suspension of the CET, the court said, "The Community is not entitled to ignore article 26 or to so hollow it out that it is rendered a meaningless shell. To accept this would be contrary to good governance, the rule of law and fundamental values and principles embedded in the RTC." at [55].

process relies on the sharing and considering of information, the court indicated that Member States have a "duty to provide the Secretary-General and COTED with accurate, relevant and timely information".[52] The Secretary-General also has a residual duty to exercise due diligence to ascertain whether the required consultation has taken place at the domestic level, and if it has not been done to encourage that it be done.[53] The tripartite duty of consultation as articulated by the court corrals all the community's public actors, enabling each to be a check on the other, all for the benefit of openness in the Community's operations and effective public management.[54]

Third, also in *Shanique Myrie*, the Court stated that Community law requires officials to give reasons promptly and in writing for a denial of entry (under the freedom of movement).[55] The requirement to give reasons for decision was also stated in *Trinidad Cement Ltd. v Caribbean Community* where the Court said that "when the Secretary-General takes a decision to authorise a suspension [of the CET] it is a good practice for his authorisation to be supported by a brief statement of the reason or reasons…"[56] This good practice that the court referred to in *Trinidad Cement Ltd.* has since crystallized into a general community obligation. In the *Derogation Ruling*[57] the CCJ found that "…the CSME has reached the stage that a general obligation on the part of Community organs to give reasons for decisions that generate legal consequences for the Community, Member States and/or Community Nationals must now be accepted".[58]

This finding was in response to the claimants' contention that a decision of COTED was flawed because it did not give reasons.[59]

---

52. *Trinidad Cement Ltd. v Caribbean Community*, at [68].
53. Ibid.
54. It seems to be common sense that effective public sector management requires the monitoring of any procedure or system created to ensure that it achieves its stated objective, while minimizing externalities, and remedying errors or defects when they arise. As a result, it is not fanciful to see these pragmatic community duties infiltrating the domestic administrative space.
55. *Shanique Myrie v Barbados*, at [77, 78, 80].
56. *Trinidad Cement Ltd. v Caribbean Community*, at [81].
57. Consolidated Judgment (in *Trinidad Cement Ltd. and Arawak Cement Ltd. v Barbados*, and *Rock Hard Cement Ltd. v Barbados and Caribbean Community*), Judgment [2019] CCJ 01 (OJ), 17 April 2019 [Judgment].
58. *Derogation Ruling*, at [47].
59. At [46] in the *Derogation Ruling*, prior to its finding that there was a general community

The Court grounded the duty to give reasons in its power of judicial review, which it says is sanctioned by the RTC.[60] The court further noted that where there is a deviation from a constant decision-making practice, there is an 'enhanced duty to give reasons'. Notably, the Court resorted to principles of good governance to support its legal conclusions. It said, "this legal rationale is supported by the fact that there are sound policy benefits to giving reasons including the fostering of transparency in the decision-making process and the encouragement of decision-making that is thought through and rational".[61] Helpfully, the Court made it clear that reasons need not be lengthy. However, they must be appropriate for the context. That is to say, the reasons must show due application of the established rules to the facts under consideration.[62]

It is apt at this point to make further observations about the governance standard that public actors must meet within the Community. These are:

1. The Secretariat has a duty to publish relevant data and statistics on the freedom of movement and make them freely available to the public.

2. The Community Council, in collaboration with the Secretary-General, has a duty to monitor the operations of the system for consultations established under Article 26, RTC.

3. The Community Council, in collaboration with the Secretary-General, has a duty to rectify any deficiencies in the system for consultations.

4. All stakeholders have a duty to comply with the established rules in the system for consultations.

5. Member States have a duty to provide accurate, timely and relevant information to advance decision-making and the consultative process.

6. The Secretary-General has a duty to exercise due diligence to ascertain (and if necessary, encourage) compliance with the consultative process at the domestic level.

---

obligation to give reasons, the court observed that there was no provision in the RTC that required a ministerial council like COTED to give reasons for their decisions.
60.   Ibid., 47.
61.   Ibid.
62.   Ibid., 48.

7. The community (and member states acting on behalf of the community) has a duty to given reasons for decisions that generate legal consequences.

The duty to give reasons is enhanced when there has been a change in policy or deviation from established decision-making practice.

A Duty to Give Reasonable and Adequate Notice

In the *Derogation Ruling*,[63] concerning the lawfulness of Barbados' decision to revert to the CET for certain cement (which meant ending the CET suspension that it was granted), the CCJ determined that Barbados had an implicit duty to give the affected private actors, those in the cement industry, reasonable and adequate notice of its intention. Specifically, the court said:

> There was an implied obligation on Member States to serve on COTED reasonable notice of their intention to revert to the CET.[64]

> A tariff incentive, approved by COTED and implemented by the Member State, and enjoyed by regional manufacturers in that Member State cannot be unilaterally and unceremoniously pulled without giving the manufacturer reasonable time to adjust its business models and operations to the changed realities. Without reasonable and adequate notice, a regional manufacturer, supplying the regional market, would not enjoy the transparency, certainty, and predictability required for tariff regimes to be compliant with… the ethos of the RTC.[65]

> While the court indicated what the contents of the notice should include in that case,[66] what constitutes reasonable and adequate notice "is a matter of fact for decision on a case-by-case basis".[67]

---

63.   Ibid.
64.   Ibid., 39.
65.   Ibid., 41.
66.   Ibid., 39: The notice should include "(i) the date on which the Member State no longer required the derogation and (ii) the date on which the Member State would apply or re-apply the CET."
67.   Ibid., 45.

Even though the decision in this case was specific to the CET for cement, one is hard-pressed not to see its immediate applicability to decisions by the Community and any Member State that have legal consequences or prejudicial effects on a right or benefit emanating from the RTC.[68] This view is fortified by one of the Court's policy reasons in support of its legal conclusion: "Notice would serve two main purposes. Firstly, it would alert COTED, the regional administrator of the CET, of the status of the State's application of the CET and secondly, it would be in the best interest of private persons and other Member States which may have some interest in the Member State deciding to re-impose the CET rate."[69]

In the context of whether notice is required, important considerations are (1) whether notice enables a Community actor to more efficiently fulfil its mandate, and (2) whether notice is in the best interest of stakeholders. In this light, the following further observations about the governance standard that public actors must meet within the Community can be made. These are:

1. Member States have a duty to give notice to the Community that it will cease the application of any exemption or benefit granted to it by the Community.

2. Member States have a duty to give reasonable and adequate notice to private actors likely to be affected that it will cease the application of any exemption or benefit granted to the State by the Community.

A Duty to Provide Independent and Effective Review System

As referred to earlier, the *Shanique Myrie* case concerned the freedom of movement; in particular, whether Barbados' denial of entry to Ms Myrie was consistent with the RTC. The court found that the denial of entry was unlawful because Ms Myrie was entitled to hassle-free entry into Barbados since she was a Jamaican national,[70] and Barbados could not show that she would have become a charge

---

68.   See *Shanique Myrie v Barbados* at [78], "The accountability principle requires Member States promptly and in writing to inform a Community national refused entry not only of the reasons for the refusal but also of his or her right to challenge that decision."
69.   *Derogation Ruling*, 43.
70.   *Shanique Myrie v Barbados*, 83.

on the public purse or that she posed a serious and present risk to national security.[71]

Regarding the denial of entry, the court said: "The accountability principle requires Member States promptly and in writing to inform a Community national refused entry not only of the reasons for the refusal but also of his or her right to challenge that decision."[72]

> Community law requires access to appropriate judicial review in a case of a denial of entry. It also requires that officials give reasons promptly and in writing for any such denial.[73]

These statements make it clear that the duty to give reasons facilitates the judicial review, which the Court noted is sanctioned by the RTC. The process of judicial review is invoked when the CARICOM National exercises the right to challenge the decision to refuse him or her entry. It naturally follows that the Member States, in taking all the necessary and appropriate measures to comply with the RTC, should establish "at the national level an effective and accessible appeal or review procedure with adequate safeguards to protect the rights of the person denied entry".[74]

In commenting on the practice in Jamaica to have a senior official review the denial of entry, the court indicated that though commendable, it is not RTC-compliant. An effective and accessible review procedure must entail independent domestic judicial oversight.[75] A clear consequence to flow from these duties is that any domestic law, regulation and administrative practice that authorizes not giving reasons or ousts judicial oversight is inconsistent with the RTC. While the member states have a large margin of discretion in policy choices for their domestic affairs, that margin is limited by the terms and ethos of the RTC where community interests are implicated. In this regard, the following further observations can be made:

1. To the extent decisions of member states implicate community rights and benefits, affected CARICOM nationals should have access to judicial review of such decisions.

---

71.   Ibid., 99.
72.   Ibid., 78.
73.   Ibid., 80.
74.   Ibid., 78.
75.   Ibid.

2. Member states should modify their laws to ensure that the domestic courts are able exercise a power of review of decisions that implicate CARICOM rights and benefits.

Conclusion

Up to this point, this essay has argued that the decisions of the Caribbean Court of Justice in its Original Jurisdiction paints a portrait of the standard of governance sanctioned by the terms and ethos of the RTC. The Court has indicated that RTC-compliant governance is imbued with a respect for the rule of law and effective public sector management, which demands both the giving of reasons for decisions and availability of judicial oversight. Certain substantive and structural implications follow from this main argument. First, Community standard of governance would become the minimum standard of governance for CARICOM member states. Second, there is a melding of the legally sanctioned standards of governance at the domestic and regional levels. Third, there is harmonization of domestic governance norms in the Community. Fourth, there is a diffusion of centres of governance in the region.

The decisions of the Court in its Original Jurisdiction bind all CARICOM Member States. In addition, Community law (which includes CCJ decisions) prevails over inconsistent domestic law.[76] It stands to reason that the standard of governance the Court sets out is the controlling law for the Community. Since nothing prevents the Member States from exceeding the standard called for by the RTC, Court's understanding of good governance and its core components is the minimum standard within the Community. This will have the effect of raising the quality of governance across the region.

The raised standard of governance is likely to lead to the melding of the domestic and the Community standards. This is likely to happen due to limited resources and the desire for effective public sector management. Limited available resources means that it is unlikely that Member States will either want to or be able to maintain two separate streams and standards of governance, one

---

76.   *Tomlinson v Belize and Trinidad & Tobago*, 56.

for domestic affairs and one for Community affairs. And, given that the Community standard controls, it is likely that domestic governance apparatus will be modified to reflect, at a minimum, the requirements of community law.

By setting a minimum standard of good governance in the community and potentially modifying the domestic governance apparatus and processes to reflect Community standards, the CCJ is likely to advance the development of regional customary law in relation to good governance. As CARICOM good governance, as defined by the court, crystallizes into a customary norm, it simultaneously contributes to the harmonization of standards of governance across the sub-region.

Finally, the rising customary norm in relation to good governance has and will continue to lead the organizing or reorganizing of centres of power in the exercise of governance activities. In doing this, it shifts or diffuses power, reshapes relationships, sways preferences and influences the allocations of resources, resulting in multi-sourced and multi-level governance. When the CCJ exercises its power of judicial review, it is an empowered actor in the field of governance. First, the RTC delegates to the CCJ a very wide scope to determine the substance of the rules. Second, through interpretation, the court is able to adjust the rule on a progressive basis without the need for constant amendment of the RTC. That is to say, in some cases, as knowledge, technology, best practices and state capacity and Community maturity change, the Court can respond to those changes through interpretation and application of the RTC without waiting for Member States to amend the rule.[77] Third, the CCJ is placed to review Member States' prioritization of preferences and, in the main, balance the relationship with the need for compliance with the RTC and the State's willingness to accept higher standards. These functions put the Court at the heart of the governance apparatus that flows out of the RTC.[78]

---

77. This has already happened with the duty to give reasons.
78. The court has already acknowledged this reality when it said: "The Court has the power to scrutinise the acts of the Member States and the Community to determine whether they are in accordance with the rule of law which is a fundamental principle accepted by all the Member States of the Caribbean Community." *Trinidad Cement Ltd. v Caribbean Community*, Judgment [2009] at [58]; see also, *Trinidad Cement Ltd. v Competition Commission*, Judgment [2012] CCJ 4 (OJ), 12 November 2012 [Judgment] at [16].

The RTC facilitates the role of other actors in determining the Community content and standard of governance. Other than States and CCJ, the RTC-compliant governance creates a space for other actors – IGOs, NGOs, transnational networks of government agencies, private actors or experts and individuals (natural and juristic) – to function in the process of elaborating the law. It is common practice for these actors to promulgate rules, regulations and best practices that aid in governance activities. Generally, these are non-binding and function as points of reference for Member States in shaping their preferences and adopting methodologies to comply with their obligations. The works of these other actors also serve as points of reference for the Court as it reviews the choices that Member States have made.[79]

In relation to the exercise of RTC-compliant governance activities, power is shifted to other actors, some more than others. Governance power can be considered diffused and multi-sourced or polar. Concomitantly, the structure of relationships among and between the actors has experienced changes. As discussed above, the other (non-State and non-judicial) actors are duly drafted into the policy-shaping matrix. As community law develops, it will be interesting to learn how the court straddles the thin, often porous border of law interpretation and policy-making.[80]

---

79. In the *Derogation Ruling*, at [18], [22] we see the court's resort to the World Customs Organization Harmonized Description and Coding System.

80. In *Shanique Myrie v Barbados*, the court said, "However, the scope of public policy and particularly that of the concept of 'undesirable persons', which is used as a justification for derogation from the fundamental principle of freedom of movement and hassle free travel of Community nationals, cannot wholly or unilaterally be determined by each Member State without being subject to control by the major Community Organs, in particular the Conference, and ultimately by the Court as the Guardian of the RTC." *Shanique Myrie v Barbados*, at [68].

Selected Bibliography

Alexander, M. Jacqui. "Redrafting Morality: The Postcolonial State and the Sexual Offences Bill of Trinidad and Tobago," in *Third World Women and the Politics of Feminism*, edited by Chandra Mohanty, Ann Russo and Lourdes Torres. Bloomington: Indiana University Press, 1991.

Ardia, David. "Reputation in a Networked World: Revisiting the Social Foundations of Defamation Law," *Harvard Civil Rights-Civil Liberties Law Review* 45 (2010): 261–328.

Baker, Roy. "Defamation and the Moral Community," *Deakin Law Review* 13, no. 1 (2008): 1–35.

Bartels, Lorand. "The Chapeau of the General Exceptions in the WTO GATT and GATS Agreements: A Reconstruction," *American Journal of International Law* 109, no. 1 (2015): 95, 109.

Beckles, Hilary. "Caribbean Anti-slavery: The Self-liberation Ethos of Enslaved Blacks," *Journal of Caribbean History* 22, nos. 1–2 (1988): 1–19.

Berman, Harold. *Law and Language: Effective Symbols of Community*. Cambridge: Cambridge University Press, 2013.

Bell, Wendell. "Equity and Social Justice: Foundations of Nationalism in the Caribbean," *Caribbean Studies* 20, no. 2 (1980): 5–36.

Berry, David. *Caribbean Integration Law*. Oxford: Oxford University Press, 2014.

Bowling, Daniel. "Lawyers and Their Elusive Pursuit of Happiness: Does It Matter?" *Duke Forum for Law & Social Change* 7 (2015): 37–52.

Breitsameter, Christof. "How to Justify a Ban on Doping?" *Journal of Medical Ethics* 43, no. 5 (2017): 287–92.

Brown-Blake, Celia. "The Right to Linguistic Non-discrimination and Creole Language Situations: The Case of Jamaica," *Journal of Pidgin and Creole Studies* 23, no. 1 (2008): 32–74.

———. "Supporting Justice Reform in Jamaica through Language Policy Change," *Caribbean Studies* 45, nos. 1–2 (2017): 183–215.

———. "Judges as Language Referees for Caribbean English Vernacular

Speakers," in *New Frontiers in Forensic Linguistics: Themes and Perspectives in Language and Law in Africa and beyond,* edited by Monwabisi K. Ralarala, Russell H. Kaschula, and Georgina Heydon, 149–73. Stellenbosch: African Sun Media, 2019.

Bulkan, Arif. "The Poverty of Equality Jurisprudence in the Commonwealth Caribbean," *Equal Rights Review* 10 (2013): 11–32.

Bulkan, Arif, and Tracy Robinson, "Equality and Social Inclusion," in *Securing Equality for All in the Administration of Justice,* edited by Janeille Zorina Matthews and Jewel Amoah. Kingston: UWI Faculty of Law, 2019.

Burgess, Andrew. *Commonwealth Caribbean Company Law.* 1st ed. Oxford: Routledge Taylor and Francis, 2013.

Carrington, Lawrence. "The Status of Creole in the Caribbean," *Caribbean Quarterly* 45, nos. 2&3 (1999): 41–51.

Carroll, Archie. "Carroll's Pyramid of CSR: Taking Another Look," *International Journal of Corporate Social Responsibility* 1, no. 3 (2016): 1–8.

Carroll, Archie, Jill Brown, and Ann Buchholtz. *Business & Society: Ethics, Sustainability & Stakeholder Management.* 11th ed. Boston: Cengage, 2022.

Casini, Lorenzo. "The Making of a Lex Sportiva by the Court of Arbitration for Sport," *German Law Journal* 12, no. 5 (2011): 1317–40.

Churchill, Robin, and Vaughan Lowe. *The Law of the Sea.* Manchester: Manchester University Press, 1988.

Clarke, John, Kathleen Coll, Evelina Dagnino, and Catherine Neveu. *Disputing Citizenship.* Bristol: Bristol University Press, 2014.

Crenshaw, Kimberle. "Mapping the Margins: Intersectionality, Identity Politics, and Violence against Women of Color," *Stanford Law Review* 43, no. 6 (1991): 1241–99.

Clarke, Thomas. "Case Study: Master of Corporate Malfeasance," *Corporate Governance: An International Review* 1, no. 3 (1993): 141–51.

Colombos, Constantine John. *The International Law of the Sea.* 6th ed. London: Longman, 1967.

Cooky, Cheryl, and Shari Dworkin, "Policing the Boundaries of Sex: A Critical Examination of Gender Verification and the Caster Semenya Controversy," *Journal of Sex Research* 50, no. 2 (2013): 103–11.

DeMerieux, Margaret. *Fundamental Rights in Commonwealth Caribbean Constitutions.* Bridgetown: UWI Faculty of Law Library, 1992.

Dodd, David J. "The Role of Law in Plantation Society: Reflections on the Development of a Caribbean Legal System," *International Journal of the Sociology of Law* 7 (1979): 275–96.

Domínguez, Jorge. "The Caribbean Question: Why Has Liberal Democracy (Surprisingly) Flourished?," in *Democracy in the Caribbean,* edited by Jorge Domínguez, Robert Pastor, and Delisle Worrell, 1–28. Baltimore: Johns Hopkins University Press, 1993.

Donnelly, Jack. "Human Rights, Democracy and Development," *Human Rights Quarterly* 21, no. 3 (1999): 608–32.

Drayton, Richard. "Whose Constitution? Law, Justice and History in the Caribbean," Judicial Education Institute of Trinidad and Tobago Sixth Distinguished Jurist Lecture 2016, https://www.ttlawcourts. org/jeibooks/books/djl2016_final.pdf (accessed 17 July 2022).

Dubner, Barry Hart, and Brian Otero, "The Human Rights of Sea Pirates: Will the European Court of Human Rights Decisions Get More Killed?," *Washington University Global Studies Law Review* 15, no. 2 (2016): 215.

Evans, R. Sandra. "'Ou ni right-la pou remain silans': The Case for a Standard Kwéyòl Translation of the Pre-trial Right to Silence," *Journal of Pidgin and Creole Languages* 36, no. 1 (2021): 175–200.

Fahner, Johannes. "In Dubio Mitius: Advancing Clarity and Modesty in Treaty Interpretation," *European Journal of International Law* 32, no. 3 (2021): 835–61.

Farquharson, Joseph. "The Black Man's Burden: Language and Political Economy in a Diglossic State and Beyond," *Zeitschrift für Anglistik und Amerikanistik: Leipzig* 63, no. 2 (2015): 172–73.

Fasken Martineau DuMoulin LLP. *Canada Business Corporations Act & Commentary 2019–2020.* Toronto: Lexis Nexis Canada, 2020.

Ffolkes-Goldson, Suzanne. "Directors' Duties to Creditors On or Near Insolvency and Duty of Care in the Commonwealth Caribbean: Should the *Peoples* Decision be Adopted?" *Oxford University Commonwealth Law Journal* 6, no. 1 (2006): 61–75.

———. *Corporate Business Principles: A Guide to the Jamaica Companies Act.* Kingston: Caribbean Law Publishing, 2020.

Fortier, Anne-Marie. "On (Not) Speaking English: Colonial Legacies in Language Requirements for British Citizenship," *Sociology* 52, no. 6 (2018): 1254–69.

Fredman, Sandra. "Substantive Equality Revisited," *International Journal of Constitutional Law* 3, no. 14 (2016): 712–38.

Frey, Klaus. "Development, Good Governance, and Local Democracy," *Brazilian Political Science Review* 2, no. 2 (2008): 39–73.

Fuller, Lon. *The Inner Morality of Law.* Rev. ed. New Haven: Yale University Press, 1969.

George, Robert. *Making Men Moral: Civil Liberties and Public Morality.* Oxford: Oxford Scholarship Online, 2012.

Girvan, Norman. "Caribbean Integration: Can Cultural Production Succeed Where Politics and Economics Have Failed?" Keynote address, St Martin Book Fair, 31 May 2012.

Gould, Kim. "Locating a 'Threshold of Seriousness' in the Australian Tests of Defamation," *Sydney Law Review* 39, no. 3 (2017): 333–63.

Goveia, Elsa. "The West Indian Slave Laws of the Eighteenth Century," *Revista de Ciencias Sociales* 4 (1960): 75–105.

Graziano, Michael. "Race, the Law, and Religion in America," in *Oxford Research Encyclopedia of Religion*. Oxford: Oxford University Press, 2017.

Hannigan, Brenda. *Company Law.* Oxford: Oxford University Press, 2009.

Heineman, Ben, William Lee, and David Wilkins. *Lawyers as Professionals and as Citizens: Key Roles and Responsibilities in the 21st Century.* Harvard Law School Center on the Legal Profession, 2014. Available at https://clp.law.harvard.edu/wp-content/uploads/2022/10/Professionalism-Project-Essay_11.20.14.pdf

Herring, Jonathan. *Legal Ethics.* 2nd ed. Oxford: Oxford University Press, 2017.

———. *Family Law (Longman Law Series),* 2nd ed. Boston: Addison Wesley, 2004.

Hymes, Dell. *Foundations in Sociolinguistics.* Philadelphia: University of Pennsylvania Press, 1974.

Jackman, Mahalia. "They Called it the 'Abominable Crime': An Analysis of Heterosexual Support for Anti-gay Laws in Barbados, Guyana and Trinidad and Tobago," *Sexuality Research and Social Policy* 13, no. 2 (2016): 130–41.

Jennings, Robert, and Arthur Watts. *Oppenheim's International Law Vol. II.* Harlow: Longman, 1993.

Jolowicz, John, Percy Winfield, and W. Rogers, *Winfield and Jolowicz on Tort.* 18th ed. London: Sweet and Maxwell, 2010.

Jordan, Jeremy, John Gillentine, and Barry Hunt, "The Influence of Fairness: The Application of Organizational Justice in a Team Sport Setting," *International Sports Journal* 8, no. 1 (2004): 139–49.

Keeper, Phillip. "Governance," in *The Sage Handbook of Comparative Politics,* edited by Todd Landman and Neil Robinson. Thousand Oaks, CA: Sage Publications, 2009.

Kerrigan, Dylan, Peter Jamadar, Elron Elahie, and Tori Sinanan, "Securing Equality for All: The Evidence and Recommendations," in *Security Equality for All in the Administration of Justice,* edited by Janeille Zorina Matthews and Jewel Amoah, 61–98. Kingston: UWI Faculty of Law, 2019.

Kodilinye, Gilbert. *Negligence Liability in Caribbean Hospitality and Tourism.* London: Polgrene Press, 2020.

Krane, V., Emma Calow, and Brandy Panunti. "Female Testosterone: Contested Terrain," *Kinesiology Review* 11 no. 1 (2021): 54–63.

Lesnick, Howard. *Religion in Legal Thought and Practice.* Cambridge: Cambridge University Press, 2010.

Lindsay, Louis. "The Myth of Independence: Middle Class Politics and Non-Mobilization in Jamaica." Working Paper No. 6. Kingston: Sir Arthur Lewis Institute of Social and Economic Studies, 1975. https://papers.ssrn.com/sol3/papers.cfm?abstract_id=1822826 (accessed 17 July 2022).

Loland, Sigmund. "Caster Semenya, Athlete Classification, and Fair Equality of Opportunity in Sport," *Journal of Medical Ethics* 46, no. 9 (2020): 584–90.

Marston, Steve. "The Revival of Athlete Activism(s): Divergent Black Politics in the 2016 Presidential Election Engagements of LeBron James and Colin Kaepernick," *FairPlay, Revista de Filosofia, Ética y Derecho del Deporte* no. 10 (2017): 45–68.

McIntosh, Simeon C.R. *Caribbean Constitutional Reform: Rethinking the West Indian Polity.* Kingston: Caribbean Law Publishing Company, 2002.

McNamara, Lawrence. *Reputation and Defamation.* Oxford: Oxford University Press, 2007.

Miller, Holly. "Homosexuality as Defamation: A Proposal for the Use of the 'Right-Thinking Minds' Approach in the Development of Modern Jurisprudence," *Communication Law & Policy* 18 (2013): 349–74.

Mills, Charles. "Smadditizin," *Caribbean Quarterly* 43, no. 2 (1997): 54–68.

Munroe, Trevor. *The Politics of Constitutional Decolonisation.* Kingston: Institute for Social and Economic Research, 1972.

Murray, Thomas. "Making Sense of Fairness in Sports," in *The Ethics of Sports Technologies and Human Enhancement,* edited by Thomas Murray and Voo Teck Chuan. London: Routledge, 2020.

Nicolaides, Angelo, and Stella Vettori, "The Duty of Lawyers: Virtue Ethics and Pursuing a Hopeless Legal Case," *Athens Journal of Law* 5, no. 2 (April 2019): 149.

O'Connell, Daniel Patrick. *The International Law of the Sea Vol. 1.* Oxford: Clarendon Press, 1982.

Peterson, Jason. "A 'Race' for Equality," in *From Jack Johnson to Lebron James: Sports, Media, and the Color Line,* edited by James Lamb, 332–56. Lincoln: University of Nebraska Press, 2016.

Pettit, Philip. *On the People's Terms.* Cambridge: Cambridge University Press, 2012.

———. *Republicanism: A Theory of Freedom and Government.* Oxford: Clarendon Press, 1997.

Post, Robert. "Democracy and Equality," *Annals of the American Academy of Political and Social Science* 603, no. 1 (2006): 28–31.

Potts, Lee. "Law as a Tool of Social Engineering: The Case of the Republic of South Africa," *Boston College International and Comparative Law Review* 5, no. 1 (1982): 1–50.

Quijano, Anibal. "Coloniality of Power, Eurocentrism, and Latin America," *Nepantla: Views of South* 1, no. 3 (2000): 533–80.

Rawls, John. "Justice as Fairness," in *Contemporary Political Philosophy*, edited by Robert Goodin and Philip Pettit, 187–202. Hoboken, NJ: Blackwell, 1997.

Roach, Kent, Benjamin Burger, Emma Cunliffe, and James Stribopoulos. *Criminal Law and Procedure*. 11th ed. Toronto: Emond Montgomery, 2015.

Robinson, Tracy, Arif Bulkan, and Adrian Saunders, *Fundamentals of Caribbean Constitutional Law*. 2nd ed. London: Sweet and Maxwell, 2015.

Rolph, David. "A Critique of the Defamation Act 2013: Lessons for and from Australian Defamation Law Reform," *Communications Law* 21, no. 4 (2016): 116–22.

Rousseau, Stéphane, Julie Biron, and Ejan Mackaay, "Lawyers as Gatekeepers," in *Company Lawyers Independent by Design: An ECLA White Paper*, edited by P. Coen and C. Roquilly, 335–44. Paris: Lexis Nexis, 2014.

Tak, Minhyeok, Michael Sam, and Steven Jackson, "The Politics of Countermeasures against Match-Fixing in Sport: A Political Sociology Approach to Policy Instruments," *International Review for the Sociology of Sport* 53, no. 1 (2018): 30–48.

Thoreson, Ryan. "The Limits of Moral Limitations: Reconceptualizing 'Morals' in Human Rights Law," *Harvard International Law Journal* 59, no. 1 (2018): 197–244.

Tokarz, Karen. "Access to Justice: The Social Responsibility of Lawyers," *Washington University Journal of Law & Policy* 16, no. 1 (2004): 1–10.

Vinten, Gerald. "The Corporate Governance Lessons of Enron," *Corporate Governance* 2, no. 4 (2002): 4–9.

Viñuales, Jorge E. "Seven Ways of Escaping a Rule," in *Exceptions and Defences in International Law*, edited by Lorand Bartels and Federica Paddeu, 65–87. Oxford: Oxford University Press, 2020.

Welling, Bruce. *Corporate Law in Canada: The Governing Principles*. 3rd ed. London: Scribblers Publishing, 2006.

Whisenant, Warren, Debbiesiu Lee, and Windy Dees, "Role Congruity Theory: Perceptions of Fairness and Sexism in Sport Management," *Public Organization Review* 15, no. 4 (2015): 475–85.

White, Dorcas. "Some Problems of a Hybrid Legal System: A Case Study of St Lucia," *International and Comparative Law Quarterly* 30: 862–81.

Wodak, Ruth, Rudolf De Cillia, Martin Reisigl, and Karin Liebhart. *The Discursive Construction of National Identity.* Edinburgh: Edinburgh University Press, 2009.

Contributors

Professor Shazeeda Ali, LLB (UWI); LLM (Cantab.); PhD (London), attorney-at-law, is currently the dean of the Faculty of Law at the University of the West Indies, Mona, Jamaica and a professor of corporate and financial law. She lectures the LLB courses "Caribbean Securities Regulation" and "Introduction to Offshore Law", as well as the LLM course, "Legal Aspects of Corporate Misconduct". Professor Ali is also a tutor in "Ethics, Rights and Obligations of the Legal Profession" at the Norman Manley Law School. She has presented and published widely on financial crime, financial services regulation, offshore financial law, and legal professional ethics. She is the author of *Money Laundering Control in the Caribbean* and *Proceeds of Crime Act: Taking the Profit Out of Crime*. She is also the editor of *Risky Business: Perspectives on Corporate Misconduct* and *The Ethical Lawyer: A Caribbean Perspective*.

Dr Celia Brown-Blake, BA and LLB (UWI), LLM (London), MA and PhD (UWI), is a senior lecturer in the Faculty of Law at the UWI, Mona, where she is currently the deputy dean for graduate studies and research. She teaches trust and insolvency and her research interests include financial regulation, insolvency law, language and the law, and corporate law. With a PhD in linguistics, a significant stream of her publications concerns language rights and language policy in the Commonwealth Caribbean. Her most recent works include "Supporting Justice Reform in Jamaica through Language Policy Change", "The Legal Matrix Governing Directors and Officers of Financial Supervisors: Understanding Their Role in Governance", and "Judges as Language Referees for Caribbean English Vernacular Speakers".

Honourable Mr Justice Andrew Burgess is a judge at the Caribbean Court of Justice and a member of the panel of the World Bank Administrative

Tribunal. He is a former Barbados Court of Appeal judge and former dean with the responsibility for the LLB and LLM programmes delivered at the Mona and St Augustine campuses. He also served as professor of corporate and commercial law at the UWI Cave Hill. He has the distinction of being the longest-serving dean at the faculty. He served as a judge on the Inter-American Development Bank's Administrative Tribunal in Washington, DC; as its vice president, and later as its president. He was a Senior Commonwealth Fellow at Oxford University. Justice Burgess is the author of *Commonwealth Caribbean Company Law* (2013), and *The Law of Corporate Receivers and Receiver-Managers* (2002). He has also published in leading law journals on legal issues, mainly corporate and commercial jurisprudence.

Gabrielle Elliott-Williams, LLB Hons (UWI), LLM (Cantab.). She is a lecturer in the Faculty of Law at the UWI, Mona, where she teaches international law and human rights law. Her teaching and research interests also includes the work of the Caribbean Court of Justice. Her numerous publications include "The Public Morality Limit in the Commonwealth Caribbean Conventional Model Constitution" and "Whether the Main Reason for Securities Legislation is the Maintenance of a Reliable and Reputable Securities Market for the Protection of the Investing Public". Her recent article, "Who Belongs?: The Caribbean Court of Justice Reveals Caribbean Identity's Inclusive Potentiality", explores how the jurisprudence of the CCJ recognizes the lack of belonging that homosexuals and trans people of the Caribbean experience while also demonstrating the regional identity's inclusive potentiality.

Suzanne Ffolkes Goldson (1961–2023), BA (Econ.) (York), LLB Hons (UWI), BCL (Oxon), was a senior lecturer and former deputy dean of the Faculty of Law at the UWI, Mona. She was the course director for the "Company Law" and "Corporate Management" courses and the postgraduate course "Corporate Governance". A recipient of the Principal's Research Award for the Most Outstanding Researcher and the Best Research Publication in the Faculty of Law, she presented extensive research on company/corporate law, corporate governance, corporate insolvency and corporate social responsibility at numerous seminars, workshops and conferences locally, regionally and internationally. Her book, *Commonwealth Caribbean Corporate Governance,* explores the development of the law and codes in Jamaica, Barbados, Trinidad and

Tobago, and the wider Commonwealth Caribbean region. Her publication, *Corporate Business Principles: A Guide to the Jamaica Companies Act,* breaks down the legislation and provides an accessible guide to incorporation, corporate finance, corporate management, complainants' remedies and winding up.

Dr Jason Haynes, LLB (Hons.), UWI, LLM (UoN), PhD (Durham), LEC, MCIArb, CEDR, attorney-at-law, is an associate professor of law and Deputy Head of Research at the University of Birmingham School of Law. Previously, he was a senior lecturer and Deputy Dean (Graduate Studies and Research) at the Faculty of the Law, UWI Cave Hill, where he taught sports law, international investment law and administrative law, entertainment law and intellectual property law. His research interests include anti-trafficking law, international investment law, sports law, and their intersectionality with marginalized, vulnerable communities. He also incorporates decolonial studies, feminist theory and intersectionality theory into his research. He is the co-author of *Commonwealth Caribbean Sports Law,* published by Routledge in 2019. He has published in various peer-reviewed journals, including *International and Comparative Law Quarterly, Journal of International Dispute Settlement, Oxford University Commonwealth Law Journal* and *Commonwealth Law Bulletin.*

Professor Gilbert Kodilinye, MA (Oxon), LLM (Lond), CIPP/E, CIPM, barrister (England and Wales), attorney-at-law (St Lucia). He is Emeritus Professor of Law at the UWI, where he taught for thirty years. He was also the general editor of the *Caribbean Law Review* for sixteen years. His current research areas are real property, civil procedure, data protection and hospitality, and tourism law. He is the author or co-author of five Routledge *Commonwealth Caribbean Law Series* texts. He has numerous articles and case notes published in leading international journals, cited in superior courts, major textbooks and legal periodicals in the United Kingdom, Australia, New Zealand and Canada. The substance of parts of his chapter was first published in *Negligence Liability in Caribbean Hospitality and Tourism* (Polgrene Press, 2020).

Dr Coleen B. Lewis, BA Hons (UWI), PGDip in Law (Exeter), LLM (Strathclyde), is a lecturer in employment law at the UWI, Mona. Her research focuses on law, technology and the internet, with special reference to legal and policy issues concerning the regulation of technology, cybercrime and commerce, privacy concerns and data protection. Dr Lewis' work and research merges her areas of interest and practice of media and technology. She started her professional career as a radio journalist then entered the legal profession as an attorney-at-law working at top law firms such as Harneys in the British Virgin Islands, and Barrow and Co. in Belize. In Jamaica, she worked with the legal department at the Gleaner Company. Her doctoral thesis, offered at the University of Leicester, was titled, "Comparative Analysis of the Approaches to Ensuring Unreasonable Limits Not Imposed on the Right to Freedom of Expression by the Defamation Legislation of Jamaica, Australia and England & Wales Within the Context of the Internet".

Dr Derrick McKoy, CD, KC, MCIArb, FAiADR, LLB, LLM, PhD, MBA, DBA, is a former dean and lecturer of the Faculty of Law, UWI, Mona. He also served as an adjunct lecturer at the Mona School of Business, the Institute of International Relations, the Norman Manley Law School, Barry University's Andreas School of Business, and Nova Southeastern University's Huizenga School of Business. In 2016, he was awarded the Order of Distinction, in the rank of Commander, for his outstanding contribution to the legal profession and public service in Jamaica. He has published in the areas of competition law, constitutional law, corruption, labour law, public management, governance and the law of computers.

André Sheckleford, BSc (UWI), LLB Hons (UWI), LLM (Cantab.), is a lecturer at the UWI, Mona. He teaches the undergraduate courses "Real Property I & II" and "Introduction to International Investment Law". His research interests include international economic law, the relationship between law and information, and property law. He has made submissions to the Caribbean Court of Justice, the Judicial Committee of the Privy Council, the Court of Appeal of Jamaica, the Supreme Court of Jamaica, and the Court of Arbitration for Sports. His most recent essay, "Biometric Identification Systems in the Commonwealth and the Right to Privacy", discusses biometric identification systems in several developing Commonwealth countries.

Professor Stephen Vasciannie, BSc (UWI), BA (Oxford), LLM (Cantab.), DPhil (Oxon), is a lecturer at the UWI, Mona, where he teaches "Public International Law" and "International Mooting". He has worked extensively in the areas of his research interests: international law, law of the sea, human rights law, and investment law. He has held various positions in academia and public life. He received the Jamaican national honour, the Order of Distinction (Commander class) for service in the fields of law, education and international relations. Professor Vasciannie has been a member of the United Nations International Law Commission and the Inter-American Juridical Committee, and chairman of the Committee on Juridical and Political Affairs of the Organisation of American States. His most recent book, *Caribbean Essays on Law and Policy*, addresses the Jamaican practice of diplomatic immunity and issues concerning the Montego Bay Convention on the Law of the Sea.

Dr Neto Waite, BSc (UWI), LLB (UWI), LLM (Harvard), JSD (NYU), is a lecturer in the Faculty of Law at the UWI, Mona, where he teaches "Law of International Organizations", "Law of International Courts and Tribunals" and "Caribbean Integration Law". His research focuses on public international law, international investment law and regional economic integration. Dr Waite served as an intern in the Appeals Chamber of the International Criminal Court from June to December 2009, undertaking research in and analysis of public international law, international human rights law, international criminal law, and international humanitarian law, as well as a comparative study into criminal procedure practice in common law and non-common law systems. One of his most recent pieces of work, "An Inquiry into the ICC Appeals Chamber's Exercise of the Power of Remand", was published in a leading international law journal.

Dorcas White, attorney-at-law and former course director for the "Law of Remedies" at the Norman Manley Law School. She has a long history of teaching at the Faculty of Law and the law school since 1974. She has written a book and several articles in regional and international journals, including "Some Problems of a Hybrid Legal System: A Case Study of St Lucia", which was cited before and applied by the Judicial Committee of the Privy Council in the matter of *Parry Husband v Warefact* (PC#74 2001).

Index

www.ingramcontent.com/pod-product-compliance
Lightning Source LLC
Chambersburg PA
CBHW021029210326

41598CB00016B/962